A History of
Middle East
Economies in the
Twentieth Century

Roger Owen & Şevket Pamuk

Harvard University Press
Cambridge, Massachusetts
1999

Printed and bound in Great Britain

Library of Congress Cataloging-in-Publication Data

Owen, Edward Roger John.
    A history of Middle East economies in the twentieth century /
Roger Owen and Şevket Pamuk.
        p.   cm.
    Includes bibliographical references and index.
    ISBN 0-674-39830-0 (cloth). — ISBN 0-674-39831-9 (pbk.)
    1. Middle East—Economic conditions—20th century. I. Pamuk, Şevket.
II. Title.
HC415.15.0935 1999
330.956'04—dc21   98-29099

To Isabel and Zeynep

CONTENTS

ACKNOWLEDGEMENTS

Roger Owen would like to acknowledge the valuable assistance of Jon Alterman, Huri Islamoglu, Tom Mullins, and Margaret Owen.

NOTE ON TRANSLITERATION

Words transliterated from Arabic follow a modified version of the system used in the *International Journal of Middle East Studies*: there are no dia-critical marks used and ta marbuta is 'a' in the construct state. Spellings commonly used in English have been retained, particularly personal and place names. The same applies where people have adopted Roman spellings of their own names.

LIST OF TABLES

LIST OF ACRONYMS

APOC	Anglo-Persian Oil Company
ARAMCO	Arabian American Oil Company
BAPCO	Bahrain Oil Company
CASOC	Standard Oil of California
CERMOC	Centre d'Etudes et de Recherches sur le Moyen-Orient Contemporaine (Beirut)
CNRS	Centre National de Recherche Scientifique (Paris)
EC	European Community
EDO	Economic Development Organization (Egypt)
EU	European Union
FDI	Foreign Direct Investment
GATT	General Agreement on Tariffs and Trade
GCC	Gulf Cooperation Council
GDP	Gross Domestic Product
GNI	Gross National Income
GNP	Gross National Product
ID	Iraqi Dinar
IME	Industrial Market Economies
IMF	International Monetary Fund (Washington)
INOC	Iraqi National Oil Company
IPC	Iraq Petroleum Company
IRFED	Institut International de Recherche et de Formation en vue de Développement Intégral et Harmonisé (Paris)
ISI	Import Substituting Industrialization
JD	Jordanian Dinar
KD	Kuwaiti Dinar
MENA	Middle East and North Africa
MESC	Middle East Supply Centre (Cairo)
NAFTA	North American Free Trade Area
NATO	North Atlantic Treaty Organization
NDP	Net Domestic Product
OECD	Organization for Economic Cooperation and Development
OPEC	Organization of Petroleum Exporting Countries
PDRY	People's Democratic Republic of Yemen
PRO	Public Record Office (London)

SABIC	Saudi Arabian Basic Industries Corporation
SOCAL	Standard Oil of California
SPO	State Planning Organization (Turkey)
RIIA	Royal Institute of International Affairs (London)
UAE	United Arab Emirates
UMI	Upper Middle Income (countries)
UNCTAD	United Nations Conference on Trade and Development
UNWRA	United Nations Relief and Works Administration
WTO	World Trade Organization
YAR	Yemen Arab Republic

GENERAL INTRODUCTION

The aim of this book is to provide a general evaluation of the growth of the Middle East economies from the end of the First World War to the early 1990s. By Middle East we mean the Arab states of Egypt, Syria, Jordan, Lebanon, Iraq, and the Arabian Peninsula as well as Turkey and Israel. It was our original intention to include Iran, but this did not prove possible. However, we continue to hope that we can add an Iranian section to a second edition.

We take our audience to be college and university students, Middle East area specialists, and economists with an interest in comparative development. We assume no more than a basic knowledge of economic theory.

Our inquiry is informed by such general questions as: what makes an economy grow? Why do some economies grow faster than others? What is the role of the state? And how does growth impact on different social groups in terms of income and welfare? It is our belief, however, that these are, and will always remain, open questions to which any number of answers can be given. Our aim is to highlight areas of controversy and to try, whenever possible, to explain actual historical outcomes rather than to criticize development by evaluating paths not taken. We will also make use of comparisons between the Middle Eastern economies and, where helpful, between the region and other similar regions of the world.

We take as our basic unit of analysis the individual national economies as they began to be created throughout most parts of the region just after the First World War. We look at them basically in terms of the growth of both national and per capita income and of the changing relationship between the three major sectors: agriculture, industry, and services. It is our belief that economic progress is best captured by the use of this three sector model pioneered by Simon Kuznets, paying particular attention to the first two, productive sectors whose growth is mutually reinforcing, providing raw material, markets, capital, and foreign exchange.[1]

Furthermore, we see economic growth in the non-European world during the twentieth century as, essentially, a three stage process beginning with the increased export of primary products, then turning towards a more enclosed system based on the policy of nurturing local manufacture known as import substituting industrialization (ISI), before a return toward a more open phase once the ISI phase is perceived to have reached its limits, a moment usually signaled by increasingly severe balance of payments crises, budget deficits, and huge distortions within the domestic market and accompanied by pressure for liberalization and structural adjustment from the IMF and the World Bank. Typically, the ISI phase was initiated during either the Great Depression of the early 1930s or the Second World War, and the return to a more open phase during the world economic crisis of the 1970s.

Finally, we follow the tradition which goes back to Kuznets and to Alexander Gershenkron in which factor accumulation is seen as the central motive force for economic growth and in which the primary impetus for increase in national income comes from a process of capital deepening by means of investments both in expanding production and in improving skills via technical and general education.[2] It follows that one of the basic factors inhibiting rapid growth is the significant distortions to the pricing system, and so the efficient allocation of resources, which became more or less institutionalized during the ISI phase and which proved exceedingly difficult to change, even when policies of economic liberalization were well under way.[3]

However, various caveats must also be underlined. First, the Middle East as we define it contains a huge variety of different economies and only a few countries – notably Turkey, Israel, and Egypt – whose growth path can be said to conform directly to the general model just described. Others, such as Syria, Iraq, Lebanon, and Jordan, exhibited some of its features and not others, while the remainder – almost all the states of the Gulf – followed a wholly different path due to their possession of a single source of great wealth, oil. Even where states did conform to the general pattern, they did so at different speeds and with somewhat different degrees of openness and closure due to such specific factors as the central role played by foreign aid (Israel) or access to money from the neighboring oil producers (Egypt).

Second, although the Middle East began to enter the statistical age soon after 1918, many of the numbers necessary to examine its economic progress are defective both in terms of the way they were collected and, very often, in terms of what they attempt to measure. For example, national income statistics record only activities to which a monetary value can be attached and so ignore much of what goes on within the household, particularly work done by women. The same is true for what economists call the 'black' or 'informal' economy where unreported, and therefore unrecorded, transactions may constitute a large part of total activity.[4] Furthermore, certain central notions such as 'employment/unemployment' and certain measures of educational achievement such as 'literacy/illiteracy' are notoriously difficult to measure. Third, national income figures, as a rule, say nothing about the distribution of national wealth among the various classes and social groups.

It is also our belief that the growth of national economies can only be understood when placed within their historical, political, and global context. It is to history that we should look for the development of such long-term variables as the control of agricultural land by different social groups, the creation of different systems of transport, and the size and location of local populations. It is to politics that we need to look for guidance as to the role of the state both as an arena for struggle between various socioeconomic interests and as a source of the growing power exercised in the form of management and control over the economy and its resources: states act to shape their economic environment just as they are themselves shaped by it. It is in the global context that we find those powerful external forces which open or close particular foreign markets, encourage aid and investment, and in so many ways act to delineate each Middle Eastern country's place within the international division of labor.

We will pay particular attention to the role of the state in providing a framework for the operation of the national economy in terms of laws, rules and regulations, and relations with the rest of the world. Then, after 1945, we will also examine the expansion of statist activity consequent on the adoption of new notions of central planning and accelerated national development, as well as the later reaction to state direction under the rubric of markets, privatization, and trade liberalization.

It is this emphasis on the role of the state, and its treatment on a country by country basis, which distinguishes our approach from that of the two other works of economic history which cover much the same period from a more general perspective: Charles Issawi, *An Economic History of the Middle East and North Africa* and Alan Richards and John Waterbury, *A Political Economy of the Middle East: State, Class and Economic Development* (details of both in the Bibliography).

Finally, as far as money and measurements are concerned, we give them both in their original form and as converted into a standard international form where possible: dollars ($) for money, acres as a measure of areas of land, etc. For further information about Middle Eastern weights and measures, see Charles Issawi (ed.), *The Economic History of the Middle East, 1800–1914*, pp 517–24 (details in the Bibliography).

Notes on General Introduction
Full details of all sources are in the Bibliography

1   See, in particular, his *Modern Economic Growth.*
2   Kuznets, *The Income Growth of Nations*; Gershenkron, *Economic Backwardness in Historical Perspective.* For more recent support for the same argument, see Abramovitz, 'Catching Up, Forging Ahead, and Falling Behind,' and Taylor, 'On the Costs of Inward-Looking Development: Price Distortions, Growth and Divergence in Latin America.'
3   This point is forcefully made in Taylor, 'On the Cost of Inward-Looking Development,' pp 9–18.
4   One contemporary estimate puts the value of unrecorded transactions in Egypt as at least equal to that of the official GDP. See Oweiss, *The Underground Economy with Special Reference to the Case of Egypt*, pp 19–20.

Part I
1918–1945

Introduction
to Part I

In the immediate aftermath of the First World War the Middle East had a population of some 40 million, the great majority of them resident in two independent (or quasi-independent) states – Turkey and Egypt – with perhaps 13–14 million each. In addition, there were some 3 million in Syria/Lebanon, another 2.5 million in Iraq, 1 million in Palestine/Transjordan, and 7–8 million either concentrated in the area now known as Yemen or scattered around the fringes of the rest of the Arabian Peninsula. After the expulsion of the Greek population from Anatolia in 1922, the only large group of persons of European origin was in Egypt: some 250,000. Unlike French North Africa, there was very little European ownership of land, although we should note the presence of a small Jewish community in Palestine with plans to purchase more land in pursuit of its scheme to establish a 'National Home.'

The vast majority of these people (70–80 percent) lived outside the large towns and made their living either from cultivation, or herding, or a combination of the two. As for the crops they grew, this depended largely on the availability of water. Most Middle Eastern agriculture depended on the annual winter rains. But there were also important areas of irrigated agriculture in the two great river valleys of the Nile and the Tigris and Euphrates, as well as small areas such as the Barada near Damascus. The major rain-fed crops were wheat, barley, and various types of maize grown for subsistence or to pay taxes. But irrigation allowed a more intensive and various pattern of output, and it was here that the most important cash crops were to be found, such as cotton and sugar in Egypt, and dates in Iraq.

In most parts of the Middle East except western and central Anatolia, the late nineteenth century had seen a concentration of ownership and control in the hands of a relatively small number of rich and powerful men, most of whom preferred to let it to tenants rather than manage it directly. Hence what were defined as large estates constituted about half the culti-vated land in the Egyptian delta and up to two-thirds of some of the riverain districts of lower Iraq. While not all the owners of such estates had yet been able to establish secure, legal title, they were well placed to do so under the aegis of the new state systems which were created after 1918.

Industry of a factory type using power-driven machines was confined to only a few plants, most of which either produced manufactured goods for export, for example sugar, cigarettes, carpets, and silk thread, or took advantage of the protection afforded by high transport costs to make such products as cement, flour, or beer for the local market. But even here the use of mechanical power was quite limited. There was also a huge range of small workshop and handicraft industry in both town and country. Some parts of this activity had been affected by European competition during the course of the nineteenth century but much of it had been able to sur-vive, often because some small change in technique allowed it to keep its old markets or find new ones among fast growing urban populations.

For most parts of the region, the nineteenth century had seen a huge increase in trade. As far as the Ottoman Empire was concerned, Pamuk's estimate shows a rise in value (at current prices) from £T 9 million in 1830 to £T 45.9 million (1910–13).[1] Meanwhile, Egypt's trade increased in money terms from £E 5 million in 1850 to £E 60 million in 1910, or some 5 percent a year.[2] These developments were accompanied by a shift in trading patterns from one of exchange within the region itself to trade with Europe. The shift was carried furthest in Egypt where over 90 percent of the value of exports in 1913 and some 70 percent of imports were with European states, notably Britain. Indeed, so close were its links with the British economy through its export of long staple cotton to the Lancashire textile mills, the finance of its cotton crop by British banks, and its early adherence to the gold standard, that it has been described as part of the 'British area' along with Portugal, Canada, and Australia.[3] Some of the same type of links existed between the major European economies and the export sectors to be found in western Anatolia, Mount Lebanon, and southern Iraq. As a rule such trade consisted of the exchange of primary products for manufactures, industrial raw materials, and a growing quantity of foodstuffs such as cereals and refined sugar.

Growing commerce with Europe allowed the Middle East to participate in the first great period of globalization which began in the 1870s and which saw world trade grow by some 3.5 percent a year between 1872 and 1914.[4] This, in turn, was encouraged by significant developments within the inter-national economy, such as the huge expansion of shipping, the growing acceptance of the common gold standard to fix exchange rates between currencies, and the laying of submarine telegraph cables which allowed a process of day-to-day trading and price-making for commodities such as cotton and tobacco. Certainly the most spectacular example of this process was Egypt, whose total trade in the period 1910–13 may well have constituted as much as 50 percent of its GDP, a figure just a little larger than that of Britain.[5]

Trade with Europe was followed by the import of capital, first on government account and then, from the 1880s onwards, by private companies investing in infrastructural projects like ports and railroads, land and mortgage, companies and, to a lesser extent, factory industry. Unfortunately, most Middle Eastern governments did not make good use of the money they borrowed from Europe, a process that led the international bankruptcy of the Ottoman and Egyptian governments in the 1870s and the subordination of parts of their economies to foreign financial control.

Economic life in the Middle East was seriously disrupted by the fighting which took place in many parts of the region during and just after the First World War. Trade flows were halted, men and animals conscripted, and, worst of all, there was a large number of deaths from fighting and forced migration, famine, and disease. The population of Anatolia was further reduced by the killing or forcible eviction of large numbers of Greeks and Armenians, declining by some 25 percent overall between 1913 and 1924.[6] Estimates of total casualties in the other battle zones are obviously imprecise, but one calculation suggests that some 500,000 people died in the Syrian provinces during the four years of war.[7] The only small compensation was the encouragement which the disruption of normal trade gave to local manufacturers and to producers of food and other necessities.

The war brought great political change as well, notably the dismantling of the Ottoman Empire and the establishment of the Republic of Turkey (founded in 1923) and a number of successor states under British and French mandatory control: Syria/Lebanon, Palestine/Transjordan, and Iraq. The war also provided the conditions for the final victory for the Saudi ruling family in its long battle for control over the Arabian Peninsula with its two main rivals, the Hashemites of the Hijaz and the Rashidis of

Najd. The result was the political division of the Middle East into two: the independent states of Turkey, Egypt, and later Saudi Arabia, on the one hand, and the mandates, colonies, and protectorates of the great powers, on the other. There were also the beginnings of a significant economic division of the region, as the new states began to introduce tariffs and other protective devices, thus putting an end to the system which, in Ottoman times, had permitted almost complete free trade between Anatolia and the Arab provinces of the Empire.

The world into which these new national economies were born had also changed in ways that had an important impact on the Middle East. The war itself had proved enormously disruptive to existing patterns of trade and output, putting an end to the gold standard, diverting production to military purposes, and setting in train a process of economic nationalism which created considerable barriers to the international flow of both goods and labor. There followed a necessary period of economic recovery and reconstruction which meant that, for example, it was not until 1925 that European manufacturing output was able to return to its pre-war level.[8] Then, just as the world economy began to revive, with most of the leading states having returned to the gold standard by 1928, there came the huge fall in prices and production which marked the first stages of the Great Depression during the early 1930s, encouraging a new round of protectionist measures and the division of the world into separate currency blocs: the dollar, sterling, the franc, and so on. International trade was divided and segmented along similar lines, forcing many countries to conduct their exchanges on the basis of bilateral arrangements and clearing schemes.[9] The result was a general slow-down in the growth of world production and commerce, the latter increasing at only 0.72 percent a year, 1913–29, and then falling for most of the 1930s before making a small recovery towards the end of the decade.[10]

The Great Depression was transmitted to the developing countries via a number of mechanisms. First, there was a decline in the volume of imports from the developing countries. Second, dollar prices of primary commodities collapsed more steeply than the prices of manufactures until 1933. Such a deterioration in the sectoral terms of trade would have represented a major loss of income even if physical output had remained unchanged. The third mechanism was the collapse of international flows to the developing countries once the Depression took hold. Fourth, and finally, the decline in world prices increased the debt burden of the many developing countries that had become net borrowers before 1929.[11]

Responses varied widely. For a number of reasons, the governments of some developing countries adopted a 'passive' stance, waiting for the end of the Depression and the return of world demand for their primary products. Others, gradually, and in varying degrees, began to expand domestic demand. Among the policy instruments used for this purpose were protectionist trade measures such as tariffs and quotas, expansionary fiscal and monetary policies, and the depreciation of the exchange rate. Many of those countries with a large external debt declared a moratorium on debt repayments and/or demanded the renegotiation of payments schedules. Recent studies have shown that countries which adopted more active policy positions during the 1930s fared better in terms of growth than those that simply waited for trade to revive.[12]

The impact on the Middle East of these changes in world conditions was considerable. To begin with, it experienced a process known as 'de-globalization', in which the flows of capital and commerce to and from Europe were much reduced. This was particularly the case with those countries that were dependent on British or French international investments, both of which saw a marked decline in value beginning during the First World War and continuing through until the Second.[13] To make matters worse, Middle Eastern countries saw the prices of their primary exports fall precipitously between 1929 and 1932 while, in the case of Lebanese silk or Gulf-produced pearls, most of what remained of their markets was taken away by cheaper, man-made, substitutes. Further problems came for those states whose currencies were tied directly to sterling or the franc, both of which were subject to drastic devaluation in the 1930s. The Second World War led to yet another period of disruption. Although there was much less fighting in the region, and less loss of civilian life than in the First World War, a shortage of shipping space caused a substantial decline in international trade including much-needed imports such as machinery and fertilizer. Allied military expenditure of some $2 billion between 1939 and 1944 provided partial compensation, but only at the expense of very high levels of wartime inflation.[14]

The result was a general tendency for GNP to grow much less rapidly than in the late nineteenth century and, in many cases, to do little more than keep pace with the increase in population. This was certainly true of Egypt, where the few tentative available estimates of GNP indicate that there was no overall growth in per capita income between 1913 and the late 1940s.[15] It may well have been true of Syria/Lebanon as well.[16] The only countries which were able to make some limited economic progress were Iraq, which began to export oil in the 1930s, and Palestine, where the wave of Jewish immigration from Germany at the beginning of the Nazi period produced an important fillip to production and investment.

Most Middle Eastern states sought to protect themselves against some of the worst consequences of the Depression by restricting imports, encouraging local industry and, in some cases, protecting local agriculture as well. This can be seen most obviously in the actions of the two main independent states, Turkey and Egypt. But even in the mandated states of Syria/Lebanon and Palestine/Transjordan, various domestic pressures forced the French and British administrators to raise existing tariffs even though, as often happened, this tended to raise the cost of living for the poorer classes.[17] One result was to encourage the beginnings of a modern industrial sector in Turkey, Iraq, Egypt, Palestine and, to a lesser extent, Syria/Lebanon. Another was a marked reduction in the ratio of trade to GDP. In Egypt, for example, this fell from some 50 percent between 1920 and 1924, to just over 40 percent between 1937 and 1939.[18]

It should be noted, however, that the Middle East's inter-war economic performance had much in common with that of many of its neighbors. One good comparison is with Eastern Europe where, just as in the Middle East itself, an old empire, the Austro-Hungarian, had been broken up after the First World War into a number of small successor states, all of which had to go through the same process of establishing their own administrations and national markets. Almost everywhere there was a similar overwhelming reliance on the agricultural sector for income and exports. These states experienced mixed progress in the 1920s, with per capita income rising modestly in Hungary and Yugoslavia but falling in Poland and Bulgaria.[19] All were then hit severely by the Depression when their commodity prices fell by more than half and they experienced a profound deterioration in their terms of trade. As in the Middle East, there was some modest progress in a few sectors during the rest of the 1930s but not enough to change the basic fact that they remained low income, agrarian, economies, highly dependent on access to world markets and with economic and social structures which provided significant barriers to further progress.[20]

To sum up, analysis of the growth performance of the Middle East economies during the period 1918–45, together with a comparison with that of the adjacent Balkan states, suggests that the major differences between one country and another can be explained largely in terms of the differential impact of the two world wars as well as by the damage caused by the Great Depression offset, in some instances, by the particular policy responses to it.

8

Notes on Introduction to Part I
Full details of all sources are in the Bibliography

1   Pamuk, *The Ottoman Empire and European Capitalism 1820–1913*, Table A1-1.
2   Issawi, *An Economic History*, Table 2.1.
3   Braga de Macedo, Eichengreen, and Reis (eds.), *Currency Convertibility: The Gold Standard and Beyond*, p 114.
4   Hirst and Thompson, *Globalisation in Question*, p 49.
5   Figures for Egypt from Owen, *The Middle East in the World Economy 1800–1914*, p 241; estimate for Egypt's GDP to be found in Hansen and Marzouk, *Development and Economic Policy in the UAR*, Chart 2.2; figures for the UK from Hirst and Thompson, *Globalisation*, p 49.
6   Based on Behar, *The Population of the Ottoman Empire and Turkey, 1500–1927*; Shorter, 'The Population of Turkey After the War of Independence'; Eldem, *Osmanlı İmparatorluğu'nun İktisadi Şartları Hakkında Bir Tetkik*; and McCarthy, *Muslims and Minorities*.
7   Schatkowski Schilcher, 'The Famine of 1915–1918 in Greater Syria,' pp 229–52.
8   Pinder, 'Europe in the World Economy, 1920–1970' in Cipolla (ed.), *Fontana Economic History of Europe: Contemporary Economies – 1*, p 326.
9   See, in particular, Kindleberger, *The World in Depression 1929–39*.
10 Issawi, *An Economic History*, p 25.
11 Maddison, *Two Crises*, pp 13–16.
12 *Ibid.* and Diaz Alejandro, 'Latin America in the 1930s.'
13 See, for example, Royal Institute of International Affairs (RIIA), *The Problem of International Investment*, pp 133–5 and 215.
14 See Wilmington, *The Middle East Supply Centre*, p 22.
15 For example, the figures provided by Ibrahim in Zimmerman, 'The Distribution of World Income 1860–1960,' p 46.
16 For example, Couland's estimate that the purchasing power of Lebanese wages declined by 100 percent between 1913 and 1937; *Le mouvement syndical au Liban 1919–1946*, pp 214–16, 279–84.
17 For an example of the problems associated with raising tariffs on the import of cheap Japanese textiles, see Shimizu, *Anglo-Japanese Trade Rivalry in the Middle East in the Inter-war Period*, p 197.
18 Figures from Mead, *Growth and Structural Change in the Egyptian Economy*, Appendix 1 and Appendix V-A-1.
19 I have drawn this information about Eastern Europe from Aldcroft, 'Eastern Europe in the Age of Turbulence, 1919–1950,' pp 592–602.
20 *Ibid.*, p 599.

1

Turkey
1918–1945

The period from 1918 until 1945 was exceptionally difficult for the society and economy of Turkey. Before the country could fully recover from the devastation of a decade of war which brought about the end of the Ottoman Empire and led to the emergence of a new nation state, it was hit by the Great Depression and the collapse of the world market for agricultural commodities. The 1930s were characterized by government interventionism and the promotion of domestic industry. The onset of the Second World War signaled another period of costly mobilization even though the country did not join the war. This chapter examines the impact of each of these major shocks, as well as the policies of the government on both the rural and urban sectors. It assesses the long-term record in terms of economic growth, structural change, distribution, and socio-economic welfare, to the extent permitted by the available evidence.

A DECADE OF WAR AND DESTRUCTION

For more than a decade beginning in 1912, Anatolia was ravaged by a series of wars. The hostilities, destruction, and death that accompanied the Balkan Wars of 1912–13, the First World War, and the War of Independence in

1920–22, had severe and long-lasting demographic, social, and economic consequences. Demographically, the population of the areas that were later included in Turkey was around 17–18 million in 1913. Total casualties, military and civilian, of Muslims during this decade are estimated at close to 2 million. In addition, most of the Armenian population of Anatolia was forcibly deported, died, or was killed after 1915. Of more than 1.5 million Armenians living in this area before 1914, fewer than 100,000 remained in 1923, mostly in Istanbul. Large numbers of Greeks also fled western Anatolia after the defeat of the Greek occupation army in 1922. Finally, in the largest peacetime agreement of population exchange between two governments, the remaining 1.2 million Greeks left Anatolia, and in return, approximately half a million Muslims arrived from Greece and the Balkans after 1923.[1]

As a result of these massive changes, the population of Turkey stood at around 13 million at the end of 1924, a decrease of about 25 percent from a decade before. Close to two-thirds of this decline was due to deaths and the rest to emigration. The large numbers of deaths amongst males meant that the resulting population included an unusually high number of females and widows. In many provinces of western Anatolia widows accounted for 30 percent of the female population, according to the 1927 census. The decline in the urban population, most prominently of Istanbul and Izmir, was proportionately greater. Urban centers of 10,000 people or more accounted for only 16 percent of the population of Turkey in the early 1920s compared with to more than 20 percent before the wars.

Ethnically speaking, the population of Turkey emerged as much more homogeneous than the Ottoman population in the same areas, with Muslim Turks and the Kurds in the southeast making up close to 98 percent of the total. Most of the remaining minorities – Greeks, Armenians, and Jews – now lived in the Istanbul area. The dramatic decline in the Greek and Armenian population meant that many of the commercialized, export-oriented farmers of western Anatolia and the eastern Black Sea coast, as well as the artisans, leading merchants, and moneylenders who linked the rural areas to the port cities and the European trading houses, had departed.[2]

Accompanying these dramatic changes in population was a sharp decline in the levels of production during the war years. Agriculture, industry, and mining were all adversely affected by the loss of human lives and by the deterioration and destruction of crops, draft animals, equipment, and manufacturing plants during the war years. It is hard to provide precise estimates for the extent of the decline in production during this difficult decade. In agriculture, where the evidence is more detailed, aggregate

11

production probably declined by more than 50 percent from 1914 levels.[3]

The decade of war also gave rise to more interventionist and protectionist economic policies, and this important legacy was to become more evident with the onset of the Great Depression in 1929. Even before the First World War, one wing of the Young Turks who had led the 1908 revolution had begun to argue against the open economy model based on trade and agricultural development, supporting instead the protection of domestic manufacturing and a more self-reliant strategy based on industrialization. The Ottoman government, however, had already committed itself under international treaties to free trade and a capitulatory regime which provided extraterritorial privileges for foreign companies and citizens. As a result, these arguments had little impact on policy until the First World War.

After its entry into the war on the side of the central powers, the Committee of Union and Progress (Young Turk) government moved unilaterally to redefine the empire's external economic relations in three key areas. First, it abrogated the capitulations and subjected foreign companies and individuals to Ottoman laws. Second, it eliminated the low-rate *ad valorem* tariff structure in favor of higher specific tariffs on selected goods. Third, it declared a moratorium on payments on the country's large and crippling external debt, most of which was held by France, Germany, and Great Britain.

The disruption of external trade and the sharp decline in agricultural output under wartime conditions brought about severe shortages. The provisioning of the army and the capital city thus emerged as key economic issues. The Young Turk government moved quickly to intervene in the economy. It also used the opportunities created by the wartime shortages to promote a Turkish bourgeoisie. Monopolies were created for the importation and distribution of many scarce commodities, and these were then awarded to the supporters of the Committee of Union and Progress. In the provinces, the emerging Muslim bourgeoisie began to acquire the land and other assets of the departing Greeks and Armenians. The government also recognized the importance of industry for national economic development.

Existing legislation for the encouragement and support of domestic industry was revised and extended. Wartime conditions and policies thus provided a significant boost to domestic industry.[4] A comparison of the Ottoman Industrial Census of 1913–15 with the Turkish Industrial Census of 1927, despite many methodological problems, reveals the extent of emerging manufacturing activity during that interval. Most of the new enterprises, however, remained small or medium-sized in scale.[5]

THE NEW POLITICAL LEADERSHIP IN ANKARA

The struggle for independence from foreign occupation, organized after the First World War under the leadership of Mustafa Kemal, culminated in the founding of a new nation state and a single-party regime under the Republican People's Party in 1923. The former military officers, bureaucrats, and intellectuals who assumed the positions of leadership in the new republic had strong political, social, and ideological ties to the Young Turk movement. They had been influenced by the ideas of the Enlightenment and the rationalist, libertarian thought of the French Revolution. During the War of Independence they had sought and obtained the support of provincial notables, large landowners, Muslim merchants, and religious and tribal leaders, both Turkish and Kurdish. They viewed the building of a new nation state and modernization through westernization as two closely related goals.

Their economic policies followed on directly from this outlook. They strove, from the outset, to create a national economy within the new borders. Construction of new railroads and the nationalization of the existing railroad companies were also seen as important steps towards the political and economic unification of the new state. Industrialization and the creation of a Turkish bourgeoisie were viewed as the key ingredients of national economic development. The Kemalist leadership was also keenly aware that Ottoman financial and economic dependence on the European powers had created serious political problems for the Ottoman state.[6]

In economic affairs, the first challenge to the new regime occurred at the Lausanne Peace Conference (1922–23) which was to define, amongst other things, the international economic framework for the new state. After protracted negotiations, agreement was reached in three key areas representing the beginning of a new era in relations with the European powers. First, the regime of capitulations which had provided special privileges to foreign concessionaries during the Ottoman period was abolished. This shift also paved the way for the gradual nationalization of some of the foreign-owned enterprises, notably the railroads. Second, the Ottoman external debt was renegotiated and apportioned between the successor states. The Turkish government assumed 67 percent of the total, to be paid in gold sterling beginning in 1929. Third, the free-trade treaties which had been renewed periodically during the nineteenth century were discontinued. It was agreed that the existing structure of low tariff rates and restrictions against quotas would continue until 1929, when the new republic would be free to pursue its own commercial policies.

13

THE RECOVERY OF THE 1920s

In terms of both world economic developments and domestic economic policy, it is best to examine the era until 1946 in three sub-periods. The first of these, lasting until 1929, is characterized by a strong economic recovery under conditions of an open economy. The second sub-period covers the decade from the onset of the Great Depression until the outbreak of the Second World War. During this period, the earlier measures to protect the domestic market were followed in 1932 by the adoption of etatism, or industrialization led by the state. Even though Turkey did not join the war after 1939, it maintained a large army and its economy came under enormous pressure as imports were disrupted and production levels fell sharply. Under these circumstances, etatism was replaced in this third sub-period by piecemeal measures to deal with shortages and the provisioning of the army and the urban areas. Tables 1.1 and 1.2 summarize the basic indicators of population, production, and economic growth for each of these three sub-periods. In the remainder of this chapter, each of them will be examined in greater detail.

Since the Lausanne Treaty imposed fixed tariff rates on imports at an estimated average rate of 13 percent, and adopted other related restrictions on commercial policy until 1929, the option of raising tariffs to promote selected sectors of domestic industry was not available to the new government. This did not mean, however, that the government would keep out of the economy. With industrialization and the promotion of a Turkish bourgeoisie considered as the new goals of economic policy, an active policy of intervention to favor the private sector was pursued. State monopolies in areas such as matches, alcoholic beverages, gasoline importation, and management of ports were transferred to private firms under favorable terms, especially to those firms with political connections to the ruling Republican People's Party. The Law for the Encouragement of Industry, passed in 1927, offered a wide variety of incentives and subsidies to the industrial establishments in food processing, textiles, cement, and other construction materials. In addition, the government embarked on an expensive, long-term effort to build new railroads that would link eastern Anatolia with the rest of the country, an important first step toward the creation of an integrated domestic market within the borders of the new nation state. The government was also eager to attract foreign capital, especially in partnership with domestic firms. More than 30 percent of the 200 joint stock companies founded during the 1920s included foreign partner.[7] Table 1.2 indicates that industrial output increased at rates exceeding 10 percent per annum during this period. While this may seem impressive at

14

first glance, most of the increases were due to the postwar boom in urban construction activity and, more generally, to the postwar recovery. Moreover, the country's industrial base was still too small for these figures to represent a broad advance in the urban sector.

The single most important act of government policy before 1929 was, undoubtedly, the abolition of the much dreaded agricultural tithe and the animal tax in 1924, and their replacement by land taxes and some indirect taxes on the basic consumer goods purchased by the rural population. The traditional tithe, which was collected at 10 percent of gross agricultural product, had represented the single most important source of revenue for the state. In the early 1920s it had accounted for more than 20 percent of all government revenues. Total collections from the peasant producers were considerably larger, however, since private tax farmers – who had purchased the right to collect the tithe for the government – appropriated a large part of the receipts. Revenues from the new taxes never approached those obtained from the tithe and the animal tax. As a result, the abolition of the tithe represented a major break from the Ottoman patterns of taxation and a significant decrease in the tax burden on the rural population. The fiscal burden began to shift, especially after the 1930s, toward the urban economy.

The abolition of the tithe has often been interpreted as a concession by the new regime to the large landowners in return for their support during the War of Independence. While this may have been a motive for some, most legislators and senior officials were aware that the tithe had placed too large a burden on the often defenseless small producers. After a decade of war and adversity, the new leadership was concerned to alleviate poverty and improve the material welfare of the small and medium-sized producers who made up the overwhelming majority of the rural population. Most historians of the period have also tended to ignore the fact that the abolition of the tithe also eliminated tax farming. The economically powerful strata of the provinces – large landowners, merchants, moneylenders, and urban notables – thus lost an important and convenient mechanism which had enabled them to appropriate a large part of the agricultural surplus. In the longer term, the abolition of both the tithe and tax farming certainly helped consolidate small peasant ownership and production in Turkish agriculture.

After a decade of war and a dramatic decline in output levels, the agricultural sector, which accounted for close to half of the national economy, experienced a sharp recovery during the 1920s. This recovery was helped by favorable price and demand trends in the world markets, and, in turn, provided an important lift to the urban economy. Sectoral growth rates,

15

summarized in Table 1.2, indicate that agricultural output almost doubled between 1923 and 1929. Nonetheless, detailed comparisons of Ottoman and Turkish production statistics suggest that by the end of the decade, per capita production levels in Anatolian agriculture were still somewhat lower than those prevailing on the eve of the First World War.[8]

THE GREAT DEPRESSION

The principal mechanism for the transmission of the Great Depression to the Turkish economy was a sharp decline in the prices of agricultural commodities. Prices of the leading crops, wheat and other cereals, declined by more than 60 percent from 1928/29 to 1932/33 and remained at those levels until the end of the decade. Prices of the leading export crops, tobacco, raisins, hazelnuts, and cotton, also showed declines averaging around 50 percent, although they recovered somewhat later in the decade. Since these decreases were greater than the decline in the prices of non-agricultural goods, the external terms of trade of the country deteriorated by around 21 percent and the domestic terms of trade shifted against agriculture by about 20 percent between 1928/29 and 1938/39 (see Tables 1.3 and 1.4B). Even though the physical volume of exports continued to rise after 1929, perhaps reflecting the continued recovery in output levels, the result was a sharp decline in the real incomes of most market-oriented agricultural producers. The adverse price movements thus produced a sharp sense of agricultural collapse, especially in the more commercialized regions of the country. Also in 1929, the economy experienced a severe foreign exchange crisis, both real and speculative, arising in part from sharply higher import volumes in anticipation of the tariff increases, and in part from the first of the large annual payments on the Ottoman debt.[9]

The severity of the agricultural and commercial crises convinced the government to undertake an important shift in economic policy and move toward protectionism and greater control over foreign trade and foreign exchange. In addition to quantity restrictions, tariffs on imports of foodstuffs and manufactured consumer goods were raised substantially, but those on agricultural and industrial machinery and raw materials were kept lower. Average tariffs on imports are estimated to have increased from 13 to 46 percent. As a result, imports declined more sharply than exports, ushering in a period of foreign trade surpluses which was to last until after the Second World War.[10] Also significant is the decline in the share of exports in GDP after 1929. This trend was primarily due to adverse movements in the prices of exports while overall export volumes continued to

16

rise. Since GDP continued to increase during the 1930s, the result was a fall in the share of exports in GDP. One significant implication of this trend is that exports failed to act as a source of recovery and growth for the national economy during the 1930s. The causes of that recovery thus have to be found elsewhere. Table 1.3 summarizes these trends, reflecting the decline of the foreign trade sector and the emergence of a more closed, more autarchic, economy during the 1930s. These developments were, of course, part of worldwide trends.

The balance of payments crisis of 1929 had a number of other important repercussions. First, concern over trade deficits and balance of payments problems moved the government increasingly towards clearing and barter agreements and bilateral trade, reflecting another worldwide trend during the 1930s. By the second half of the decade, more than 80 percent of the country's foreign trade was conducted under clearing and reciprocal quota systems. These bilateral arrangements also facilitated the expansion of trade with Nazi Germany, which offered more favorable prices for Turkey's exports as part of its well-known strategy towards southeastern Europe. Germany's share of Turkey's exports rose from 13 percent in 1931–33 to an average of 40 percent in 1937–39. Similarly, its share of Turkey's imports increased from 23 percent in 1931–33 to 48 percent in 1937–39. In contrast, shares of other leading European countries such as Italy, Britain, and France averaged less than 10 percent each during the 1930s. Turkish trade with countries in the Middle East also remained limited.[11]

Government concern with the balance of payments also led to a cessation of payments on the external debt and a demand for a new settlement after the first annual payment in 1929. The subsequent negotiations, aided by the crisis of the world economy and demands for resettlement by other debtors, produced a favorable result, reducing the annual payments by more than half for the rest of the decade.[12]

The Kemalist regime was not opposed to foreign capital. On the one hand, the government placed high priority on purchasing back European-owned enterprises in public utilities, mining, and above all in railroads. At the same time, it sought foreign funds and expertise for its industrial projects. Inflows of foreign capital declined after 1929, however, and remained quite low during the 1930s. The government succeeded in attracting funds only from the Soviet Union for the financing of the first five-year plan, and from Great Britain for an iron and steel complex beginning in 1938.[13] The most important reason for the limited volume of foreign capital inflows was the world economic crisis.

ETATISM

The difficulties of the agricultural and export-oriented sectors quickly led to popular discontent with the single-party regime, especially in the more commercialized and export-oriented regions of the country: in western Anatolia, along the eastern Black Sea coast, and in the cotton-growing Adana region in the south. The wheat producers of central Anatolia who were connected to urban markets by railroad were also hit by the sharply lower prices. With the creation, albeit temporarily, of a second political party, the pressure on the Kemalist leadership to adopt a new economic strategy to deal with the Depression intensified. Until that point, the mostly small-scale manufacturing enterprises consisting of textile mills, flour mills, glass works, brick factories, tanneries, and others had experienced reasonably high rates of growth as a result of the protectionist policies pursued since 1929. Nonetheless, this performance was not considered sufficient to meet the economic and political challenges posed by the Depression. The unfavorable world market conditions continued, and the government announced in 1932 the beginning of a new strategy, etatism.

Etatism promoted the state as a leading producer and investor in the urban sector. A first five-year industrial plan was adopted in 1934 with the assistance of Soviet advisers. This document consisted of a detailed list of investment projects to be undertaken by the state economic enterprises but did not provide a macroeconomic framework. A second five-year plan was initiated in 1938 but its implementation was interrupted by the war. By the end of the decade, state economic enterprises had emerged as important, and even leading, producers in a number of key sectors such as iron and steel, textiles, sugar, glass works, cement, utilities, and mining.[14]

Etatism has undoubtedly had a long-lasting impact in Turkey. The Turkish experiment also proved to be inspirational for other state-led industrialization attempts in the Middle East after the Second World War.[15] From a macroeconomic perspective, however, the contribution of the state sector to the industrialization process in Turkey remained modest until the Second World War. For one thing, state enterprises in manufacturing and many other areas did not begin operations until after 1933. The total number of active state enterprises in industry and mining on the eve of the Second World War did not exceed 20. Official figures indicate that in 1938 total employment in manufacturing, utilities, and mining remained below 600,000, or about 10 percent of the labor force. State enterprises accounted for only 11 percent of this amount, or about 1 percent of total employment in the country. Approximately 75 percent of employment in manufacturing continued to be provided by small-scale private enterprises.[16]

Etatism involved the extension of state-sector activities and control to other parts of the urban economy as well. Railroads, both those that were nationalized after being removed from European ownership and the newly constructed lines, were transformed into state monopolies. Most of the state monopolies which had been handed over to private firms in the 1920s were taken back. In transportation, banking, and finance, state ownership of key enterprises was accompanied by increasing control over markets and prices. At the same time, the single-party regime maintained tight restrictions on labor organization and labor union activity. These measures paralleled the generally restrictive social policies of the government in other areas. It is significant that, despite considerable growth in the urban sector during the 1930s, real wages did not exceed their levels of 1914.[17]

Despite the tensions between the two, it would be difficult to argue that the private sector was hurt by the expansion of the state sector. Even though the largest of the private enterprises in the foreign trade sector were adversely affected by the contraction of foreign trade during the 1930s, this was due more to the disintegration of international trade than to etatism itself. Elsewhere in the urban economy, most private enterprise remained small in size. By investing in large, expensive projects in intermediate goods and providing them as inputs, state enterprise actually helped the growth of private enterprise in the manufacturing of final goods for the consumer. Private investments continued to be supported and subsidized during the 1930s. Nonetheless, the private sector remained concerned that the state sector might expand at its expense. Tensions between the two sides continued.

There is some, admittedly crude, evidence on the rates of investment by the state and private sectors which sheds additional light on their respective roles. These estimates show that total gross investment in Turkey averaged more than 12 percent of GDP between 1927 and 1929. Private investment accounted for about 9 percent, and the rest came from the state sector. With the onset of the Depression, private investment dropped sharply to 5 percent of GDP and stayed at that level for the rest of the decade. State investments, on the other hand, rose modestly to an average of 5 percent of GDP by the end of the decade.[18] These estimates suggest that the state sector made up for some of the decline in private investment during the Depression but was not able to raise the overall rate of capital formation. It is also possible that the investment rates of the late 1920s were unusually high due to the postwar reconstruction and recovery. If so, one may conclude that the aggregate rate of investment fully recovered in the second half of the 1930s, even though it had declined immediately after 1929.

A sectoral breakdown of public sector investment is also instructive. Close to half of all fixed investments by the public sector during the 1930s went to railroad construction and other forms of transportation. This substantial commitment reflects the overriding desire of the single-party regime to create a politically and economically cohesive entity within the new boundaries. In comparison, industry received limited resources, attracting no more than a one-fourth of all public investment, or slightly above 1 percent of GDP, during the second half of the 1930s. This low figure supports our earlier argument that the contribution of etatism to the industrialization process remained modest in the 1930s.

Similarly, government macroeconomic policies can hardly be characterized as expansionary during the 1930s. In fiscal and monetary policies, etatism represented rather modest shifts in broad aggregates. Government revenues and expenditures increased from about 13–15 percent of GDP in the late 1920s to a new range of 17–19 percent during the 1930s. Government budgets were, on the whole, balanced, and no attempt was made to use deficit financing as an additional mechanism for generating savings. The nominal amount of currency in circulation remained stable and was linked closely to the gold and foreign currency reserves of the Central Bank until 1938. There was some increase in the real money supply, however, due to the decline of the aggregate price level. Nonetheless, since annual rates of GNP growth exceeded 5 percent during this decade, the real money supply did not keep pace with economic growth.[19] The most important reason behind this approach to macroeconomic policy was the bitter legacy of the Ottoman experience, with budget deficits and large external debt until the First World War and the inflationary experiment with paper currency during the war itself. Ismet Inönü, a close associate of Atatürk and prime minister for most of the inter-war period, was a keen observer of the late Ottoman period and was largely responsible for this cautious, and even conservative, policy stance.

ECONOMIC GROWTH AND ITS CAUSES

It is difficult to be precise about the rate of growth of industrial output and, more generally, the rate of growth of the urban sector during the 1930s. Tuncer Bulutay and his colleagues, who have constructed the only available series of national income accounts for the period before 1948 from incomplete official statistics, assumed, in the absence of other evidence, that the entire manufacturing sector grew at the same rate as those, mostly large, establishments which received subsidies from the government under the Law for the Encouragement of Industry, and for which data were available.[20] This method thus sharply overstated the extent of increase in manufacturing output, because it incorrectly assumed that the small establishments enjoyed the same rate of growth as their larger counterparts. In fact, other independent evidence has since become available showing that the small manufacturing establishments achieved only a modest increase in output during the 1930s. The consequent revisions to the Bulutay calculations bring down the overall rate of growth for manufacturing industry from around 10 percent to 5 percent per annum.[21] This is undoubtedly a significant correction, but the latter rate is still remarkable for the decade of the Great Depression. The revised estimates presented in Table 1.2 still point to a strong performance for the economy as a whole. GNP and GNP per capita grew at average annual rates of 5.2 and 3.0 percent respectively during the 1930s.

We thus have an apparent puzzle on our hands. Aggregate figures show that the contribution of the state sector to the urban economy, both as an investor and as a producer, was rather modest during the 1930s. Moreover, fiscal and monetary policies were not significantly expansionist. Indeed, balanced budgets and stable money supply reflect a cautious approach to macroeconomic policy. At the same time, however, we have evidence of strong performance by the industrial sector, the urban economy, and the national economy. How can these high growth rates be explained?

One important cause of the output increases after 1929 was the adoption of strongly protectionist measures by the government, which sharply reduced the import volume from 14.4 percent of GDP in 1928/29 to 8.7 percent by 1932/33 and 6.8 percent by 1938/39.[22] The most effectively used instruments in this process were quotas and tariffs on a wide variety of manufactured goods. An increasingly restrictive foreign exchange regime and a growing reliance on bilateral trading arrangements also served to limit import volumes. Domestic prices, which had moved sharply against agriculture and in favor of the urban sector, owing to trends in international markets, moved still further in the same direction as a result of these measures. Severe import repression thus created very attractive conditions for the emerging domestic manufacturers after 1929. These mostly small and medium-sized producers, which belonged overwhelmingly to the private sector, were able to achieve relatively high rates of output growth for the entire decade until the Second World War.[23]

There is yet another explanation for the overall performance of both the urban and the national economy which has frequently been ignored by economists and economic historians in their often heated debates over etatism and its meaning.[24] For that we need to turn to agriculture, the largest sector of the economy, employing more than three-fourths of the labor force during the 1930s and accounting for close to half of GDP.

AGRICULTURAL EXPANSION DURING THE DEPRESSION

The story of the agricultural sector during the inter-war period has two parts. First, as already pointed out, the collapse of commodity prices and the deterioration of the intersectoral terms of trade after 1929 had severe consequences for most producers. Not only did the market-oriented producers, both small and large, in the more commercialized, export-oriented regions of the country experience a decline in their standards of living, but so too did the more self-sufficient producers of cereals in the interior. Price movements in cereals were especially important since they accounted for more than half of the country's crop output in value terms (Table 1.4B). The sharp decline in agricultural prices also increased the burden of the indebted peasantry, forcing many to give up their independent plots and accept sharecropping arrangements.

One of the responses of the government was to initiate, after 1932, direct and indirect price support programs in wheat and tobacco. It began to purchase wheat from the producers, first through the Agricultural Bank, and later via an independent agency established for this purpose, Toprak Mahsulleri Ofisi (Soil Products Office). Until the end of the decade, however, such purchases remained limited, not exceeding 3 percent of the wheat crop in any given year. These purchases may have prevented an even further decline in wheat prices, but they certainly did not reverse the sharp deterioration of the terms of trade faced by the wheat producers. Whereas the domestic price of wheat had been above world prices before 1929, by the end of the 1930s it had fallen well below. It appears that the sharply lower agricultural prices were seen by the government as an opportunity to appropriate the agricultural surplus in order to accelerate the industrialization process in the urban areas. Prices of export crops and, more generally, of the non-cereal crops did not fare as poorly. The terms of trade faced by the producers of non-cereals improved after 1934, regaining their pre-1929 levels by the end of the decade (Table 1.4B).[25]

The second part of the story of agriculture during the Great Depression is less well known, but equally important. Evidence from a variety of sources, including official statistics, shows that agricultural output increased by 50–70 percent during the 1930s, after adjustments are made for fluctuations due to weather. The evidence thus indicates an average rate of growth of more than 4 percent per year for aggregate agricultural output during the decade. Foreign trade statistics corroborate this upward trend, as they show that Turkey turned from being a net importer of cereals at the end of the 1920s into a net exporter of wheat and other cereals on the eve of the Second World War, despite a population increase of 20 percent during the 1930s (Tables 1.1 and 1.4A).

The next task is to explain these substantial increases in output in the face of unfavorable price movements. Two different and not mutually exclusive explanations appear possible, although it may not be easy to assess the contribution of each without more detailed research. First, government policies could have played a role. Most importantly, the abolition of the agricultural tithe in 1924 may have contributed to the recovery of the family farm by improving the welfare of small and medium-sized producers and helping them to expand the area under cultivation or to raise yields. Another important contribution of government policy was the construction of railroads, which helped integrate additional areas of central and eastern Anatolia into the national market. Railroads must have encouraged the production of more cereals in these areas. The government was also involved in a number of other programs in support of the agricultural sector, such as the expansion of credit to farmers through the state-owned Agricultural Bank, and promotion of new agricultural techniques and higher yielding varieties of crop. Despite the rhetoric from official circles, these programs did not receive large resources, however, and their impact remained limited.

The second explanation focuses on the long-term demographic recovery of the family farms and their response to lower prices. In the inter-war period, Anatolian agriculture continued to be characterized by peasant households which cultivated their own land with a pair of draft animals and the most basic of implements. Most of the large holdings were rented out to sharecropping families. Large-scale enterprises using imported machinery, implements, and wage laborers remained rare. Irrigation and the use of commercial inputs such as fertilizers also remained very limited. If one reason for the strength of family farms was the scarcity of labor, the other was the availability of land, especially after the death or departure of millions of peasants, both Muslim and non-Muslim, during the decade of war. Under these circumstances, increases in production were achieved primarily through the expansion of cultivated area, so that the shortage of labor emerged as the effective constraint in blocking higher agricultural output in most parts of the country.

After the wars ended and the population began to increase again at annual rates of around 2 percent, the agricultural labor force followed suit, albeit with a time lag, thus facilitating the expansion of the area under cultivation. The basic agricultural trends summarized in Table 1.4A confirm this simplified picture. They show that while yields remained little changed, the area under cultivation expanded substantially during the 1930s. Numbers of draft animals increased by about 40 percent during the same period, confirming the material recovery of the peasant household and facilitating the expansion in cultivated area.[26] Recent comparisons of the late Ottoman and early Turkish statistics indicate that per capita agricultural output did not return to pre-First World War levels until the early 1930s. It took somewhat longer for total output to reach pre-war levels, most probably until the middle of the decade.[27] The availability of land also helps explain why land reform and redistribution of land did not become an important issue in Turkey during the inter-war period, except in the southeast where Kurdish tribal leaders controlled extensive tracts.[28]

An additional factor contributing to output growth arises from the economic behavior of peasant households. It is likely that the peasant households responded to the lower cereal prices after 1929 by working harder to cultivate more land and produce more cereals in order to reach certain target levels of income, very much like the peasant behavior implied by the Russian economist A.V. Chayanov.[29]

Sharply lower prices and rising output levels in agriculture thus created very favorable conditions for the urban sector during the inter-war period. Underlying the high rates of industrialization and growth in the urban areas were the millions of family farms in the countryside which continued to produce more, despite lower prices. These increases in crop output, in turn, kept food prices low for longer periods of time. After the abolition of the tithe, the agricultural surplus thus continued to be transferred to the urban sector with the help of the price mechanism. Protection of domestic industry alone, without this performance from the countryside, would not have allowed the urban sector to achieve such high rates of growth.

ECONOMIC CONTRACTION DURING THE WAR

Although Turkey did not participate in the Second World War, full-scale mobilization was maintained during the entire period. The sharp decline in imports and the diversion of large resources for the maintenance of an army of more than one million placed enormous strains on both industry and agriculture. The available estimates on national income indicate that GDP declined steadily and dramatically until 1945, when it stood at 35 percent below its pre-war level. Decreases in cereal production were even more dramatic, with wheat output apparently declining by more than 50 percent between 1939 and 1945. In response, prices of foodstuffs climbed rapidly and the provisioning of the urban areas emerged as a major problem for the government. Under these circumstances, the priorities and concerns of etatism were quickly pushed aside. The five-year industrialization plans were discontinued and the struggle with wartime scarcities, shortages, and profiteering, accentuated by economic policy mishaps, became the order of the day.[30]

Turkey's economy had already experienced a substantial decrease in the relative size of the foreign trade sector during the 1930s. Due to the difficulties facing wartime maritime transport and the shortages created in Europe by the mobilization, imports declined further during the war to less than 3 percent of GNP. As a result, the availability of many of the critical raw materials, intermediate goods, and manufactures decreased considerably, creating bottlenecks in all sectors of the economy. At the same time, Germany and the Allies competed for whatever minerals and agricultural commodities Turkey could export: wheat early in the war, and then chrome. As a result, the trade surpluses which had emerged in the early 1930s increased substantially, while gold and currency reserves continued to accumulate until the end of the war (see Table 1.3).

The agricultural sector, which had benefited from the demographic expansion of the inter-war years, was hard hit by the wartime mobilization. Even though women assumed a greater share of the burden, the conscription of males and the requisitioning of draft animals by the military adversely affected both the area under cultivation and yields, especially those of cereals. With the decline in production and increased demand from the larger army, the internal terms of trade moved sharply in favor of agriculture for the first time since the late 1920s (see Tables 1.4A and 1.4B).

In order to secure foodstuffs for urban areas and the military, the government attempted different forms of coercion, such as taxation in kind and forced deliveries at below-market prices. In response, producers of all strata tried to resist by deception, bribery, and more general evasion. Shortages in the large urban centers became more severe, forcing the government to reverse its policies and rely more on the price mechanism. In the end, small subsistence-oriented producers who could not take advantage of higher market prices bore the heaviest burden of government policies. While their consumption levels declined, the middle farmers and large landowners, especially those who could evade government demands, benefited from the sharply higher prices.[31]

The shortages created by the decline in imports also placed enormous strains on the industrial sector. Without the importation of raw materials, intermediate goods, and machinery, earlier levels of production could not

25

be sustained. Manufacturing industry output declined by more than 35 percent between 1939 and 1945. With the spread of bottlenecks and shortages, black markets thrived, and stockpiling and profiteering spread. Under these circumstances, the government was forced to abandon earlier plans for new investments in manufacturing industry. Another reason for the abandonment of etatism was financial. Wartime expenditures could not be met with the existing revenues, and the budget deficits began to be financed by printing money. The result was spiraling inflation, which accelerated the decline in the standard of living of the great majority of the urban population.[32]

In 1942, both as a partial solution to its fiscal difficulties and as a response to wartime profiteering, the government devised a major initiative called Varlik Vergisi, a one-off wealth levy on leading merchants, industrialists and other businessmen in the large urban centers. In practice, however, the Muslim businessmen were treated lightly and the levy was assessed mostly on the non-Muslim bourgeoisie of Istanbul. Seventy percent of the revenues were collected in Istanbul and 65 percent of the collections in this city came from non-Muslims. During the process, many non-Muslims, given short notice to raise cash, were forced to sell their real estate and businesses. These emergency sales proved to be an important source of accumulation for many of the prominent Turkish businessmen of the post-Second World War era. After causing much embarrassment to the government, the levy was discontinued the following year.[33]

When declining production and sharply lower standards of living combined with increasing inequalities in the distribution of income, large segments of the urban and rural population turned against the single-party regime. At the same time, the commercial and industrial bourgeoisie, as well as the larger, market-oriented producers in the countryside, many of whom had benefited from the wartime opportunities, began searching for alternatives to etatism and government interventionism. The war years, rather than the Great Depression and etatism era, thus appear to be the critical period in the demise of single-party rule. After the transition to a multi-party electoral system, the Republican People's Party was defeated in the first openly contested elections in 1950.

LONG-TERM TRENDS AND EQUITY

It is generally agreed that those developing countries in Latin America and Asia which abandoned the export-oriented model of the nineteenth century and adopted more interventionist, inward-looking policies during the

Great Depression fared better than those which continued with the earlier formula.[34] With its economic strategy as well as growth performance, Turkey certainly belongs to the former category. At the same time, however, the foregoing analysis, based on national income accounts not hitherto used for these purposes, reveals that the state sector itself was not responsible for the strong performance of the national economy. Instead, it has been argued that the high rates of growth were generated primarily through the repression of imports and the impressive expansion of small peasant production in agriculture.

It also needs to be emphasized that, while Turkey's economic performance during the inter-war period was favorable, it was bracketed by two extended periods of war and costly mobilizations. From a long-term perspective, these wars took their toll. The 1914 levels of per capita GDP were not attained again until the early 1930s. Similarly, per capita levels of production in 1948 and 1950 were only 25 percent higher than the levels attained on the eve of the First World War. In other words, the long-term growth rate of per capita GDP during these decades was approximately 0.6 percent per annum.[35] Resources allocated by the government to health care and education also remained limited. For this reason, one should not expect major improvements in the average or national levels of socio-economic and human development indicators, such as life expectancy at birth, during this period. Numbers of doctors, nurses, midwives, and other health care personnel increased modestly from 1.9 per 10,000 population in 1928 to 2.5 in 1945. At the same time, some progress was clearly made at all levels of education. Enrollment in elementary schools increased from approximately 22 percent of school age children in 1925 to 45 percent in 1945. Overall illiteracy rates declined from 81 percent in 1935 to 70 percent in 1945, and those for women, from 90 percent to 83 percent during the same period.

The national aggregates inevitably hide a good deal of regional, sectoral, and rural–urban differentiation. Unfortunately, however, we do not have reliable evidence with which to pursue these distributional issues in detail. One important statistical series that does cast light on them is the intersectoral terms of trade. It is clear that, owing to the sharp decline of prices in international commodity markets, the Great Depression had the most severe impact on agriculture. Within the rural areas, the more commercialized regions and the more market-oriented producers fared worse than others. Despite the rhetoric of the Republican People's Party to the effect that the peasant was the true master of the country, the rural areas did not receive significant levels of compensating support from the government after 1929. In contrast, the urban economy benefited from the favorable price movements, the severe repression of imports, and the beginnings of import substituting industrialization (ISI), as well as the policies of etatism. It is difficult, however, to determine how income distribution within the urban economy may have changed after 1929. The reliance on protectionism and the resulting rents of scarcity as the driving force of industrialization, coupled with the fact that real wages did not exceed their 1914 levels despite considerable growth in the urban economy, suggests that not only the rural-urban differences but also the inequalities within the urban economy may have increased during the 1930s. These broad trends in income distribution also suggest that if gains were made in life expectancy, health, and education during the inter-war period, these must have occurred primarily in the urban areas. Government policies must have reinforced this pattern since the health and education spending of the single-party regime favored the city population.

Notes on Chapter 1
Full details of all sources are in the Bibliography

1   See references in Introduction to Part I, note 6.

2   Keyder, *State and Class in Turkey*, pp 71–90.

3   Based on a comparison between the Turkish agricultural statistics of the 1920s as summarized in Bulutay et al., *Türkiye Milli Geliri (1923–1948)*, 2 vols, and the Ottoman agricultural statistics before the First World War as given in Güran, *Agricultural Statistics of Turkey During the Ottoman Period*.

4   Toprak, *Türkiye'de Milli Iktisat, 1908–1918*, pp 267–344; Ahmad, 'War and Society under the Young Turks,' pp 265–86; Zürcher, *Turkey, A Modern History*, pp 125–31.

5   Ökçün, *The Ottoman Industrial Census of 1913, 1915*; Turkey, State Institute of Statistics, *The Industrial Census of 1927*.

6   Tezel, *Cumhuriyet Döneminin Iktisadi Tarihi (1923–1950)* exp. 2nd ed., pp 389–97; Keyder, *State and Class in Turkey*, pp 91–101.

7   Boratav, 'Kemalist Economic Policies and Etatism,' chs 3 and 4.

8   Based on the sources cited in note 3 above. See also Özel, 'The GNP for Turkey, 1907–1939,' ch. 3.

9   Tekeli and Ilkin, *1929 Dünya Buhranında Türkiye'nin Iktisadi Politika Arayişlari*, pp 75–90; Tezel, *Cumhuriyet Döneminin Iktisadi Tarihi (1923–1950)*, pp 98–106.

10   Boratav, 'Kemalist Economic Policies and Etatism,' pp 170–76; Kazgan, 'Türk Ekonomisinde 1927–35 Depresyonu, Kapital Birikimi ve Örgütleşmeler,' pp 231–73.

11   Tezel, *Cumhuriyet Döneminin Iktisadi Tarihi (1923–1950)*, pp 139–62; Tekeli and Ilkin, *Uygulamaya Geçerken Türkiye'de Devletçiliğin Oluşumu*, pp 221–49.

12   Tezel, *Cumhuriyet Döneminin Iktisadi Tarihi (1923–1950)*, pp 178–86.

13   *Ibid.*, pp 165–89.

14   Boratav, 'Kemalist Economic Policies and Etatism,' pp 324–35; Hershlag, *Turkey: The Challenge of Growth*, chs 4 and 9; Tekeli and Ilkin, *Uygulamaya Geçerken*, pp 134–220; Tezel, *Cumhuriyet Döneminin Iktisadi Tarihi (1923–1950)*, pp 197–285.

15   For the influence of etatism on the state-led industrialization strategies in other Middle Eastern countries after the Second World War, see Richards and Waterbury, *Political Economy*, pp 174–201.

16   Tezel, *Cumhuriyet Döneminin Iktisadi Tarihi (1923–1950)*, pp 233–7.

17   Pamuk, 'Long Term Trends in Urban Wages in Turkey, 1850–1990,' pp 96–102.

18   Tezel, *Cumhuriyet Döneminin Iktisadi Tarihi (1923–1950)*, pp 362–88.

19   Yücel, 'Macroeconomic Policies in Turkey during the Great Depression, 1929–1940,' pp 46–73.

20   Bulutay et al., *Türkiye Milli Geliri (1923–1948)*, tables.

21   Zendisayek, 'Large and Small Enterprises in the Early Stages of Turkey's Industrialisation, 1929–1939,' ch. 4.

22   Table 1.3 and Tezel, *Cumhuriyet Döneminin Iktisadi Tarihi (1923–1950)*, pp 102–3.

23   Yücel, *Macroeconomic Policies*, pp 74–130.

24   For the debate, see, amongst others, Hershlag, *Turkey*, ch. 4; Boratav, 'Kemalist Economic Policies and Etatism'; Keyder, *State and Class*, ch. 5; Tezel, *Cumhuriyet Döneminin Iktisadi Tarihi (1923–1950)*.

25   Also see Boratav, 'Kemalist Economic Policies and Etatism,' pp 180–6. For a different perspective on state-peasantry relations and state policies towards agriculture during the 1930s, see Birtek and Keyder, 'Agriculture and the State,' pp 446–68.

26   Shorter, 'The Population of Turkey After the War of Independence.'

27   Güran, *Agricultural Statistics of Turkey During the Ottoman Period*; Özel, 'The GNP for Turkey, 1907–1939,' ch. 3.

28   Keyder and Pamuk, '1945 Çiftçiyi Topraklandırma Kanunu Üzerine Tezler,' pp 61–3.

29   Chayanov, *The Theory of Peasant Economy*, ed. Thorner, Smith, and Kerblay.

30   Boratav, *Türkiye Iktisat Tarihi, 1908–1985*, pp 63–72.

31   Pamuk, 'War, State Economic Policies and Resistance by Agricultural Producers in Turkey, 1939–1945,' pp 131–7.

32   Tezel, *Cumhuriyet Döneminin Iktisadi Tarihi (1923–1950)*, pp 156–60.

33   Aktar, 'Varlik Vergisi ve Istanbul,' pp 97–149.

34   Maddison, *Two Crises*, ch. 2; Diaz Alejandro, 'Latin America in the 1930s,' pp 17–49.

35   Based on statistical series and other evidence presented in Eldem, *Osmanlı Imparatorluğu'nun Iktisadi Şartlari Hakkında Bir Tetkik*; Güran, *Agricultural Statistics of Turkey During the Ottoman Period*; Bulutay et al., *Türkiye Milli Geliri (1923–1948)*; Özel, 'The GNP for Turkey, 1907–1939.'

2

Egypt
1918–1945

THE EGYPTIAN ECONOMY AT THE END OF THE FIRST WORLD WAR

According to its 1917 census, Egypt had a population of nearly 12.72 million, of whom only a small proportion – some 1.86 million (14.6 percent) – lived either in the two major cities of Cairo and Alexandria or in 13 other towns with a population of over 20,000. The rest were crammed into some 5.2 million acres of agricultural land along the banks of the Nile (Upper and Middle Egypt) or in the triangular-shaped delta (Lower Egypt), where population densities of up to 700 persons per square kilometer were among the highest in the world. The vast majority of this population – 86.4 percent of men and 97.9 percent of women – were classified by the census takers as 'illiterate.'[1] There was also a widespread incidence of disease including the water-borne affliction, bilharzia (schistosomiasis), the harmful effects of which had been greatly intensified by the spread of perennial irrigation to most of Lower and Middle Egypt during the nineteenth century. When the first National Life tables were produced for insurance purposes in the 1930s they revealed an average life expectancy at birth of thirty-one years for men and thirty-six years for women.[2]

Egypt was thus a predominantly agricultural country. According to the 1917 census, 2.4 million men were classified as workers in agriculture –

30

nearly 70 percent of those aged five years and over in full-time employment. Figures for the number of women at work in the same sector are more problematic but must have been well in excess of the 500,000 or so given in the census.[3] Agriculture also provided an estimated two-thirds of GNP, about one-third of government revenues (through the land tax), and nearly all exports.[4] In addition it acted as a major focus for foreign investment with well over half of the £E 100 million placed in Egypt's joint stock companies used to finance mortgages or other transactions connected with agricultural land.[5] Agriculture itself was dominated by the production of long staple cotton which had been introduced in the early part of the nineteenth century and was now grown as part of a two- or three-year rotation in most parts of Middle and Lower Egypt. Other important crops were wheat and barley, maize, rice, sugar, and the birsim (clover) grown for animal fodder. However, none of these produced anything like as high a return as cotton, which had the additional advantage that it could always be sold for cash and so was excellent security for loans or prompt payment of rent.

It was cotton, too, that acted as the spur for the vast expansion of dams, barrages, and canals built after the British took effective control of Egyptian administration in 1882. This in turn had allowed cotton production to increase from under 3 million cantars in the early 1880s to some 7.5 million just before the First World War (1 cantar = 99 lbs). However, the provision of all this extra water had not been accompanied by the necessary improvements in drainage. Hence salination and waterlogging had begun to have a serious effect on soil fertility and yields, at the very moment when supplies of new cultivable land were coming to an end. In such circumstances of incipient crisis it was clear that a large investment was needed to repair the damage. But, unfortunately for Egypt, all such works had to be postponed for the duration of the war.

Another feature of nineteenth-century agricultural development was the creation of what, in terms of the income they provided, were classified as large estates of 50 feddans and over, held as legally recognized private property (1 feddan = 1.038 acres = 0.42 hectares). These occupied some 45 percent of the total land area in 1907. As a rule they were administered as a single unit by their owners using a system which combined the direct cultivation of some of their fields through the use of service tenants and seasonal laborers, with renting out the rest to tenants on a yearly (verbal) contract related to the price of cotton. Another 30 percent of the land was held in what were classified as 'medium' properties of 5–50 acres, leaving only one-fourth for the smaller plots of 5 acres and under. The result was a highly unequal distribution of ownership, with some 150,000 persons holding three-fourths of the land and over 1.4 million small peasant holders the rest. Landlessness was also an increasing problem, with over half the families in Upper Egypt, and between 36 and 40 percent in Middle and Lower Egypt, owning no land at all.[6]

Returning to the 1917 census, only 489,695 persons (421,543 males and 68,152 females), or 5.9 percent of the active labor force, were classified as employed in the manufacturing sector, although here, too, there were considerable problems of definition.[7] Of these, the vast majority were to be found in small plants, or simply in the rooms of houses or shops, involved in the processing or working up of local agricultural produce such as cotton, sugar-cane, cereals, or leather. Others were employed in the salt and soda works or the various small factories producing bricks and cement from local materials. A last group worked in plants working up imported products such as silk or tobacco, most notably the numerous small cigarette factories, some of which produced hand-rolled 'Egyptian' brands for export and others machine-rolled cigarettes for the local market.[8]

Only a tiny proportion of the manufacturing labor force was employed in the small numbers of larger enterprises of a modern factory type. These were confined to the refinery belonging to the French-owned sugar company, the Société Générale des Sucreries et de la Raffinerie d'Egypte, just south of Cairo, which employed some 17,000 workers in 1916, the cotton spinning and weaving mill of the British-owned Fabrique Nationale d'Egypte at Alexandria (800 workers), the factory run by the Belgian Société Anonyme des Ciments d'Egypte near Helwan (260 workers), and a number of smaller plants making cement, ceramics, bricks, soap, or chemical products based on the alcohol distilled from sugar.[9] Such enterprises generally shared the local market with many smaller competitors, for example some 600 small sugar refineries or the products from the 13,000 hand looms.[10]

Given that so little of Egypt's manufactured products could be exported, industrial activity was almost exclusively directed towards a domestic market subject to only the most minimal protection from the 8 percent duty laid down in the international Commercial Convention of 1861 to which Egypt remained committed until 1930. But as was the case elsewhere in the non-European world, the First World War provided its own form of protection in the shape of reduced foreign competition, allowing Egyptian manufacturers to increase production to meet the extra demand from local consumers as well as the large number of British and other foreign troops stationed in the country.

Nevertheless, there were bound to be real worries as to whether such a high level of production could be sustained once foreign competition resumed in 1919. And, in the event, a number of the larger firms, such as the Sucreries and the Fabrique Nationale, only managed to keep going in this difficult period by running down their considerable wartime reserves, while many of the smaller ones were forced out of business.[11]

Although Egypt was only formally established as a British protectorate shortly after the outbreak of war in 1914, it had developed in ways which bore a striking resemblance to those of the typical colonial economy described by A.G. Hopkins. This he characterizes as an 'open' economy exporting a limited range of agricultural or mineral products, dominated by expatriate interests, and with low tariffs and minimal restrictions on trade. Other features of his definition include an unwillingness by the metropolitan power to shoulder any of the fiscal burden of running the colony, and a monetary system which is no more than an appendage of that of its colonial master.[12]

Turning to the Egyptian case, we can point not only to the low external tariff and the heavy emphasis on the export of cotton, but also to the British insistence on a balanced budget with only minimal expenditures on education, health, and welfare. In addition there was no central bank with powers to set interest rates or otherwise control the supply of money. Instead the right to issue notes had been given to a private organization, the National Bank of Egypt, which worked closely with the Bank of England (the British central bank) through an advisory board established in London. Foreign influence was further maintained by the British advisers attached to the main ministries, as well as by the presence of an expatriate community of some 250,000 foreigners, the majority of them, Italians and Greeks, who enjoyed a legally privileged position under nineteenth-century capitulatory treaties and tended to dominate most of the more profitable parts of the economy.

Lastly, Egypt's economic progress was hugely dependent on foreign direct investment, a fact which was brought home with particular force following the world financial crash in 1907, after which there was a marked slow-down in capital imports, particularly from Britain and France, with only the large mortgage companies able to attract significant new funds. This situation was made worse during the First World War when there was a further retreat of European capital from the non-European world.[13]

THE GENERAL PERFORMANCE OF THE EGYPTIAN
ECONOMY, 1918–1945

The first attempt to measure Egypt's national income was made by an economist for 1921/22 and the second – which included an index going back to 1937–39 – in 1950.[14] However, both are only very rough approximations and for the first reliable calculation we have to wait for the official government figures for 1959/60. Nevertheless, given the existence of good statistics from the decennial censuses, and the more regular recording of agricultural output and foreign trade, it has since been possible for economists to create indices which provide some guide to economic performance after 1913 (see Table 2.1).

Such indices indicate that both national income and GDP may have doubled between 1913 and 1950. Bent Hansen then divided this period into three sub-periods in each of which an initial shock to the economy was followed by a short period of recovery. These are: 1913–28, beginning with the deleterious economic effects of the First World War followed by a decade of recovery during which GDP is estimated to have increased at an overall rate of 1 percent a year; 1929–39, which began with the impact of the Depression before another period of recovery (with overall GDP increasing at 1.5 percent a year); and 1939–50, when the Second World War had much the same harmful impact as the First but was succeeded by another even stronger spurt of growth (overall GDP increasing at 2.5 percent a year).[15]

Turning to the main components of this economic performance, the major factor at work was clearly the slow growth of agricultural output over the period as a whole, as Egypt struggled to raise yields per acre in order to compensate for both the decline in soil fertility before the First World War and the fact that it had reached the limit as far as supplies of easily cultivable land were concerned. Other activities such as manufacturing provided too small a proportion of total product to have made anything but a small impact from 1930 onwards. It is also the gloomy conclusion of economists from Charles Issawi to Hansen that whatever gains were made in terms of income and output were almost completely negated by two other factors.[16] One was the rise in population which grew at a steady rate of 1.1 percent a year between 1917 and 1937 before increasing rapidly to perhaps 1.8 percent a year from 1937 to 1950 – although this may have been a little exaggerated as a result of over-counting in the 1947 census. The other was the huge deterioration of 31.5 percent in the country's terms of trade (the ratio of the index of export prices to the index of import prices) during the 1930s.[17] The impact of the first factor (population growth) was enough to cause GDP per capita (the measurement of domestic output) to fall slightly between 1913 and 1928, to rise at only 0.25 percent in the 1930s, to fall back by some 5 percent during the Second World War, and only to begin to advance significantly from 1945 onwards.[18] As for per capita national income (a measurement which also takes into account international factors, notably the balance of foreign trade), Hansen calculates that this fell by 10 percent during the 1930s and then by a similar amount during the Second World War.[19] Calculations such as these support Issawi's early argument that the standard of living of individual Egyptians showed no improvement whatsoever during the first half of the twentieth century.[20] More recently they have been used to underpin Robert Tignor and Hansen's melancholy characterization of the period as one of 'development without growth.'[21] By this they mean that the small amount of structural change – which raised industry's contribution to some 8 percent of GDP in 1937–39 and then to perhaps 10 percent in 1945 – was not enough to generate any significant increase in income.

There has been less consensus as to the reasons for this relatively poor performance, with various conclusions depending on the methodology and point of view of the analyst concerned. The evidence would suggest that there were three main *economic* reasons which need to be explored. These are: a low level of investment (perhaps 5–6 percent of GDP) which was insufficient to do more than offset the depreciation of existing assets (particularly in the agricultural sector) and to meet the needs of a steadily expanding population;[22] the outflow of foreign capital during and after the First World War, followed by only a gradual increase thereafter, leading to what one contemporary economist described as a 'starvation of funds,'[23] and Egypt's vulnerability to adverse changes in the world economic environment, particularly the adverse impact on foreign investment and agriculture of two world wars and the Great Depression.

One note of caution is also in order. Even though Egypt's economic performance can be considered poor during this period, this was a characteristic it shared with any number of other countries including India and a whole host of other so-called 'tropical' exporters.[24]

GOVERNMENT AND THE ECONOMY

Egypt's nominally independent governments remained subject to considerable constraints when it came to the formation of economic policy from 1923 onward. They did not gain autonomy to set tariffs until 1930 for freedom to impose new taxes which might affect the foreign community until 1937. In addition, they remained subject to varying degrees of British pressure, exercised either by the few remaining British advisers or by the British High Commission which changed only its name (not its role) to that of the British Embassy after the ratification of the Anglo-Egyptian Treaty in 1936, which phased out the British occupation. Finally, the country was essentially reoccupied by the British during the Second World War and subjected to economic measures designed to promote the Allied campaign against Germany.

Nevertheless, the fact that the vast majority of the British officials left government service in 1922–23, to be replaced by Egyptian nationals, did mark an important difference. It is true that policy-making initially lacked coherence and was subject to the rapid turnover of cabinets that was a major feature of the political life of the 1920s and 1930s. It is also true that, at least to begin with, there were few civil servants capable of providing the kind of continuities which successful new initiatives required. But this did not stop successive cabinets from trying to follow certain general principles concerning the promotion of national economic growth, urged on by an increasingly vocal public opinion. Nor did it prevent a complex struggle for influence and privilege conducted by a wide range of pressure groups and private commercial interests.

As far as the major principles were concerned, there was near universal agreement within the country's political class that government should take a more active role in the economy and that it should concentrate particularly on efforts to restore agricultural productivity and to encourage diversification through the promotion of manufacturing activities along the lines suggested by the government's Commission on Commerce and Industry at the end of the First World War. In addition, there was a general belief that, where possible, Egyptian rather than foreign interests should receive the more favorable treatment. Nationalism had rapidly become a potent force, something of which Egyptian entrepreneurs soon became keenly aware, particularly after the formation of the Bank Misr in 1920 with its stated aim of raising Egyptian capital to finance purely Egyptian projects. However, such activities were always more self-conscious than many later historians have allowed: they were engaged in with an eye to local economic and political advantage, and did not mean that anyone, from the members of the Commission on Commerce and Industry on, imagined that Egypt could do without foreign capital or foreign technical assistance for a very long time to come.[25]

Nevertheless, if there was agreement over general principles, there was much less about how they ought to be implemented. Here a major factor was the domination of government and policy-making by the large landowners whose economic and social influence was now augmented by the power they could bring to bear on a predominantly rural, peasant electorate. They exercised control through their association with the various political parties, as well as their strong presence in both senate and parliament. To give only one example, according to calculations by Asim Dasuqi, large landowners (by his definition anyone owning over 100 acres) constituted an average of 58.5 percent of all parliamentary committees between 1924 and 1952.[26] In these circumstances it was only common sense for advocates of economic diversification to try to encourage landlord support by stressing the compatibility of the agricultural and manufacturing interests, with new industry justified in terms of its role in processing locally produced crops for a mainly rural market. However, as the 1930s progressed, there were signs of growing contradictions between the two interests, particularly over the allocation of the government's limited financial resources. This in turn led to a fierce debate over the proposals for tax reform which had been made possible by the ending of the capitulations in 1937 and the completion of the period of fixed land tax rates established by the British at the time of their original land settlement 30 years before. Should the weight of any new taxes fall on the agricultural or the urban industrial interest? Under pressure from all sides, the government of the day settled for a small tax on income and wages, and only the most limited readjustment of rates on different qualities of land, leaving the old maximum of £E 1.64/feddan untouched. However, this temporary victory for the landed interests was soon to be challenged by those who argued that the large estate-owners should shoulder more of the fiscal burden. Such pressures were further intensified by the wartime suffering of Egypt's peasant population which was sufficient to encourage the first proposals for reforms aimed at redistributing agricultural land, of which at least one was justified in terms of the fact that further industrial expansion was dependent on the creation of a prosperous rural market.[27]

Let us turn now to a more detailed examination of the actual policies pursued. During the 1920s, governments concerned themselves with three major priorities. First, they provided more money for those areas where the British had come under nationalist criticism for being particularly parsimonious in their expenditure, notably education. Public elementary schooling was made notionally compulsory in the 1923 constitution. More importantly, spending on education rose from 3 percent of total expenditure in 1921/22 to 7 percent in 1929/30, although it was still not enough to provide teaching for more than a small proportion of the school age population.[28] Second, successive governments provided money for the long-postponed drainage scheme which began to be taken seriously in hand from the mid-1920s onwards. Third, governments continued to bow to pressures from the agricultural lobby to attempt to maintain the price of cotton by restricting its acreage for most of the 1920s and by purchasing part of the crop with public funds.[29]

Another area which received government attention was the approaching possibility of tariff reform in 1930. Once again, as a result of pressure from commercial interest groups, notably the Egyptian Federation of Industries, the administration was encouraged to hurry along with the preliminary work so as to be ready to present a bill to parliament at the first possible moment. The resulting legislation erected a three-tier structure with reduced rates (usually 4 percent) for necessities, medium rates (6–10 percent) on semi-manufactures and machines, and higher rates (usually 15 percent) on most finished manufactured goods.[30]

Successive governments during the 1930s were then faced with more pressure to continue to raise these rates, particularly from the expanding textile sector which was worried not only by competition from Europe but also by the increasing importation of cheap Japanese textiles. Hence as early as February 1931 tariffs were raised on the lower quality, heavier cotton cloths, and then again in 1933. But this was not enough to halt the Japanese tide, and in September 1935 the government imposed a 40 percent depreciated currency surcharge on Japanese products on the grounds that they had benefited unfairly from the huge 1930 devaluation of the yen.[31] This led to an immediate reduction in the volume of such imports. Other measures of government support for local industry followed, many along the lines of the recommendations made by the Commission on Commerce and Industry, for example reduced railroad rates for raw materials, government purchases of finished products and, in the case of textiles, sales of raw cotton from government warehouses at subsidized prices.

However, the governments of the 1930s were soon forced to confront a much more serious problem in the shape of the agricultural crisis brought on by the huge fall in the price of cotton at the beginning of the Depression. This had an immediate knock-on effect in terms of falling land prices, higher real tax rates and increased indebtedness for those forced into renewed borrowing to meet existing obligations, such as mortgages. The government's initial response was to continue the previous policy of restrictions on cotton acreage in 1931 and 1932. But this policy was abandoned when its opponents were able to demonstrate that, given Egypt's tiny share of the total world market, such measures could have no effect whatsoever on price.[32] Whether this was in fact the case continues to be a matter for debate. Efforts to estimate the elasticity of demand for Egyptian cotton do not, as yet, seem to have found a way of coming to terms with the fact that, while the superior grades enjoyed a partial monopoly in certain well-defined markets (for example, the manufacture of automobile tires), others had to compete with the better grades of American cotton which provided possible substitutes.[33]

Nevertheless, if the price of Egypt's cotton was left to market forces, the government intervened to raise the prices of other agricultural products by such measures as the prohibitive tariff placed on imports of cereals and flour in 1932 and the 1931 agreement with the sugar company to provide total protection for the Egyptian domestic market in return for increased government control over sugar prices and sugar-cane acreage as well as a share of the profits. The result, of course, was a marked increase in the cost of foodstuffs which had serious consequences for the poorer classes. Government attempts to meet some of the immediate financial problems of the agriculturists also involved the temporary remission, or reduction, of taxes and support for landowners faced with the threat of expropriation for non-payment of mortgage interest. Later, as the 1930s progressed, more long-term measures of relief for the agricultural sector were implemented. These included the creation of new sources of credit, notably a government-financed bank, the Crédit Agricole, founded in 1931, and a series of agreements with the three largest mortgage companies, beginning in 1933, to reduce interest rates and to extend repayment periods in exchange for government financial support.

Lastly, the agricultural sector soon began to benefit from continued government investments such as the extension of the drainage system, which by 1938 had been made to cover almost all of Lower Egypt. Meanwhile, new measures to increase the supply of water were also set in train, notably the doubling of the capacity of the Aswan Dam, completed by 1933, and the opening of the Gabal Aulia Dam in 1937, which paved the way for the further conversion of parts of Upper Egypt from winter-only flood irrigation to the perennial system found in the rest of the country. The result, as will be seen in later sections of this chapter, was that Egyptian agriculture survived the Depression much better in aggregate terms than might initially have been supposed, but, as in many other parts of the non-European world, at the heavy cost of increasing poverty for the bulk of its peasant population.[34]

The outbreak of the Second World War and the direct threat posed to Egypt by the Axis advance across North Africa brought new problems. These were tackled most directly by the Wafd Party government of Nahas Pasha, which was brought to power at British insistence as a result of the direct pressure imposed on King Farouk though the Abdin Palace ultimatum of February 1942. It chose to manage the economy through an

increasing system of controls and limited rationing, as well as by the imposition of restrictions on cotton production combined with compulsory
grain deliveries to meet the food crisis of the early war years. It was this
same Wafdist administration which was the first to recognize the need for
government intervention to regulate relations between workers and
employees. This involved the legalization of trade unions in a system of
binding arbitration to settle labor disputes through the establishment of
Conciliation and Arbitration Committees.[35]

THE PERFORMANCE OF THE AGRICULTURAL AND
MANUFACTURING SECTORS 1919–1945

AGRICULTURE

Tables 2.2 and 2.3 provide some of the data needed to evaluate the performance of the agricultural sector between 1919 and 1945. Four general
points stand out.

(1) Although there was no increase in the cultivated area during most of the
    two inter-war decades, this tendency was then reversed by an addition
    of some 500,000 acres between 1937 and 1947, probably as a result of
    the extra water stored in the Aswan Dam and, perhaps, the greater use
    of pumps to irrigate marginal land. Furthermore, the size of the
    cropped area (i.e. the total area planted with field crops of all kinds)
    continued to increase – except for some hiccups in the early 1930s and
    again during the Second World War – as farmers used their land more
    intensively, aided by the widespread employment of fertilizers, better
    techniques, and, in the case of Upper Egypt, the introduction of peren-
    nial irrigation.
(2) There was only a small increase in the output of the major field crops
    up to the end of the 1930s and then a fall during the Second World War.
    However, agriculture's performance looks better if we include, like
    Hansen and Wattleworth, a wider range of products such as birsim,
    fruit, and vegetables (Table 2.3, column 2).
(3) The agricultural labor force increased at least as rapidly as the output
    of the major field crops in the 1920s and 1930s with the result that there
    was only a tiny increase in agricultural output per capita during the
    Second World War.
(4) The main constraint imposed on faster agricultural advance was the
    need to compensate for the impact of more intensive cultivation and

soil exhaustion on yields in the decade just before 1914. The effect of the two world wars was also considerable, causing the postponement of vital public works schemes and cutting off the supplies of imported fertilizers and other much-needed inputs.

These aggregate figures, however, hide some of the important variations in agricultural practice which took place over time. They also raise interesting questions about the organization of production and the efficiency with which the various types of farming units were managed.

Far and away the most important crop in terms of income was cotton, which in a normal year occupied at least a third of the cultivated land. From the late nineteenth century onwards it was increasingly grown as part of a two-year rotation in conjunction with one or two cereal crops – usually wheat and maize – as well the birsim used for animal feed. Expansion was held back by the acreage restrictions employed during most of the 1920s, but increased rapidly after they were abandoned in 1933. Acreage was cut again during the Second World War, although output remained high owing to the fact that cotton was still grown on the best quality land. It was cotton which was affected most by the pre-1914 decline in agricultural yields when it had suffered not only from the general over-watering but also from an intensification of attacks from pests such as the cotton worm and the boll weevil. It took some time for the impact of drainage, increased use of fertilizer, and earlier planting (to reduce worm attack) to produce an effect, so that yields did not return to their pre-war level until the late 1920s. There was another fall in the early 1930s before a strong recovery towards the end of the decade, helped also by the appearance of new, and more prolific, varieties such as Giza 7 which had been developed by the Ministry of Agriculture as a substitute for older types whose yields continued to decline.

The area devoted to most of Egypt's other crops depended largely on their place within the system of cotton rotation. Of these, wheat was the second most important in terms of acreage and maintained a steady average of some 1.3–1.4 million feddans for most of the inter-war period, sufficient to provide all Egypt's domestic requirements. Other cereals, particularly maize, declined in importance during the 1930s. Meanwhile, cotton's only competitors in terms of value were rice, the production of which began to expand rapidly in the northern part of the delta once more water was available from the new dams, and sugar. Citrus acreage also increased during the period, although it was constrained by the relatively large investment required to start production and the fact that local demand was confined to the urban population.

41

Economists continue to argue about whether such a pattern made the best use of Egypt's scarce agricultural land. Yields were high by international standards but, given the fertility of the country's soil, the good transport system, and the well-developed mechanisms for marketing and finance, could productivity and income not have been even higher? One line of argument which continues to the present day is whether Egypt should substitute more high value crops for the cereals and fodder needed to feed its people and draft animals.[36] However, as far as the period under discussion its concerned, this can only be seen as a counsel of perfection: for more than half a century almost all of Egypt's resources had been devoted to the cultivation of one high-value crop, cotton, a situation which it would have been extremely difficult to change, the more so as there seems to have been little opportunity to increase the production of other high value crops like rice and citrus at a faster rate.

An equally intense argument focuses on the question of land management. Here many writers have tended to assume that, just because the large estates were a base for the exploitation and coercion of their workers, they had to be economically inefficient as well. Such arguments received a considerable boost from the political campaign conducted before and after the 1952 revolution against 'feudalistic' and 'absentee' owners in the interests of some form of land redistribution. Unfortunately there is an almost complete absence of data which would allow the question to be settled one way or the other. Nevertheless a few important points can be made. One concerns the operation of the large estates themselves and the observation that they were units which could avail themselves of economies of scale when it came to essential inputs (credit, fertilizers, pumps, etc.) while still benefiting from some of the advantages of small-scale production through renting part of their land to tenants.[37] A second underlines one of the findings of the 1950 agricultural census, which showed that, whereas Egypt's land was divided into 2.7 million individual properties, these were farmed as only 1 million units. From this economists have concluded that peasants – perhaps belonging to the same family – consciously tried to offset some of the obvious disadvantages of parcelized ownership by working several of their plots in common. As a result it is possible to conclude, with Robert Mabro, Patrick O'Brien, and others, that the inter-war system, though extremely inequitable, was reasonably efficient in terms of the organization of production and the allocation of resources.[38]

MANUFACTURING

Analysis of the growth of Egypt's manufacturing sector is also greatly handicapped by the absence of reliable indices of size and performance. All that exist are the census figures for the number of persons employed in this sector, Samir Radwan's calculation of capital investment in industry, and some statistics relating to the output of the large factories producing refined sugar and cotton cloth (Table 2.4). The establishment of the complete picture has also been hampered by concentration on the expansion of the modern sector to the exclusion of research into developments in the smaller-scale enterprises.

Scattered figures show that, during the 1920s, and in spite of the absence of both protection and significant government assistance, there was a continuation of the previous trend by which local manufacturers sought to increase their share of the domestic market wherever they possessed some particular advantage over their foreign competitors. This included the producers of cement, who had managed to meet half of the local demand by the end of the 1920s, of alcohol and related chemicals, of soap, and of shoes. To this should be added certain processors of local raw materials such as the cotton ginners and pressers, and the millers of flour.[39] Another significant development was the takeover by the Anglo-American Eastern Tobacco Company of all but one of the main local cigarette factories, keeping their brand names but redirecting their sale almost entirely towards the local market using machines which rolled imported Virginia tobacco.[40]

Egypt's two largest factory industries also managed to expand their output during the 1920s, although with some difficulty. Thus the Filature Nationale increased the number of its spindles from 20,000 in 1918 to 40,000 in 1922 and 60,000 in 1930. But if the output of yarn was raised by such an investment, that of cloth declined, falling from 9 million square meters in 1922 to only 6 million in 1930. This was in marked contrast to the concomitant increase in production by Egypt's hand loom weavers, which grew from an estimated 15 million square meters in the mid-1920s to a possible 23 million in 1930.[41] As for the sugar company, it was forced to reduce production at the end of the First World War, but then managed to expand again in the 1920s before running into serious difficulties in 1929 as a result of the collapse of the international price.[42]

One reason for the Filature Nationale's decision to increase capacity in the late 1920s was the desire to position itself so as to be able to take advantage of the fact that it would enjoy a much better protected domestic market once the new tariff rates were introduced in 1930. To this end it also made a strategic alliance with the British Calico Printers' Association in 1934 to establish a new enterprise, the Société Egyptienne des Industries Textiles, to spin, weave, bleach, dye, and print a much higher quality type of cloth than it had managed to do before.[43] Meanwhile, the Bank Misr had established its own textile subsidiary, the Misr Spinning and Weaving Company, with mills in the delta town of Mehalla el-Kubra. Later it too made an alliance with a British concern, Bradford Dyers, to produce its own higher quality cloth in two new companies, Misr Fine Spinning and Beida Dyers, which began operations in the late 1930s. The result was a considerable increase in Egyptian textile output in which the use of Egyptian cotton grew from 1 to 12 percent of the local harvest between 1930 and 1940/41, and the market share from 12 to 75 percent between 1931 and 1941.[44]

Other industries also expanded to take advantage of the more protected market. Apart from the sugar company, which enjoyed a monopoly position as a result of its 1931 agreement with the government, the proportion of local demand supplied by local manufacturers in 1939 was 100 percent for alcohol, cigarettes, and sugar, 90 percent for boots and shoes, cement, soap, tarbushes, and furniture, 80 percent for matches, and 65 percent for beer.[45] Most of these firms then continued to expand their operations to meet the still larger demand created by the Second World War during which Egyptian industrial production may have increased by as much as another 35 percent.[46] Considerable help was provided by the Anglo-American Middle East Supply Centre established in Cairo in 1941 in terms of access to scarce machinery and raw materials.

As elsewhere in the world, the small size of Egypt's protected market encouraged monopolies, high costs, and inefficiency. Certainly the most obvious example of this were the Misr mills at Mehalla, which were not only badly located as far as transport was concerned but relied on a predominantly agricultural workforce with labor allowed to come and go as it chose, a situation requiring considerable overmanning of the spindles and looms.[47]

Economists have also raised the larger question of whether Egypt had a natural advantage in textile production in the first place. The industry was forced to use high value, long staple Egyptian cotton to produce low quality cloth when there were many other countries, notably Japan and India, which used less good cotton to produce similar cloth much more cheaply. In Tignor's opinion Egypt received some offsetting benefit from its association with foreign capital which allowed the establishment of joint enterprises to weave better quality cloth.[48] But this still leaves the question of whether, in ideal circumstances, it would not have been wiser to try to miss out the low quality stage altogether, the more so as the initially poor organization of the Misr mills seems to have established a pattern which continues to handicap the Egyptian textile industry to the present day.[49] Nevertheless, in the real world of the 1920s and the 1930s, it seems doubtful whether Egypt could have proceeded in any other fashion, given the prestige that was attached to the establishment of a modern industry by politicians and businessmen alike, as well as the key role which the textiles factories (with their use of local cotton) played in cementing the central alliance between agriculturists and entrepreneurs.

SOCIETY, INEQUALITY AND WELFARE

During the inter-war period Egyptian society can be visualized as a very flat pyramid with an extremely broad base. At the apex were the 2,750 or so families, according to Dasuqi's estimates, who owned over 100 feddans (104 acres) of land, dominated by an even smaller group, 282 families plus the king and a few members of the ruling household, who owned 500 feddans or more.[50] Their numbers seem to have remained remarkably stable through the period with just a few families dropping out to be replaced by others headed by men who either married into wealth or were able to buy land after a career in government or business.

It was these families who dominated the rural areas on the basis not only of their control over land and agricultural employment but also of their occupancy of most of the important posts in the local administration, from umda (village mayor) to provincial governor. As a result they were able to combine economic with coercive power, and it is this which has often encouraged misleading parallels with feudalism of the European mediaeval type. What in fact seems to have happened is that they enjoyed complete authority over the inhabitants of their own estates, directing their working lives with a large force of overseers, supervisors, and others, and being able to exert extra discipline over the permanent estate workers using the threat of instant ejection from their houses which the owner himself provided.[51] More generally, they were well placed to ensure that any government initiative to help the agricultural sector, for example the provision of cheap credit for the smaller landholders, could be redirected to their own benefit.[52] As already noted, the large landowners were also able to use their rural position to exert strong influence on the government in Cairo. This they used to defend their own interests, whether by demanding government assistance for the agricultural sector or by defeating the claims of other interest groups for equally favorable attention. A good example of their power is provided by the official decision that the opportunity taken to amend the land tax rates in 1937–39 should not be used to raise the aggregate amount of tax paid by any one owner. As Andrew Holden, a British official who assisted in this operation, noted, the government of the day was particularly anxious to ensure the cooperation of those who controlled the countryside in order to make the revision of rates a success.[53] It was usual for large landowner members of parliament or the senate to present themselves as good nationalists – 'We are all Egyptians' or 'We are all fellahs (peasants)' – when arguing for government support. But they were also quick to demonstrate the distance which separated them from the peasants when it mattered, for example by conducting a spirited campaign against any increase in expenditure on education for those living in the rural areas.[54]

Below the very rich lay a growing stratum of professionals working either for the government or a private individual. Using census figures, Jean-Jacques Waardenburg calculates that this consisted of 53,000 persons in 1937 and 88,000 in 1947.[55] The majority, 35,300 in 1937, were teachers in schools and universities, after which came engineers, doctors, and dentists, and then lawyers. Viewed from a somewhat larger perspective, this stratum can be seen as forming the top layer of a much larger urban middle class of property owners and employers which Morroe Berger estimated to consist of some 500,000 employed persons in 1947, or 6 percent of the Egyptian labor force.[56] Of these, about half were classified as 'merchants,' an elastic term which could also mean shopkeeper or small trader. Another 25 percent were described as 'clerks.'

Finally, at the base, lay the workers, the unemployed and then the many millions of peasants. According to census figures, the numbers of adult males (aged over 14) engaged in agriculture increased from 1.9 million in 1917 to 2.9 million in 1937, followed by a small fall during the Second World War. Of these, an increasing proportion owned no land at all while, of the remainder, the vast majority possessed properties of less than the 3 feddans which Alan Richards estimates was necessary to provide a single family with its subsistence.[57] Such persons were thus forced to work either as day laborers and service tenants on the big estates, or to rent land from those more fortunate than themselves. Meanwhile, even peasant families who did possess a holding large enough to provide them with food and clothing still suffered from a great variety of obstacles, most notably the 1913 law which made it impossible for them to pledge properties of 5 feddans and under as security for official loans, thus forcing them into the hands of village moneylenders who charged them much higher interest rates. There is much evidence to suggest that the standard of living of the poorer peasants, while remaining more or less steady during the 1920s, fell away seriously in the 1930s as agricultural wages declined more rapidly than rents or the price of the maize from which they made their daily bread.[58] According to Hansen's calculations, Egypt's consumption of cereals and pulses fell by over 12 percent between 1929 and 1937, tobacco by 30 percent and sugar by nearly 40 percent.[59] This must certainly have led to increased risk from the many diseases endemic in the countryside. The same trend then continued into the early years of the Second World War, made worse in Upper Egypt by regular epidemics of malaria between 1942 and 1944, before a small increase in wages led to the beginnings of a recovery at the end of the war.

A last feature of Egypt's system of social stratification was the minimal opportunities it offered for upward mobility. In spite of the increased funding for education, the proportion of the population attending state schools had only reached 6.9 percent by 1940/41.[60] Of these, some 80 percent were attending overcrowded rural elementary schools with very poor quality teaching. At the same time there were no more than 8,500 students in the whole of the Egyptian higher educational system.[61] Other barriers to mobility included the shortage of employment opportunities in the towns and the fact that land prices were so high – some 20 times their annual rental – as to make their purchase virtually impossible for a landless peasant.[62] Hence it was only in the special conditions of the Second World War, when nearly 300,000 Egyptians found work with the British and American armies, that rural people began to leave the land in any significant numbers, swelling the proportion of those living in towns to about a third of the total population by 1947.[63]

Notes on Chapter 2
Full details of all sources are in the Bibliography

1   Egypt, Ministry of Finance, Statistical Department, *The Census of Egypt Taken in 1917* II, Introduction by Craig, p liii. 'Literacy' was officially defined as the ability to read and write a 'short letter.' It is unlikely that this could have been adequately assessed by the census enumerators. To make matters more difficult, the ability to read and then to write were assessed in two different columns which then had to be aggregated at the tabulation stage.

2   El-Shanawany, 'The First National Life Tables for Egypt,' p 240. El-Shanawany gives the comparative figures for England as 56 for men and 60 for women.

3   The census gives a figure of another 1.1 million women classified as agricultural laborers 'by inference,' i.e. they did not give this as their occupation but might reasonably be assumed to have been engaged in such work by virtue of the fact that they lived on agricultural properties of 10 feddans and under. *The Census of Egypt Taken in 1917*, II, p liii.

4   Hansen, *Egypt and Turkey*, p 42.
5   Crouchley, *The Investment of Foreign Capital in Egyptian Companies and the Public Debt*, pp 72–4.
6   Thomas, 'Agricultural and economic position of Egypt,' in Milner Papers, Bodleian Library, Oxford.
7   For example, many problems arose from trying to fit Egyptian occupations into categories drawn from the international 'Code alphabétique des professions et occupations,' *The Census of Egypt Taken in 1917* II, Introduction, p liii.
8   Vallet, *Contribution à l'étude de la condition des ouvriers de la grande industrie du Caire*, pp 103–4.
9   Data to be found in Government of Egypt, *Rapport de la commission du commerce et de l'industrie*, 2nd ed., Annexes X, XI, XIII, etc.
10 Sugar refinery figures in Tignor, *State, Private Enterprise and Economic Change in Egypt, 1914–1952*, p 34. Hand loom figures (for mid 1920s) in Tignor, *Egyptian Textiles and British Capital 1930–56*, p 11.
11 Tignor, *State, Private Enterprise and Economic Change in Egypt, 1914–1952*, p 54.
12 Hopkins, *An Economic History of West Africa*, pp 168–9.
13 Crouchley, *The Investment of Foreign Capital in Egyptian Companies and the Public Debt* pp 182–3; Radwan, *Capital Formation in Egyptian Industry and Agriculture, 1882–1967*, Tables 4.2 and 5.2.
14 Lévi, 'L'augmentation de revenues de l'état: possibilités et moyens d'y parvenir,' p 428ff. Lévi's calculations were subject to serious criticism by Baxter, 'Notes on the Estimate of the National Income of Egypt for 1921–1922' and then defended by Lévi in his 'Evaluation du revenu national de l'Egypte: réponse à Monsieur J. Baxter.' See also Anis, 'A Study of the National Income of Egypt.'
15 Hansen, 'Income and Consumption in Egypt, 1886/1887 to 1937,' Table 1; Hansen, *Egypt and Turkey*, Table 1/1. See also Hansen and Marzouk, *Development and Economic Policy*, Chart 1.1.
16 Issawi, *Egypt at Mid-Century*, p 80; Hansen and Marzouk, *Development and Economic Policy*, pp 4–5.
17 Hansen, *Egypt and Turkey*, p 10.
18 Hansen and Marzouk, *Development and Economic Policy*, pp 4–5.
19 *Ibid.*, p 5.
20 'The economic development of Egypt, 1800–1960,' p 368.
21 This is the title of both Tignor's 'Conclusion' in *State, Private Enterprise and Economic Change*, p 243, and Hansen's ch. 3 in *Egypt and Turkey*, p 64.
22 Hansen, *Egypt and Turkey*, p 69.
23 Crouchley, *Investment of Foreign Capital*, p 200.
24 Maddison, *The World Economy in the 20th Century*, Table 1.3.
25 This point is well covered in Vitalis, 'On the Theory and Practice of Compradors: The Role of Abbud Pasha in the Egyptian political economy,' pp 291–315.
26 Dasuqi, *Kibar mullak al-aradi al-zira'iyya wa dawrahum fi-al-mujtama' al-misri, 1914–1952*, pp 212–13.
27 For the wartime suffering from malaria and cholera exacerbated by rural poverty, see Gallagher, *Egypt's Other Wars*, chs 2 and 7. For an early proposal for land redistribution see Ghali, *Al-islah al-zira'i*. For a summary of this work in French, see Ghali Bey, 'Un programme de réforme agraire pour l'Egypte.'
28 Tignor, *State, Private Enterprise and Economic Change*, Table A/15; Abdalla, *The Student Movement and National Politics in Egypt*, Tables 2/1 and 2/2.

29 Large landlords generally did not suffer from these restrictions which confined cotton growing to a third of Egypt's fields as they tended to practice a three-year cotton rotation. But the smaller growers, who were more likely to practice a two-year cotton rotation, were unable to grow as much as they wanted (to the extent that they obeyed the law) and so suffered a loss of income. For a discussion of the different patterns of rotations see Richards, *Egypt's Agricultural Development, 1800–1980*, pp 112–20.

30 Mabro and Radwan, *The Industrialization of Egypt 1939–1973*, pp 50–1.

31 Shimizu, *Anglo-Japanese Trade Rivalry*, pp 103–4, 110 and Table 15.

32 Egypt, Ministry of Finance, *Twenty Years of Agricultural Development in Egypt (1919–1939)*, pp 127–8.

33 For a good discussion of this point, see Issawi, *Egypt at Mid-Century*, pp 115–16. He himself bases many of his remarks on two contemporary attempts to estimate the elasticity of demand for Egypt's cotton: Zahra and al-Darwish, *A Statistical Study of Some of the Factors Affecting the Price of Egyptian Cotton*; Brescia-Turroni, 'Relations entre la récolte et le prix du coton égyptien.'

34 This is the general argument to be found in Rothermund, *The Global Impact of the Great Depression, 1929–1939*, especially pp 80–1.

35 Beinin and Lockman, *Workers on the Nile*, pp 291–4.

36 For example, Issawi, *Egypt at Mid-Century*, pp 124, 248.

37 For example, Mabro, *The Egyptian Economy: 1952–1972*, pp 62–3.

38 *Ibid.*, pp 62–4; O'Brien, *The Revolution in Egypt's Economic System*, p 11.

39 Tignor, *State, Private Enterprise and Economic Change*, pp 49–55.

40 El-Gritly, 'The Structure of Modern Industry in Egypt,' p 510.

41 Tignor, *Egyptian Textiles*, pp 11–13. Figures for capacity have been inferred from those for the number of looms.

42 Tignor, *State, Private Enterprise and Economic Change*, pp 99, 130–2.

43 *Ibid.*, p 32.

44 *Ibid.*, pp 45–6.

45 Calculations made by the Egyptian Ministry of Commerce and Industry quoted in Great Britain, Department of Overseas Trade, *Egypt: Review of Commercial Conditions (May 1945)*, pp 21–2.

46 Mabro and Radwan, *The Industrialization of Egypt 1939–1973*, Table 5.1. But see also p 82, where they say that the wartime increase might have been as much as 40 percent.

47 Tignor, *Egyptian Textiles*, pp 34–5; El-Gritly, 'Structure of Modern Industry,' pp 482–4, 534.

48 Tignor, *Egyptian Textiles*, pp 31, 41–4.

49 Hansen, *Egypt and Turkey*, p 89.

50 Dasuqi, *Kibar mullak al-aradi al-zira'iyya wa dawrahum fi-al-mujtama' al-misri, 1914–1952*, pp 212–13.

51 For example, Saad, 'Social History of an Agrarian Reform Community in Egypt,' pp 39–44.

52 Owen, 'Large Landowners, Agricultural Progress and the State in Egypt, 1800–1970,' pp 79–80.

53 'Report on Land Tax Assessment,' Holden Papers, St Antony's College, Oxford.

54 For example, debates of 22 and 24 May 1933 and 9 June 1937, *Madabit majlis al-shuyukh wa-al-nuwwab*.

55 Waardenburg, *Les universités dans le monde arabe actuel* II, p 81.

56 Berger, 'The Middle Class in the Arab World.'

57 Richards, *Egypt's Agricultural Development, 1800–1980*, pp 151, 160.

58 *Ibid.*, Table 5/12.

59 Hansen, 'Income and Consumption in Egypt, 1886/1887 to 1937,' Tables 3.5 and 3.6.

60 Waardenburg, *Les universités dans le monde arabe actuel* II, Table 109.

61 Abdalla, *The Student Movement and National Politics in Egypt*, p 27.

62 El-Ghonemy, 'The Egyptian State and Agricultural Land Market 1810–1986,' p 184.

63 At its peak in November 1943 the number of Egyptians employed by the British army reached 263,000, with another 25,000 or so employed by the Americans; Beinin and Lockman, *Workers on the Nile*, p 260.

3

The Economies of the British and French Mandates 1918–1945

The award of League of Nations mandates to Britain for the new states of Iraq and Palestine/Transjordan, and to France for Syria/Lebanon, had two major economic consequences. First, the creation of these new political entities entailed the creation of new national economies as well, each with its own boundaries, and each with its own centralized system of laws, taxes, and fiscal management. One result was the growth of separate national markets in which the prices paid for particular goods and the wages paid for particular types of work gradually tended to converge. Another was the development of barriers to the large movement of goods and labor that had been such a prominent feature of the region in the last years of the Ottoman Empire.

Second, these economies were submitted to what was very much like a common system of colonial economic management, tempered only by the need to respect the various international obligations imposed by the League of Nations itself. As far as the Middle Eastern mandates were concerned, the two obligations which had the most important implications for economic management were the general need to provide most favored nation treatment to members of the League and the particular requirement written into the Mandate for Palestine that Britain should respect the promise made in the Balfour Declaration of November 1917 to 'encourage' the establishment of a Jewish 'National Home.'

Writers on the British and French empires have identified a number of major principles underlying colonial economic practice, all of which were in evidence in the management of their Middle Eastern mandates as well:[1]

(1) Colonies should pay for themselves without recourse to special financial assistance from the metropolis. This produced pressures for fiscal conservatism including the need to make sure that they balanced their budgets. This, in turn, ensured that, given the fact that the first call on their resources was to spend money on administration and the police, there were usually only small sums left for welfare or public works (Table 3.1).

(2) The colonial currency should be tied closely to that of the metropolis to facilitate trade and exchange. As a result colonies could easily suffer either from an overvalued currency or from its sudden loss of value at a time of imperial devaluation. Typically a colonial currency was managed by a currency board in London or Paris. There was no central bank and so no mechanism for controlling the colonial money supply or the rate of interest.

(3) Every effort was made to try to monopolize the trade in goods and services between metropolis and colony even though, in the case of the Middle Eastern mandates, this was strictly forbidden by the League of Nations. Mandated territories were also incorporated in the sterling and the franc areas when these were established in the 1930s. But Palestine, not being part of the British Empire, could not be included in the British Scheme for Imperial Preference which would have given its exports privileged access to the empire's markets.

(4) Political management was likely to be easier and cheaper in alliance with the large landowners, tribal shaykhs, and others who controlled the rural areas where the majority of the population lived. Colonial administrations should be prepared to cement this alliance by reducing taxes or other financial concessions including, on occasion, the award of state land.

Beyond this, both mandatory powers shared a common commitment to the development of the economic resources of the territories under their control, subject to a number of major constraints. One was fiscal, involving the need to balance the budget. A second was the priority which colonial administrations always had to give to political over economic considerations. This encouraged economically wasteful policies of 'divide and rule' such as the French division of Syria/Lebanon into a number of mini-states, and the British creation of separate legal systems for the tribal areas in Iraq and Transjordan. And it tended to produce mixed feelings about pushing through policies which could threaten the social peace, for example, the extension of commercial agriculture or the creation of individual private property which might endanger what the administrators took to be well-established traditional or customary communal relations.

Lastly, both the British and the French mandates were encouraged to adopt a common approach to certain legacies they inherited from their Ottoman predecessors. They were obliged to take responsibility for the share in the Ottoman debt allocated to the various successor states they now controlled. They both maintained parts of the Ottoman legal system although subjecting it to considerable change over time. Both began their administration by collecting taxes in the Ottoman way, notably the system of payment in kind, the tithe, imposed on large sections of the rural population.

THE BRITISH MANDATES IN THE INTER-WAR PERIOD

IRAQ

The new state of Iraq was created out of an amalgamation of the three Ottoman provinces of Basra, Baghdad, and Mosul. At the time of the award of its mandate to Britain in 1920, it contained some 2.5 million people, the great majority of whom lived in rural areas and earned their livelihood from agriculture or animal husbandry.[2] Those in the north and the east of the country practiced rain-fed farming involving the cultivation of a winter cereal crop complemented by sheep rearing, and small amounts of tobacco and other cash crops. Those who lived between the Tigris and the Euphrates rivers south of Baghdad grew cereals, rice, and dates on land which was badly drained, often salinated, and subject to the additional hazard of huge and unruly spring floods. The small urban population was engaged largely in commerce and trade, with some handicrafts but no mechanized factory industry.

53

The British, who administered the country directly until its limited independence in 1932, concentrated their efforts mainly on establishing better security, improving internal transport, and creating a small central administration. Given the time available, and the complexities of the existing systems of taxation and control over land, they could do no more than continue the Ottoman practice (as they understood it) while setting in train certain processes of registration and settlement which were then taken over and adapted by their Iraqi successors. It was the same with the much-needed measure of flood control, where they were only able to embark on a limited number of small drainage schemes as well as the repair of the Hindiya Barrage designed to regulate flooding along the middle Euphrates. They made one innovation of great consequence, however, and that was the encouragement given to the establishment of irrigation pumps by means of fiscal incentives contained in a 1926 law. As a result, the number of such pumps increased from just 140 in 1921 to over 2,000 in 1929, reducing dependence on flood irrigation and allowing an immediate extension of the cultivated area by about one million dunums (1 Iraqi dunum = 2.5 hectares = 0.618 acres).[3] It was only much later that experts began to recognize the harmful side-effects of this innovation in terms of the high rates charged by the pump owners to their impoverished peasant customers and the damage to soil fertility due to over-watering without proper attention to drainage.[4]

As independence approached, the British also began to pay serious attention to measures which would secure their position of economic advantage well into the future. This was one of the main purposes of the Anglo-Iraqi Treaty of 1930 which sought to establish a monopoly over the provision of loans, military equipment, and expert advice. Other measures included the creation of a currency board in London to manage the new currency based on parity between the pound sterling and the Iraqi dinar (ID) introduced in 1932.

Just as important was the agreement reached between the new Iraqi government and the largely British-controlled Iraq Petroleum Company (IPC) in March 1931.[5] This replaced an earlier agreement of March 1925 under which exploration had started in the Kirkuk region leading to the discovery of a huge field at Bab Gurgur in October 1927. The company was allowed to keep its original concession area east of the Tigris river in exchange for a promise to build a pipeline to the Mediterranean. Royalties were to remain at the original 4s/ton (ID 0.2 or $0.80) payable in gold. Given the great inequality in power between the two parties, it seems that the Iraqi negotiators drove quite a hard bargain. Even though they were unable to obtain an owner's share in the IPC itself, they did manage to ensure that the oil was exported in sufficient quantity to make a substantial contribution to government revenues during the 1930s (Table 3.2).[6] In the event, exports began in 1934 and soon reached a level of 80,000 barrels a day.

The first Iraqi governments of the post-independence period immediately introduced programs designed to redress some of the lacunae which they identified in colonial economic policy by spending more money on education and welfare, as well as on schemes designed to promote greater agricultural production. Fortunately, they were in a position to use some of the new oil revenues for this purpose even though, in the event, a portion of these funds had to be redirected to meet shortfalls in the central budget. As a result, several large irrigation and drainage projects were initiated south of Baghdad while government spending on health and education was considerably increased.[7]

The other main task for the post-independence governments was to complete the project for creating a national system of land registration and taxation. A major step was taken in 1932 with the passage of a law implementing an essential recommendation made by the British expert Sir Ernest Dowson, that the award of rights over land should maintain what he termed 'beneficial occupation and use.'[8] Just how this was actually interpreted by the newly established land settlement committees is another matter. Registration of title proceeded slowly in the 1930s and only began to accelerate during the Second World War. But there is some evidence that, in many areas, it was used to favor tribal shaykhs and others with local political power.[9] Dowson's other major recommendation, the legalization of a form of tenure known as *miri lazma*, was also instituted in 1932 and, like the regulations pertaining to the registration of title, was implemented in such a way as to facilitate the award of large tracts of land to shaykhs and politicians with influence in Baghdad.[10]

Attempts to replace the Ottoman land tax also favored those with local power. An early effort by the British to introduce a comprehensive land tax in 1929 was soon abandoned, to be replaced in 1931 by a new tax (the *istihlak*) levied at a rate of 10 percent on goods brought to market, a regressive measure in that it was the same for rich and poor alike. A second attempt to introduce a combined land and water tax on government-owned and government-irrigated land in 1936 was soon abandoned as well. The government then decided to relinquish the idea of such a tax entirely and to introduce legislation in 1939 which allowed a one-off extinction of tax liability in ten annual installments, with an enormous reduction if it were paid in one lump sum.[11] The result of these measures was that revenue from taxes on land fell from over 20 percent of total government receipts in the 1920s to less than 10 percent in the 1930s, a situation which would have been impossible to sustain had it not been for the additional revenue from oil.[12]

Data which would permit an evaluation of the performance of the Iraqi economy in the 1920s and 1930s are sadly lacking. The first modern census was not carried out until 1947, and even then there are suggestions of considerable undercounting.[13] The first, and very imperfect, national income statistics were calculated for the year 1956.[14] However, reasonably good figures for trade and government finances do exist, both of which demonstrate that the most dynamic force acting on the economy during this period was an increase in oil exports and its consequent impact on governmental revenues. There was an associated increase in the value of imports, which almost doubled from ID 5.7 million in 1930 and 1932 to around ID 9.5 million in 1937 and 1938.[15] Items which showed a particular increase included consumption goods like tea and sugar, as well as capital goods such as electrical machinery required for irrigation, railroad construction, and improvements in municipal water and electricity supply.[16]

Data concerning industrial and agricultural output are much more limited. There is a little evidence of the beginning of a small degree of import substitution as far as cigarettes and shoes are concerned once protective tariffs started to be raised in 1933.[17] There may also have been an increase in the production of barley, one of the two main cereal crops, during the 1930s.[18] However, this has to be balanced by the fact that most sources agree that crop yields were falling as a result of declining soil fertility in the riverain areas of the south while cultivators also had to contend with the huge fall in cereal prices during the early years of the Depression.[19]

It is here that we begin to notice the beginnings of a paradox which continues to haunt Iraq today: the disparity between the possession of large quantities of oil, water, and land, and the inability of successive regimes to create the institutional structure which would bring them all together in a process of sustained development. As it was, in the 1920s and 1930s the agricultural sector can be seen to have suffered from an interlocking mix of problems – natural, technological, and social – which kept the yields and quality of its major crops low, and much of its peasant population in dire poverty and subject to some of the most intense forms of exploitation to be found anywhere in the Middle East.

PALESTINE

The territory awarded to Britain by the League of Nations in 1922 was carved out of the Ottoman Empire's south Syrian provinces and had previously not existed as a separate economic or political entity. This area was then immediately divided in two – Palestine west of the river Jordan and Transjordan to the east – although both remained within a single customs union with free movement of goods between them, a single currency, and a common external tariff.[20]

According to the first census, conducted in 1922, Palestine's population stood at just over 750,000 of whom 83,790 (11 percent) were Jewish.[21] The vast majority lived in rural areas with only about one-fourth in the 23 largest towns.[22] For most of the Ottoman period the bulk of the population had been concentrated in the hills which ran north-south from Jenin to Hebron, where the main crops were olives and small quantities of cereals and vegetables. But in the late nineteenth century there had been the beginnings of a more extensive settlement of the maritime plain which allowed a great expansion of cereal cultivation, especially wheat and barley. Apart from some small areas of irrigated land along the coast used for growing citrus fruits – notably 'Jaffa' oranges, Palestine's most valuable export – the bulk of the agricultural land relied on the winter rains which generally fell in a cycle of three to four good years followed by three to four bad. A second important crop was olives which experienced a shorter, two-year cycle of good and bad harvests. Manufacturing activity was confined to some 15,000 workshops producing soap, textiles, souvenirs for religious pilgrims, and food products.[23]

As a British mandate, Palestine shared many of the colonial features characteristic of neighboring Syria and Iraq. During the 1920s and 1930s some 58 percent of expenditures were devoted to administration and security, with only 10–12 percent allocated to education and health, and very little to infrastructure apart from the items required for imperial defense, such as the deep water harbor at Haifa completed in 1933.[24] Meanwhile, the bulk of the revenues came from indirect taxes, principally the customs tariff, with a much smaller amount from the new taxes on rural property which began to replace the tithe in 1935.[25]

There was also much the same administrative timetable as in Syria and Iraq, with the introduction of a new unit of currency, the Palestine pound, in 1927 and some of the same difficulties in organizing the survey and settlement of rural land, intensified in the case of Palestine by the fact that, by the 1930s, the whole subject of land ownership and land rights had become a highly contentious issue between the resident Arabs and the

57

incoming Jews. Hence, by 1936, the government had only managed to survey 2.6 million dunums (650,000 acres; 1 Palestinian dunum = 1000 square meters = 0.25 acres) and settle 1.5 million dunums (375,000 acres) out of a total of 13.6 million (3.4 million acres) subject to the 1935 agricultural property tax.[26] But a further 3.3 million (825,000 acres) had been settled by 1945.[27]

The slow rate of settlement also meant slow progress in dealing with a form of co-ownership known as *musha'*, in which land of half the villages in Palestine (mostly on the plains) was held in undivided shares, giving owners the right to cultivate plots of land in several different sections.[28] To most British officials this system stood in the way of proper agricultural progress – a notion which has never been subject to proper economic analysis – and they believed it should be transformed by the partition of village land among those holding shares, granting each an individual title.[29] Be that as it may, the question of sorting out rights proved too difficult and probably too politically charged – for example, shares were endlessly subdivided and many of them had passed into the hands of outsiders including Jewish land purchasing agents – and the plan was more or less abandoned even before the Arab revolt of 1936 brought settlement operations largely to a halt.[30]

What made Palestine particularly unusual was the obligation, written into the Mandate itself, to facilitate the establishment of a Jewish 'National Home.' This, in turn, required the British administration to pay special attention to Jewish immigration and Jewish land purchase, and to do so in consultation with a body representing the interests of the Jewish community which came to be known as the Jewish Agency. To begin with, some senior officials, including the first High Commissioner, Herbert Samuel, believed that this commitment could best be carried out within the context of an expanding economy, and it was for this reason that they were willing to do much more than the conventional colonial government in amending the tariff structure (in 1924 and 1927) to encourage the development of local industry.[31] But after the anti-Jewish riots in Jerusalem and Hebron in 1929 (the Wailing Wall Incident, in which over 200 people died), which demonstrated the extent of growing Palestinian Arab opposition to further Jewish immigration and land purchase, the British began to introduce policies designed specifically to protect the interests of the local rural population. Such policies became even more prominent in the early 1930s as Jewish immigration increased rapidly in response to the Nazis' coming to power in Germany, but were not enough to prevent the full-scale Arab revolt which broke out in 1936 and continued in many parts of the country until 1939.

The presence of a growing Jewish population with its own proto-national institutions (notably the Histadrut, the general federation of Jewish labor), and its own project for establishing a self-sufficient economic enclave based on the exclusive employment of Jewish labor and the purchase of what was made into inalienable Jewish land, has helped to fuel an ongoing debate about the structure and performance of the Palestinian economy in the Mandate period.[32] For some, it is best seen as a species of 'dual economy' containing two quite distinct economic entities, the Arab and Jewish, with only minimal interaction between them.[33] For others, it is better analyzed as a single colonial economy but one containing a sector (the Jewish) subject to a set of proto-national practices which differentiate it to some extent from the more usual white-settler enclave to be found elsewhere in the colonial empire, for example in Kenya.[34]

The subject is, of necessity, highly political, with Israeli economists, by and large, supporting the first argument and Arab ones the second. But the discussion has now been going on for long enough to allow a judgment to be made on the economic merits of the case. It is our opinion that the case for two separate economies has not been made and that the most useful way to analyze economic activity in Palestine, as well as to understand the many intercommunal relationships involved, is to do so within the context of the single economy with its single currency, single tax structure, and single legal system.

Nevertheless, before examining Palestine's economic performance in the inter-war period in unitary terms, it would be useful to set out some of the essential features of the Jewish activity simply because it had such a large impact on the development of the economy as a whole. As shown in Table 3.4, the Jewish population in Palestine increased via several waves of immigration to some 450,000 by 1939 out of a total of about 1,500,000.[35] Unlike the indigenous Palestinian Arab population, the great majority of the Jewish community (around 75 percent) lived in towns. It also exhibited a very different employment structure with, on average, only just over 20 percent working in agriculture (compared with over half of the Palestinian Arabs), another 20 percent in industry and manufacturing, and the rest in services.[36] Other salient features included the high levels of capital and skill brought into the country by individual immigrants and the fact that, by 1937, the Jewish community controlled some 10 percent of Palestine's cultivated land, mostly along the coastal plan between Tel Aviv and Haifa, in the Marj Ibn Amr (Jezreel Valley) and in the Galilee in the northeast.[37] To begin with, the bulk of this land had been bought in large estates from several hundred landlords, the vast majority of them living outside Palestine. But by the early 1930s it had become necessary to buy it in much smaller lots from different groups of local people, a process which increased the displacement of those who rented such land, so leading to an intensification of the Arab/Jewish conflict.[38]

There was only one official attempt to produce national income figures in Palestine during the Mandate, those by the government statistician, P. J. Loftus, for the year 1944.[39] However, indices constructed by Jacob Metzer show that the country enjoyed a steady rate of economic growth in the inter-war period, with NDP increasing from £P8.4 million (at 1936 prices) in 1922 to a high of £P34.9 million in 1935 before falling away to £P31.4 million in 1939.[40] (£P1 = £1 sterling = $4) This same series gives per capita income at £P11.5 (1922), £P26.7 (1935) and £P20.9 (1939).[41] But, in fact, much of this rise in income was concentrated in the Jewish sector, producing an increasing disparity between the two communities, with Jewish per capita income almost three times of that of Arab income by 1936 (£P47.1 to 16.1).[42] Two other features of this development are worth noting. One is the accompanying process of structural change, with the contribution of industry rising to 15.4 percent of GDP in 1935 and then to 18.2 percent in 1939.[43] The other is the fact that the growth of the Palestinian economy was largely counter-cyclical in world terms, slowing down during the international boom in the late 1920s and then picking up again during the Depression of the early 1930s, largely as the result of increased Jewish migration from Germany.

Developments in the agricultural sector present particular problems of analysis owing both to the absence of precise statistics and to the intrusive influence of the rainfall cycle, which makes the establishment of trends more difficult. Nevertheless, there does seem to have been a steady growth in the value of output due to a combination of the expansion of the cultivated area – from perhaps 5 million dunums (1.25 million acres) in the mid-1920s to over 7 million (1.75 million acres) a decade later – and of a progressive shift towards the production of higher value and more marketable crops.[44] The most obvious example of this latter process is the expansion in the area of the citrus groves to nearly 300,000 dunums (75,000 acres) by 1939, owned almost equally by Arabs and Jews. So profitable were these groves that they constituted just over a third of the value of total Arab agricultural output in 1939 and more than two-thirds of Jewish output.[45] But output from other commercial crops such as olives, vegetables, potatoes, and tobacco was also on the increase, fed by expanding local demand.[46]

Industrial growth was much more spectacular, with output increasing in value sevenfold in the period 1922–1939 according to Metzer and Kaplan's calculations.[47] Here it was Jewish-owned industrial activity which clearly provided the major stimulus, contributing 44 percent of total output in 1928, a proportion which had risen to 70 percent by 1939.[48] Data from the General Census of Industry and Handicrafts conducted by the government in 1927 can be compared with a Jewish census of a somewhat narrower range of industry in 1937 to provide a general picture of the scope of this development.[49] Apart from a few large establishments the general picture is of one dominated by small labor-intensive units. In 1927 the number of persons employed per establishment was 6.7 in the Jewish-owned and 4.2 in the Arab, while only 17 percent of establishments used motor power of any kind.[50] At this time, the major share of output (by value) was accounted for by food, drink, and tobacco followed a long way after by 'chemicals and allied trades,' and then the production of various building materials such as bricks, stones, and timber.[51] By 1937 industry was still dominated by small units but its range was greatly expanded to include metals and machinery, chemicals, and textiles.[52] Two years earlier, in 1935, this industry was sufficiently broad in scope to produce half of the country's demand for manufactured goods.[53]

A final set of questions concerns income distribution and welfare. Here there were a number of factors which prevented the general rise in income from being translated into an across-the-board improvement in the standard of living. First, there was the large and growing gap between average Arab and Jewish income, with the latter being able to call upon much larger financial resources to sustain a much higher level of health, education, and employment. To give only one example, while the best the government could do was to provide a minimum of four years of elementary schooling to two-thirds of Palestinian boys (and only 7.5 percent of the girls living in the rural areas), the Jewish community was able to provide nine years of education for over 90 percent of its children aged between five and fourteen.[54] Second, there were clearly huge disparities of income on the Palestinian Arab side with a small group of landowners, citrus-growers, and merchants enjoying a standard of living vastly superior to that of the bulk of the rural population. Large sectors of the latter were particularly hard hit during the early 1930s when a combination of new tax rates and falling agricultural prices drove many of them into debt.[55]

TRANSJORDAN

The territory defined as Transjordan in 1922 took several decades to develop into a single independent state with a single economy. To begin with it was too poor to support anything but the most minimal of administrations, while its boundaries remained contested well into the 1930s by important tribal groups often supported by the rulers of the new kingdom of Saudi Arabia to the south. Furthermore, it remained closely bound to the Palestinian economy while also becoming part of a larger free trade area with, in effect, no tariffs on the movement of goods between it and Syria and Saudi Arabia, or on the transit trade with Iraq after 1934.

The population was small, rising from some 250,000 in 1922 to 375,000 in 1947. The official estimate for 1922 was 225,380 but excluded people living in the Ma'an district in the south.[56] By the late 1930s there were still only four towns with more than 10,000 people – the largest being Salt and the capital, Amman, with some 20,000 each – while perhaps half of those who lived in the rural areas could be classified as nomadic.[57]

The main economic activities were agriculture and herding, which provided about half of the national product in a good year.[58] According to the fiscal survey completed in 1933 there were then some 4.6 million dunums (1.15 million acres) of cultivated land, almost all of which was reliant on the uncertain winter rains.[59] Meanwhile, conditions among the nomads in the south of the country were beginning to deteriorate dramatically, with the reduction in the need for camel transport and the losses caused to their flocks by fierce raids conducted by rival tribes now living on the other side of the new borders with Iraq and Saudi Arabia.[60]

A small population and a lack of natural resources also made for a very limited tax base, leaving the government heavily dependent on external support, notably the Palestinian government which provided a number of small subsidies including the financing of the Transjordanian Frontier Force. Hence between 1924/25 and 1938/39, nearly 30 percent of government revenues came from outside funding while much of the rest came from its share of receipts from the common Palestinian/Transjordanian tariff.[61]

Given such constraints, the development of national economic institutions was bound to be slow. Beginning in 1927, the major administrative effort was devoted to surveying the country's land, registering it in individual title and imposing a uniform tax system upon it. This process was much more rapid than in Palestine due largely to the administration's success in obtaining the cooperation of the peasant population in the process of partitioning the large quantities of undivided (*musha'*) land which occupied some 50 percent of the total cultivable area. The price for this was the creation of new inefficiencies consequent on the division of each person's new holding into several long strips, the peasants' way of ensuring that all those with shares obtained a selection of lands of roughly equal quality.[62] With settlement came the progressive introduction of the provisions of the Land Tax Law of 1933 with rates the equivalent of 6 percent of gross yields.

What is not clear is the impact of the new land regime on either revenues or total output. Figures for the sums collected in tax show only a small increase after the new rates were enforced.[63] These, together with the fees for land registration, contributed about 23 percent of locally-raised revenue in the late 1930s: £P 80,000 out of a total of some £P 350,000.[64] The impact on output is similarly unclear. Official figures for output exist only from 1934 to 1935 while, as elsewhere, analysis is complicated by the effects of the rainfall cycle and, in particular, the unusually dry period from 1929 to 1936. Unofficial estimates, however, would suggest a decade of irregular increase in the production of wheat and barley from 1927 to 1939, although probably exaggerated by the two bumper harvests in the late 1930s.[65] It would seem reasonable to suggest that, in such an economy, the value of trade is closely associated with the value of agricultural output. This is certainly the case for the period 1936–1939, when movement in the value of exports (consisting largely of wheat and barley) correlate quite closely with the size of the cereal harvest.[66]

Not surprisingly, the government could only afford small sums for welfare and development. Almost certainly its main contribution was the improvement in transport and public security. Beyond that it spent some 12 percent of its budget on education and public health, a figure which allowed school building to increase more or less in line with population growth and to provide elementary schooling for perhaps half of those whose parents wanted it.[67] Finally, Richard Bocco and Tariq Tell have argued for the important role played by Glubb Pasha, the commander of the Desert Patrol from 1930 onward, in alleviating the near famine conditions among the camel nomads of the southern desert through a combination of subsidies, military employment, and the provision of small amounts of seeds to allow a shift to a more settled pattern of agriculture.[68]

FRENCH MANDATES IN THE INTER-WAR PERIOD

SYRIA AND LEBANON

French occupation of parts of the Syrian provinces of the Ottoman Empire between 1918 and 1920 was recognized by the award of a League of Nations Mandate in 1922. A year previously, in 1921, they had divided their new conquest into two parts: Greater Lebanon (Grand Liban) and Syria, which was itself sub-divided into smaller statelets of which the two most important were those centered on Aleppo in the north and Damascus in the south.[69] From an economic point of view, however, the whole area was administered more or less as a single unit with a common external tariff and a common currency (the Syrian pound, linked to the French franc) but with freedom allowed to the separate statelets to raise their own taxes and, after 1936, to impose some restrictions on the movement of goods and labor.[70] In what follows we will call Greater Lebanon simply Lebanon and deal with the varying number of Syrian statelets as a single unit called Syria.

All parts of the region had suffered greatly during the First World War with population losses estimated at as much as 300,000 out of a pre-war total of some 3 million.[71] In addition, the new states had become host to some 150,000 Armenian refugees who had been forcibly deported from Turkey.[72] To make matters worse, the boundaries established between Syria and its new neighbors, Turkey and Iraq, created huge barriers to the free flow of goods as a result of the high tariffs now imposed.[73] Further economic disruption was then caused by the widespread revolt against French rule between 1925 and 1927. Hence, as in many other parts of the Middle East, it is unlikely that economic activity regained its pre-war vitality until the very end of the 1920s.

According to the one and only census conducted by the French in 1921–22 there were then some 2.14 million people in Syria. Later estimates show that this may have risen to some 3 million in 1932.[74] Meanwhile, Lebanon was estimated to have a population of 630,000 in 1921–22 and 855,000 at the time of the second (Lebanese) census held in 1932.[75] In the early 1930s just over a third of each population lived in towns with over 5,000 inhabitants. Another significant feature was the renewal of the pattern of emigration which had been so much a feature of the pre-1914 period, with some 16,000 persons leaving Syria/Lebanon each year between 1923 and 1926. A few years later, however, this number fell to only a few thousand as the impact of the Depression made the Americas a much less attractive destination so that, for some years in the early 1930s, more migrants were returning to Syria and Lebanon than leaving.[76]

The basic instrument of French economic management was a system by which the revenues raised from the common external tariff were put into a single budget (*Comte de gestion des services d'intérêt commun*) administered by the high commissioner and then allocated between the separate statelets to support certain common interests such as the railroads, the telegraphs, and the customs administration itself. It was also used to provide subsidies for the ten or so large, French-owned, concessionary companies which provided a range of monopoly services such as the railroads, urban tramways, gas and electricity, and the banking of state revenues.[77] Details about the distribution of these common funds, or even the principle upon which it was carried out, remained a closely guarded secret making evaluation almost impossible.[78] In addition, each of the statelets raised its own revenues from a variety of taxes and impositions, most notably the tithe on agricultural products inherited from the Ottomans and then commuted at a fixed rate based on an average of the amounts collected between 1921 and 1924 but still levied on the village community as a whole. As in Palestine, the great fall in the price of most agricultural crops in the early 1930s forced the authorities to remit up to a third of this each year.[79]

Again, as in the case of the British mandates, agricultural tax reform was accompanied by an attempt to survey, and then to establish title to, rural land according to the rules set out in the Land Code of November 1930. Some 3 million hectares (7.41 million acres) had been surveyed by 1938, representing most of the area then under cultivation.[80] Less progress had been made in establishing individual title, particularly in those regions subject to *musha'* cultivation in the south and middle of Syria, where each villager's share was registered, but without title to any specific piece of land, a practice justified by the director of the Bureau de Cadastre on the grounds that *musha'* had a 'real basis in the social life of the country.'[81] As a result, although a new fiscal regime is said to have been established on 2.6 million hectares (6.42 million acres) of the surveyed land, it seems likely that this still depended largely on an assessment based on the village community rather than on the individual cultivator.[82]

Like their British counterparts in Iraq, the French colonial administrators also began by making little effort to influence the pattern of local economic activity. During most of the 1920s, the external tariff was used almost exclusively for revenue-raising purposes while expenditures on welfare and public works remained low.[83] But from 1928 onward, the high commissioners began to come under increasing pressure from well-organized Syrian interest groups to respond to the growing crisis, first in the agricultural sector, then in the industrial, where a combination of

falling prices and foreign competition was driving many small manufacturing enterprises out of business. Their response was twofold. First, they
began to introduce a protective element into the tariff structure, raising the
rates on such imports as silk thread, cement, and shoes, while being careful
not to put barriers in the way of the consumption of the very cheap Japanese
textiles which were all some of the poorer Syrians could afford.[84] Second,
from 1934 onward, they allowed a considerable increase in the public
works budget, particularly for road building and the expansion of Beirut
port, which can be seen as part of a larger project for developing that city
as the major commercial center on the eastern Mediterranean coast.[85]

Turning to the performance of the Syro-Lebanese economy during the
inter-war period, there are two main problems. The first is the absence of
reliable statistics for production in both the agricultural and manufacturing
sectors. The second is the high degree of polemic which, not surprisingly
in a situation of colonial dependence, tends to make it difficult to find a
middle path between French exaggeration and Syrian and Lebanese
nationalist rhetoric. In these circumstances it is perhaps not surprising that
only one attempt has been made to estimate the national product of Syria
(excluding Lebanon) and that just for the years 1936–38.[86] For the rest, what
we are left with is the general impression that, given the general difficulties
under which all parts of the economy labored, there is unlikely to have
been any advance in per capita income from 1919 to 1939. No sooner had
conditions begun to return to normal in 1928, with the beginnings of
a more regular administration and the stabilization of the French franc,
than Syria/Lebanon was hit by the repercussions of the Depression with
disastrous results given its reliance on trade, emigrant remittances, and
workshop industry, the collapse of which in the face of foreign competition
also greatly reduced the demand for several locally produced agricultural
crops, such as the mulberry leaves used to feed the silk worms raised in the
Lebanese mountains.

Reading the French and other foreign economic reports from Beirut
and Damascus in the early 1930s is to read of declining trade, growing
unemployment, falling government revenues, and a sense of general
impoverishment.[87] Nevertheless, there are also signs of something of an
economic revival from the mid-1930s onward, assisted by the recovery of
the international economy, the devaluation of the French franc in 1935
(which automatically reduced the value of the Syrian pound, making
exports cheaper); and the investments made in the creation of a new, more
modern, factory industry. Agriculture too seems to have revived, with
the return of better winter rains after the mid-1930s, the opening up of
newer markets for industrial crops such as cotton and tobacco, and a rapid

66

expansion of the cultivated area around Homs and, more especially, in the fertile region known as the Jazira to the east of Aleppo.[88] Let us look at the industrial and then the agricultural sector in turn.

From the late 1920s onward, French publicists developed the notion that Syro–Lebanese industry could be divided into two sections, the 'old' and the 'new.'[89] Such a division had the great advantage of making the transition from one to the other seem both progressive and inevitable, and has provided the framework for much of the economic analysis which has followed.[90] In some formulations, however, it can become dangerously over-simplified, depending as it does on the basic dichotomy of old/traditional/workshop versus new/modern/factory. Nevertheless, if used with care, it can also be employed to provide a way of analyzing the structure of manufacturing activity which existed in 1913, revived after the First World War, and then forced to transform itself under pressure of the changed economic environment of the early 1930s.

During the 1920s, Syro–Lebanese industry consisted largely of plants working up local agricultural produce by hand. The largest of these were the so-called silk 'factories,' located mostly in the Lebanese mountains, only a few of which contained machines to turn their reels. There were 113 of these at their postwar peak in 1927/28, producing some 330,000kg of thread, or three-fourths of their pre-First World War average.[91] Other, smaller, enterprises produced cotton or silk woven cloth, soap, leather goods, and tobacco products. All then came under huge pressure from shrinking local and foreign demand after 1929 and many either disappeared or were forced to transform themselves by adopting new methods of production and investing in new machinery like the power loom. In addition, larger plants, also using newer methods of production and organization, began to be constructed in the late 1920s, a trend which intensified greatly in the early 1930s. These included two cement works, various textile factories, and plants for producing flour, jams and confectioneries, soap, beer, cigarettes, and shoes.[92] To contemporary observers, enterprises of this type all tended to get classified as 'new' or 'modern.' But exactly how these are to be distinguished from the older, updated plants remains unclear, as both might use low-cost machinery and employ roughly the same (small) number of workers. What can be said with greater confidence is that the revival of Syrian manufacturing activity in the 1930s represents the beginnings of a process of import substitution which, by 1938, was able to meet half the local demand for cotton thread, a third for cotton textiles, and about half for cement.[93]

As already noted, the major agricultural activity was the cultivation of a cereal crop of wheat or barley which occupied perhaps 75 percent of the total cultivated area.[94] For such crops the main determinant of output was the area sown, which itself depended on the volume and timing of the winter rains. What figures exist show no appreciable increase in the area planted to wheat before the late 1930s but a small increase in that devoted to barley.[95] However, such estimates obscure the considerable fluctuations resulting from the regular three- or four-year rainfall cycles as well as the fact that agricultural prices fell very sharply through the late 1920s and early 1930s. Where there was much greater change was in the cultivation of the so-called 'industrial' crops, notably mulberry leaves, cotton, and tobacco. Some, like the new type of 'Lonestar' American cotton which had been introduced to the Akkar plain in northern Lebanon in the mid 1920s, suffered greatly in the early 1930s, only to recover their earlier position by the end of the decade.[96] Other crops, like the mulberry leaves, remained largely unpicked, causing some farmers to replace them with higher value crops such as vegetables and bananas but leaving others, particularly those living at higher altitudes, to abandon their terraced fields entirely and either to migrate or to seek other forms of economic activity, such as that connected with the summer tourist industry as it began to expand in the mid-1930s.[97]

Given the likelihood of at least stagnant personal incomes over the whole inter-war period, as well as the serious limitations on public expenditure, it is impossible to imagine any significant increase in welfare except for those connected directly with the mandatory administration or the French concessionary companies, or those like certain tribal leaders who were able to benefit from their own local power to obtain title to large tracts of agri-cultural land. By and large, the French administrators were content to leave education and, to some extent, health in the hands of the various foreign missionary and local communal/religious organizations. But such a policy clearly discriminated against members of the Muslim population even if some small effort was made to increase the number of government schools on which they were forced to rely. This situation was reflected directly in the figures for educational attainment which show that, for example, in the mid-1930s about half of Lebanon's Maronite Christian population was literate compared with only a third of the Sunni Muslims and 17 percent of the Shi'is.[98]

THE MANDATES DURING THE SECOND WORLD WAR

The Middle East became a major field of military activity during the Second World War as a base for the large British, Free French and, later, American armies fighting the German and Italian forces seeking to invade it through North Africa. There were also important political changes as Iraq was virtually re-occupied by Britain in 1941 while the Vichy French administration was ousted from Syria and Lebanon that same year and replaced by joint British/Free French wartime management.

As far as economic life was concerned, the major impact of the war was felt in two main areas. The first was the disruption of pre-war trading patterns following the German closure of the Mediterranean to Allied shipping. The result was a severe shortage of both consumption goods and important agricultural and industrial inputs, such as chemical fertilizers and spare parts. The second area was the presence of very large numbers of Allied troops and the demands they placed upon the local economies for accommodation, labor, food and, in the case of Palestine, the production of essential military supplies such as petrol cans, mines, and barbed wire. Some idea of the impact of such purchases can be seen from the calculation that, at their peak in 1942, military purchases contributed about a third to Syro-Lebanese national income and some 15–20 percent in Iraq.[99] As for Palestine, which became the second most important British military base after Egypt, one estimate puts the number of local people (both Arabs and Jews) either serving directly in the British armed forces or engaged in some other military-related activity at 130,000, while another places the military contribution to national income from 1940 to 1945 at just under 25 percent.[100]

One immediate consequence of this combination of shortages and military expenditures was a huge expansion in the money supply and the very high rates of inflation that persisted throughout the war. In Iraq, for example, the general price index increased by 580 percent between 1938/39 and 1943, while the Damascus retail price index grew by an even larger 830.5 percent between 1938/39 and 1945.[101] Governments did their best to try to control this situation but, on the whole, lacked the administrative means to impose a regime of forced savings either through increased taxation or the sale of bonds, although both were tried. A more effective measure taken in an effort to mop up excess purchasing power was the sale of $80 million in gold bars bought specially for this purpose from India, especially in Iraq where such sales were estimated at some 18 percent of local British military purchases in 1943/44.[102] For the rest, the best each government could do was to rely on a combination of price controls, limited food rationing, and the subsidizing of certain basic necessities in order to ensure that populations continued to be able to obtain what they needed for everyday life at a price they could afford.

For the purposes of the Allied war effort, the whole Middle Eastern region stretching from North Africa to Iran was placed under the economic control of the Anglo-American Middle East Supply Centre (MESC) established in Cairo in 1941.[103] By and large it relied on the mandatory governments to carry out its directives but in Syria/Lebanon it was also assisted by the newly created Office de l'Economie de Guerre in Beirut. The MESC's major aim was to reduce non-military imports into the region, thus saving scarce shipping space. This it did, first by a system of licensing and controls, and second by efforts to increase local production to make up the shortfall. To judge by its own figures, it was remarkably successful as far as the former aim was concerned, engineering a reduction in the tonnage of civilian goods shipped into the region from 5.5 million to 1.5 million tons during the course of the war.[104] Trade figures for the individual states show much the same story with, for example, imports into Syria/Lebanon declining by 50 percent in weight between 1938 and the beginning of 1943.[105]

As for the efforts to increase production, while the activities of the MESC in allocating scarce supplies of fuel, spare parts, and raw materials were certainly of some importance, the major stimulus was clearly provided by a combination of shortages, high prices, and military purchases. This can be seen most clearly in the industrial sector and, in particular, in those states where manufacturing activity was already quite well developed, notably Palestine. By 1942 the output of Jewish-owned factories had increased by some 200 per cent compared with 1939 and that in Arab-owned factories by 77 percent, while the numbers of workers employed in manufacturing industry had grown from 48,000 to 64,000 during the same period.[106] As a result, by the war's end, the industrial sector was contributing almost one-fourth of GNP.[107] It should be noted, however, that this figure also includes the output of the 34 diamond polishing enterprises which had been established by Jewish refugees from Holland and Belgium at the beginning of the war and which, by 1945, were producing cut diamonds worth £P7 million and providing over 40 percent of total exports.[108] Elsewhere, in Syria/Lebanon and Iraq, the types of manufacturing which expanded most quickly during the war were those which required only small amounts of capital and machinery, such as cigarettes, beer, textiles, and building materials.

In agriculture, the major effort was directed toward increasing local supplies of food crops, mainly through the extension of cereal cultivation on to new land but also, as in Palestine, by encouraging more efficient methods.[109] Results differed from country to country. Hence, while there is no clear evidence of any great increase in the volume of the cereal harvest in Syria and Iraq, there was much better success in Palestine, where agricultural output is estimated to have increased by about a third during the war years, and in Lebanon and Transjordan.[110]

Given their important role in the Allied military effort, the overall impact of the Second World War on the mandatory economies was bound to be profound. On the one hand, it stimulated increased output, brought full employment to Lebanon and Palestine, and greatly extended the sphere of wage labor and commercial agriculture. On the other, there was high inflation, severe shortages, and a huge amount of postponed consumption saved up for after the war's end. For those whose wartime income outstripped inflation there were many positive aspects, for example, the ability enjoyed by Palestinian peasants and others to get rid of almost all of their accumulated debt. But for others on fixed incomes and unable to obtain many of the goods and services they had previously enjoyed, the war brought only hardship and suffering.

The war also had an important effect on postwar economic management. As elsewhere in the world, many of the administrative mechanisms developed to plan, to supervise, and to tax were retained after 1945 as the newly independent governments of Syria and Lebanon sought to play a greater role in shaping the economies they now controlled.[111] Something of the same influence can be seen in the case of Iraq and Transjordan as they emerged from direct British control as well as inside the Jewish community in Palestine where the intense wartime mobilization of resources became the basis for the drive towards its own national state. We will return to a discussion of this topic in Part II.

Notes on Chapter 3
Full details of all sources are in the Bibliography

1   For example, Hopkins, *Economic History of West Africa*, ch. 5; Meredith, 'The British Government and Colonial Economic Policy, 1919–1939,' pp 484–99; Betts, *France and Decolonisation*, p 2.

2   Sassoon, *Economic Policy in Iraq 1932–1950*, p 3.

3   Government of El-Iraq, *An Inquiry into Land Tenure and Related Questions: Proposals for the Initiation of Reform*, p 11.

4   Warriner, *Land Reform and Development in the Middle East*, pp 113–16; Hasan, *Al-tatawwur al-iqtisadi fi al-'Iraq: al-tijara al-kharijiyya wa-al-tatawwur al-iqtisadi, 1864–1958*, Table 18.

5   Each of the following held 23.5 percent of the shares: the Anglo-Persian Oil Co., Anglo-Dutch Shell, Compagnie française de pétroles and what was originally a consortium of six US companies which by the early 1930s had been reduced to Standard Oil of New Jersey and Socony.

6   Penrose and Penrose, *Iraq*, p 73.

7   Sassoon, *Economic Policy*, pp 74–5.

8   Government of El-Iraq, *An Inquiry into Land Tenure and Related Questions*, p 77.

9   For example, Pool, 'From Elite to Class: The Transformation of the Iraqi Political Leadership,' pp 78–83.

10   Government of El-Iraq, *An Inquiry into Land Tenure and Related Questions*, p 76; Batatu, *The Old Social Classes and the Revolutionary Movements of Iraq*, pp 102–10; Sassoon, *Economic Policy*, pp 161–2.

11   Rasheed, 'Development of Agricultural Land and Taxation in Modern Iraq,' pp 262–5.

12   Sassoon, *Economic Policy*, p 79 and Table 3.3.

13   *Ibid.*, p 3, quoting Food and Agricultural Organization (FAO), Mediterranean Development Project, Country Report: *Iraq* (Rome, 1959), p 7.

14   Haseeb, *The National Income of Iraq 1953–1961*, particularly pp 13–22.

15   Sassoon, *Economic Policy*, Table 5.1.

16   *Ibid.*, p 188.

17   *Ibid.*, pp 236–7.

18   *Ibid.*, p 139.

19   Hasan, 'The Role of Foreign Trade in the Economic Development of Iraq, 1864–1964,' p 352; Warriner, *Land Reform and Development*, pp 113–14; IBRD (World Bank), *The Economic Development of Iraq*, p 5.

20   There were some barriers to movement of persons between Palestine and Transjordan, particularly from 1937 onward.

21   McCarthy argues that this represents considerable undercounting and that the total should really be 823,684: *The Population of Palestine*, pp 27–30.

22   Hopkins, 'Population,' p 13.

23   Himadeh, 'Industry,' p 223.

24   Gross, *The Economic Policy of the Mandatory Government in Palestine*, p 7.

25   *Ibid.*, p 10; Government of Palestine, *A Survey of Palestine* I, p 246.

26   Gross, *The Economic Policy of the Mandatory Government in Palestine*, p 57.

27   Government of Palestine, *A Survey of Palestine* I, p 237.

28   For useful background to this form of landholding, see Firestone, 'The Land Equalising Musha' Village: A Reassessment,' particularly pp 92–4 and 98–110; Mundy, 'Village Land and Individual Title: Musha' and Ottoman Land Registration in the Ajlun District,' pp 58–79; 'La propriété dite musha' en Syrie: à propos des travaux de Ya'akov Firestone,' pp 273–87.

29   One of the best reasoned arguments of this kind was presented by Tute, 'The Law of State Lands in Palestine,' pp 171–73.

30   Granott, *The Land System of Palestine*, pp 239–43; see also Owen, 'Aspects of Ottoman Law in Mandatory Palestine,' pp 122–8.

31   Smith, *The Roots of Separatism in Palestine*, ch. 8.

32   For example, Owen, 'Economic Development in Mandatory Palestine, 1918–1948,' pp 13–15.

33 This case is well argued by Metzer, *The Divided Economy of Mandatory Palestine*, pp 1–27.

34 For example, Lockman, 'Railway Workers and Relational History: Arabs and Jews in British-Ruled Palestine,' pp 602–8. See also Shafir, *Land, Labor and the Origins of the Israeli-Palestinian Conflict 1882–1914*, pp 1–21, for a discussion of the Jews in Palestine as constituting a 'settler society' operating a split labor market.

35 Government of Palestine, *Survey* I, p 141.

36 Metzer, 'The Divided Economy of Mandatory Palestine,' pp 1–29.

37 There is a useful map showing the pattern of Jewish agricultural settlement in Atran, 'Le masha'a et la question foncière en Palestine 1858–1948,' p 1371.

38 Porath, 'The Land Problem as a Factor in Relations among Arabs, Jews and the Mandatory Government,' pp 178–80.

39 Government of Palestine, *National Income of Palestine 1944*.

40 Metzer, *The Divided Economy of Mandatory Palestine*, Table A/22. Their figures exclude the salaries of British nationals and the value of official government imports.

41 *Ibid*. For per capita income I have divided Metzer's figures by those for total population to be found in Government of Palestine, *Survey* I, p 141.

42 *Ibid.*, Table A/22.

43 Gross and Metzer, 'Palestine in World War II: Some Economic Aspects,' Table 4.4.

44 Metzer and Kaplan, 'Jointly but Severally,' pp 338, 342–4.

45 Metzer, *The Divided Economy of Mandatory Palestine*, Table A/12.

46 Metzer and Kaplan, 'Jointly but Severally,' pp 342–4.

47 Metzer and Kaplan, 'The Jewish and Arab Economies in Mandatory Palestine,' p 11.

48 *Ibid*.

49 Data collected in 1927 but published in 1928. It was not broken down by ethnic ownership when published but since 1979 Israeli economic historians have had access to the original, disaggregated, figures. See Gross, 'Some New Light on the Palestine Census of Industries 1928,' pp 264–75.

50 *Ibid.*, p 266.

51 *Ibid.*, Table 1.

52 Government of Palestine, *Survey* I, p 502.

53 Himadeh, 'Industry,' p 223.

54 Gross, *The Economic Policy of the Mandatory Government in Palestine*, p 46.

55 Government of Palestine, *Survey* I, p 364; Granott, *The Land System of Palestine*, pp 66–8.

56 IBRD, *The Economic Development of Jordan*, p 3.

57 Konikoff, *Trans-Jordan*, p 15n; Epstein, 'The Bedouin of Transjordan: Their Social and Economic Problems,' p 228.

58 IBRD, *Economic Development of Jordan*, p 12.

59 Fischbach, 'British Land Policy in Transjordan,' pp 86–9.

60 Bocco and Tell, 'Pax Britannica in the Steppe,' particularly p 123.

61 Konikoff, *Trans-Jordan*, p 116.

62 Walpole, 'Land Problems in Transjordan,' p 56.

63 Fischbach, 'British Land Policy in Transjordan,' pp 102–5.

64 Konikoff, *Trans-Jordan*, p 118.

65 *Ibid.*, Table VII.

66 Compare Konikoff's Table VII with Table XV.

67 *Ibid.*, p 119; Amadouny, 'Infrastructural Development under the British Mandate,' p 155.

68 Bocco and Tell, 'Pax Britannica in the Steppe,' pp 120–6.

69 Apart from Aleppo and Damascus, other entities were the Sanjak of Alexandretta (ceded to Turkey in 1938) and the governments of Latakia (along the Mediterranean coast) and of Jabal Druze (in the south). Aleppo and Damascus were later joined to make the single state of Syria in 1924. Latakia and Jabal Druze were also attached to them politically from 1936 to 1939 (and then again in 1942) but retained their own budgetary authority.

70 Hakim, 'Fiscal System,' pp 234–5. There were some barriers to trade between Lebanon and Syria after 1936; see note in *L'Asie française* (May 1938), p 158.

71 Figure for all Syrian provinces in Antonius, *The Arab Awakening*, p 241.

72 Widmer, 'Population,' p 23.

73 Sadowski suggests that Aleppo's trade with Turkey fell two-thirds by volume between 1924 and 1928; 'Political power and economic organization in Syria,' p 152.

74 Widmer, 'Population,' pp 5–6.

75 *Ibid.*

76 *Ibid.*, p 16.

77 Sir H. Satow, Beirut 17 March 1933, PRO/FO 406/71/Syria.

78 United States Department of State, 'Study of the Financial Situation of Syria and Lebanon.'

79 Hakim, 'Fiscal System,' pp 344–50.

80 Helbaoui, *La Syrie: mise en valeur d'un pays sous-développé*, pp 63–4.

81 Quoted in Warriner, *Land and Poverty in the Middle East*, pp 91–2. The same comment can also be found in Murray, 'Land Tenure in the Fertile Crescent.'

82 Figures from Weulersse, *Paysans de Syrie et du Proche Orient*, 2nd ed., p 189.

83 Syro-Lebanese tariff rates were: 15–30 percent (1924–26) and 25–50 percent (1926–28); Burns and Edwards, 'Foreign Trade,' pp 254–6.

84 Burns, *The Tariff of Syria, 1919–1932*, pp 47–51; Shimizu, *Anglo-Japanese Trade Rivalry*, pp 195–7.

85 Buheiry, *Beirut's Role in the Political Economy of the French Mandate*, pp 8–15.

86 Makdisi, 'Syria,' pp 158–61.

87 For example, United Kingdom, Department of Overseas Trade, 'Economic Conditions in Syria'; Bagh, *L'Industrie à Damas entre 1928–1958*, pp 348, 375, 397.

88 Helbaoui, *La Syrie*, pp 64–5.

89 See France, Ministère des affaires étrangères, *Rapport à la Société des Nations sur la situation de la Syria et du Liban*, pp 2–23.

90 For example, Hakim, 'Industry,' pp 122–36; Grunwald and Ronall, *Industrialization in the Middle East*, pp 297ff.

91 Owen, 'The Silk-Reeling Industry of Mount Lebanon, 1840–1914,' pp 282–3.

92 Hakim, 'Industry,' pp 147–69.

93 Charani, 'Points de vue successifs sur l'économie syrienne,' pp 236–8.

94 Khuri, 'Agriculture,' pp 75–8; Warriner, *Land and Poverty*, p 81, 83.

95 This is based on figures to be found in Whitaker, 'The Union of Demeter with Zeus,' Appendix.

96 Khuri, 'Agriculture,' pp 75–8; Warriner, *Land and Poverty*, pp 79–80; Republic of Syria, Ministry of Agriculture, Cotton Bureau, *A Report on the Cotton Situation in Syria*, pp 1–3.

97 Latron, 'La Production et le commerce de soie au Levant,' p 81.

98 Note in *L'Asie française* (March 1935), p 96.

99   United States Department of State, 'Study of the Financial Situation of Syria and Lebanon,' pp 4, 7–8; Hunter, 'Economic Problems,' p 189.

100 Government of Palestine, *A Survey of Palestine* III, p 1308; Gross and Metzer, 'Palestine in World War II,' Table 4.2.

101 Sassoon, *Economic Policy*, pp 116–18; Asfour, *Syria*, pp 48–9.

102 Lloyd, *Food and Inflation in the Middle East 1940–45*, p 212; Sassoon, *Economic Policy*, p 123.

103 The Americans joined the center in 1942. It then played a very important role in facilitating US lend-lease aid to eligible countries of the Middle East.

104 MESC, *Some Facts about the MESC*, quoted in Kingston, 'Pioneers in Development,' p 12.

105 United States Department of State, 'Annual Economic and Financial Review (Syria-Lebanon) 1942,' p 2.

106 Nathan, Gass, and Creamer, *Palestine*, p 198.

107 Calculations by Metzer and Kaplan quoted in Gross and Metzer, 'Palestine in World War II,' Table 4.4.

108 Ben-Ami, 'The Palestinian Diamond Industry,' p 96; Gross and Metzer, 'Palestine in World War II,' Table 4.8.

109 Lloyd claims that the MESC was responsible for bringing an extra 2 million acres into cultivation throughout the whole Middle East (including Iran), *Food and Inflation*, p 108.

110 For example: figures in Charani, 'Points de vue successifs sur l'économie syrienne,' p 22; Sassoon, *Economic Policy*, p 139; Gross and Metzer, 'Palestine in World War II,' Table 4.6 and pp 71–3; Amawi, 'The Consolidation of the Merchant Class in Transjordan during the Second World War,' pp 169–70.

111 This point is made most forcefully by Sadowski in his dissertation 'Political Power and Economic Organization in Syria: The Course of State Intervention 1946–1958,' pp 159–64.

4

The States of the Arabian Peninsula 1918–1945

INTRODUCTION

The Arabian Peninsula is a land mass of more than one million square miles, almost all of which is desert. In 1918 its population of between 6 and 7 million was largely confined to the coastal fringe along the Red Sea, the Indian Ocean and the Persian Gulf, with a smaller number living in a string of large oasis towns in the north, from al-Hufuf in the east to Medina in the west.[1] Much the largest concentration – several millions – was to be found in what is now Yemen, where the monsoon provided sufficient spring and autumn rainfall for an intensive pattern of cultivation along the thin coastal plain and then up the sides of the high mountain range which stood behind.[2] A smaller population of no more than 1.5 to 2 million lived in the four regions which were to be brought together by 'Abd al- 'Aziz Ibn Sa'ud to form the modern kingdom of Saudi Arabia: Najd and al-Hasa in the east, and the Hijaz and Asir in the west.[3] Finally, around another 750,000 lived along the Arabian side of the Gulf, some 175,000 in Kuwait, Bahrain, and Qatar, 80,000 on the Trucial Coast between Abu Dhabi and Ra' sal Khaymah, and 500,000 in what was then known as Muscat and Oman.[4]

At this same time, a fragile power to control and tax was exercised over parts of the settled regions by ruling families established in one or other of the larger towns, almost all of them in some type of formal or informal treaty relationship with Britain. This pattern had begun with separate treaties along the Trucial Coast itself and with Bahrain in 1820, and was then generalized with the Perpetual Maritime Truce of 1853, and a second series of treaties between 1880 and 1892 in which the separate rulers bound themselves and their heirs not to enter into negotiations with any foreign power without prior British consent. It was further extended to Muscat and Oman (1891), Kuwait (1899), and Qatar (1916). Thereafter a final series of treaties between 1913 and 1922 bound the same rulers to award concessions only to companies appointed by Britain. Meanwhile, the British also exercised a form of legal protection over many of the non-native inhabitants of the Gulf, for example, the Indian merchants established in Bahrain, Dubai, and Muscat.[5]

Much the same pattern was replicated along the coastal plain to the east of British India's one Arabian colony, Aden, where the various rulers also entered treaty relationships in what was later (in the later 1930s) to become the Aden Protectorate. However, as such treaties concerned the conduct of external relations alone, direct British interference in domestic government was still minimal. British influence was also a factor in the successful struggle for dominance in the northern peninsula in which the Saudis defeated the Hashemites for control over the Hijaz and the Islamic Holy Cities of Mecca and Medina. Only the Imam Yahya, strenuously trying to build up a centralized administration of the northern part of Yemen after the enforced departure of the Ottoman Turks in 1918, felt secure enough to challenge Britain's position in and around Aden before reaching a *modus vivendi* with it in 1934.

British influence was equally important in the establishment of the peninsula's first political frontiers: that between Aden and Ottoman-controlled Yemen negotiated in 1905, and then those between Saudi Arabia, Kuwait, and the mandatory states of Iraq and Transjordan negotiated in a series of conferences between 1922 and 1925. Such boundaries meant little to begin with, but gradually assumed an increasing significance as local governments tried to exercise greater control over border security as well as over the movement of goods and people. However, it was only with the granting of the first concessions for oil exploration in the early 1930s that the exact position of the frontiers between Saudi Arabia and its Gulf neighbors became a matter for serious concern and growing dispute.

The main areas of settled agriculture were in Yemen (including the western end of the British protectorate and the disputed province of Asir to the north), Oman, and the oasis towns of northern Arabia. Yemen contained three distinct regions: the plain, the maritime hills, and the mountain terraces, all of which were used to grow cereals and vegetables as well as, at higher altitudes, Mocha coffee, its major export crop, and the mild narcotic, qat.[6] The coastal regions of north-east Oman also benefited from adequate rainfall and were used to grow dates, citrus fruits, cereals, and vegetables. As for the oasis towns, a good example is Medina, which was described in a book first published in 1917 as a 'city of agriculturalists' producing dates, maize, and vegetables.[7] However, far and away the largest concentration of such agriculturalists lived in the extensive oasis of al-Hufuf with its seven enormous springs which provided enough water for perhaps 27,000 acres of cultivated land and 2 million date palms.[8] For the rest, agriculture was conducted only on small, isolated patches of cultivated land either in the bottoms of wadis and mountain valleys, containing soil washed down from nearby mountains, or wherever wells could be dug to allow access to the considerable quantities of underground water.

Many parts of Arabia also contained a substantial nomadic population which raised camels as well as sheep and goats. They were also important in the intensive caravan trade which linked the oasis cities and provided them with the rice, salt, and manufactured goods such as arms and cooking pots they were unable to produce themselves. Then, round the coasts, a considerable part of the population took part in some type of sea-going activity, whether as fisherman, traders or, in the Persian Gulf, divers for pearls.

Production, for the most part, catered to the needs of immediate consumption, providing a basic diet of dates, cereals, vegetables, and some dried fish. Manufacturing followed the same lines with the greater part of it consisting of the weaving of rough cloth or the making of basic goods such as pottery storage jars and metal cooking pots. However, there was also a significant commercial sector involved either in exchange of locally produced goods like coffee, dates, and pearls, for imports of rice, textiles, and other basics, or in an entrepôt trade linking the peninsula with neighboring communities in Asia and Africa. In addition, Jiddah, on the Red Sea, derived much of its prosperity from providing services for the annual pilgrimage to nearby Mecca, while Aden was a major coaling station for ships using the Suez Canal.

One commercial activity of great significance to the coastal population of the Gulf was pearling. In the first decade of the century, there were over 2,000 pearling dhows which spent the season from April/May to September/October diving off the oyster bank which stretched 400 kilometers from just south of Kuwait in the north to Ra's al-Khaymah on the Trucial Coast.[9] The pearls themselves were then sold along a chain of merchants which took them finally to Bombay and beyond.[10] As Fuad Khuri describes the organization of this activity in Bahrain, the main pearling center of the Gulf before 1914, the boats were usually owned by their pilots who then employed a crew of around 20 men with whom, after deducting his expenses, the owner was customarily supposed to divide the profits on the basis of five shares for himself, three for the divers, and two for the 'pullers.' But as the pilots often kept no written records, and as the crew were usually deeply in their debt for loans granted them at the start of the diving season, it is unlikely that this ideal division was ever properly adhered to.[11] By the early twentieth century, the pearling industry as a whole was based largely on credit, a development which had led the rulers of the Trucial Coast shaykhdoms to sign an agreement in 1899 jointly committing themselves to return any absconding debtors to their original place of residence.[12]

Figures to be found in early twentieth century official reports, as well as the books written by contemporary travelers, provide a very rough guide to the value of the various types of commercial activities just described. For example, the government of India's Persian Gulf political residency put the average annual export of pearls from Bahrain for 1898–1902 at Rs6,240,975 (£416,065).[13] A few years later, one British report estimated that Jiddah imported £1.75 million of goods a year while another put the value of Hodeida's in 1909 at just over £1million.[14]

It was this trade, too, which provided rulers with the bulk of their public revenues through customs duties farmed out to some of the influential local merchants, whether Arabs or, in Bahrain and Muscat, men of Indian origin. Nevertheless, given the fact that tariffs were kept low in order to encourage trade, the sums involved were generally small, only Rs 8,000 (just over £533) from the Sharjah customs farm just before the First World War and a minuscule Rs 800 at Ra's al-Khaymah.[15] Such low official receipts placed an obvious premium on private sources of ruling family income, such as the date gardens owned by the al-Khalifas in Bahrain and the al-Sabahs in southern Iraq, or their participation in the profits to be derived from pearling or commerce.

ECONOMIC CHANGE BEFORE OIL, 1918–1939

SAUDI ARABIA

No sooner had 'Abd al-'Aziz gained control of the Hijaz in 1925 than he instituted a process of political and economic centralization, assisted by the establishment of new institutions, staffed by new (often foreign) advisers, and the employment of modern methods of communication such as the automobile, the radio, and the telegraph.[16] He also issued countrywide rules and regulations, for example the Commercial Code of 1931–32 based on Ottoman precedent, and a new currency, the silver riyal, first introduced in 1928.[17]

The revenues to pay for these and other expenditures were raised in a variety of ways. One was the duties levied on trade, either from customs or from direct levies on the merchants themselves. It was to this end that 'Abd al-'Aziz also instituted a trade boycott of Kuwait from 1920 to 1937 in an effort to force his subjects to use either his own ports or those of entities like Bahrain with which he had concluded favorable transit agreements. Other taxes included those on animals and dates as well as various types of forced loans. But far and away the most important source of revenue was the money obtained from taxing the pilgrims, either directly at various stages of their journey or by charging them for the provision of various government-sponsored services such as the automobiles which ferried the more wealthy the 46 miles from Jiddah to Mecca.[18]

Nevertheless, it would be wrong to exaggerate the bureaucratic efficiency of the new institutions. Government offices still contained only tiny staffs. There were, for example, just 182 state employees in the Hijaz in 1930,[19] and in the 1920s at least, the royal archives containing all the important official correspondence could still be transported about the country in a number of large boxes.[20] Just as important, when it came to finance, there was no budget and no distinction between the moneys used by the royal family, the government in its official capacity, and the government in its role as importer and provider of various commercial services.[21] According to St John Philby, certainly one of the best-informed foreign residents, Shaykh 'Abdullah Sulayman, the so-called minister of finance, carried all the figures for the country's revenue and expenditure 'in his head.'[22] It was this same 'Abdullah Sulayman who, some years later, is said to have had Saudi Arabia's oil revenues paid directly into his personal account in a New York bank to which he alone had access.[23]

There were also considerable problems involved in the use of the Saudi riyal. First, the government was unable to achieve its aim of making it the sole currency so that it was forced to coexist with a number of other coins, notably the Turkish majidi in the Hijaz, the Indian silver rupee (which was very popular in Najd and along the Gulf coast), and the British gold sovereign.[24] Second, its exchange rate varied enormously, particularly during the pilgrimage season when the foreign pilgrims sought to convert their own coins into riyals in order to defray their local expenses. There were further difficulties following the devaluation of the British pound – to which the riyal was nominally linked – in 1931, leading to the issue of a new version of the same coin in 1933 with exactly the same silver content as the Indian rupee.[25]

To make matters worse, the first attempts at institutionalized centralization were soon overtaken by the great economic crisis of the early 1930s when the numbers of foreign pilgrims able to afford to visit Mecca fell away sharply, from a peak of 132,109 in 1927 to 21,065 in 1932, and only 20,705 in 1933.[26] As even the poorest pilgrim was estimated to spend at least £30 on local expenses, this was a huge blow not only to the government finances but also to the Hijazi economy as a whole.[27] Imports declined, customs revenues fell sharply and, even though the government made every effort to raise more taxes, it experienced increasing difficulty in paying both its own officials and those merchants to whom it owed money. According to Philby, who was himself vitally concerned to obtain the moneys due to him for importing automobiles on government account, revenues fell from some £1 million in the late 1920s to just £250,000 in 1933; another estimate put the amount owed to the government's official creditors at the end of 1932 at nearly £220,000.[28] Moreover, all this was at a time when there was a sharp rise in expenditures needed to pay the soldiers engaged in the 1933–34 campaign against the Yemenis in Asir.

The financial crisis of the 1930s had another important effect; this was the encouragement it gave 'Abd al-'Aziz to seek out foreign companies which might be offered concessions of one type or another in exchange for ready cash. Certainly the most important example of this new policy was the award of the first oil exploration concession to Standard Oil of California in July 1933 for an immediate advance of £50,000 plus £5,000 a year (see later section). Further advances followed, augmented from 1938 onwards by the first royalties for oil actually produced and exported, a sum which had already reached $1.9 million for the year 1939.[29] Meanwhile, the number of foreign pilgrims slowly began to revive, rising to nearly 50,000 by 1937, each of whom was required to pay a tax of £2 in gold.[30] Tax receipts also began to rise again in the mid-1930s, particularly those collected in the main towns.[31] But if revenues increased, so too did government expenditure, leading to a continued demand for more advances met by substantial amounts of British and American financial aid during the Second World War.

THE GULF COAST

During the inter-war period the economic life of the Gulf shaykhdoms was subject to two powerful external influences: growing British interference in domestic administration and the severe impact of the Depression, including the sudden collapse of the pearl trade. But then, at this time of great difficulty, the economies of Bahrain, and to a lesser extent those of Kuwait and Qatar, received a substantial boost from the revenues they began to receive as a result of concessions awarded to foreign oil companies (see later section).

The 1920s were a boom period as far as the profits from the Gulf pearling industry were concerned. Over 2,500 boats were usually involved, with crews which accounted for a very large proportion of the economically active population. Meanwhile, one estimate puts the total value of Gulf pearl exports at $1.2 million in1925 and $1 million in 1926.[32] Some of the ruling families – for example the al-Sabahs in Kuwait – benefited directly from taxes and from their customary share in profits.[33] Others, like the al-Khalifas in Bahrain, did not tax the pearling industry directly but shared in the general prosperity through the customs revenues levied on the increase in trade.[34] There was also one notable attempt to regulate the terms under which the pilots managed their affairs: this was the Bahraini regulations of 1924, which forced boat owners to keep proper records of their profits and expenses and set limits on the duration and size of the loans they gave to their divers and the rate of interest they were allowed to charge.[35] This produced an annual protest at the beginning of each season from 1926 to 1932, from both pilots and crews, without, as far as can be seen, doing anything to damage the size of the harvest itself.[36]

There were two shaykhdoms, however, where the profits from pearls were offset by other factors. One was Kuwait, where the Saudi trade boycott considerably reduced the sums which the al-Sabahs received from the tariff on imports.[37] The other was Muscat and Oman where, after a brief revival in the early 1920s, the general decline in commercial activity which had begun in the late nineteenth century continued, made worse by the reduction of the market for Omani dates and the insecurity produced by the uneasy coexistence of two rival centers of political power: the British-protected Sultan who ruled along the coast and the Imam who controlled much of the interior.[38]

Pearl prices began to fall in 1929, partly because of the reduced demand for luxury goods in Europe and America at the beginning of the Depression, partly because of competition from lower-priced cultured pearls. For a couple of seasons, Gulf merchants held much of the catch off the market hoping for a revival. However, as the downward trend continued, the number of boats in operation started to fall, and both pilots and divers began to look for other sources of income. The consequences were felt throughout the local economies: fewer boats were built by local craftsmen, loans could not be repaid, and the value of imports greatly declined leading, in turn, to a sharp fall in government revenues.[39] To make matters worse, many of the Gulf merchants began to suffer from the effects of falling silver prices on the value of some of the coins used most commonly in trade, notably the Maria Theresa dollar. Dispatches from the British Political Agent in Kuwait, Colonel Dickson, provide vivid evidence of the impact of all this on the local population. In 1931, he reported that a few Bedouin pearl divers had died of starvation and in 1932 that the town now contained 'beggars' as well as 2,000 starving Persian refugees.[40]

The pearl trade experienced a brief revival towards the end of the 1930s and through the Second World War. However, by and large, those Gulf communities which managed to survive the Depression the best were those which were able to find alternative sources of income, whether from oil royalties or from a return to long-distance trade, including the hazardous business of smuggling goods into Persia and Iraq, where the high tariff barriers meant large profits for those who could avoid detection. In these new circumstances, it was Bahrain and Dubai where incomes held up the best: Qatar, Abu Dhabi, and Oman possessed fewer opportunities to compensate for the loss of their pearling income and so experienced great hardship as well as a loss of population to their now better-off neighbors.

YEMEN AND ADEN

Information about the experience of Yemen and Aden in the inter-war period is difficult to find. This is due partly to the fact that Imam Yayha, who ruled Yemen from 1918 to 1948, deliberately attempted to isolate his newly independent country from European influence. Internally, his main concern was an attempt to create a small army and police force which he then used both to create greater security of communication and to tax his largely agricultural population. Figures obtained by Gamal Eddine Heyworth-Dunne from the Imam's own records show an increase in local revenues from the 1930s to the 1940s, much of which came from direct taxes, and under one-fourth from trade.[41] Kiren Chaudhry describes the extractive agencies as 'highly developed' with the Yemeni government at one stage employing 2,000 non-military officials of whom some 60 percent were revenue collectors.[42] The result was considerable over-taxation in the south of the country and substantial out-migration to Aden.[43] This movement was accelerated by the impact of the world Depression, falling export prices, and a further effort to maximize revenues through the creation of state monopolies, a process which did much to sever the remaining ties between the Imam's Yemen and the outside world.[44]

To the south there were two spheres of economic activity. The first centered on the port of Aden which earned its livelihood from various internationally based activities, such as bunkering foreign ships or conducting a flourishing entrepôt trade with its Arabian and African neighbors, exchanging locally produced hides, coffee, and sea salt for imported textiles. The second involved much of the interior where the population practiced a largely subsistence agriculture dependent on rains whose regularity seems to have become more and more uncertain as the 1930s progressed.

Both Yemen and Aden shared some of the major economic problems produced by the Depression: falling trade, falling export prices, problems with silver coinage, and a huge reduction in the remittances sent home by members of the rich Yemeni merchant communities resident in Southeast Asia. It was Aden which was able to survive with the least harm, thanks largely to the fact that its harbor had been dredged between 1928 and 1930 to allow much larger European ships to anchor there, as well as to its ability to provide an oil-bunkering service to complement the coal which declined rapidly as a marine fuel in the 1930s. There was also profit to be had from an expansion of evaporated sea salt which, by 1937, was providing half the requirements of the whole British colonial empire.[45] Some of this wealth was then spread to the rest of the region via the reopening of the border between Aden and Yemen in 1934 and the better security provided by the British along the major tracks and roads.

THE IMPACT OF OIL

The Arabian Peninsula began a rapid process of economic change with the award of the first major oil concessions in the Persian Gulf beginning with Bahrain in 1930, Saudi Arabia in 1933, Kuwait in 1934, Qatar in 1935, Oman in 1937, three of the Trucial States (Dubai, Sharjah, and Ra's al-Khaymah) in 1938, and Abu Dhabi in 1939.[46] The majority were shared between two major oil companies, Standard Oil of California (SOCAL) and Iraq Petroleum Company (IPC), each of which then created wholly owned subsidiaries for the purpose of exploration and development. Hence SOCAL established the Bahrain Petroleum Company (BPC; generally known as BAPCO) and the Californian Arabian Standard Oil Company

(CASOC: renamed ARAMCO in 1944) while IPC created Petroleum Development Qatar and Petroleum Development Trucial Coast. The only exception was the firm operating in Kuwait, the Kuwait Oil Company, initially set up by the Anglo-Persian Oil Company (APOC) and Gulf Oil.

By and large the concession agreements followed the principles established by the IPC and APOC in their concurrent agreements with Iraq and Iran during the early 1930s. They provided the company in question with the exclusive right to explore for oil within a specified area and then to conduct further operations for a given period of years, for example 60 years for the SOCAL/CASOC concessions in Saudi Arabia, and 75 years for the companies in Kuwait and Qatar. They would pay a standard royalty of either 4 English gold shillings, equivalent to £0.20 (Saudi Arabia), or Rs 3/8 annas (Bahrain) per ton of oil produced. And they would employ local workers where this was 'practicable' or 'consistent with efficiency.' In spite of the fact that some rulers, such as King 'Abd al-'Aziz and the Amir of Kuwait, had been able to organize some small amount of competition between two rival companies, they were not in a strong bargaining position and were unable to insist on a number of more remunerative terms, for example their right to tax the concessionaires directly. What they did get, however, was a reasonable assurance that the companies would explore for, and then export, oil without significant delay.[47]

The economic impact of these concessions began well before oil was actually discovered. For one thing, there was usually an initial lump sum payment to the ruler against future royalties as well as additional, annual payments until oil was found. Small though these sums may now seem, they were of enormous importance during negotiations and, in the Saudi case, were certainly enough to persuade King 'Abd al-'Aziz to accept the SOCAL offer rather than that of its rival, the IPC.[48] Secondly, the act of exploration itself had important local consequences, providing employment for local labor, bringing in small numbers of foreign workers and creating new towns, jetties, and harbors. To most European and American writers this whole process is usually presented as a triumph of technology in adverse geographical circumstances. Another much more critical perspective is provided by the Saudi exile 'Abd al-Rahman Munif, whose fictional quintet entitled *Cities of Salt* chronicles the disruptive character of the process from the point of view of the local people concerned.[49]

Oil was discovered in Bahrain in 1931 and first exported in 1934. Work then continued on a series of developments including the building of a refinery in 1936–37 which was then enlarged after 1938 to process some of the oil discovered at Dhahran in Saudi Arabia less than 30 miles away. Given the small size of the local labor force, most of the first workers were migrants from Persia, followed, after a shift in policy, by the employment of Indians. This in turn soon raised questions which have continued to occupy the rulers of the Gulf oil states ever since, notably the problem of how to balance the cost, skills, and availability of such foreign workers against the possible political consequences of their presence and their ability to organize a system of collective bargaining backed, on occasion, by a willingness to go on strike.[50] In the rather simple-minded (even racialist) terms in which these matters were then discussed, Persians were thought of as politically troublesome because they could be used by the Shah in support of his claim to Bahrain, while Indians were seen as the most likely to lead the workers in demands for higher wages. It was as a result of calculations of this kind that, by 1939, Indians had come to occupy over 90 percent of the jobs defined as 'clerical and technical' or involving payment by the month, while the overwhelming majority of the non-contract daily-paid workers were either Persian or Bahraini.[51]

There were also considerable ups and downs in the total number of BAPCO employees, rising briefly in 1936/37 and 1944/45 when work was being undertaken either on building or expanding the refinery and then falling away thereafter. It was in this way that Bahrain began to experience one of the basic features of an oil economy – a tendency towards sharp fluctuations of income – first observed in 1937 when a temporary surge in the number of foreign engineers alternately swelled demand for housing and other local services, and then dampened it down again when they left.[52]

As oil production began to increase (see Table 4.1) so too did the government's oil royalties, growing from some $9,000 in 1933 to $173,000 in 1936 (a third of total revenues) to $1 million in 1940.[53] At the urging of the British financial adviser Charles Belgrave, these sums were allocated in a three-way division: a third to the ruling family's civil list, a third to current expenditures, and a third invested for future use. Belgrave himself makes the point that Bahrain was fortunate in the relatively slow build-up of oil revenues which allowed it to plan for their proper use.[54] However, others were more critical of what the under-secretary to the government of India described as Bahrain's 'extreme financial conservatism' even though it was clearly based on the necessity of building up its reserves in the expectation that its oil fields would only have a 15-year life.[55] Certainly it is not easy to find signs of any significant increase in spending on public services during these years except in the case of education where the numbers of pupils in government schools increased threefold between 1930 and 1938.[56] Later, the exigencies of the world war, and the need to import quantities of food on government account, are probably enough to account for the continued low levels of expenditure on public works in spite of the fact that Bahrain's oil exports continued at just under 1 million tons a year between 1940 and 1945 (see Table 4.1).

In spite of considerable effort, oil was not discovered in Saudi Arabia until the strike at Dhahran in the eastern province of al-Hasa in March 1938. A year later this field was producing 10,000 barrels a day, some of which was shipped by barge to Bahrain for refining.[57] Two other fields were then discovered at Abqaiq and Abu Hadriya although both were immediately shut down at the beginning of the Second World War. Oil operations had a considerable impact on the economy of al-Hasa, bringing jobs to men who had previously been employed in the pearling industry along the coast or who had lost their livelihood as a result of the fall in the demand for Arabian dates in the late 1930s. But there was also considerable economic disruption when shipping activity at the little ports of al-'Uqayr, Qatif and al-Jubayl declined in favor of the new CASOC facility at Ra's Tannurah.

It was not until 1939 that the Saudi government began to receive significant royalty payments on the 4 million barrels produced.[58] Before that, the much smaller sums obtained from CASOC as advances had done little to alter a situation in which, as one American observer described it, the ministry of finance conducted a 'rolling credit' until the annual pilgrimage season, at which point some of its debts were paid off by the main pilgrim bank, the Netherlands Trading Society.[59]

Oil was discovered at Kuwait's Burgan field in 1938 and was first located in Qatar in 1939. However, in both cases, activity was soon put on hold at the beginning of the Second World War. Nevertheless, the rulers continued to receive relatively small sums as advances against future royalties. In the case of Kuwait, for example, the 1939 advance came to just under 10 percent of total revenues.[60]

The only state where there were significant oil-related developments during the Second World War was Saudi Arabia. First, after an initial period of retrenchment, there was an expansion of local production facilities beginning in 1943, including the construction of a major new refinery at Ra's Tannurah with a capacity of 50,000 barrels a day designed to provide aviation fuel for the Allied forces fighting in the Far East. The result was a huge increase in the size of CASOC/ARAMCO's work force, from 2,882 in 1943 to 11,892 in 1945 (including close to 7,500 Saudi nationals).[61] Second, the government developed a close relationship with the company as a source both of technical advice and of further advances against future royalties. As far as the former was concerned, company engineers began to drill artesian wells in al-Hasa province and to assist in the larger al-Kharj irrigation project south-east of Riyadh. It also helped to improve Jiddah harbor and to distribute imported food using its own company trucks.[62]

The provision of advances was even more important given the rise in government expenditure at the beginning of the war and the inevitable reduction in the number of foreign pilgrims. According to one source, the value of such advances had reached a total of $6.4 million by 1941, followed by a further $2.3 million in 1942.[63]

Oil was also the main reason why both Britain and, later, the United States were willing to provide the Saudi government with larger subsidies than SOCAL itself was able to contemplate at this time. To begin with, it was Britain which assumed most of this burden, supplying an estimated $38 million up to the end of 1943.[64] By this time, however, the United States government had become alerted to the country's huge oil potential, a fact signaled by President Roosevelt's extension of the lend-lease program to Saudi Arabia in February 1943. The United States then stepped in to provide much needed silver and Arabian silver riyals when Britain proved unable to meet the king's demand.[65] Hence, by 1944, both countries were contributing more or less equally to an annual subsidy worth some £4–5 million.[66] Only in 1945 did American influence finally become paramount when the British treasury, anxious to reduce the country's overseas financial commitments at the end of a long, draining war, insisted that the British subsidy be cut by 50 percent.

Notes on Chapter 4
Full details of all sources are in the Bibliography

1 Issawi estimates the total population as 7 million in 1914 and 8 million in 1930; *An Economic History of the Middle East*, Table 6.1.

2 Figures for Aden and Protectorates for 1946 are 750,000: Colonial Office, *Annual Report on Aden and Aden Protectorate for the Year 1946*, pp 11, 57, 71. One estimate for Yemen gives between 3.5 and 4 million in the late 1940s: Heyworth-Dunne, *Al-Yemen*, p 9.

3 Figure for 1930s from McGregor, 'Saudi Arabia: Population and the Making of the Modern State,' p 221.

4 Lorimer, *Gazetteer of the Persian Gulf, Oman and Central Arabia* 2, *Geographical and Statistical*, A, pp 1051, 1412, 1437; B, pp 238, 410, 489.

5 Zahlan, *The Making of the Modern Gulf States*, pp 8–10.

6 Bury, *Arabia Infelix or the Turks in Yamen*, ch. 6, pp 100–12.

7 Hogarth, *Hejaz Before World War I*, new ed., pp 26–7.

8 The (1942) figure for date palms is from Twitchell, *Saudi Arabia with an Account of the Development of its Natural Resources*, p 6. The figure for the cultivated area also relates to 1942: United Kingdom, Naval Intelligence Division, *Western Arabia and the Red Sea*, p 474.

9 Lorimer, *Gazetteer of the Persian Gulf, Oman and Central Arabia* 2, *Geographical and Statistical*, A, pp 243, 490; II, B, p 1,533 for numbers of boats. Not all boats were used for pearling every season.

10 Khuri, *Tribe and State in Bahrain*, p 57.

11 *Ibid.*, pp 59–63.

12 Heard-Bey, *From Trucial States to United Arab Emirates*, pp 211–12.

13 'Administrative Report on the Persian Gulf Political Residency and Muskat Political Agency for 1901–1902,' p 62. As a result of the 1893 currency reform, the exchange value of the Indian rupee was fixed at £1=15 rupees; Keynes, *Indian Currency and Finance*, p 6.

14 Figures cited by Issawi from diplomatic and consular reports in 'Trade of Hijaz at the Turn of the Century' and from Great Britain, Admiralty War Staff, *A Handbook of Arabia 1916* (London, 1916) in 'Yemen, Aden, and Bahrain in the 1900s,' pp 321 and 327.

15 Heard-Bey, *From Trucial States to United Arab Emirates*, pp 190–1.

16 See Kostiner, 'On Instruments and Their Designers,' pp 310–11. Also the same author's *The Making of Saudi Arabia 1916 to 1936*, pp 141–5.

17 Sir A. Ryan, Jidda, 29 March 1935, PRO FO 406/74, pt 38.

18 According to British sources, revenues from customs and pilgrimage reached £520,000 in the early 1920s under the previous reign of King Hussein; Chaudhry, *The Price of Wealth*, p 55, n18.

19 *Ibid.*, pp 63–4, Table 2.1.

20 Almana, *Arabia Unified*, p 181.

21 Mikesell, 'Monetary Problems in Saudi Arabia,' p 171.

22 Quoted in 'Saudi Arabia: Annual Report, Economics (B), for 1938' in Sir Reader Bullard, Jedda, 10 December 1938, PRO FO 371/23268.

23 Grafftey-Smith, *Bright Levant*, p 265. Grafftey-Smith was British Minister to Saudi Arabia in 1945.

24 'Saudi Arabia: Annual Report, Economics (A) for 1938' in Sir Reader Bullard, Jedda, 28 March 1939, PRO FO 371/23268; Mikesell, 'Monetary Problems in Saudi Arabia,' p 172.

25 *Ibid.*, p 171.

26 Pilgrim numbers from 'Analysis of Mecca Pilgrimage,' 18 April 1945, PRO FO 371/45535.

27 'Saudi Arabia: Annual Report, Economics (B) for 1938' in Sir Reader Bullard, Jedda, 10 December 1938, PRO FO 371/23268.

28 'Economics of Araby,' 8 March 1933 in Philby Papers, Private Papers, Box XXXII/4, Middle East Centre, St Antony's College, Oxford; Sir A. Ryan, Jedda, 31 January 1933, PRO FO 406/71.

29 Stocking, *Middle East Oil*, p 89.

30 'Saudi Arabia: Annual Report, Economics (B) for 1938' in Sir Reader Bullard, Jedda, 10 December 1938 and 'Saudi Arabia: Annual Report for 1937' in Sir Reader Bullard, Jedda, 26 March 1938, PRO FO 371/23268.

31 Chaudhry, *The Price of Wealth*, p 65.

32 Bowen, 'The Pearl Fisheries of the Persian Gulf,' p 163.

33 More, 'Administrative Report of the Kuwait Political Agency for the Year 1918,' Dickson Papers, Box 3, File 6, Private Papers, Middle East Centre, St Antony's College, Oxford.

34 Khuri, *Tribe and State*, pp 66, 106.
35 *Ibid.*, pp 107–8; Belgrave, *Personal Column*, pp 50–1.
36 *Ibid.*, pp 51–3.
37 The Shaykh of Kuwait told the British Resident in 1929 that the Saudi blockade had reduced his revenues by 70 percent but this might be an exaggeration; quoted in Crystal, *Oil and Politics in the Gulf*, p 39.
38 Landen, *Oman Since 1856*, p 405.
39 According to the British Resident, Kuwaiti customs revenues fell from Rs8–9 million in the early 1920s to Rs2 million in the early 1930s; 'Administrative Report of the Kuwaiti Political Agency for 1931,' p 13, Dickson Papers, Box 3, File 5.
40 *Ibid.*, p 32; 'Administrative Report of the Kuwait Political Agency for the Year 1932,' Dickson Papers, Box 3, File 5, p 15.
41 Heyworth-Dunne, *Al-Yemen*, p 9.
42 Chaudhry, *The Price of Wealth*, p 106.
43 *Ibid.*, pp 108–10.
44 *Ibid.*, p 110.
45 Gavin, *Aden under British Rule 1839–1967*, p 291.
46 There had been previous concessions awarded but none that led to actual exploration. See Longrigg, *Oil and the Middle East*, pp 99–101.
47 Stocking, *Middle East Oil*, pp 81–3.
48 *Ibid.*, pp 78–9.
49 For example, Munif, *Mudun al-milh: riwaya*, translated as *Cities of Salt* by Theroux.
50 Seccombe, 'Labour Migration in the Arabian Gulf: Evolution and Characteristics,' pp 5–7.
51 Seccombe and Lawless, *Work Camps and Company Towns*, p 21 and Table 2.3.
52 Zahlan, *Making of the Modern Gulf States*, p 52.
53 Penrose, 'Oil and State in Arabia,' p 135.
54 Belgrave, *Personal Column*, pp 84–5.
55 Under-Secretary to Political Resident, Persian Gulf, New Delhi, 22 August 1945, PRO FO 371/45193.
56 Zahlan, *Modern Gulf States*, p 51.
57 Saudi Arabia, 'Annual Economic Report (B) for 1939' in R.W. Bullard to Viscount Halifax, Jedda, 4 December 1939, PRO FO 371/23268.
58 Stocking, *Middle East Oil*, p 959.
59 Quoted in Malone, 'Involvement and Change,' p 44n.
60 Crystal, *Oil and Politics*, p 55.
61 Seccombe and Lawless, *Work Camps and Company Towns*, pp 16–17; Anderson, *ARAMCO, the United States and Saudi Arabia*, p 117.
62 Malone, 'Involvement and Change,' pp 36–7.
63 Stocking, *Middle East Oil*, pp 92, 95.
64 *Ibid.*, p 95.
65 Another shipment of 3 million riyals and silver ingots was torpedoed by a German submarine in the Gulf in 1944 and only rediscovered in 1994: *Boston Globe*, 10 November 1994.
66 Baxter, Foreign Office to British Ambassador, Washington, February 1945 (draft), PRO FO 371/45523.

Part II
1946–1990

Introduction
to Part II

THE WORLD ECONOMY AFTER THE SECOND WORLD WAR

Even before the end of the Second World War, the United States and its Western allies had begun focusing on the design of a new international economic order. The structure of this order was greatly influenced by the perceived lessons of history, most notably the problems created during the inter-war period by war debts, reparations, and beggar-my-neighbor policies which were instrumental in the breakdown of the world trade and payments system. The absence of a leading power was also viewed as an important reason for the persistence of the Great Depression.

The 1944 conference at Bretton Woods aimed at creating a liberal international economic system based upon multilateral, non-discriminatory trade. Three institutions were to play key roles in the implementation of this vision. The International Monetary Fund was given responsibility for maintaining the stability of a new fixed exchange rate system with the dollar at the center and for facilitating international adjustments. The IMF was to provide reserves for countries facing short-term balance of payments difficulties. Another institution, the International Bank for Reconstruction and Development, later known as the World Bank, was originally designed to help finance postwar reconstruction and to support

long-term investments for productive purposes. It later assumed responsibility for extending loans and aid to developing countries. The third
institution was the General Agreement on Tariffs and Trade (GATT)
which held its first session in 1947. It sought the liberalization of international trade through the reduction of tariff and non-tariff barriers. The
GATT remained in existence until the 1990s as an instrument for promoting simultaneous tariff concessions through multilateral negotiations.[1]

The late 1940s, overshadowed by the escalation of Cold War tensions
and the difficulties associated with the reconstruction of Europe and its
periphery, was a difficult period for the world economy. The recovery of
Western Europe was encouraged by the Marshall aid program and efforts
to promote greater European integration were then placed on a new footing
in 1952 with the establishment of the European Coal and Steel Community
which aimed at the reduction of tariffs and the gradual abolition of quotas
between member countries. The outbreak of the Korean War in 1950
provided a major stimulus to the world economy by raising demand and
leading to a short-lived, but powerful, commodity boom which, in turn,
provided a major boost to the incomes and balance of payments of the
developing countries. By the early 1950s the first stage in the postwar
recovery of the world economy had been largely completed.[2]

From 1950 until the first oil price increase of 1973, the world economy
experienced an unprecedented period of prosperity and expansion. In the
industrialized countries, real GDP increased at rates above 4.5 percent per
annum and increases in per capita GDP exceeded 3 percent per annum.
These rates were almost twice as fast as in any previous period since 1820.
They were accompanied by similar increases in labor productivity which
also rose twice as fast as ever before and increases in real wages. These
trends were supported by an investment boom of historically unparalleled
length and vigor as well as technological progress. The Keynesian macroeconomic policies of the period underscored the greater importance
attached to full employment. Another important development with long
lasting significance was the rapid recovery of Japan which established itself
as a world economic power by the 1970s.[3]

THE DEVELOPING COUNTRIES IN THE POSTWAR ERA

Rates of growth in the developing countries were also exceptionally high
during this same quarter century. The average rate of GDP growth in the
developing countries as a whole was about 5.5 percent per annum. Due to
the higher rates of population growth, however, per capita GDP increased

at about 3 percent per annum, a rate quite similar to those of the industrialized countries.[4]

Stimulated by the deterioration of the terms of trade against primary commodities after the end of the Korean War, import substituting industrialization (ISI) became the most frequently adopted strategy for economic development during the postwar era, especially in the medium-sized and larger developing countries. Even in those countries that had not embraced the strategy during the 1930s, ISI quickly demonstrated its ability to generate rapid growth of output and employment in the manufacturing sector. With a heavily protected domestic market and the establishment of infant industries made up of public as well as private firms, ISI found strong allies both domestically and internationally. It involved the diversion of resources away from the traditional raw materials exporting producers, and, more generally, the agricultural sector, to the emerging industrialists and a rapidly expanding bureaucracy created to administer the new economic apparatus. The transition to ISI probably produced more opportunities than costs for the multinational companies as well. In addition to licensing and patent arrangements, many were able to set up subsidiaries in the developing countries behind protective barriers and exploit the opportunities created by a captive domestic market. In this early stage, the newly industrializing countries did not need to export manufactures as the traditional exports of primary commodities continued to pay for the imported capital and intermediate goods.[5]

Even though these inward looking policies often appeared to be in conflict with the policies favored by the IMF, the fixed exchange rate systems actually made it possible for the ISI regimes to coexist with the international monetary and trade arrangements of the Bretton Woods era, including GATT. Most developing countries successfully resisted IMF pressures to eliminate quotas and multiple exchange rates until the 1980s.

By the 1970s, however, the problems and bottlenecks of ISI were becoming more apparent. Even though ISI aimed to reduce foreign exchange bottlenecks, in practice the result was often the opposite. Typically imports of consumer goods declined, but the need to import raw materials, intermediate, and capital goods increased due to the growing volume of domestic production of manufactures. Moreover, domestic industry was unable to compete in the international markets because of inefficiencies and overvalued exchange rates. While this was not a problem for the oil exporters pursuing ISI, countries without large and steady export revenues often faced chronic foreign exchange scarcities. In addition, the ISI strategy often contributed to inflation, neglect of agriculture, and unequal distribution of income.

THE END OF BRETTON WOODS AND THE ERA OF STRUCTURAL ADJUSTMENT PROGRAMS

The fixed exchange rate regime which sustained the postwar expansion came under considerable pressure in the late 1960s with the American balance of payments deficits of the Vietnam era and the accompanying weaknesses of the dollar. In the absence of strong measures by the United States to adjust its balance of payments, the Bretton Woods system came to an end in the early 1970s. The innovations that occurred in the early 1970s can hardly be called a conscious redesigning of the international monetary system, however. The transition to floating rates took place gradually through improvisations that fitted together in a rough and ready way. Managed floating remained the norm and the dominance of the dollar continued.[6]

The weakened international monetary and trading system received a major shock when the oil producers of the Middle East within OPEC decided to demonstrate their recently acquired power by bringing about a substantial raise in the price of crude oil. Governments of the industrialized countries chose to respond to the price increases of 1973 and 1979 by contracting domestic demand. The global recession that followed brought about the end of a long period of expansion of the world economy. These contractive policies failed, however, to bring inflation under control. The outcome, instead, was the worst of both worlds, a combination of stagnation and inflation, accompanied by a slow-down in productivity growth and a leveling off of real wages, which lasted well into the 1980s.

In the aftermath of the oil price increases, the large trade surpluses of the oil exporting countries created new liquidity in the international markets and these so-called petrodollars were offered to potential borrowers at low interest rates, often below the levels of dollar inflation. Many developing countries attempted to take advantage of this new liquidity and borrowed large amounts in order to extend the ISI related boom. This strategy could not be sustained for long, however. The second round of increases in oil prices brought about severe monetary tightening in the United States and pushed interest rates sharply higher.

The rapid escalation of the outstanding debt and the growing difficulties of servicing and repayment in many developing countries thus gave the IMF and the World Bank renewed power for bringing about long-term structural changes in these economies.

The stabilization and structural adjustment programs advocated by these institutions promoted greater international integration and openness, as well as the liberalization of trade and payments regimes and of financial·

markets, greater emphasis on exports, and more generally, greater reliance on markets, both international and domestic, for resource allocation.[7]

In most cases, however, the abandonment of ISI and the adoption of a new long-term strategy cannot be explained by the increased leverage of the international organizations alone. The slow and often painful shift towards new policies was also due to the growing recognition on the part of governments that the earlier model could not be sustained any more. Demands for change also came from those segments of the private sector that stood to gain from the new policies and from those who had benefited from the ISI policies but now recognized that these had been exhausted.[8]

It is thus safe to say that, since the mid-1970s, the nature of the linkages between the developing countries and the rest of the world economy has been undergoing changes as fundamental as those that began in the early 1930s and were consolidated during the 1950s. Whereas the period after 1929 witnessed a move towards inward-looking policies and greater government interventionism, the shift in the recent period has been in the opposite direction, toward greater integration with the world markets and greater reliance on markets per se.

Another important trend since the 1970s has been the increasing differentiation between the developing countries and the emergence of successful industrialists who were able to adjust to the changing conditions and to achieve high rates of per capita growth. Most notably, the developing countries in East and Southeast Asia, including China, have combined export-oriented policies with government interventionism in trade, industrial policy, and technology to transform this area into the most dynamic economic region of the world since the early 1970s.[9] As a result, it has become increasingly difficult to talk about the world economy in terms of a simple cleavage between a developed metropolis and an underdeveloped periphery in recent decades.

THE MIDDLE EAST IN THE POSTWAR PERIOD

During the half century since the Second World War, the population of the Middle East has grown more rapidly than ever before. The annual growth rate averaged approximately 1.5 percent in the inter-war years and considerably less during the Second World War. In contrast, it rose above 2 percent from the end of the war until 1960 and above 3 percent during the 1960s and 1970s, although then it declined somewhat during the 1980s, averaging 2.9 percent from 1960 to 1990 as a whole. As a result, the total population of the region under study in this volume has almost tripled from approximately 63 million in 1950 to 184 million by 1990.

Despite rapid overall growth, the two large countries of the region, Egypt and Turkey, continued to account for well above half of the total population, although their share declined somewhat from 69 percent in 1950 to 61 percent in 1990. While rates of growth have been slowing down in Egypt and Turkey, population has grown most rapidly in the small and medium-sized oil exporting countries which have attracted considerable amounts of immigration since the early 1970s.[10]

The population increases of the postwar period can be explained in terms of a pattern well known throughout the developing world. Overall growth in population was almost entirely due to the decline in the death rates, while birth rates fell only modestly, although there were significant variations in this respect between countries of the region.

By contrast, migration into and out of the region has played a small role in the overall changes of numbers. Turkey received close to half a million immigrants from Bulgaria, while a much larger number of Turks, as many as 2 million, emigrated to Europe in search of jobs from the early 1960s until the recession of 1974–75 when European governments placed severe restrictions on these labor flows. Syrians and Lebanese continued to migrate to the New World at a modest pace of about 4,000 per annum. Israel attracted as many as 1.5 million Jewish immigrants from outside the region until 1990 in addition to the several hundred thousand who came from Iraq, Yemen, Egypt, and elsewhere in the region, although approximately 500,000 Israelis left the country during the same period to live in Europe and North America. Beginning in the 1960s, but especially after the oil price increases, the Gulf countries and Saudi Arabia received as many as four million Asian workers, most importantly from India, Pakistan, and the Philippines.[11]

A considerable amount of migration has also occurred within the region since the Second World War and these flows accelerated considerably after 1973. Most important were the departure of 700,000 Palestinians from their homeland after 1948 and then flows of unskilled and skilled workers, including professionals, from elsewhere in the region and the Maghreb towards the oil exporting countries. These latter flows increased substantially after 1973 with the development of a major construction boom in the Gulf countries, Saudi Arabia, and Iraq. Most migrating workers were from Egypt, Yemen, and Jordan. It is difficult to estimate the numbers of people who have moved within the region since the early 1970s but the figure may be of the order of 5 million.[12]

Much more important than these flows, in terms of sheer numbers, has been the rural to urban migration within the individual countries. In 1950, close to 80 percent of the population of the region lived in rural areas. By 1990, the share of rural population in the total had declined below 50 percent. These flows were absorbed not only by Cairo and Istanbul, the largest metropolitan centers whose populations reached 13 and 7 million respectively by 1990, but also by the second-tier urban centers of the region. Whereas no city in the region had a population exceeding 1 million in 1925, and only two in 1950 (Cairo and Istanbul), eleven cities had populations of over this size by 1990.

From an economic perspective, rural-to-urban migration has meant the movements of people and resources from agriculture to other sectors of the economy, that is, long-term structural change. In the aftermath of the Second World War, agriculture was the most important economic sector in the Middle East, employing close to 75 percent of the labor force. That share has steadily declined ever since, to below 40 percent by 1990. The share of agriculture in total GDP has also declined, from approximately 50 percent or lower to less than 20 percent during the same period.[13] These aggregate figures conceal, of course, the large differences within the region between the small and medium-sized oil exporters, on the one hand, and the medium and large countries that are not major exporters of oil, on the other.

In the urban economy, ISI was the most commonly adopted strategy of economic development in countries without significant amounts of oil. Manufacturing industry typically began its ascent in textiles and food processing and soon spread to intermediate goods and consumer durables. In the oil exporting countries, in contrast, by far the most important industry was oil extraction for export although it did not rank very high in terms of employment. Similarly, refining and petrochemicals became important in the 1970s in value added terms but not in terms of employment.[14]

One important feature of ISI in the Middle East was the central role played by the public sector. Until the Second World War, Turkey was the only country in the region that began building a large public sector to lead its ISI strategy. Elsewhere it was only after that war that it assumed an increasingly important role in the urban economy. In this post-colonial era, it was seen as the task of the state to mobilize material and human resources to overcome economic 'backwardness,' build a diversified economy, and attain a more equitable distribution of income and wealth.

Obviously these concerns are not unique to the Middle East but common to most developing countries. In fact according to World Bank estimates the output of the public sector, excluding banks and other financial institutions, in the developing countries averaged close to 10 percent of GDP in 1980 in the developing countries as a whole. Similarly, state-owned enterprises frequently accounted for one-fourth to one-half of total value added in manufacturing. In many countries of the Middle East, however, the share of the state sector was considerably higher than these averages.[15]

The rapid expansion of the state sector and the growth in publicly owned assets was due to a number of factors, some internal and some external. The absence of a strong private sector due to the departure or expulsion of the existing bourgeoisie, the nature of the single party or Arab socialist regimes, and externally, the rapprochement with the Soviet Union were the most important. The growth of the state sector was not limited to the Arab countries, however. In Israel, too, the doctrine of etatism that was developed soon after independence led to the emergence of a large welfare state with vaguely socialist objectives and extensive public ownership.

Many states in the region soon began to employ large numbers of people as civil servants, workers and managers, sometimes – as in the case of Egypt – as much as half of the non-agricultural labor force. They also controlled large investment budgets, strategic parts of the banking system, virtually all subsoil minerals and the basic infrastructure in roads, railroads, power, and ports.

In most of these countries, market forces were considered inferior to planning and other centralized mechanisms of resource allocation. Similarly, the large scale private sector was seen as untrustworthy and governments nationalized this sector or sharply curtailed its activities. Foreign investment was also viewed with suspicion and generally considered undesirable. As a result, entire sectors of the economy such as metals, chemicals, and minerals were closed off to private activity and foreign capital and reserved exclusively for state economic enterprises.

In the 1950s and 1960s the state sector-led ISI process achieved rapid growth and structural change as measured, for example, by the rise in the share of industry in total employment and output. By the middle of the 1970s, however, the problems of ISI, compounded by the problems of the state sector, were becoming increasingly apparent. The infant industries had difficulties growing up to become competitive adults. International comparative advantage was often ignored. Various types of state intervention, most notably overvalued exchange rates and various subsidies, led to misallocation of resources in both agriculture and industry.

The quadrupling of the international price of oil in 1973 precipitated one of the largest and most rapid transfers of wealth in the twentieth century. In the Middle East, the inflow of unprecedented amounts of foreign exchange led to a major economic boom, first in the oil exporting countries and then in other parts of the region, as the labor-scarce oil exporters and capital-scarce labor exporters became tightly linked through massive flows of labor and capital including remittances across national borders. When oil prices plummeted in the 1980s, however, the regional boom was quickly transformed into a regionwide recession. As the oil revenues of the exporters fell, government expenditures dropped, and workers' remittances and other types of capital flows followed. The Gulf War of 1990–91 then formally severed many of the intra-regional links that had been weakening through the 1980s.[16]

The increases in oil prices after 1973 only exacerbated the problems of ISI and the inefficiencies of the state sector in the oil importing countries. Even though growing import bills coupled with stagnating exports increased the need for adjustment, the first reaction in many parts of the region was to take advantage of the low interest rates in the international markets arising from the availability of petrodollars to continue the domestic expansion with external finance.

Sooner or later, though, the need for structural adjusment was bound to assert itself with or without a debt crisis. Since the end of the 1970s, all countries of the region, initially the oil importing countries and later the oil exporters, have been forced to come to terms with the need to adjust their economic development strategies to the changing global realities.

The timing, pace, and content of efforts for economic reform have varied across the region. The uneven progress of structural adjustment programs needs to be examined in a political economy framework as the complex interaction of domestic and external forces rather than reflecting economic logic alone.[17]

Despite the poor economic performance and growing costs associated with ISI and the public sector, such as economic stagnation, growing urban unemployment, foreign exchange difficulties, and the accumulation of external debt, it has not been easy for governments to take action on their own. For one thing, the political leadership has often been reluctant to abandon or reduce the leverage they exert over the resources and people that the public sector provides. Secondly, it has been very difficult to build and sustain the political coalitions necessary for the initiation and implementation of the structural adjustment programs. As a result, the progress of these programs often depended on the external pressures and the leverage enjoyed by international agencies such as the IMF and World Bank.[18]

In turn, the leverage of the international forces demanding more rapid and more extensive policy changes generally depended on the severity of the economic crisis, most typically a foreign exchange crisis or default on the outstanding external debt. Such crises often helped overcome some of the obstacles in the way of structural adjustment by helping to bring together domestic forces demanding reform and forcing governments to take action.

One major risk as perceived by the governments in the region has been that the austerity demanded by these programs will provoke violence especially amongst the urban population, thus severely testing their regimes. Since the decline in the price of oil in the 1980s, the oil exporting countries of the region have also been forced to undertake austerity measures and implement, in various degrees, aspects of the structural adjustment programs.

Finally, in terms of economic growth, the region has experienced significant increases in GDP per capita during the second half of the twentieth century. Levels of GDP per capita for the region as a whole had changed little between the early 1920s and the late 1940s. In contrast, it increased at an average rate close to 3 percent per annum between 1950 and 1990. By 1990 GDP per capita for the region had reached approximately three times its level in 1950. These long term rates of growth are close to the averages for the developing countries as a whole during the same period. The many gaps in available statistics make it impossible, however, to be more precise about the growth record of the region.[19]

As important as the rise in this average figure was the changing distribution of the gains between the national economies and between different groups across the region. After the increase in oil prices, differences within the region between the oil exporting and oil importing countries widened considerably as did the strategies for dealing with the consequences. While many of the oil exporting countries channelled their resources towards an investment and construction boom, the others struggled to adjust at a time when the world economy was experiencing a slowdown in growth. In the following chapters, we will be examining these far-reaching changes on a country by country basis.

Notes on Introduction to Part II
Full details of all sources are in the Bibliography

1   Foreman-Peck, *A History of the World Economy since 1850* 2nd ed., pp 235–92; Kenwood and Lougheed, *The Growth of the International Economy, 1829–1990,* pp 235–60; Block, *The Origins of International Economic Disorder*, pp 32–108.
2   Milward, *The Reconstruction of Western Europe, 1945–51.*
3   Van der Wee, *Prosperity and Upheaval*, pp 48–280; Arrighi, *The Long Twentieth Century*, pp 269–324. For a European perspective on this exceptional period, see Crafts, 'The Golden Age of Economic Growth in Europe, 1950–1973,' pp 429–47.
4   Based on the tables in World Bank, *World Development Report*, various issues.

5 Hirschmann's 'Political Economy of Import Substituting Industrialization in Latin America,' pp 1–29, remains a classic on the achievements and limitations of ISI. For different perspectives see Kemp, *Industrialization in the Non-Western World* 2nd ed., chs 4–9 and Chenery, Robinson, and Syrquin, *Industrialization and Growth*.

6 Block, *Origins*, pp 140–225; Foreman-Peck, *A History of the World Economy since 1850* 2nd ed., pp 305–22; and Van der Wee, *Prosperity and Upheaval*, pp 479–512.

7 Stallings, 'International Influence on Economic Policy' and Kahler, 'External Influence, Conditionality and Political Adjustment.' Toye examines the implications of this shift for the developing countries in *Dilemmas of Development* 2nd ed.

8 Haggard and Kaufman, 'Introduction,' in Haggard and Kaufman (eds.), *Politics of Economic Adjustment*, pp 13–27; see also Nelson (ed.), *Economic Crisis and Policy Choice*, passim.

9 Wade, *Governing the Market, Economic Theory and the Role of Government in East Asian Industrialization*.

10 For greater detail on demographic as well as economic trends within the Middle East since 1950, see the Statistical Appendix at the end of this volume.

11 Owen, *Migrant Workers and the Gulf*, Table 2.

12 Yapp, *The Near East Since the First World War*, pp 23–5.

13 For more detailed statistics on economic trends in the Middle East since 1950, see the Statistical Appendix at the end of this volume.

14 For a regional overview, see Issawi, *An Economic History of the Middle East and North Africa*, pp 154–69 and Richards and Waterbury, *A Political Economy of the Middle East* 2nd ed., pp 173–212.

15 Richards and Waterbury, *A Political Economy of the Middle East* 2nd ed., pp 177–201.

16 Chaudhry, *The Price of Wealth*, pp 1–9.

17 Haggard and Kaufman, 'Institutions and Economic Adjustment,' pp 18–37.

18 Stallings, 'International Influence on Economic Policy.'

19 Based on the tables in World Bank, *World Development Report*, various issues.

5

Turkey
1946–1990

INTRODUCTION

This chapter will examine the evolution of the economy of Turkey in the postwar era in three sub-periods: agriculture-led growth, 1947–1962; the high age of import substituting industrialization (ISI) and its crisis, 1963–1979; economic liberalization and increasing macroeconomic instability, 1980–1990. For each sub-period the focus will be on the domestic and international forces that gave rise to a specific economic model and the evaluation of economic performance. A concluding section will briefly review the record for welfare and distribution.

TOWARDS A MORE LIBERAL ECONOMY

After the end of the Second World War, domestic and international forces combined to bring about major political and economic changes in Turkey. Domestically, many social groups had become dissatisfied with the single-party regime by 1946. In the countryside, poorer segments of the peasantry had been badly affected by wartime taxation and government demands for the provisioning of the urban areas. The gendarme and the tax collector had become more hated and feared than ever.[1] In an attempt to mend fences with these groups, the regime passed through parliament a bill which gave the government the power to redistribute all holdings above 50 dunums (4.5 hectares or 11 acres). The parliamentary debate on the bill was very heated and gave rise to strong criticism of the government, especially from members with landowning connections. This bill played an important role in the emergence of an open opposition to the single-party leadership within the parliament.

In the urban areas, the wealth levy of 1942 had caused unrest and suspicion amongst the Muslim bourgeoisie even though the measure had been used to discriminate against non-Muslims. After more than two decades of rule by the Republican People's Party, the bourgeoisie was no longer prepared to accept the position of a privileged but dependent class, even though many of them had benefited from the wartime conditions and policies. In addition, laborers, who constituted a small minority, and other waged and salaried workers, including civil servants, had been hard hit by the wartime inflation and profiteering.[2]

The opposition to the regime thus began to demand, *inter alia*, greater emphasis on private enterprise, the agricultural sector, and a more open economy. In response, the single-party regime led by President Inönü decided to allow competition within the political system and began to move towards a multi-party electoral system. The opposition, led by the representatives of large landowners and merchants, founded the Democrat Party in 1946.

International pressures also played an important role in the shaping of new policies. The emergence of the United States as the dominant world power after the Second World War had shifted the balance toward a more open political system and a more liberal and open economic model. At this juncture, Soviet territorial demands pushed the Turkish government towards closer cooperation with the United States. As the country began to be drawn increasingly into the American sphere of influence, Marshall Plan aid was extended to Turkey for military and economic purposes, beginning in 1948. Numerous foreign experts and official missions visited the country during this period to express their preference for a more liberal and open economy. Perhaps the most influential intervention was the report prepared for the World Bank by a commission of American experts led by the industrialist Max Thornburg, which called for the dismantling of a large number of the etatist manufacturing establishments, including the country's only iron and steel complex, as well as greater emphasis on private enterprise, encouragement of foreign capital, a more liberal foreign exchange and trade regime, and greater reliance on agricultural

105

development. These changes, the report stated, were necessary if Turkey was to benefit from United States aid and the inflow of private American capital in the postwar era.[3]

It has been argued by many that the electoral victory of the Democrats in 1950 was the major turning point for the economy. In fact, in terms of both policy and performance, the true turning point came in 1947 when the Republican People's Party decided to set aside the etatist third five-year plan, which had been prepared during the previous summer, and began to move in the direction of greater reliance on private capital and greater emphasis on agriculture. It also offered a new definition of etatism which still reserved for the state such activities as public works, mining, heavy and military industry, and energy, but assumed the transfer of all other enterprises to private capital.

Even before the elections of 1950, therefore, the single-party regime had begun to adopt some of the basic positions of the opposition. But the Democrats pursued the same trail with greater enthusiasm once they came to power. One important change by the Democrat Party was the liberalization of imports, especially of consumer goods.[4] In this, the new government was aided by the substantial volume of foreign reserves accumulated during the austerity years of the Second World War, the improvements in the external terms of trade which began in 1947, and the favorable world market conditions of the Korean War boom that supported a strong expansion of Turkish exports until 1953. The Democrat Party platform had also called for the sale of state economic enterprises to the private sector. This goal was soon abandoned, however; because in the early 1950s the private sector was not interested in acquiring these enterprises (see Table 5.1).

AGRICULTURE-LED GROWTH, 1947–1962

Another important change instituted by the Democrat Party was the strong emphasis placed on agricultural development. Official statistics show that agricultural output more than doubled from 1947, when the pre-war levels of output had already been attained, through 1953. The most important reason for this strong performance was an increase in the cultivated area by 55 percent thanks to the availability of marginal land.[5] The expansion of the agricultural frontier was supported by two complementary government policies, one for the small peasants and the other for larger farmers. First, even though the Land Distribution Law of 1946 included a clause for the redistribution of large holdings, it was used instead to distribute state owned lands and open up communal pastures to peasants with little or no land. The land distributed under this law, and the transfer of communal pastures to peasants and village cooperatives, together accounted for about half of the postwar increase in the area under cultivation. This aspect of government policy also served to strengthen small ownership across Anatolia, except for the southeast, where the Kurdish landlords and tribal leaders were dominant. Secondly, the Democrat Party government used the Marshall Plan aid to finance the import of agricultural machinery, and especially tractors, whose numbers jumped from fewer than 10,000 in 1946 to 42,000 at the end of the 1950s. Most of these were purchased by the prosperous farmers who were given favorable credit terms through the Agricultural Bank, and were used to expand the area under cultivation. According to a rule of thumb of the period, while a pair of oxen could cultivate 5–10 hectares (12.5 to 25 acres) in a given year, a tractor raised that figure to 75 hectares (185 acres). The tractors were also rented by smallholders who paid for their use by sharecropping.

Agricultural producers also benefited from favorable weather conditions, increasing demand, and improving terms of trade during this period. Domestic prices began to move in favor of agriculture in the late 1940s, and the country's external terms of trade improved by as much as 44 percent from 1948–50 to 1951–53 as world demand for wheat, chrome, and other export commodities rose as a result of America's stockpiling programs during the Korean War.[6] In a country where three-fourths of the population lived in the rural areas, the agriculture-led boom of the early 1950s meant good times and rising incomes for all sectors of the economy. It seemed in 1953 that all would go well and that the promises of the liberal model of economic development would be quickly fulfilled. GNP increased by an average annual rate of 8.7 percent from 1947 through 1953. Urban groups shared in this growth as evidenced by the increases in wages and salaries (see Tables 5.3 and 5.4).

These golden years did not last very long, however. The favorable conjuncture quickly disappeared after 1953. With the end of the Korean War, international demand slackened and the prices of export commodities began to decline. At the same time, the weaknesses of the agricultural sector began to assert themselves. The Anatolian countryside continued to rely on dry farming with virtually no use of chemical fertilizers during the 1950s. Irrigation did not yet rank high on the list of government investments. Only 5.5 percent of the total cropped area was being irrigated at the end of the decade. With the disappearance of the favorable weather conditions, agricultural yields began to stagnate and even decline. Moreover, the rate of expansion in cultivated area slowed down considerably in the

107

second half of the 1950s as the bounds of profitable cultivation were approached. Agricultural production levels thus fluctuated and did not show an upward trend until the early 1960s. For sustained increases in yields, Turkish agriculture had to wait until after the mid-1960s when the limit of land availability encouraged a shift to more intensive techniques of production, including the use of fertilizers and high yielding varieties of seeds (see Tables 5.2 and 5.3).

It was at this juncture that, rather than accept lower incomes for the agricultural producers who made up more than two-thirds of the electorate, the government decided to shield them from the adverse price movements by initiating a price support program for wheat. Such supports became, after 1954, the most important government program affecting agricultural incomes. They were not financed directly out of the budget but by Central Bank credits to the Soil Products Office, the state agency responsible for the purchase of low priced wheat, as well its distribution to urban areas. The extent to which these subsidies may have caused the inflationary wave that began in the mid-1950s has been the subject of much debate. Earlier observers point out that the outstanding Central Bank credits to the Soil Products Office account for most of the increase in the money supply in this period.[7] More recently, however, Bent Hansen has argued that the main culprit was the credit extended from deposit banks to the private sector, including the cooperatives.[8]

Through the continued expansion of domestic demand, the government was able to maintain economic growth for several additional years. In the meantime, however, exports declined even further owning to the overvaluation of the currency, and foreign exchange reserves were quickly exhausted under the liberalized import regime. As imports began to be curtailed, the economy moved from the relative abundance of the early 1950s into a severe balance of payments crisis, characterized by shortages of many items of basic consumption.

One casualty of the crisis was the political and economic liberalism of the Democrat Party. Just as it responded to growing political opposition with the escalation of political tensions and restrictions on democratic freedoms, in most economic issues the government was forced to change its earlier stand and adopt a more interventionist approach. Quantitative restrictions on imports were generalized and controls on the use of foreign exchange were tightened. In the domestic market, price and profit controls were initiated and credit began to be allocated through non-price mechanisms. The government also rediscovered the state economic enterprises as useful instruments for relieving some of the bottlenecks and for capital formation in manufacturing, infrastructure, and mining.

108

With the balance of payments crisis of the mid-1950s, the experimental move towards a more open economy came to an end. Amidst the shortages and bottlenecks induced by the severe restrictions on imports, domestic industry began to produce some of the goods which had been imported in large volumes only a few years earlier. There thus emerged a return to ISI, not yet as explicit government policy but as a *de facto* shift that arose out of necessity. Even though the annual rates of growth for manufacturing industry were not very different for our two sub-periods, at 6.5 percent for 1947–1953 and 7.6 percent for 1954–1962, there was in fact a qualitative difference between the two (see Table 5.3). The former was characterized by high rates of growth of primary exports, incomes, and imports. The increases in value added in manufacturing were due to increases in demand and the value of output. The latter period, by contrast, was characterized by strict import restriction, which created more suitable conditions for increasing the value added per unit of output in manufacturing.

The government negotiated with the International Monetary Fund (IMF) and the Organization for Economic Cooperation and Development (OECD) for loans and foreign exchange relief from 1956 until 1958, but refused to undertake the major devaluation they demanded until after the elections of 1957. As a result, the crisis lasted for several years. The magnitude of the devaluation of 1958 reflected the extent of the overvaluation of the currency, the value of the Turkish lira being reduced from 2.80 to 9.00 to the dollar. In addition to the devaluation, the stabilization program also included most elements of something which later came to be referred to as the IMF package: import liberalization, changes in the export regime, removal of price controls, increases in the prices of state economic enterprises, and consolidation and rescheduling of the external debt.[9] While the balance of payments picture improved, and the rate of inflation declined as a result of these measures, the economy plunged into a severe recession which was prolonged by the military coup of 1960 and lasted until 1961. The annual rate of growth of GNP declined to 4.0 percent per annum and that of per capita GNP to 1.3 percent per annum between 1954 and 1962 (see Table 5.3).

Foreign direct investment remained limited during the 1950s, at well below $10 million per year, despite occasional modifications of the existing laws to provide more flexibility for profit transfers and the repatriation of the original investment. United States firms accounted for about 40 percent of the total, followed by Switzerland, Germany, and Holland. In contrast, Turkey received substantial amounts of public funds in the form of military and economic aid in the postwar period, beginning with the Marshall Plan and continuing with other bilateral funds from the United States,

NATO assistance, and some multilateral loans. These public capital inflows averaged over $100 million per year, or more than one-third of the country's annual export earnings during the 1950s.

Despite the stagnation in agricultural output and the decline in international prices after 1954, the domestic terms of trade remained favorable to agriculture because of the government price support policies, allowing the rural producers to hold on to their gains until 1957. The countryside was thus the real beneficiary of the Democrat Party era, although it is difficult to establish how this affected the distribution of wealth within the rural economy. In contrast, inflation squeezed wages and salaries in the urban areas.[10] The decline in the standard of living and social status of civil servants, especially of military personnel, played an important role in the organization of the armed forces against the government and the military coup of 1960.

The Democrat Party thus emerges as the first example of a populist government in twentieth century Turkey. Not only did it target a large constituency and attempt to redistribute income towards it, but it also tried to sustain economic growth with short-term expansionist policies, with predictable longer-term consequences. To this day, the Democrat Party government and especially its leader, Prime Minister Adnan Menderes, originally a large landowner, continue to be viewed most favorably by the agricultural producers and many of their descendants who now live in the urban areas, as the first administration to understand and respond to the aspirations of the rural population.

The 1950s also witnessed the dramatic acceleration of rural to urban migration in Turkey. It has long been debated whether the Turkish domestic migration was due to push or pull factors. There were undoubtedly both, and the conditions prevailing in rural areas varied widely across the country. Nonetheless, the distribution of land to peasants with small holdings, the substantial increases in land under cultivation, and the strong increases in agricultural incomes all suggest that pull factors played the more important role in the process. The development of the road network also contributed to the migration process.[11]

THE GOLDEN AGE OF IMPORT SUBSTITUTING INDUSTRIALIZATION, 1963–1977

One criticism frequently directed at the Democrats was the absence of any coordination and long-term perspective in the management of the economy. Hence, the military regime was quick to establish the State Planning

Organization (SPO) in 1960. The idea of development planning was supported by a broad coalition: the Republican People's Party with its etatist heritage, the bureaucracy, the large industrialists, and even the international agencies, most notably the OECD. Planning methodology and target setting were strongly influenced by Professor Jan Tinbergen, who was invited as the chief consultant to the SPO to coordinate the preparation of the first five-year plan.

The economic policies of the 1960s and 1970s aimed, above all, at the protection of the domestic market and at industrialization through import substitution. Within this framework, the five-year plans constituted attempts to coordinate investment decisions. The planning techniques made heavy use of a restrictive trade regime, investments by state economic enterprises, and subsidized credit as key tools in achieving ISI objectives. The plans were based on medium-term models and did not give much weight to short-term policy issues, most notably fiscal and monetary policy. They were binding for the public sector but only indicative for the private sector. In practice, the SPO played an important role in private sector decisions as well, since its stamp of approval was required for all private sector investment projects which sought to benefit from subsidized credit, tax exemptions, and import privileges, and to obtain access to scarce foreign exchange. The agricultural sector, dominated by peasant ownership, was left mostly outside the planning process.[12]

With the resumption of import substitution, the state economic enterprises once again began to play an important role in industrialization. They accounted for more than 20 percent of the value added and about half of fixed investment in manufacturing industry until the end of the 1970s. Their role, however, was quite different in comparison to the earlier period. During the 1930s, when the private sector was weak, industrialization was led by the state enterprises and the state was able to control many sectors of the economy. In the postwar period, in contrast, the big family holding companies, large conglomerates which included numerous manufacturing and distribution companies as well as banks and other services firms, emerged as the leaders. Some of these, such as the Koç group, had emerged in the 1920s but entered industry in the postwar years either independently or in joint ventures with foreign capital. The Sabanci group began its rise manufacturing textiles in the cotton-growing Adana region during the 1950s. Eventually there emerged a crude division of labor between the two sectors. The state enterprises were directed to invest in large-scale intermediate goods industries, while the private firms took advantage of the opportunities in the heavily protected and more profitable consumer goods sector. From food processing and textiles in the 1950s, the emphasis shifted increasingly to radios, refrigerators, television sets, cars, and other consumer durables. Foreign capital in the ISI industries remained modest. A large part of the technology was obtained through patent and licensing agreements rather than direct investment.

The years 1963–77 thus represent for Turkey what Albert Hirschman has called the easy stage of ISI.[13] While the opportunities provided by a large and protected domestic market were exploited, the ISI program was not carried into the technologically more difficult stage of a capital goods industry. The export orientation of manufacturing industry also remained weak.[14] Foreign exchange necessary for the expansion of production was obtained from traditional agricultural exports and workers' remittances.

The ISI policies were successful in bringing about economic growth, especially in the early stages. GNP increased at an average annual rate of 6.8 percent during the period 1963–77. Even if the crisis years of 1978–79 are included in the calculations, the average rate of GNP growth of 6.0 percent still compares well with the two other periods in the postwar era (see Table 5.3). The rate of growth of manufacturing industry was considerably higher, averaging more than 10 percent per annum between 1963 and 1977 and more than 9 percent between 1963 and 1979. Since the population growth rate was 2.4 percent per annum during this period, the average rate of growth of GNP per capita was 4.3 percent for 1963–77 and 3.5 percent for 1963–79. This performance is close to the average rates of per capita growth of 3.6 percent for the middle income countries as defined by the World Bank, and above the 3.4 percent for the industrialized countries and the 1.4 percent for the low-income countries during the same period.[15]

The role played by the domestic market during this period deserves further attention. Despite the apparent inequalities in income, large segments of the population, including the civil servants, workers, and to a lesser extent, agricultural producers, were incorporated into the domestic market for consumer durables. Perhaps most importantly, real wages almost doubled during this period (see Table 5.5). Behind this exceptional rise were both market forces and political and institutional changes. While industrial growth increased the demand for labor, the emigration of more than one million workers to Europe before 1975 kept conditions relatively tight in the urban labor markets. At the same time, the new rights obtained under the 1961 Constitution, including the increased ability to organize at the workplace and strike, supported the labor unions at the bargaining table. For their part, the large industrial firms, which were not under pressure to compete in the export markets, reasoned that they could afford these wage increases, as they also served to broaden the demand for their own products. By the middle of the 1970s, however, the industrialists had begun to complain about the high level of wages and an emerging labor aristocracy. Similarly, in the rural areas, the small and medium-sized peasant producers, as well as the larger landowners, were able to share in the expansion of the domestic market, thanks to government price support programs and the manipulation of the domestic terms of trade in favor of agriculture, especially during election years.[16]

Another important contribution to the expansion of the home market came from remittances sent by workers in Europe.[17] These inflows remained modest during the 1960s when the workers began arriving in Europe. After the devaluation of 1970, however, they jumped to more than $1.4 billion per year, or 5 percent of GNP, and began to exceed the economy's total earnings from exports. But the balance sheet for the remittances remains mixed. While they supported the balance of payments and growth in the short term, they also contributed to the over-valuation of the domestic currency, thereby reducing the competitiveness of the tradable sectors. The aggregate demand they generated was met by the importation of intermediate goods, which ended up hurting the import substitution process. Their impact was thus very similar to that of the 'Dutch disease' frequently observed in the oil-exporting economies. Remittances began to decline in the second half of the 1970s, however, as immigration restrictions in Europe forced the workers to re-evaluate their savings behavior. The overvaluation of the Turkish lira also discouraged remittances, at least those sent through the official channels.

While industry and government policy remained focused on a large and attractive domestic market, exports of manufactures were all but ignored, and this proved to be the Achilles' heel of Turkish industry. Throughout the 1960s and 1970s, the share of exports in total manufacturing output remained below 12 percent. Similarly, the share of industrial exports in GDP remained below 2 percent until 1980.[18] A shift towards exports would have helped Turkish industry in a number of critical ways. It would have increased its efficiency and competitiveness, acquired the foreign exchange necessary for an expanding economy, and even supported the import substitution process itself in establishing the backward linkages towards the technologically more complicated and more expensive intermediate and capital goods industries. There existed an opportunity for export promotion in the early 1970s, especially in the aftermath of the relatively successful devaluation of 1970. By that time, Turkish industry had acquired sufficient experience to be able to compete, or at least to learn to compete, in international markets.

113

For that major shift to occur, however, a new orientation in government policy and the institutional environment was necessary. Not only the overvaluation of the domestic currency but many other biases against exports needed to be eliminated. Instead, the successes obtained within a protected environment created the vested interests for the continuation of the same model. Most of the industrialists, as well as organized labor, which feared that export orientation would put downward pressure on wages, favored the domestic market-oriented model. Moreover, political conditions became increasingly unstable during the 1970s. The country was governed by a series of fragile coalitions with short-term horizons. As a result, no attempt was made to shift towards export-oriented policies or even adjust the macroeconomic balances after the first oil price shock of 1973.[19]

THE CRISIS OF ISI

When oil prices rose in 1973, the total oil bill was still small and the balance of payments awash with remittances. The government could thus afford to ignore oil price hikes without major short-term consequences. Instead, the weak coalitions chose to continue with expansionist policies at a time when many of the industrialized economies were taking painful steps to adjust their economies. With the support of the foreign exchange reserves and an accommodating monetary policy, the Turkish public sector embarked on an investment binge, eventually pulling along private sector investment as well. As the share of investment the GDP rose from 18.1 percent in 1973 to 25.0 percent in 1977, the growth rate of the economy reached its peak at 8.9 percent in 1975 and 1976.[20]

This drive was then sustained by a very costly external borrowing scheme. Just as the foreign exchange reserves were being depleted in 1975, the right-wing coalition government of Süleyman Demirel launched the so-called convertible Turkish lira deposit project, in which private firms were given exchange rate guarantees by the government for all the external loans they could secure. Under inflationary conditions where the domestic exchange rate was already perceived to be overvalued, this was a signal to the private sector to borrow abroad and finance its day to day operations at the cost of the treasury. In less than two years it became clear that the government was in no position to honor the outstanding external debt stock, which had spiraled from 9 percent to 24 percent of GNP.[21]

Just as striking as the behavior of the government was the willingness of the international banks, admittedly overflowing with petrodollars, to play along. It is clear that they did not pay much attention to the repayment capacity of the ultimate borrower when they agreed to provide loans under terms which must have seemed very attractive at the time. As foreign lenders began to lose their nerve early in 1977, the stage was set for a debt crisis.

In 1978 and 1979 Turkey found itself in its most severe balance of payments crisis of the postwar period. The IMF made three fundamental demands in return for rescheduling Turkey's outstanding debt and giving the green light for new credits: the implementation of a full-scale stabilization program including a major devaluation, extensive cutbacks in government subsidies, and elimination of controls on imports and exports. The Social Democrat-led coalition government of Bülent Ecevit was conscious of the costs to be borne by its political constituencies if these radical measures were adopted; at the same time it was too divided to implement any feasible alternative. As rising budget deficits were met with monetary expansion, inflation, which had been averaging 20 to 30 percent per annum earlier in the decade, jumped to 90 percent in 1979, and the government responded with various foreign exchange and price controls. Both investment and exports collapsed. The second round of oil price increases only compounded the difficulties. As oil became increasingly scarce, frequent power cuts hurt industrial output as well as daily life. Shortages of even the most basic items became widespread owing to the declining capacity to import and to the price controls. The economic crisis coupled with the continuing political turmoil brought the country to the brink of civil war.[22]

Perhaps the basic lesson to be drawn from the Turkish experience is that an ISI regime becomes difficult to dislodge, owing to the power of vested interest groups which continue to benefit from the existing system of protection and subsidies. To shift towards export promotion in a country with a large domestic market required a strong government with a long-term horizon and considerable autonomy. These were exactly the features lacking in a Turkish political scene characterized by weak and fragile coalitions during the 1970s. As a result, the economic imbalances and the costs of adjustment increased substantially. It then took a crisis of major proportions to move the economy towards greater external orientation.

AGRICULTURE AND MIGRATION

The agricultural sector reached the limits of available land in the 1960s and 1970s. From that point on, a shift had to be made from extensive to intensive agriculture. Increases in output began to depend on increases in yields

115

through the intensification of cultivation and the use of improved plant varieties, along with increased inputs of chemical fertilizers, increased mechanization, and some expansion of irrigated lands. As a result, wheat yields increased by 70 percent and overall yields in agriculture increased by an unprecedented 65 percent during the period 1960–80 (see Table 5.2). The intensification was partly a response to market forces from both small and medium-sized producers, but it was also supported by the government policy of subsidizing inputs through favorable exchange rates and interest rates. The most important form of subsidy was given to chemical fertilizers whose prices were kept well below world prices in the face of rising petroleum prices during the 1970s.

After the frontier was reached, increases in output became more difficult and costly. The long-term trend rate of growth of agricultural output declined from 4 to 5 percent per year in the earlier decades to 3.5 percent in the 1960s and 1970s, although the actual figure varies according to the exact period chosen. The share of agriculture in the overall economy also declined substantially from 38 percent in 1960 to 25 percent in 1980. By the end of the 1970s, agriculture was no longer the leading sector in terms of contribution to total growth. Nonetheless, it continued to provide employment for more than 50 percent of the labor force (see Tables 5.1 and 5.2).[23]

Despite the slow-down in the rate of growth of output, the long-term performance of Turkish agriculture has been impressive. During the half century from the early 1930s until the end of the 1970s, agricultural output per person in the country increased at an annual rate of 1.6 percent and doubled for the period as a whole. This performance has enabled Turkey not only to increase per capita consumption but also to remain self-sufficient in foodstuffs, a rare achievement in the Middle East (see Tables 5/2 and 5/3 and compare with Tables 1/1 and 1/2 in Chapter 1). The availability of additional land until the 1960s was an important factor in this outcome. At least equally important, however, was the success of small peasant ownership and production supported by government policies.

Agrarian property relations continued to be dominated by independent peasant ownership, except in the Kurdish southeast where tribal nomadism gave way to rent-collecting landlords. This overall pattern made it more appealing for the politicians to use government programs as an electoral instrument. With the help of government manipulation of the intersectoral terms of trade, the incorporation of the rural population into the national market accelerated. The villages became important markets for textiles, clothing, and food industries, and gradually for consumer durables, radios, TV sets, and even refrigerators. Another important component of demand came for the domestically produced tractors whose numbers jumped ten-fold in less than two decades, from 42,000 in 1960 to 430,000 in 1980 (see Table 5.2). Remittances from family members in Europe also contributed to this trend.

Patterns of rural to urban migration were strongly influenced by the strength of independent peasant ownership. The average migrant continued to have claims to some land in his village which was typically rented out or left to family members. More often than not, he came to the urban area with sufficient resources to build an instant squatter house (*gecekondu*, literally, 'landed at night') in an area already colonized by the migrants from his own province, or even his own village. After the initial move, the migrant and his family did not easily lose contact with the village. They returned during the annual vacation and regularly received supplies in kind, often as compensation for their claims to the land in the village. The average migrant thus served to expand the internal market to a greater extent than would have been possible had the urbanization process been characterized primarily by the migration of the landless poor.

Only a minority of the migrants found employment in the new indus-tries, however. Instead, they faced a hierarchy of jobs as they arrived in urban areas. The unionized blue collar jobs were at the top of that hierarchy and thus out of the reach of a recent migrant. At the lower echelons were a variety of jobs in the informal sector with low pay, such as work as a day laborer or street vendor. Only in time did some of the migrants begin to move up this urban ladder. Most migrants chose to remain in the cities, however, although they often returned to their villages to help with the harvest.[24]

LIBERALIZATION AND INCREASING INSTABILITY DURING THE 1980s

Against the background of import and output contraction, commodity shortages, and strained relations with the IMF and international banks, the newly installed minority government of Süleyman Demirel announced a comprehensive and unexpectedly radical policy package of stabilization and liberalization in January 1980. Turgut Özal, a former chief of the SPO, was to oversee the implementation of the new package. The Demirel government was unable to gain the political support necessary for the successful implementation of the package, but the military regime that came to power after a coup in September of the same year endorsed the new program and made a point of keeping Özal as deputy prime minister responsible for economic affairs.

117

The aims of the new policies were threefold: to improve the balance of payments, to reduce the rate of inflation in the short term, and to create a market-based, export-oriented economy in the longer term, thus putting the economy on an outwardly oriented course, a sharp change of direction from the previous era of inwardly oriented growth and industrialization. Implementation of this package began with a major devaluation followed by continued depreciation of the currency in line with the rate of inflation, greater liberalization of trade and payments regimes, elimination of price controls, substantial price increases for the products of the state economic enterprises, elimination of many of the government subsidies, freeing of interest rates, subsidies, and other support measures for exports and the promotion of foreign capital.

Bringing about reductions in real wages and the incomes of agricultural producers was an important part of the new policies. The Demirel government had little success in dealing with the labor unions, and strikes and other forms of labor unrest, often violent, became increasingly common in the summer of 1980. But the military regime prohibited labor union activity and brought about sharp declines in labor incomes. Most observers agree that, without military rule, an elected government could not have carried out the January 1980 package to its conclusion.[25]

Improvements were obtained rather quickly on three fronts. The balance of payments improved as the external debt was rescheduled after negotiations with the IMF and the international banks, and fresh credit was obtained. The rate of inflation was reduced from 100 percent in 1980 to a low of 30 percent in 1983, and then fluctuated at around 40 percent, although it rose again to over 70 percent at the end of the decade. The doubling of exports within two years, and sustained increases thereafter, not only improved the balance of payments but also helped output levels recover from the initial impact of the stabilization measures.[26]

With the shift to a restricted parliamentary regime in 1983, Özal was elected prime minister as the leader of the Motherland Party, which he had formed. He launched a new wave of liberalization of trade and payments regimes, including unprecedented reductions of quantity restrictions on imports. These measures began to open up the existing ISI structure to competition for the first time. The frequent revisions in the liberalization lists, the arbitrary manner in which these were made, and the favors provided to groups close to the government created a good deal of uncertainty regarding the stability and durability of these changes, however. The response of the private sector to import liberalization was mixed. While export-oriented groups and sectors supported it, the ISI industries, especially the large-scale conglomerates such as the Koç group, whose products included consumer durables and automobiles, continued to lobby for protection. The government also introduced measures aimed at further liberalization of the financial system including virtually complete liberalization of capital inflows and outflows, and the introduction of foreign currency deposits within the domestic banking sector.[27]

From the very beginning, the program of January 1980 benefited from the close cooperation and goodwill of international agencies such as the IMF and the World Bank, as well as the international banks. One reason for this key support was the increasingly strategic place accorded to Turkey in the aftermath of the Iranian revolution. The Islamic revolution moved Turkey from its disadvantaged position in international politics, and it became an indispensable ally of NATO. Other reasons were the close relations between Özal and the international agencies, and the special status accorded to Turkey. For most of the decade Turkey was portrayed by these agencies as a shining example of the validity of the orthodox stabilization and structural adjustment programs they promoted, and enjoyed their good will. As far as the economy was concerned, this support translated into better terms for rescheduling the external debt and substantial amounts of new resource inflows. As a result, the foreign exchange constraint disappeared practically overnight and the public sector had less need for inflationary finance at home. These were undoubtedly vital ingredients for the success of the program.[28]

One area of success for the new policies was in export growth. Merchandise exports rose sharply from a mere $2.3 billion, or 2.6 percent of GNP in the crisis year of 1979, to $8.0 billion in 1985 and $13.0 billion, or 8.6 percent of GNP in 1990 (see Table 5.4). Turkey in fact ranked first in the world in rate of export growth during this decade. Equally dramatic was the role of manufactures, which accounted for approximately 80 percent of this increase. Among exports, textiles, clothing, and iron and steel products dominated. It is thus clear that the success in export growth was achieved by reorienting the existing capacity of ISI industries towards external markets. During this drive, exporters were supported by a steady policy of exchange rate depreciation, credits at preferential rates, tax rebates, and foreign exchange allocation schemes. The latter mechanisms amounted to a 20 to 30 percent subsidy on unit value, although their magnitudes gradually declined during the second half of the decade. It should be noted, however, that some of the reported increase in export volume during the middle of the decade was fictitious, due to over-invoicing designed to take advantage of the incentives.

The export drive also benefited from the war between Iraq and Iran, which provided a captive market for Turkey. Between 1982 and 1985,

Turkish exports to the Middle East exceeded those to the European Community (EC), with Iran and Iraq emerging as the biggest markets. Thereafter, the earlier pattern re-established itself, and the EC once again became the main export market for Turkey. An econometric study by Robin Barlow and Fikret Şenses concludes that, from a longer-term perspective, the policy measures, especially the real exchange rate depreciation and export subsidies, and not the external demand conditions, emerge as the most important explanations for Turkey's strong export performance during the 1980s.[29]

Aside from export performance, however, the impact of the new policies on the real economy was rather mixed. Most importantly, the new policies were unable to mobilize the level of private investment necessary for long-term growth. In manufacturing industry, high interest rates and political instability were the most important impediments. Even in the area of exports, new investment was conspicuously absent; most of the increase was achieved with the existing industrial capacity. In the aftermath of financial and trade liberalization, foreign investments in banking, especially in foreign trade financing and investment banking, where the international banks have a competitive advantage, increased considerably. On the whole, however, the response of foreign capital to the new policies was not very strong, apparently for reasons similar to those affecting domestic capital.[30]

As a result, the growth performance of the economy was less than impressive. GNP increased at the annual average rate of 4.6 percent and GNP per capita at 2.3 percent during the 1980s. Moreover, these increases were only obtained at the cost of accumulating a large external debt which climbed more than fivefold from less than $10 billion in 1980 to more than $50 billion in 1990. These rates of growth are lower than those of earlier decades but in line with trends toward distinctly lower rates of growth in other parts of the developing world during the 1980s, with the notable exception of East and Southeast Asia (see Table 5.3).[31]

Another important area where the record of the new policies was bitterly contested was that of income distribution. From the very beginning, the January 1980 package set out to repress labor and agricultural incomes, and these policies were maintained until 1987 thanks to the military regime and the limited nature of the transition back to multi-party politics. Real wages declined by as much as 34 percent and the intersectoral terms of trade turned against agriculture by more than 40 percent from 1977 until 1987, although some of this deterioration took place during the crisis and high inflation years just before the 1980 coup (Table 5.5). The decline in household incomes was not as dramatic, however, as wage and salary earners in the urban areas attempted to compensate, as far as possible, by working longer hours and having other members of the household, including school-age children, find employment within the informal sector. Similarly, there was a shift in the countryside toward more intensive techniques and more labor-intensive crops in order to compensate for declining crop prices. Part of the benefits of wage and agricultural price repression was captured by net lenders through higher interest income. In addition, a new class of wealthy entrepreneurs emerged, based on exports and international construction projects.[32]

The new policies had been given much-needed support from two significant interventions in the early part of the decade: labor repression by the military and generous foreign capital inflows by the international financial institutions. These opportunities were not adequately utilized, however, to bring the state finances and the public sector under further control. With the transition to a more open electoral regime, the opposition began to criticize not so much the basic thrust of the policies but the arbitrary manner in which Özal often implemented them and the growing inequality of income distribution. As the political system became more competitive towards the end of the 1980s, the government resorted increasingly to old-style populism and lost much of its room for maneuver. Public sector wages, salaries, and agricultural incomes were raised sharply. Real wages almost doubled from their decade low point in 1987–1990 (see Table 5.5). In addition, an escalating war against the Kurdish guerrillas in the southeast began to take its toll. These trends, in turn, sharply increased the deficits and borrowing requirements of the public sector, which began to be financed by higher levels of internal and external borrowing as well as the printing of money. By the end of the decade, inflation had once again jumped to levels above 70 percent per annum. One important factor that reinforced the link between public sector deficits and inflation was the introduction of foreign exchange deposit accounts in 1984 as part of the policies of financial liberalization. By reducing the demand for domestic money, this measure increased the inflationary impact of the public sector deficit.[33] By the end of the decade, macroeconomic balances had sharply deteriorated. In these circumstances, the accumulation of a large external debt, increasing financial liberalization, and the open invitation to short-term capital flows made the system increasingly vulnerable to a balance of payments crisis.[34]

The agricultural sector, which continued to provide employment to about half of the labor force, was all but ignored by the military regime and the Motherland Party. The most important change for the sector was the virtual elimination of the subsidies and price support programs after 1980 which combined with trends in the international markets to produce a

121

sharp deterioration in the sectoral terms of trade. As a result, the agricultural sector showed the lowest rates of output increase during the postwar era, averaging only 1.4 percent per year for the decade (see Tables 5.1 and 5.2). Agricultural output thus failed to keep pace with population growth for the first time in the twentieth century. One investment program which was pursued energetically by the government was the large South-East Anatolia Project, originally planned in the 1960s. It envisaged the construction of a number of interrelated dams and hydroelectric plants on the Euphrates river and the irrigation of 1.6 million hectares (4 million acres) in the plain of Harran, which would double the total irrigated area under cultivation in the country. Because the government could not reach an agreement with the downstream countries regarding the sharing of the water, however, the project was continued without financial assistance from international agencies.[35]

WELFARE AND DISTRIBUTION

Despite recurring crises and fluctuations, the Turkish economy has experienced reasonably high rates of growth averaging 5.7 percent per annum during the postwar era. Per capita incomes have increased at more than 3 percent per year, approximately tripling between 1947 and 1990 (see Table 5.3). Basic indicators of social and economic development have also shown steady increases. For example, calorific intake per capita increased by more than 50 percent, or about 0.7 percent per year, during the same period. By the end of the 1980s, per capita calorific intake in Turkey was well above the average for upper to middle income countries but still below that of the industrialized countries.[36] Similarly, life expectancy at birth rose from around 44 in 1950 to 65 in 1990 (see Table 5.1).[37] Part of this increase was due to the decline in rates of infant mortality from the exceptionally high levels of 160 per 1,000 live births until the late 1960s to 60 in 1990, even though this is still quite high in comparison to other industrialized countries.[38] Basic indicators for education have also registered considerable, but not exceptional, increases. Illiteracy rates at age 15 or older have declined from 55 percent for men, 86 percent for women and 72 percent overall in 1960 to 10 percent for men, 29 percent for women and 19 percent overall in 1990.[39] (For more detailed indices of social and economic development and a comparison with the indices of other countries of the region, see the Statistical Appendix at the end of this volume.)

The quality of information on how these gains in incomes and standards of living have been distributed is not very good. Nonetheless, it is

122

possible to draw some general conclusions. A good place to begin is the persistently large productivity differentials between the agricultural sector and the rest of the economy. Calculations based on national income accounts show that the Kuznets' K ratio, which is obtained by dividing the production per capita in the non-agricultural sector by the production per capita in the agricultural sector, has been above 4 in Turkey throughout the postwar period. This gap has not closed despite considerable rural to urban migration because the productivity increases in the non-agricultural or urban sector have been much higher than those in the agricultural sector. Some caution is necessary in interpreting these figures, however. The existing estimates for the Kuznets' K ratio based on national income data tend to overstate the income differentials between the two sectors. Some of the measured difference in average productivity has been due to the inclusion of most women in the rural labor force but their exclusion in the urban areas. Higher taxation of the urban sector further reduces the gap between the agricultural and non-agricultural or rural and urban incomes. Nonetheless, the available estimates for Kuznets' K still suggest that average incomes are considerably higher in the urban areas, contributing to countrywide patterns of inequality in income.[40]

Within the agricultural sector, the evidence on land distribution confirms what has been argued earlier: there is a relatively equitable distribution of land especially outside the predominantly Kurdish southeast. Despite the limitations of existing estimates, it also appears that the Gini coefficient for the distribution of land has changed little since the 1950s. The degree of inequality of the distributions by holdings and by ownership also appears to be similar: while some large plots are now being cultivated by small and medium-sized tenants, some of the small plots have been consolidated into larger holdings with the spread of tractors and more recently by the entry of other machinery into agriculture.[41]

Within the non-agricultural sector, the absence of a uniform methodology and the changing assumptions of the different surveys or other indirect studies make it difficult to determine the temporal changes in income distribution. On the one hand, the Gini coefficients for income distribution calculated by a leading economist for both the agricultural and non-agricultural sectors, as well as the overall economy, have been remarkably stable from 1973–78 to 1983.[42] At the same time, there is a good deal of indirect evidence suggesting that income distribution within the non-agricultural sector became more unequal and that the gap between the agricultural and non-agricultural sectors increased considerably owing to high inflation followed by the stabilization and structural adjustment programs. Trends in two important indicators suggest that income

123

distribution became more unequal from the late 1970s until the late 1980s. Both urban real wages and the intersectoral terms of trade between agriculture and the rest of the economy declined sharply between 1977 and 1987. Studies by Süleyman Özmucur based on national income accounts and other data also point to a sharp decline in the shares in national income of both agricultural incomes and non-agricultural wages and salaries during the same period. With the return of more open politics, however, both real wages and agricultural prices registered sharp increases after 1987 (see Table 5.5).[43]

Large regional inequalities are yet another dimension of income distribution in Turkey. Through the 1980s, the private sector-led industrialization remained concentrated in the western third of the country. Commercialization of agriculture also proceeded further in the western and coastal areas. In contrast, the eastern third of the country had lower incomes and was lacking in government-provided infrastructure and services, especially education and health. The development of tourism in the west, the deterioration of the terms of trade against agriculture, and above all, the rise of Kurdish insurgency in the south-east during the 1980s further increased the already large regional disparities, adding to the pressures for rural-to-urban as well as east-to-west migration. The large irrigation projects are expected to transform the south-east into a significant center of economic growth in the longer term. In 1990, however, these expensive projects remained years and if not decades away from completion.

In sum, income distribution in Turkey from 1960–1990 was characterized by large rural-urban and regional differentials. The available evidence also suggests that the distribution within the urban economy became increasingly more unequal than that of the rural areas. This pattern should also tell us a good deal about the distribution of the gains made in socio-economic and human indicators, such as life expectancy, health, and education during the postwar period.

Notes on Chapter 5
Full details of all sources are in the Bibliography

1   Pamuk, 'War, State Economic Policies and Resistance by Agricultural Producers in Turkey, 1939–1945,' pp 131–7.
2   Keyder, *State and Class*, pp 112–14; Boratav, *Türkiye İktisat Tarihi, 1908–1985*, pp 63–7.
3   Thornburg, Spry, and Soule, *Turkey*.

4   Boratav, *Türkiye Iktisat Tarihi, 1908–1985*, pp 73–81.
5   Turkey, State Institute of Statistics, *Statistical Indicators*, 1923–1992; see also Table 5.2.
6   Hansen, *Egypt and Turkey*, pp 338–44; Keyder, *State and Class*, pp 117–35.
7   Hershlag, *Turkey*, pp 163–5.
8   Hansen, *Egypt and Turkey*, pp 344–6.
9   *Ibid.*, pp 344–8; Boratav, *Türkiye Iktisat Tarihi, 1908–1985*, pp 73–81.
10 Boratav, *Türkiye Iktisat Tarihi, 1908–1985*, pp 90–93.
11 Zürcher, *Turkey*, p 235; Keyder, *State and Class*, pp 135–40.
12 Hansen, *Egypt and Turkey*, pp 352–3; Barkey, *The State and the Industrialization Crisis in Turkey*, ch. 4; Öniş and Riedel, *Economic Crises and Long Term Growth in Turkey*, pp 99–100. The political factors behind the introduction and evolution of development planning are discussed in Ahmad, *The Turkish Experiment in Democracy, 1950–1975*, ch. 10.
13 Hirschman, 'The Political Economy of Import-Substituting Industrialization in Latin America,' pp 1–26.
14 For more detail on the export performance of manufacturing industry, see Table 5.4 and later parts of this chapter.
15 World Bank, World Development Report, various years. Also Çeçen, Doğruel, and Doğruel, 'Economic Growth and Structural Change in Turkey, 1960–88,' pp 37–56.
16 Hansen, *Egypt and Turkey*, pp 360–78; Keyder, *State and Class*, ch. 7; Barkey, *State and the Industrialization Crisis*, ch. 5.
17 Paine, *Exporting Workers*; Keyder and Aksu-Koç, *External Labour Migration from Turkey and Its Impact*, Report No. 185e.
18 Turkey, State Institute of Statistics, *Statistical Yearbook*, various years.
19 Barkey, *State and the Industrialization Crisis*, pp 109–167.
20 Celasun and Rodrik, 'Debt, Adjustment and Growth,' *Developing Country Debt and Economic Performance*, vol. 3, pp 641–55.
21 *Ibid.*, p 639.
22 Keyder, *State and Class*, ch. 8.
23 The official labor force statistics tend to exaggerate the share of the agricultural sector in overall employment by including peasant women working in the family farms but excluding urban women who work within the household.
24 Keyder, *State and Class*, pp 156–63.
25 For example, Aricanli and Rodrik, 'An Overview of Turkey's Experience with Economic Liberalization and Structural Adjustment,' pp 1343–50.
26 *Ibid.*; Hansen, *Egypt and Turkey*, pp 383–420; Çeçen, Doğruel, and Doğruel, 'Economic Growth and Structural Change in Turkey, 1960–88,' pp 44–52.
27 Öniş and Webb, *Political Economy of Policy Reform*, pp 33–8.
28 Aricanli and Rodrik, 'An Overview of Turkey's Experience with Economic Liberalization and Structural Adjustment.'
29 Barlow and Şenses, 'The Turkish Export Boom,' pp 111–33.
30 Boratav, Türel, and Yeldan, 'Dilemmas of Structural Adjustment and Environmental Policies under Instability,' pp 373–93; Aricanli and Rodrik, 'An Overview of Turkey's Experience;' Öniş and Riedel, *Economic Crises*, pp 83–90.
31 One important problem in the utilization of the national income accounts in this as well as earlier periods is the existence of a large and growing underground economy in Turkey which has not been included in the national income accounts. Various studies estimate its size at the end of the 1980s at 30 to 50 percent of the GNP.

32 Celasun, 'Income Distribution and Domestic Terms of Trade in Turkey, 1978–1983,' pp 193–216; Boratav, 'Inter-Class and Intra-Class Relations of Distribution Under Structural Adjustment.'
33 Rodrik, *Premature Liberalization, Incomplete Stabilization*, pp 10–20.
34 Öniş and Webb, *Political Economy of Policy Reform*, pp 38–47. Also Waterbury, 'Export-Led Growth and the Center-Right Coalition,' pp 127–45.
35 Mutlu, 'The Southeastern Anatolia Project (GAP) in Turkey,' pp 59–86.
36 Hansen, *Egypt and Turkey*, pp 281–82.
37 In recent years female life expectancy has been five years longer than that of males; World Bank, World Development Report, 1994.
38 Turkey, State Institute of Statistics, *The Population of Turkey*, pp 37–41.
39 World Bank, World Development Report, various years.
40 The calculations are based on national income accounts published in Turkey, State Institute of Statistics, *Statistical Yearbook*, various years; see also Derviş and Robinson, 'The Structure of Income Inequality in Turkey, 1950–1973,' pp 285–7 and 497–9.
41 Hansen, *Egypt and Turkey*, pp 275–80 and 495–501.
42 Merih Celasun has estimated that the Gini coefficient for the overall distribution has changed from 0.50 in 1973 to 0.51 in 1978 to 0.52 in 1983; 'Income Distribution and Domestic Terms of Trade in Turkey, 1978–1983'; Derviş and Robinson, 'The Structure of Income Inequality in Turkey, 1950–1973.' For an overview of the available evidence see Hansen, *Egypt and Turkey*, pp 275–80 and 494–504.
43 Özmucur, *Gelirin Fonksiyonel Dağılımı, 1948–1991*.

6

Egypt
1946–1990

During the period 1945–1990 Egypt was divided into three distinct political regimes: the monarchical regime of King Farouk, 1945–1952, the revolutionary regime which was increasingly dominated by Gamal Abdel Nasser until his death in 1970, and the successor regimes of Anwar Sadat, 1970–1981, and Hosni Mubarak, president since 1981. There is considerable disagreement, however, about how best to periodize the economic history of these same decades. Some analysts base their periodization on types of economic management (particularly as it relates to efforts to promote industrial development) and others on shifts in economic performance. This in turn has produced further disagreement about how best to characterize what they see as key turning points, for example, the impact of the 1952 revolution itself or the moment at which the swing from private to state-centered development began in earnest. Hence, for Robert Mabro, the whole period from 1952 to 1961 is one of what he calls 'partial planning,' while others see a more significant shift beginning as a result of the nationalizations of foreign property following the Anglo-French-Israeli military attack of November-December 1956.[1] There is more agreement about the characteristics of the long boom beginning in 1974/75 which lasted until the downturn in world oil prices in 1985/86, to be followed by five years of much slower growth.

For the purposes of this analysis these four and half decades are divided into the five sub-periods during which management and performance are considered to fit most closely together: 1945–56, 1957–67, 1968–73, 1974–85 and 1986–90.

SYSTEMS OF ECONOMIC MANAGEMENT

PRIVATE SECTOR-LED GROWTH, 1945–1956

Once the Second World War was over, Egypt's economy enjoyed a short period of rapid growth during which agriculture and industry recovered from their wartime difficulties, allowing national income to increase by some 40 percent between 1945 and 1952. Activity was particularly intense in the manufacturing sector where high rates of capital accumulation not only allowed entrepreneurs to replace worn out machinery but also to expand capacity, particularly in the textile sector, as well as to introduce new products, such as rayon, nitrogen fertilizers, and plastics.[2] Growth in GDP slowed down in 1948, however, as agricultural output stagnated while industry began to suffer from a combination of over-capacity and a revival of foreign competition. Analysts are divided about whether this represented part of a normal cycle or a more basic structural crisis in which Egyptian manufacturers had reached the limits set by the country's limited domestic market.[3]

What makes the question more difficult is the fact that, during the early 1950s, Egypt experienced not only the destabilizing effects of the Korean War boom, which pushed cotton prices to a new high, but also a period of political uncertainty which continued through the Free Officers' coup of July 1952. This, in turn, raises the question of what, if any, was the impact of the new regime on the revival of economic growth that took place after 1953? Would it have happened anyway? Or was it the direct result of the policies put in train by the Free Officers to promote industrialization and to diversify activity? Once again, there is a mixture of evidence which seems to point in both directions. Supporters of the first view can point to the fact that most of the key decisions affecting the growth of output in both the agricultural and manufacturing sectors remained firmly in private hands. Supporters of the second can argue that the Free Officers took immediate steps to provide more capital for entrepreneurs through the industrial bank, to raise tariffs, to put larger sums into infrastructural investments such as electricity, and to start several joint ventures of their own, most notably the Iron and Steel Complex begun at Helwan in association with a German Company, DEMAG, in 1954.

Just how the private sector responded to the regime's measures to increase investment is yet another subject for discussion and debate. On the one hand, there is statistical evidence of a return to higher rates of growth of manufacturing output: some 40 percent from 1952/53 to 1956/57.[4] On the other, there seems to have been a steady decline in new investment by the private sector beginning in 1950 and continuing until 1956.[5] Furthermore, part of this trend consisted of a process of significant disinvestment by some of Egypt's largest firms, notably the Misr Group, through increased amortization, the build-up of reserves, and the payment of larger dividends to shareholders.[6]

Whether this is also evidence of a general breakdown of confidence between the private sector and the regime is equally unclear. Major enterprises like the Bank Misr are known to have maintained large reserves even before 1952. However, this tendency could well have been augmented either by misperceptions on both sides or, more likely, by a basic distrust of the new regime's intentions.[7] As Robert Vitalis notes, with power shifting to unknown military officers after 1952, and especially with the abolition of the old parliamentary regime in 1953, private sector entrepreneurs lost most of the important channels they had once used to influence state policy in order to secure their own interests.[8] In addition, the leaders of the Free Officers in general, and Nasser in particular, made no attempt to hide their dislike of those monopolies which, in many areas, were the inevitable consequence of the strategy of using tariffs to promote industrialization in a country with only a limited domestic market which could easily be filled by the output of just one firm.[9] Nevertheless, having said all this, business confidence clearly fluctuated during the period. Hence John Waterbury's figures for private investment show a small increase from 1952 to 1956, then a decline, followed by another small increase in 1958 and 1959, although it is possible that the last trend was less voluntary than a response to regime pressure.[10]

Another regime measure which sowed the seeds of considerable mistrust among Egypt's entrepreneurs was the first Land Reform Law of 1952. This was first and foremost a political measure, designed to destroy the rural power of the large landowners (many of whom where successful businessmen) as well as to create greater social justice by giving land to the landless and placing a ceiling on rents. Its economic impact was bound to be slow. Given the fact that the large landowners were allowed to keep up to 300 feddans (311 acres) of their property for themselves and their children, only some 450,000 feddans (467,000 acres) was taken into state ownership, or just 7.5 percent of the total cultivated area (see Table 6.2). Even this relatively small amount was only redistributed in small lots at a rate which never exceeded 65,000 feddans (67,000acres) a year (see Table 6.2).

What may be said with confidence is that it was a major feat to effect even such a limited transfer of ownership without any adverse consequence on agricultural output. Although regime propaganda highlighted the role of the absentee – and therefore inefficient – landowner, Mabro's observation that most large estates in the pre-reform era were 'well managed' is certainly much closer to the mark; it was thus more difficult for the new owners to make much immediate improvement.[11] That those responsible for carrying out the reform were able to make any progress at all owes a great deal to their creation of a new institution, the supervised agricultural cooperative, membership in which was compulsory for all those who received redistributed land. This undoubtedly had a progressive impact on production over time, allowing the land it controlled to be farmed as a single unit as far as cultivation and harvesting were concerned, as well as to benefit from the wholesale application of inputs like fertilizers and improved seed.

THE MOVE TO PLANNING AND PUBLIC OWNERSHIP
1957–1967

In 1956, the new regime, now firmly identified as the managers of a national political and social revolution, faced its first great crisis as a result of the Anglo-American decision to deny it the promised financing for the construction of a new high dam on the Nile at Aswan, the cornerstone of its plans for accelerated agricultural and industrial development. Its leader, the newly elected President Nasser, responded swiftly by nationalizing the assets of the foreign-owned Suez Canal Company, an event which led, in turn, to the Anglo-French and Israeli invasion in October–November of the same year. This time the Egyptian riposte was to take over the assets of most of the companies which it identified as being British, French, or Jewish owned. These consisted of a heterogeneous collection of enterprises including banks, insurance companies, and factories making chemicals, textiles, and cement.

The sequestered companies were placed under the jurisdiction of a new body, the Economic Development Organization (EDO), which was also given control over companies in which the government already held shares. In this way the EDO became responsible for a mixed bag of manufacturing concerns producing 12 percent of Egypt's industrial output, representing a major extension of state control.[12] Further expansion followed as a result of a program to create still more enterprises, some as joint ventures with private capital, until, by 1960, the organization controlled 64 companies with a total capital value of £E 80m.[13] In addition, the EDO was given the remit to draw up Egypt's first comprehensive five-year plan to begin in 1960. But, in spite of all this activity, its role as a catalyst for an expansion of public ownership was challenged by the ministry of industry created in 1956 under the ambitious technocrat 'Aziz Sidqi, who soon became one of the regime's leading exponents of state-directed development.[14]

Economic historians continue to debate the extent to which these initiatives set the stage for the further wave of nationalizations (this time of Egyptian-owned property) which began in 1960 with the Bank Misr and the National Bank of Egypt and then moved on, in July 1961, to include all Egypt's banks, and insurance companies, and 42 of its largest industrial and commercial concerns.[15] Political considerations obviously played a part as the 1961 laws were also applied to Syria, at that time joined to Egypt as part of the short-lived United Arab Republic. So too did the simple logic of bureaucratic expansion as promoted by 'Aziz Sidqi and others.[16] Nevertheless, it is also important to note that these new nationalizations came at the beginning of the implementation of the first five-year plan (1960–65) and may just as easily have been prompted by the discovery that the state still lacked sufficient leverage over the private sector to ensure that it met the investment targets assigned to it.[17]

In any case, the nationalizations marked the final breakdown of the regime's attempt to cooperate with private capital, as well as the introduction of a system of statist control which was much more far-reaching than that in most other areas of the non-European world, where business property was not subject to wholesale confiscation and where the practice of public/private cooperation was still maintained.[18] By 1964, the state owned most of the enterprises within the modern sector of the economy, while a few years later, in 1966/67, public sector firms contributed 90 percent of the value added by plants employing ten workers or more.[19]

The newly nationalized companies were placed, briefly, under the direction of three giant holding companies, and then under 38 smaller ones, each responsible to a particular ministry, with the largest number subject to the ministries of industry and of the economy. This in turn became the foundation for an increasingly complex network of controls over public sector prices, investment decisions, and access to scarce foreign currency, transforming the limited import substitution strategy of the previous 30 years into a thoroughgoing attempt to manage almost every aspect of economic life, including, most importantly, all transactions with the outside world. One result was the abandonment of any attempt to use either the price system or a parallel system of incentives to allocate resources, thus relinquishing all criteria of economic efficiency for the more straightforwardly political logic of using the state sector to reward loyal supporters of the regime.[20]

As for the first five-year plan itself, its stated aim was to lay the groundwork for the ambitious target of doubling Egypt's national income within ten years. The first stage, an increase of 40 percent, was almost achieved by 1965 with impressive gains in industry (50.2 percent between 1959/60 and 1964/65) and those sectors closely associated with the completion of the Aswan Dam, such as electricity (128.6 percent) and construction (96.6 percent).[21] But by then the system was floundering as a result of its own contradictions and it proved impossible for the leaders of the regime to agree on what should follow. The result was that no second five-year plan was implemented but a series of smaller, annual follow-up plans were put in place until economic priorities were completely altered following Egypt's disastrous defeat by Israel in the June 1967 war.

Major criticisms of the first five-year plan have proceeded along two main lines. First, it is said to have been little more than a set of hastily, and often rather badly, chosen projects, many of which had actually been in the pipeline before 1960.[22] Second, little serious thought seems to have been given to the provision of regular sources of funding, particularly foreign currency.[23] Plan targets also implied a rise in the domestic savings rate which, as Mourad Wahba argues, Egypt would have been unlikely to sustain for long given the fact that the regime had also committed itself to spend large sums of money on social welfare, including health and education, as well as providing large numbers of new public sector jobs at well above the minimum wage.[24] Indeed, as a number of the regime's supporters were quick to point out, one of the basic ways in which Egypt's newly announced 'Arab socialism' differed from the Soviet or Chinese model was in just this fact, that it was unwilling to sacrifice the needs of the present generation in order to raise money for future development.[25]

The regime's intensification of control over the economy during this period can also be seen in the agricultural sector, where the second Land Reform Law of 1961 not only reduced the ceiling for family holdings to 200 feddans (208 acres) but also extended the system of supervised cooperatives to the whole of the country. This created a system by which the government created monopolies for itself over all agricultural inputs (credit, seeds, fertilizers, etc.), as well as over the marketing of all major crops, ordering them to be delivered to its own warehouses at prices that the government itself fixed. Once in place, such a system had many advantages for improving agricultural production, albeit at the cost of limiting most peasants' ability to grow what they chose on their own piece of land. It also provided a mechanism for extracting part of the rural surplus by selling inputs at above market prices while purchasing the crop at well below market prices. Just how much money it was able to raise using this method still remains a matter of controversy. However, Mabro cites one survey conducted by the Egyptian Institute of National Planning which suggests that, as a group, agriculturalists lost £E 44m of their gross income in this way between 1960 and 1967, equal to some 7 to 8 percent of the total value of their output.[26]

Apart from the work of the new cooperatives, the agricultural sector also benefited from a significant expansion in both the cultivated and the cropped area as a result of the increase in water from the new Aswan High Dam. Average yields rose too, partly thanks to increased watering, and partly because of the use of larger quantities of fertilizer and improved seeds.[27] Meanwhile, the process of distributing agricultural land continued at a steady pace so that by 1967 some 750,000 feddans (778,500 acres) had been allocated to peasant cultivators, or 8 percent of the total cultivable land (Table 6.2). In addition, peasants had gained extra land from forced sales by the large landowners (107,000 feddans, or 111,066 acres) and from the sale or distribution of newly reclaimed land (453,000 feddans, or 470,000 acres).[28]

MILITARY DEFEAT AND ECONOMIC STAGNATION
1968–1973

Egypt's comprehensive military defeat by Israel in June 1967 was an economic as well as a political disaster. Apart from the losses sustained in the war itself, the Egyptian economy suffered further damage from the enforced closure of the Suez Canal, the loss of the Sinai oil fields as a result of the Israeli occupation, and the reduction in revenues from tourism. Further losses followed during the so-called Canal War of 1969–70 when Israeli bombardment caused widespread destruction in the cities of Port Said, Ismailia, and Suez, forcing a million or so of their inhabitants to flee westward to the safety of Cairo and elsewhere. To this should be added the extra military expenditure involved in strengthening the armed forces to the point where they could establish a bridgehead across the canal in the war of October 1973. Finally, there was a great decline in the previous levels of Western aid to Egypt although, in this case, there was some compensation

133

from the increase in the aid provided by both the Soviet Union and Egypt's richer Arab neighbors following the Khartoum Summit of 1968.

The huge loss of Egyptian resources was immediately reflected in a sharp drop in imports, as well as a longer-term decline in new investments, greater underutilisation of capital, and a severe suppression of domestic consumption. Industrial output is estimated to have grown at less than 1 percent a year between 1969–70 and 1973, while agricultural production slowed down to an annual rate of growth of 1.7 percent between 1971 and 1974.[29]

The shift in policy required to deal with these new circumstances was announced in President Nasser's statement of 30 March 1968. Priority was to be given to the rebuilding of the armed forces, to economic steadfastness, and to what was called 'reconstruction' on the domestic front, notably the improvement of public sector efficiency. But underlying this display of regime resolution was a major polarization within the leadership between those who advocated some relaxation of economic regulation and those who pressed for an even greater intensification of state activity in the name of Arab socialism. In the event, President Nasser took steps in both directions at once. On the one hand, he announced measures to provide limited encouragement to the private sector, for example allowing private entrepreneurs to act as subcontractors for state enterprises.[30] On the other, he gave the go-ahead to a third and last act of Land Reform in 1969, reducing the maximum holding to 100 feddans (104 acres) per family. However, in the event, this entailed only the sequestration of another 28,500 feddans (29,600 acres) of land.[31]

Anwar Sadat, who succeeded Nasser as president on his death in September 1970, had no option but to continue the main lines of his predecessor's policy. But already by 1971 he was beginning to give signs of his support for advocates of a more liberal trend by instituting measures to open up the economy to foreign trade and investment. One result was a steady growth in imports which increased the non-military component of Egypt's international debt from $1.8 billion in 1970 to $6.3 billion in 1975.[32] Of this, a growing portion was used to pay for imports of wheat and other foodstuffs sold on to the population at heavily subsidized prices. Just as important, the Sadat regime began a process of trying to encourage foreign investment by passing a law (Law 65) in 1971 establishing 'free zones' in which new companies could be offered special privileges such as tax holidays and a guarantee of freedom from arbitrary action by the government, for example nationalization.[33] Other steps included those taken to underline the regime's new-found respect for private property, notably official encouragement to the courts to pass judgment in favor of individuals seeking the return of their buildings and other assets sequestered by the state in the 1960s.

THE 'INFITAH' ECONOMY 1974–1985

President Sadat took advantage of the prestige accruing to him from Egypt's limited victory over Israel in the October 1973 war to announce the introduction of a new economic policy known by its Arabic name, 'infitah' (literally 'opening up', but also translated as 'liberalization'). As he described this policy in his 'October paper' of April 1974, its basic aim was to overcome Egypt's economic stagnation by measures designed to encourage foreign (and especially Arab) investment, as well as to promote local private sector activity.

The new policy was given concrete form in June 1974 with the passage of Law 43, which set out the terms on which foreign capital could now operate. These included exemption from nationalization and sequestration, a five-year tax holiday and, most important of all, the provision that all companies founded under the law would be considered private, whatever the source of their capital. As Wahba notes, this placed Egyptian capital invested in Law 43 companies on much the same basis as that coming from abroad.[34] Later amendments, particularly Law 32 of 1977, provided still more concessions to both local and foreign capital, such as exemption from Egypt's strict laws governing foreign exchange transactions.

As a signal that Egypt would now welcome foreign investment, the new law must be considered only a qualified success. Even though it was designed to encourage private participation in enterprises of all kinds, the only sectors in which foreigners proved to be really interested were petroleum and, to a lesser extent, tourism and consultancy. This left the greater part of the money invested in Law 43 companies – roughly two-thirds overall – to come from Egyptian capital itself, both private and state (see Table 6.3).

Fortunately for the Sadat regime, as well as for its successor under Mubarak, other sources of revenue became available in such quantities that the period from 1974 to 1985 was one of sustained economic growth. The first of these, from a chronological point of view, was the Arab aid and investment which poured into the country until the decision to boycott Egypt after President Sadat signed a peace agreement with Israel in 1979. However, this was then replaced by almost equally large quantities of American aid. In addition, and over time, Egypt obtained increasing revenues from its oil exports and from the transit dues charged on ships passing through the Suez Canal, the combined total of which grew from $641 million to $6.784 billion between 1974 and 1981/82. Moreover, both the banking sector and private individuals began to benefit from the increasing flow of remittances sent back by the growing numbers of

Egyptians – perhaps 10 percent of the labor force by the early 1980s – who went off to work in Libya and the oil rich economies of the Gulf (Table 6.4).[35] Finally, the regime continued to borrow from abroad, augmenting the country's international civilian debt from $8.1 billion in 1977 to $14.3 billion in 1981 and $33 billion in 1986, and its military debt to some $11 billion at the end of the same period.[36] As a result, the proportion of exogenous capital flows to Egyptian GDP almost doubled from 6.7 percent between 1971/72 and 1973 to 12.3 between 1979 and 1983/84.[37]

Given the size of these capital flows there has inevitably been much debate about their proper use. While all analysts agree that one early result was to remove many of the bottlenecks preventing the proper utilization of capital in the pre-infitah period, it has also been pointed out that much of the money was spent on defense, imports, housing, and consumption.[38] Perhaps the best way to evaluate such claims is to follow Heba Handoussa's argument that what Egypt was experiencing at this stage was its own version of 'Dutch disease,' in which large capital inflows, rising wages, high inflation, negative real rates of interest, and an over-valued currency encouraged a vast misallocation of resources – both public and private – given a structural bias in favor of non-traded goods, which led to investment in infrastructure, housing, electricity, and transport rather than agriculture and industry.[39]

Nevertheless, as Handoussa is also quick to point out, there was a great improvement in welfare at the same time.[40] This can easily be seen in the improvements in the housing stock, in better rural access to electricity and potable water, and in a significant increase in enrollment in primary education.

What is also of importance is the way in which the Sadat regime vastly extended the system of subsidies it had inherited from its predecessor. These ranged from the sale of imported wheat and other foodstuffs at well below market prices to the indirect subsidies consequent on the provision of cheap, state sector goods such as petrol and electricity at well below cost.[41] By 1980/81 the size of the direct subsidies alone had come to equal some 10 percent of Egypt's GDP and just over 25 percent of current government expenditure (see Table 6.5).

While transfers of this magnitude undoubtedly did much to enable the poor to negotiate a period of high inflation, the policy can also be criticized on other grounds. First, no attempt was made to target those in particular need, rather than making subsidized food available to rich and poor alike, while the sale of cereals from abroad encouraged a switch from the use of locally produced maize in bread to much more expensive imports. Second, the subsidies formed only a part of a much bigger system in which a large section of Egypt's population was offered cheap public sector goods in exchange for their political acquiescence, a policy which became even more essential following the widespread popular rioting in January 1977 which greeted the announcement that subsidies on cereals and other foodstuffs were to be reduced in order to obtain financial support from the IMF. The plan was immediately reversed.

Economists also remain puzzled about the basic thrust of Egypt's liberalization. Given the way the new policy was presented, it could well be assumed that it was supposed to lead directly to dramatic changes in the management of the public sector as well in its relationship with private capital. This was not the case. While a 1975 law represented a small attempt to increase the independence of public sector managers by replacing the unwieldy General Organizations with Higher Sectoral Councils, its purpose was largely undercut by the fact that there was no parallel move to introduce either meaningful competition or pricing policies which reflected real costs and real profits. To make matters worse, the regime continued to rely on the Nasser period policy of providing university graduates and others with government jobs from which it was almost impossible for them to be dismissed. In this way the numbers of people in government employment rose from 9 percent of the labor force in the early 1960s to 27 percent in 1976 and perhaps as much as 32 percent in 1981.[42] Indeed, there is a reasonable suspicion that, once the regime found itself in possession of huge new funds towards the end of the 1970s, all pressure for public sector reform evaporated. Meanwhile, the private sector, now heavily dependent on public sector patronage, was unable to increase its own contribution to total investment, and its share remained at between 20 and 21 percent from 1977 to 1981/82.[43]

The principles underlying government policy toward agriculture are similarly difficult to discern. On the one hand, there was a great deal of talk of what became known as 'food security,' a concern aroused by Egypt's growing inability to feed itself without recourse to foreign – and particularly North American – supplies. To cite just two of the most dramatic examples, the proportion of local demand for wheat provided by the Egyptian agricultural sector declined from 70 to 25 percent between 1960 and 1980 and that of sugar from 114 to 57 percent.[44] On the other hand, government expenditures on agriculture declined as a proportion of total expenditure during the Sadat years while the state continued to manipulate the prices of agricultural inputs and outputs in such a way as to abstract a considerable part of the rural surplus.[45]

ECONOMIC SLOW-DOWN, 1986–1990

Egypt's decade of rapid economic growth ended in 1985/86 with the collapse of the price of oil – the government's oil revenues fell by 70 percent in 1986 – followed by various knock-on effects, such as a reduction in the value of the remittances sent back by Egyptians working in Saudi Arabia and the Gulf.[46] To make matters worse, there was a simultaneous drying up of international credit and foreign aid. The result was a period of much slower growth, with GDP rising at only 2.9 percent a year between 1985 and 1990, and private consumption advancing at a slower 1.9 percent. Meanwhile, government attempts to reduce expenditure led to a reduction of imports by an average of 4.7 percent a year and of gross investment by nearly 6 percent.[47]

Among the many short-term problems which confronted the Egyptian government, undoubtedly the most pressing was that of servicing its international debt at a time when repayments of principle and interest were costing the equivalent of 70 percent of the country's export earnings. It was this which finally forced it to enter into new negotiations with the IMF, leading to the signing of an 18 month stand-by agreement in May 1987 in which, in return for a new World Bank loan and IMF assistance in rescheduling part of Eygpt's international debt, the government promised to reduce public expenditure and to make a significant move towards unifying the system of multiple exchange rates begun under the Nasser regime.

In the event, however, such promises proved hard to deliver and, as early as the spring of 1988, the IMF refused to release the second tranche of the agreed loan on the grounds that the government had failed to meet its targets as far as both the budget and exchange rate unification were concerned. This, in turn, led to a new series of negotiations in 1989, in which the IMF and the World Bank widened their concerns from stabilization to structural adjustment and, in particular, the creation of markets through the rolling back of state control over the economy. However, the Mubarak regime remained extremely sensitive to the strong opposition to further liberalization to be found both within and outside the government apparatus. It was only once the international situation had changed to Egypt's advantage following its participation in the anti-Iraq coalition during the Gulf War 1990–91 that a real breakthrough could be made in terms of the production of a credible plan for reducing subsidies and price controls, as well as granting greater autonomy to public sector enterprises in preparation for their eventual privatization.

EGYPT'S ECONOMIC PERFORMANCE 1945–90
NATIONAL INCOME

Egypt only began to produce official national income statistics at the start of the first five-year plan period in 1959–60.[48] Until then we have to rely on series produced by a number of economists, most of whom either worked together or were familiar with each other's calculations. We have chosen those by Hansen (see Table 6.1).

As the figures in Table 6.1 indicate, Egyptian GNP increased at 5.3 percent a year from 1945 to 1951, 3.8 percent from 1952/53–1959/60, 5.7 percent from 1959/60 to 1981/82, before slowing down to some 2–3 percent during the rest of the 1980s. However, long-run figures of this type hide the fact that there were shorter periods of high and low growth, with particularly good periods from 1945 to 1951, 1959/60 to 1964/65 (the first five-year plan period), and 1973 to 1981/82. We should also note that, from 1945 onward, Egypt's population was growing at an increasing rate, rising from 2.1 percent between 1939 and 1955 to reach a high of 2.7 percent in the mid-1980s. This reduced growth in per capita national income to 3.2 percent between 1959/60 and 1981/82.

A second index of economic growth and development is provided by sectoral figures (see Table 6.6). These reveal the normal pattern of an increasing share of industry in GDP and a declining pattern in agriculture until the early 1970s when the explosion of income derived from the rents from the Suez Canal and from oil begin to distort the picture in a significant fashion, causing the share of industry and mining to drop again, from just under 20 percent in 1974 to nearer 15 percent in 1978 and 1983/84, while services, the main recipient of these rents, continued their rapid advance.[49]

Turning now to the movements underlying these particular developments, it is Hansen's opinion that, apart from the period of the first five-year plan, industry has not been a driving force within the Egyptian economy since 1952, after which the high growth sectors have been petroleum, electricity (particularly after the completion of the Aswan High Dam), and transport and communications (including revenues from the Suez Canal).[50] This in turn raises important questions about the development of Egypt's agricultural and industrial sectors which, for most of the period in question, were still regarded by economists and politicians as of central importance to economic advance. Their performance must be considered both singly and then in tandem via their mutual involvement in the continuing problem of how to make the best use of one of the country's most important assets – long staple cotton – and whether it should simply be exported or also used as the basis for a flourishing local textile industry.

INDUSTRY

From 1945 to 1952, Egypt's entrepreneurs continued to base their invest-ments on a process of import substitution, moving from simple consumer goods (textiles and food processing) towards more complex products (chemicals, rayon, and plastics). To these the revolutionary regime which came to power in 1952 soon added tires and then iron and steel. The pro-ductivity of such industries grew only slowly – at some 0.5 percent a year in 1947–65 – but, as Mabro points out, this is true of the industrial experience of most developing countries.[51] What is more to the point is that Egyptian factories were becoming increasingly competitive in international terms, an argument made by a 1954 UN report which asserted that the majority of them could exist without any tariff protection at all.[52]

Thereafter, however, little was done to deepen Egypt's industrial capa-city, apart from the establishment of a few more joint ventures assembling such consumer durables as cars, refrigerators, and television sets from imported kits. This lack of ambition was continued during the period of public ownership when, as Mabro and Radwan note, the first five-year plan contained no proposals for the production of machinery or other capital goods.[53] Just why this should have been so at a time when the regime was trumpeting its industrial policy with such slogans as 'From the needle to the rocket' remains unclear.[54]

Be that as it may, the regime's policy of expanding the output from existing lines seems to have been quite well conceived, at least in its early stages. It was only later that the industrial sector as a whole began to mani-fest severe structural weaknesses of the type found in most other countries where the state sector was in the ascendant. Managers were given few incentives to run their enterprises efficiently. Indeed, with administered prices and low standards of accountancy it was soon virtually impossible to calculate profit and loss in any meaningful way. By the same token, as soon as private activity was allowed to revive from the late 1960s onward, the majority of businessmen found it easier to make money by attaching them-selves, in parasitic fashion, to the state sector than by trying to produce for either the domestic or the foreign market on their own. In addition, from the late 1960s onward, the industrial sector seems to have suffered from a species of administrative neglect.

It is difficult to go beyond such easy generalizations owing to a lack of more specific information. But the few studies that have been carried out seem to show that there was a considerable gap not only between the dif-ferent sectors of Egyptian public industry but also between different firms within the same industry, with a few (notably in chemicals) managing to keep quite close to best international practice even if the majority fell far below.[55]

What is also clear is that the huge textile sector (providing 27 percent of industrial value added in the early 1970s) was unable to transcend the structural imperfections of its pre-revolutionary past, notably overmanning and the vexed problem of having to use high quality Egyptian cotton for low quality woven goods.[56] Indeed, all the evidence goes to show that these problems only intensified over time, with the factories being forced to act as a dumping ground for anyone whom the regime chose to employ, while being denied access to those Western markets which could have provided an outlet for any of their higher quality products.

It is easy to see with hindsight that the Nasser regime should either have reinforced the pre-revolutionary movement of Egypt's textile industry toward the upper end of the market or, even more radically, concentrated the bulk of its attention and resources on the relatively more efficient chemical sector.[57] It can also be argued that it would have been more profitable to export much more of Egypt's own cotton crop than to allow its use by domestic industry. But this is simply a council of perfection and not a set of policies likely to have commended itself to the Nasser regime facing as it did the particular political and economic choices of its time.

AGRICULTURE

According to World Bank figures, Egyptian agricultural output increased by 2.9 percent annually 1960–70, 3.0 percent 1970–80, and 2.6 percent 1980–89.[58] Most other calculations, however, show a significantly weaker performance.[59] Given such discrepancies, only two general assertions can be made with any confidence. One is that even the higher World Bank figures suggest that the growth of output barely kept pace with that of population. The second is that this performance must be considered disappointing when viewed in terms of the hopes raised by the revolutionary regime's two great interventions in rural life: the land reform and the construction of the Aswan High Dam. Just why this was so remains difficult to explain. But the subject is best approached by examining in turn five of the key variables which affected agriculture's performance – the size of the cultivated and cropped area, the mix of crops, yields, inputs, and units of production.

Let us begin with changes in the cultivated and cropped area. The revolutionary regime attached great importance to efforts to increase the amount of available land. This began with the Tahrir ('liberation') province

141

scheme initiated in 1953 and continued with increasing effort until, between 1965 and 1980, nearly two-thirds of the sector's investment budget was devoted to this end.[60] But in spite of the large sums of money expended the results remained disappointing. Of the just over 800,000 feddans (830,000 acres) reclaimed between 1952 and 1967–68, only a third was being farmed by 1965–66 and this with an average yield of only half that of Egypt's older land.[61] Further efforts during the 1970s were hardly more satisfactory while, to make matters worse, there began to be significant land loss as a result of building and other encroachments on the cultivated area.[62] If Alan Richard's figure of 900,000 feddans (934,000 acres) for the amount of agricultural land surrendered to urban sprawl during the 1970s is correct, then all the effort and expense of the Nasser and Sadat period reclamation were just sufficient to maintain Egypt's stock of arable land at its 1952 level, and then only by replacing the good land lost with fields of much lower fertility.[63]

To this we should add the fact that the Aswan High Dam, far from encouraging the better drainage of Egypt's fields, as originally intended, actually intensified the existing process of salination by encouraging over-watering unrestrained by any system of water taxation.[64] Efforts to remedy the situation took years to get going and, as late as 1976, more than half of Egypt's cultivated area was still without adequate drains.[65]

In these circumstances, hopes for an increase in production rested on a more intensive use of the existing land. This could be achieved in one or all of three different ways: by growing more crops on a given piece of land, by improving their yields, or by changes in Egypt's overall crop mix. The first of these, involving an increase in the cropped area, proceeded only slowly, from an average of 9.4 million feddans (9.8 million acres) between 1950 and 1954 to just over 11 million feddans (11.4 million acres) between 1978 and 1981, an increment of 18 percent.[66] And even this was only managed at the probable expense of some decline in soil fertility. Yields, too, improved just as slowly, although, given the fact that they tended to vary greatly from year to year, comparison between one period and another is often difficult. However, in very general terms, it seems that it was not until the mid-1960s that most crops were back to the levels achieved in the late 1930s, after which only cotton and wheat made any significant progress thanks to the introduction of improved seeds and, in the case of cotton, to a great increase in the use of pesticides.[67]

As for changes in land use, the main trend was one of a small decline in the proportion of the cropped land allocated to field crops, notably cotton and wheat, and a rise in that of fruits and vegetables.[68] The reasons for this are clear: not only did the production of fruits and vegetables yield higher returns, but the gap was widened still further by government policy which continued to purchase the cotton crop at well below market prices. It should be noted, however, that only the larger landholders had either enough land or enough capital to make the switch, leaving their smaller neighbors to allocate all of their own plots to that production of cotton and cereals which membership of the cooperatives made compulsory.[69] All things being equal, the move towards the cultivation of higher value crops should have been very welcome, being just the policy that many economists had been advocating for years so as to make the best use of the country's limited amount of highly fertile soil.[70] However, in the event, it placed the government on the horns of a considerable dilemma. Cotton was required as a raw material for Egypt's textile industry, while cereals were needed to feed a rapidly expanding population with increasing amounts of money to spend on food. Here, as elsewhere, the regime found it impossible either to trust the market to allocate resources or to devise administrative policies best capable of meeting a variety of competing demands.

Lastly, there is the role of inputs and of the size of the unit of production. As far as the former were concerned, two trends were important. First, there was an enormous growth in the use of nitrogenous fertilizer, of pesticides, and of improved seeds, complemented by an increasing investment in agricultural machinery, particularly tractors and pumps. This did something to offset a second trend, the development of a shortage of male labor during the 1970s as men were drawn away from the land by the higher wages they could earn either in the domestic construction industry or by migrating to Libya and the Gulf. One result was a doubling of the real agricultural wage between 1973 and 1980; another was the increased employment of women and children in the fields.[71] But, given the fact that the majority of Egypt's farm units were of a very small size (under 3 feddans = 3.1 acres), and that cotton cultivation remained largely resistant to mechanization with a high, seasonal demand for labor, particularly at harvest time, there were limits beyond which mechanization could not go (see Table 6.7).

This brings us to some of the basic constraints which faced Egyptian agriculture during the period. The evidence given above about the limited increase in the size of the cropped area and in yields suggests that, even before 1945, the country was bumping against a technological barrier which made any further increase in productivity both expensive and, in so far as the provision of extra water was concerned, highly problematic. In a sense, a great deal of the regime's investment in the agricultural sector was a kind of 'running to stand still' with more effort going into the preservation of existing gains than into encouraging marginal improvements in output. Moreover, there was the further handicap of having to allocate valuable land to cotton and cereals in order to meet an urban demand for food and raw materials which could probably have been better accommodated by imports.

Finally, for all their initial appearance of success, it can be argued that the system of supervised cooperatives simply froze an existing pattern of land ownership and land use in such a way that it remained highly resistant to technical improvements or, indeed, any further movement toward a more efficient use of the available resources. Hence, as so often happens, an inflexible system was left to try to accommodate pressures from the market, and from the larger and more influential owners, without any real attempt at reform. As a result, its role in the management of Egyptian agriculture was seriously impaired.

COULD THE EGYPTIAN ECONOMY HAVE GROWN ANY FASTER?
CONCLUDING REMARKS

Most economists conclude that the Egyptian economy could, and should, have developed faster between 1945 and 1990. And most, but not all, tend to blame government policies for this lack of success. By and large, the main culprit is taken to be the inward-looking, import substitution strategies pursued throughout the period, as well as the huge increase in the public sector which, by 1985, was consuming just under half of total GNP.[72] To this should be added the impact of the two major wars fought against Israel in 1967 and 1973.

Hansen's sensible approach is to identify the key economic variables and then to try to provide a political economy explanation for them.[73] In his account, it is the low growth of factor productivity which is the main culprit, particularly in agriculture where he sees no improvement over the whole period between independence in 1923 and the mid-1980s. Manufacturing industry fared only a little better, with its factor productivity growing by about 2 percent a year from 1945 to 1962, and declining by about the same amount from 1962 to 1970, before increasing at 5.3 percent from 1973 to 1981/82.

Why should this be so? Here Hansen blames what he calls the 'negative' aspects of Egypt's statist policies, exacerbated by a suspicion of foreigners and foreign capital and a bias towards higher education which left Egypt with one of the highest illiteracy rates in the Middle East, at just over 50 percent.[74] In addition, as far as the agricultural sector was concerned, he points to the lack of a powerful lobby, after land reform in 1952, which could put pressure on the government to look after the rural interest. The result was continued investment in irrigation and drainage projects which, he argues, produced declining returns, when the proper answer was to increase expenditures on rural extension services and elementary education.

These are powerful arguments even if they do not exhaust the whole range of possible relevant factors. As in so many countries of the non-European world, the desire to reverse the legacy of colonialism produced an excessive concern with protection and control. In the hands of a regime such as Nasser's, this led to a breakdown of good relations with the business community, both local and foreign, an unreal belief in the power of scientific planning, and the creation of a system which was driven by politics rather than economics, seeking rent rather than profit and giving rise to, in a relatively short period of time, a powerful set of vested interests which proved enormously difficult to set aside.

WELFARE

Two facts stand out concerning the distribution of income in Egypt during most of the period. One is that during the 1960s and 1970s, it remained stable as well as remarkably equitable by international standards.[75] The second is that responsibility for this state of affairs belongs largely to the post-revolutionary regime which presided over a large transfer of resources to the poorer strata of the community.

The impact of state policy can be seen most clearly and unambiguously in the indices relating to health, education, and welfare. According to official figures, the proportion of Egyptian children attending primary school increased from 66 to 76 percent between 1960 and 1981, while that in secondary education grew from 16 to 52 percent during the same period, and that in higher education from 5 to 15 percent.[76] Even though the quality of the education provided by some parts of the system declined, this remains a significant achievement. So too do efforts to improve the reach of medical care by the spread of rural health centers and the provision of more doctors.[77] One result was a significant rise in the life expectancy at birth between 1960 and 1982: from 46 to 56 for males and 47 to 59 for females.[78]

Both the Nasser and Sadat regimes contributed to these developments, but in different ways. The former pursued an increasingly aggressive policy of redistributing income from the rich to the poor, placing a cap of £E5,000 on all salaries and, of course, taking land from the large owners and parceling it up into much smaller units. As a result, the proportion of land held in plots of 10 feddans (10.4 acres) or more decreased from 63.5 percent in 1950 to only 20 percent in 1977/78 while that held in small plots

145

of under 3 feddans increased from 13.2 percent to 38 percent (see Table 6.7). The welfare policy of the Sadat regime, in contrast, was to spend an increasing proportion of the budget on expanding primary education and on subsidizing essential foodstuffs as well as trying to reduce unemployment by the provision of an increasing number of government jobs.

Nevertheless, there were limits: 40 percent of Egypt's rural families still remained landless after the reform and, as Radwan and Lee have pointed out, landlessness was highly correlated with poverty.[79] Their calculations also show that although the proportion of families living below the poverty line decreased to about 17 percent during the mid-1960s, it then rose again to 28 percent by 1974/75.[80] What seems to have happened as a result of the post-revolutionary efforts at redistribution was the creation of a two-tier system among Egypt's lower strata in which those with land or with state employment were significantly more secure and, mostly, better off than those without such advantages.

Developments during the 1980s suggest a return to greater inequality. For one thing, the Mubarak regime was forced to abandon the previous policy of providing guaranteed employment in the state sector for those with university or intermediate degrees. The result was nearly a doubling of the official rate of unemployment between 1976 and 1986, from 7.7 percent of the labor force to 14.7 percent, much of it concentrated among youths with secondary and tertiary education and no previous work experience.[81] Meanwhile those at work suffered from a significant decline in the real value of their wages, particularly after 1985, with employees of the government and public enterprises doing significantly less well than those in the private sector.[82] The progressive removal of subsidies on basic necessities after 1987, accompanied by rising inflation, created still further inequality as they tended to affect the poor much more than the rich and well-to-do.

Notes on Chapter 6
Full details of all sources are in the Bibliography

1   For example, Mabro, *The Egyptian Economy*, p 113; O'Brien, *The Revolution in Egypt's Economic System*, p 60; Wahba, *The Role of the State in the Egyptian Economy 1945–1981*, ch. 3 and especially pp 70–75.

2   Tignor, *Egyptian Textiles and British Capital 1930–56*, pp 53–7; Mabro and Radwan, *The Industrialization of Egypt 1939–1973*, pp 84–5.

3   The cyclical view is exemplified, *inter alia*, by Mabro and Radwan, *The Industrialization of Egypt 1939–1973*, pp 85–7, the structural by Hansen and Marzouk, *Development and Economic Policy*, p 2 and Wahba, *The Role of the State*, p 85.

4   Hansen and Marzouk, *Development and Economic Policy*, Table 5.3, p 87.
5   Wahba, *The Role of the State*, Table 2.6, p 55.
6   Ducruet, *Les Capitaux européens au Proche-Orient*, p 317; Mead, *Growth and Structural Change in the Egyptian Economy*, p 121.
7   Waterbury, *The Egypt of Nasser and Sadat*, pp 61–2; Vitalis, 'The End of Third Worldism in Egyptian Studies,' p 25.
8   Vitalis, 'The End of Third Worldism in Egyptian Studies,' pp 24–5.
9   El-Gritly, 'The Structure of Modern Industry in Egypt,' pp 502–28; Vitalis, *When Capitalists Collide*, p 196.
10 Waterbury, *The Egypt of Nasser and Sadat*, p 62.
11 Mabro, *The Egyptian Economy*, p 62.
12 Wahba, *The Role of the State*, p 57.
13 Waterbury, *The Egypt of Nasser and Sadat*, p 71.
14 Sidqi completed his graduate work at Harvard in the late 1940s, where he wrote a PhD dissertation entitled 'Industrialization of Egypt and a Case Study of the Iron and Steel Industry' (May 1950).
15 The nationalization continued, in less dramatic form, through 1964, including a number of private companies which voluntarily accepted partial state ownership in order to be able to bid for public sector contracts; Wahba, *The Role of the State*, pp 102–3.
16 For example, Mabro, *The Egyptian Economy*, pp 127–9.
17 Hansen and Marzouk, *Development and Economic Policy*, pp 170–1; O'Brien, *The Revolution in Egypt's Economic System*, p 125.
18 Vitalis, 'The End of Third Worldism in Egyptian Studies,' p 25.
19 Mabro and Radwan, *The Industrialization of Egypt*, pp 96–7.
20 *Ibid.*, pp 71–2; Waterbury, *Exposed to Innumerable Illusions*, ch. 4 and especially pp 132–4.
21 Hansen, 'Planning and Growth in the UAR (1960–5),' p 22.
22 Mabro, *The Egyptian Economy*, p 121; Mabro and Radwan, *The Industrialization of Egypt*, pp 69–70.
23 Hansen, 'Planning and Growth in the UAR (1960–5),' pp 36–8.
24 Wahba, *The Role of the State*, p 97.
25 For example, the article on 'Arab Socialism' in *Scribe* (Cairo), 23 July 1962, quoted in Hanna and Gardiner (eds), *Arab Socialism*, pp 336–7.
26 Mabro, *The Egyptian Economy*, pp 77–9.
27 Richards, *Egypt's Agricultural Development*, pp 202–3, including Table 6.11.
28 Abdel-Fadil, *Development, Income Distribution and Social Change in Rural Egypt 1952–1970*, p 23.
29 Ikram, *Egypt*, pp 172, 240.
30 Wahba, *The Role of the State*, p 121.
31 *Ibid.*, p 122.
32 Amin, *Egypt's Economic Predicament*, p 7.
33 Wahba, *The Role of the State*, pp 132–3.
34 *Ibid.*, p 190.
35 The government kept no official records of the numbers of Egyptians working abroad. This guesstimate comes from Handoussa, 'Crisis and Challenge: Prospects for the 1990s,' p 5.
36 Amin, *Egypt's Economic Predicament*, p 11–12; Butter, 'Debt and Financial Policies,' p 2. At least half the military debt was borrowed short-term at very high rates of interest (12–14 percent).

37 Amin, *Egypt's Economic Predicament*, Table 2.1, p 22 (quoting from Hansen, *Political Economy*, p 192).

38 For example, Amin, *Egypt's Economic Predicament*, p 12.

39 Handoussa, 'Crisis and Challenge,' pp 3–5. Hansen also gives qualified support to the 'Dutch disease' hypothesis: *Egypt and Turkey*, pp 526–8.

40 Handoussa, 'Crisis and Challenge,' p 3.

41 Wahba, *The Role of the State*, p 149.

42 Commander, *The State and Agricultural Development in Egypt Since 1973*, p 26.

43 *Ibid.*, p 17.

44 *Ibid.*, Table 2.12, p 38.

45 *Ibid.*, pp 30–2.

46 Butter, 'Debt and Financial Policies,' p 4.

47 Karshenas, *Structural Adjustment and Employment in the Middle East and North Africa*, Table E1.

48 See Sharaf, 'The Development and Present Structure of National Income Accounts in the United Arab Republic' in Khan (ed.), *Middle East Studies in Income and Wealth*, pp 1–29.

49 I have excluded petroleum from Hansen's figures for 1978 and 1983–84; see his *Egypt and Turkey*, Table 1.4.

50 *Ibid.*, pp 14–15.

51 Mabro, *The Egyptian Economy*, p 151.

52 Quoted in Hansen and Marzouk, *Development and Economic Policy*, p 157.

53 *The Industrialization of Egypt*, pp 105–6.

54 For the quotation, see Waterbury, *The Egypt of Nasser and Sadat*, p 81.

55 For example, Handoussa, 'Reform Policies for Egypt's Manufacturing Sector,' pp 107–8.

56 Figure from Ikram, *Egypt*, p 241.

57 These points are addressed, *inter alia*, by Hansen and Marzouk, *Development and Economic Policy*, pp 153–5; Ikram, *Egypt*, pp 241–3; Mabro, *The Egyptian Economy*, p 150; Mabro and Radwan, *The Industrialization of Egypt 1939–1973*, pp 104–5.

58 World Bank, *World Development Report 1981*, pp 136–7; 1991, pp 206–7.

59 For lower estimates see Hansen, *Egypt and Turkey*, p 16; Ikram, *Egypt*, p 172; Commander, *The State and Agricultural Development in Egypt Since 1973*, p 34. For one of the few higher ones see Radwan and Lee, *Agrarian Change in Egypt*, p 10. The differences stem from the use of different official figures, different methods of calculation, and differing systems of weighting.

60 Commander, *The State and Agricultural Development in Egypt Since 1973*, p 35.

61 El-Barawy, *Economic Development in the United Arab Republic (Egypt)*, pp 97–8.

62 For example, Commander, *The State and Agricultural Development in Egypt Since 1973*, p 35.

63 Richards, 'Agricultural Employment, Wages and Government Policy During and After the Oil Boom,' p 64.

64 Waterbury, *Hydropolitics of the Nile Valley*, pp 131–2. But note also that the dam did much to save Egypt from the consequences of low floods like the one in 1972–73 which could well have cut the value of the harvest by 40 percent if it had not been for the water stored from previous years; Waterbury, *Egypt*, p 103.

65 Waterbury, *Hydropolitics of the Nile Valley*, pp 132–3.

66 Commander, *The State and Agricultural Development in Egypt Since 1973*, Table 4.1.

67 Richards, *Egypt's Agricultural Development*, p 200. But see also Ikram on the problems of introducing the new HYV wheat in the 1970s; *Egypt*, pp 189–90.

68 Commander, *The Political Economy of Food Production and Distribution in Egypt*, Table 4.
69 Richards, *Egypt's Agricultural Development*, pp 182–3. Richards also notes that richer cultivators often found it in their interest to pay a fine rather than plant the compulsory, but lower value, crops; *ibid.*, p 183.
70 For example, Issawi, *Egypt at Mid-Century*, pp 123–4.
71 Commander, *The State and Agricultural Development in Egypt Since 1973*, Table 5.1.
72 Hansen, *Egypt and Turkey*, Table 15.2. The figure for 1952–53 was 22.3 percent.
73 *Ibid.*, ch. 15.
74 The actual figure for illiteracy in the late 1980s was 52 percent for those aged over fifteen; World Bank, *Claiming the Future*, p 92.
75 Hansen, *Egypt and Turkey*, p 25; World Bank, *Claiming the Future*, pp 3, 92.
76 World Bank, *World Development Report 1984*, Table 25.
77 For example, *ibid.*, Table 24 and Mabro, *The Egyptian Economy*, pp 159–60.
78 World Bank, *World Development Report 1984*, Table 23, pp 262–3.
79 Radwan and Lee, *Agrarian Change in Egypt*, p 9.
80 Based on a sample of 1,000 families; *ibid.*, p 13.
81 Karshenas, *Structural Adjustment and Employment in the Middle East and North Africa*, pp 30–1 and Table E2.
82 *Ibid.*

7

Syria, Lebanon, and Iraq 1946–1990

SYRIA AND LEBANON 1946–1990

THE CUSTOMS UNION 1946–1950

Although Syria and Lebanon obtained their formal independence in 1941, it was not until the final withdrawal of British and French troops early in 1946 that they were free to manage their two economies without direct interference from the colonial powers. Even this left them with complex problems involving their relations with each other as well as with France, with which they remained closely linked in a number of important ways.

As far as the first of these issues was concerned, one of the early decisions taken by their new national governments in 1943 was to continue the customs union between the two countries with their 'common interests' (mainly the collection and distribution of the duties levied on foreign trade) to be managed jointly by a Supreme Economic Council. Meanwhile, all other aspects of their new relationship were to be left to future arrangement.

Some of the larger questions involved were soon put to the test by the breakdown of their initial decision to act together in negotiations with

150

France; these included such vital issues as the future of their substantial monetary reserves held in the Bank of France, the French central bank, and that of the French concessionary companies still occupying important positions within their two economies.[1] However, the Lebanese soon broke ranks and signed their own monetary accord with France in February 1948, assuring themselves of the gradual release of their share of the reserves until 1953. This, in turn, encouraged them to dissolve the monetary union with Syria and then to establish their own independent currency, the Lebanese lira, in 1949, with an unusually high (50 percent) gold and foreign exchange cover.[2] Syria had no alternative but to follow suit, signing its own monetary accord with France in February 1949 and creating its own currency, the Syrian lira, shortly thereafter, but on somewhat less favorable terms.[3] The result was to permit both governments to obtain control over their country's money supply for the first time. Meanwhile, Lebanon allowed the Banque de Syrie et du Grand Liban (BSL) to continue its privileged role as government banker until its concession ran out in 1964, while Syria was able to persuade the French to terminate the concession in 1956.

The existence of two separate national currencies within a single customs union created new sets of problems and was followed quickly by the Syrian decision to dissolve the union in March 1950.[4] Given the benefit of hindsight, the formal separation of the two economies now seems to have been inevitable. For one thing, the postwar economic policies pursued in Beirut and Damascus tended to intensify the pre-existing differences in structure between Lebanon, with its growing emphasis on banking and commerce, and Syria, with its more conventional concentration on the development of agriculture and industry.[5] For another, certain international events, notably the intensification of the Arab boycott of Israel in 1948 and the arrival of a great influx of Palestinian refugees, both rich and poor, created an incipient competition between the Syrians and Lebanese for economic power and influence along the Mediterranean coast, exemplified most notably by the commercial rivalry between Beirut and the Syrian port of Latakia.[6] To make matters still more difficult, these were also years of considerable political turmoil as a result of the humiliation of both armies by the Israelis in 1948 followed quickly by a series of three military coups in Syria in 1949.

Nevertheless, it is also important to note that the decision to break up the union between the two partners was not – and could not have been – taken lightly, given their mutual reliance on each other's markets and export of raw materials.[7] Hence both economies suffered greatly from the brief Syrian boycott which was imposed immediately after the dissolution of the customs union. The two governments moved quickly to repair the damage in a series of negotiations which culminated in the agreement of 1952 re-establishing free trade in agricultural goods and creating a sliding tariff for industrial goods according to which those containing a high proportion of local raw materials could be transported across their mutual border duty free.

THE SYRIAN ECONOMY 1950–1990

Systems of economic management

The economic policies pursued in the first decades after Syria's independence were heavily dependent on the character of its political regime. Until 1958, successive governments sought to promote private enterprise-led development. But, beginning with the three-year union with Egypt from 1958 to 1961, the state started to assume a much more salient role in the management of the economy, before coming to a new accommodation with private capital in the 1970s.

From 1945 to 1958 it was agriculture which provided the main engine of economic growth as more and more land was brought into cultivation, particularly in the Jazira to the east of Aleppo and along the Euphrates. This was underpinned by a political system still heavily dominated by landlord and merchant interests. Nevertheless, there was also a small but steady move toward greater state involvement. This was encouraged, first, by the nationalization of most of the French concessionary companies which controlled the railroads, the water and electricity systems, and the important state tobacco monopoly, and then by the visit of a World Bank mission in 1954 whose report pointed to the existence of certain serious problems which only the government had the resources to address. These included an inadequate transport network and the need to switch toward a more intensive system of agriculture based, if possible, on an expansion of the land subject to perennial irrigation.[8] Many of the Bank's recommendations were immediately implemented in a series of schemes focused on road building, water resource development, and the expansion of port facilities at Latakia. However, the government's contribution to national income remained modest – perhaps 7.5 percent in 1950 rising to 8.5 percent in 1957 – while successive governments proved most unwilling to accept foreign loans for fear of compromising Syria's newly won independence.[9]

The union with Egypt provided an important catalyst for change as the Nasser government sought to impose its own, increasingly statist, systems of management on its junior partner. This can be seen in the creation of a ministry of planning in 1960 with responsibility for implementing the first five-year plan, from 1960/61 to 1964/65, which directed 60 percent of its investments towards new dams and canals.[10] It can also be seen, in more spectacular fashion, in the Land Reform of 1958 which, following the Egyptian model, imposed fixed limits of ownership – 80 hectares (198 acres) for irrigated land, 300 hectares (741 acres) for rain-fed – while also seeking to regulate the rents and crop-sharing contracts which affected 75 percent of the cultivated area.[11] The result was the sequestration of some 1.5 million hectares (3.76 million acres) of land, an area almost eight times larger than that subject to the 1952 law in Egypt, much of it along the Euphrates frontier with problems of access and few facilities for the many thousands of new owners. Not surprisingly, implementation remained slow and only 10 percent of the expropriated land had actually been distributed by 1962.[12]

There is no doubt that one of the major aims of the reform, as in Egypt, was to destroy the rural power of the 3,000 or so families who controlled the bulk of the country's land.[13] Their resistance not only slowed down its implementation but also fed into a larger movement of protest by members of the country's old political elite, excited still further by the Egyptian decision to include Syria in its bank nationalizations of 1960–61 (see p 131). It was opposition to measures of this type which lay behind Syria's secession from the union in 1961. But the triumph of the old economic elite was only short-lived. Successor governments, from 1963 onward, presided over a rapid extension of state economic power under pressure from the radical wing of the Ba'th party. Hence the re-nationalization of the private banks was followed, in 1964, by a more sweeping measure which took into state ownership the foreign oil company (the Iraq Petroleum Company) and most of the country's major manufacturing and commercial enterprises. This, in turn, required the creation of new institutions and mechanisms of control: the Syrian Petroleum Company, the government trade agency, and departments, known as unions, to manage groups of nationalized industries.[14]

Not every member of the Ba'thi regime which finally came to power in 1966 was happy with the political fall-out from these measures, however. One such was minister of defense, Hafiz al-Asad, who seized power in November 1970 and immediately implemented what he called a 'Corective Revolution' designed to obtain the support of those many sections of Syrian society alienated by his more radical colleagues. This, in effect, was an earlier, though tamer, version of Sadat's Egyptian 'infitah,' a set of measures designed to encourage both private and foreign investment by removing many restrictions on trade and opening up certain sections of the economy – notably tourism and construction – to non-state actors. As in the case of Egypt, the regime obtained major dividends from the timing of this new policy, which allowed the economy to recover rapidly from the vast expenditure ($1.8 billion) occasioned by the 1973 Arab-Israeli war, and then to benefit enormously from the oil boom which followed.[15]

The economic policies pursued by the Asad regime during the 1970s had two major features. The first was the consolidation of many of the important policy initiatives taken since 1958. As far as the agricultural sector was concerned, this meant pushing on with the land reform until, by 1975, over half of the sequestrated area (795,000 hectares or 1.964 million acres) had either been distributed in small plots or sold, with much of the rest placed under the management of cooperatives and other government agencies.[16] Peasants given reform land were required to become members of agricultural cooperatives which, by the end of the 1970s, controlled one-fourth of the cultivated area, deciding what was to be sown and buying up the field crops at prices decided by the state. According to Ian Manners and Tagi Sagafi-Nejad, these organizations had made something of a 'shaky' start in the 1960s owing to a combination of unusually low rainfalls and the inexperience of many of the officials placed in charge.[17] The situation improved in the 1970s, helped by greater government support in the form of increased credit, larger supplies of machinery and fertilizer, and a more realistic pricing policy concerning the cereals and other field crops over which the state exercised a marketing monopoly.

The second feature was the drive to increase the productive powers of industry and agriculture by completion of major projects such as the Tabqa Dam on the Euphrates (1973) and the expansion of the Homs refinery (1975–76) to process the increasing amounts of oil pumped from the wells in the northeast of the country which had begun production in 1968.

However, in the event, the main stimulus to economic activity in the 1970s was the influx of money from outside, notably several billion dollars in aid from the Arab states, but also large sums from international investment and the remittances sent back by Syrians working in the Gulf.[18] It was this which allowed the regime to cement its new alliance with private businessmen on the basis of providing privileged access to public sector contracts.[19] The downside, however, was that this flood of money led to an increasing chorus of usually well-justified accusations of official corruption that not only disturbed the regime's more socialist-minded supporters but also helped to fuel a growing opposition, culminating in the civil discontent in Aleppo in 1979 and then the brief insurrection by Islamic militants in Hama in 1982.

The political difficulties of the late 1970s also proved to be a precursor to a decade of economic problems in which a number of factors combined to depress revenues and output. One was the continuous fall in oil prices which produced the familiar knock-on effects of a substantial reduction in Arab aid and in the remittances sent back by Syrian workers in the Gulf.[20] A second was several years of below average winter rains in 1982–85, which produced a considerable decline in the cereal harvest. These, in turn, led to a fall in government revenues and a crippling foreign exchange crisis which prevented the import of essential stocks of machinery, spare parts, and raw materials required by the manufacturing sector.

The regime's response was to introduce a series of policies which bore some resemblance to the conventional stabilization programs then being introduced in other parts of the world but without the support of the World Bank and the International Monetary Fund (IMF). Indeed, the whole point was that the process could be managed in such a way as to protect the position of those powerful interests upon which President Asad relied for political support, notably the army, the Ba'th party bureaucracy, and the managers and workers within the public sector.[21] The first stage, 1982–85, was marked by cuts in public expenditure designed to reduce the deficit on the current account, while a second, initiated in a year of particular difficulty, 1986, began a process of what Steven Heydemann has called 'selective liberalization' aimed at encouraging greater private sector participation in areas such as agriculture and trade.[22] Progress was slow to begin with.[23] However, by the end of the decade, the private sector's contribution to gross investment and output had overtaken that of the still sluggish public sector.[24]

Economic performance

The first official calculation of Syria's national income was made for the year 1950.[25] But production of a regular annual series only started in 1956.[26] Unfortunately, owing to frequent changes in the political regime, as well as to numerous alterations in definition and method, their overall reliability cannot be considered very great.[27] What they seem to show is a period of quite rapid growth – perhaps 5–6 percent a year – up to 1956, followed by a slight slowing down, in 1956–68, and then a sharp increase again for most of the 1970s when GDP may have been growing at a rate of some 9 percent a year. Finally, the economic difficulties of the 1980s reduced growth to only an annual 1.6 percent, in 1980–89 (See Table 7.1A).

Estimates of Syria's population before the first census of 1960 are also problematic. The census itself produced a figure of 4.5 million, followed by

155

one of 8.6 million in 1980 and 12 million in 1990, implying increasing annual growth rates of 3.2 percent (1960–72), 3.3 percent (1970–82) and then 3.6 percent (1980–89).[28] Rates of this kind restrained the parallel growth in per capita income to some 2.2 percent, in 1960–76, followed by a long period of falling real incomes in the 1980s.[29]

Analysts are generally in agreement that the main stimulus to the rapid growth of the first ten years of independence was the huge expansion of the cultivated area towards the Euphrates frontier. Thereafter the agricultural sector ran into serious problems (to be discussed below) so that the small increase in national income during most of the 1960s was only possible as the result of a growth of services, notably public administration which expanded by an extraordinary 17.5 percent a year between 1956 and 1968, as one authoritarian regime succeeded another.[30] Lastly, the return to faster growth in the 1970s owed much to outside funds supplemented by improvements in agriculture, electricity, and oil (See Table 7.1B).

An evaluation of the performance of the agricultural sector presents particular problems involving both data and definition. For example, as Manners and Sagafi-Nejad argue, the question of what exactly constitutes 'cultivated' land is a particularly difficult one in the context of a country with an eccentric rainfall cycle and a fluctuating desert frontier.[31] Nevertheless, it is possible to draw some rough conclusions from an examination of the three key variables: cultivated area (and its division into irrigated and rain-fed), cropped area, and yields (Table 7.2). As far as the first is concerned, there seems to have been a period of rapid expansion through most of the 1950s, a retreat in the 1960s due to the abandonment of some of the more marginal areas, and then a revival in the 1970s.[32] Changes in the amount of irrigated land followed something of the same trajectory with a period of rapid increase, from 250,000 to nearly 675,000 hectares (617,750 to 1.67 million acres) between 1945 and 1963, followed by a second period in which the area fell to a level of 500–600,000 hectares. In both cases, the supposition must be that expansion reached a limit which was extremely difficult, as well as expensive, to sustain, owing to persistent land loss caused by waterlogging and salination.

The situation with regard to the area actually placed under crops is more puzzling. On the one hand, there was undoubtedly an increase over the whole period, from some 2 to 4 million hectares (4.94 to 9.88 million acres). On the other, progress was extremely uneven as, to begin with, landowners responded to the increase in the cultivated area by allowing more of it to remain fallow, a proportion which had begun to exceed 50 percent in the early 1960s.[33] Only with the arrival of new inputs of fertilizers and machinery in the 1970s was it possible to arrest this trend and to begin to use the existing land more intensively.[34] And yet this was just the moment when the regime was engaged in a campaign to achieve food security by promoting the cultivation of cereals at the expense of higher value crops like cotton. To make matters worse, it proved extremely difficult to raise yields on rainfall land and so the only real improvement in productivity came from the employment of new HYV Mexican wheat grown under irrigation.

Turning to industry, the period of private enterprise development promoted modest growth in the output of a limited range of consumer goods, mainly textiles (which employed some 70 percent of the industrial work force in 1964–65) and food. Subsequent Ba'thi regimes then tried to engineer a more rapid expansion based on their belief that industry was the key to modern economic development. The existing capacity of the newly nationalized industries was increased, notably in textiles and cement, while new lines were added in metallurgy, chemicals (particularly fertilizers), and the iron and steel complex at Hama. Later, increasing attention was paid to the development of an oil refinery, also located at Hama, which received something like two-thirds of public sector investment in the 1970s.[35]

Most analysts see the performance of Syria's public sector industry as poor and there is particular criticism of the considerable under-utilization of capacity stemming from bad management, old machinery, and problems with uncertain supplies of electricity and raw materials.[36] Nevertheless, care is needed when interpreting local data as there is reason to suppose that Syrian critics on both the right and left may have wished to exaggerate the problems for their own purposes in a situation in which both public and private sectors still coexisted somewhat uneasily. Hence supporters of the public sector, particularly the trade unionists, seemed to fear that the system was being undermined by the way its managers formed mutually beneficial associations with private capital. It may well also have suited private entrepreneurs to exaggerate the extent of public sector mismanagement in order to widen their own sphere of operations.[37]

For all their failings at the political level, there is no doubt that the statist regimes were responsible for a considerable redistribution of income from 1958 onward. This can be seen most obviously in the rural sector, where the land reform reduced the area held in properties of 100 hectares and over from something like 50 percent in the early 1950s to less than 20 percent by 1970.[38] Meanwhile, according to Raymond Hinnebusch's calculations, the proportion of those rural families without land fell to something like 15 percent.[39] There was substantial progress in the area of health, education, and welfare as well. For example, primary education was made compulsory in 1970, making it possible to get almost every child to

157

elementary school by 1988, with over half going on to the secondary stage, and 18 percent to university.[40]

THE LEBANESE ECONOMY 1950–1990

The creation of a laissez-faire economy 1950–1974

By the time of the breakup of the customs union with Syria, many of the features of Lebanon's laissez-faire economic system were already in place. These included a strong currency, minimal direct taxation, and limited public spending on either development or defense. Then, after 1950, came a policy of low tariffs (except where they were required to protect existing industry) and the Bank Secrecy Law of 1956 designed to attract foreign capital. As Nadim Shehadi has argued, such measures provide good evidence that 'openness' was a deliberate policy and not simply the result of inaction or inertia.[41] However, in another sense it can also be seen as a direct expression of material interests. For, as Albert Badre's first efforts to calculate the country's national income for 1956 clearly showed, two-thirds of this income came from banking, commerce, and other services, but only 20 percent from agriculture and 13 percent from industry.[42]

Once implemented, the new system was able to feed upon its own success and in particular from the fact that Lebanon was now well placed to benefit from the postwar rise in oil revenues in Kuwait, Bahrain, and Saudi Arabia. On the one hand, Lebanese merchants quickly found ways of replacing their links with Syria by a direct connection with their opposite numbers in the Gulf. On the other, Gulf elites preferred to invest their new revenues with the help of Lebanese middlemen whom they trusted more than the Western bankers in London and New York. According to one estimate, almost two-thirds of the Arab oil surplus found its way to Beirut between 1956 and 1965.[43] Further benefit came from Lebanon's relative political stability compared with most of its Arab neighbors; it soon became a haven for private capital in flight from coups and revolutions in Syria, Egypt, and Iraq.[44]

The only serious attempt to change the country's economic orientation came during President Chehab's six-year term of office from 1958 to 1964. Alarmed by the evidence of social tensions which emerged during the brief political crisis in 1958, he sought ways to reduce the country's wide disparities in income between different classes, regions, and sects through planning and increased state intervention. The key to the whole process was the report of a French-based consultancy group, Institut International de Recherche et de Formation en Vue de Développement Intégral et Harmonisé (IRFED) which he invited to visit Lebanon in 1960–61. Its initial report provided what seemed to be damning evidence of the existence of just those inequalities that Chehab was worried about, calling particular attention to the disparities in income and living standards between parts of Beirut and what it called the 'misery belt' of poorer villages all around.[45] But the program of action it put forward was only officially adopted in 1965, the year after the president's retirement from office, and received neither the funds nor the administrative support to make more than a minimal impact on economic conditions. Indeed, as many have argued, the main lesson to be drawn from this episode was that the status quo was supported by so many powerful vested interests as to be unreformable without a radical change in the political structure as well.[46]

Lebanon's long period of economic growth came to a temporary halt in 1966 with the crash of its largest bank, Intra, which contained somewhere between 13 and 17 percent of the system's total deposits.[47] It was widely believed at the time that the crash was politically inspired by enemies of the bank and of its president, Yusuf Beidas.[48] What was certainly the case was that Lebanon's new Central Bank – created in 1964 once the BSL's concession had finally run out – made no effort to help. The general impact of the banking crisis was exacerbated by the fall-out from the sweeping Israeli military victories of June 1967, and it was not until the early 1970s that the Lebanese economy started a new period of rapid growth, stimulated once again by a sharp increase in the oil revenues of the Gulf states. Exports and tourism experienced an enormous expansion, while the boom also produced a new source of income from the remittances sent back by the 150,000 Lebanese working in Saudi Arabia and elsewhere. Another sign of the times was the arrival of foreign banks anxious to profit from the huge increase in capital passing through Beirut.

The economic impact of the civil war, 1975–1990

The outbreak of the civil war in 1975 and the accompanying foreign interventions put an immediate end to these few years of unprecedented economic growth, as an accumulation of destruction, forced migration, loss of trade and tourism, and the increasing division of the country into separately controlled units led to a huge reduction in income and output. The damage and disruption were particularly bad during the first phase of the war, 1975–76, the Israeli invasion and occupation, in 1982–84, and then during the last phase of intense fighting, in 1989–90. During the whole

15 year period, over one million Lebanese emigrated from the country, among them a high proportion of people with professional and technical skills, including 22 percent of the country's doctors.[49] Even more were forced to leave their homes for shorter or longer periods.[50] One result was a substantial reduction in the economically occupied population: from 750,000 in 1975 to just over 450,000 ten years later.[51]

What little compensation there was for the suffering citizens of Lebanon came from three sources: continued remittances, the money sent to support the rival militias, and, most important of all, a dramatic increase in public expenditure which, by 1982, had reached some 37.6 percent of GDP, more or less double the proportion of the early 1970s.[52] Not only did the government keep adding to the numbers on its payroll (including more soldiers) but it also spent large sums on subsidizing the price of such necessities as petrol, sugar, and wheat. Nevertheless, it was only possible to sustain such a policy at a time when tax revenues were in sharp decline by the inflationary process of borrowing more and more from the Central Bank. Hence prices rose dramatically during the 1980s, with inflation reaching a peak of nearly 500 percent in 1987 before falling to some 50 percent at the war's end.[53]

Lebanon's economic performance 1950–1974

Lebanon's first official national income statistics were calculated for 1964 and then only for a number of particular years thereafter. Prior to that there are various unofficial estimates, mostly by economists such as Badre connected with the American University of Beirut. Most are agreed that there was a long period of strong growth at roughly 7 percent a year from 1950 to 1964.[54] However, the United Nations Statistical Office insists on a somewhat lower figure of 5.2 percent between 1961 and 1964.[55] Growth then declined from 1965 to 1970 before picking up again dramatically in the early 1970s, when it expanded at well above 10 percent a year. The movement of per capita income is still more difficult to calculate given the fact that there were no accurate population figures after Lebanon's one and only census, held in 1931. But if Chaib's calculations are more or less correct, it could have increased at something like 3–4 percent over the whole period from 1950 to 1974.[56]

As for changes in the sectoral composition of the national product, the figures show banking and services remaining at somewhere between two-thirds and three-fourths of GNP, with the main change involving a decrease in the contribution of agriculture and an increase in that of industry (see

Table 7.3). In agriculture, the main feature was a major reduction in the labor force, from some 50 percent of the total to 20 percent between 1950 and 1974, accompanied by a movement away from the cultivation of cereals toward higher value crops like fruit and vegetables.[57] Industry's trajectory is more difficult to discern owing to the existence of rival sets of often incompatible data.[58] But, by and large, three tendencies can be identified. One is a steady increase in investment, employment, and output through the 1950s and 1960s, followed by a period of more rapid development in the early 1970s. Second, there was a partial movement toward the introduction of more complex processes, often involving the working up of imported raw materials or spare parts. Hence, although the more traditional lines such as textiles, clothing, and shoes maintained their old importance, new lines such as vehicle assembly and pharmaceuticals developed rapidly as well. Third, the main stimulus to the huge expansion in activity in the early 1970s was the opening up of new markets for Lebanese manufactures in the Gulf.

Growth in the services sector was the result of a rapid expansion in banking and trade. While the number of individual banks (of Lebanese, foreign, or mixed ownership) increased from 17 to 46 in the 1950s and then to 93 at the time of the Intra crash in 1966, the ratio of deposits to national income leapt from 20 to nearly 100 percent during the same period.[59] The system was almost entirely unregulated until the creation of the Superior Banking Council in the wake of the Intra crisis, after which laws were tightened and 14 of the more risky banks forced into liquidation. It was this which created the conditions for the arrival of large Western banks, generally as partners of the existing Lebanese banks, after 1967. As for foreign trade, it provided nearly a third of GDP from 1950 to the early 1970s, a very high proportion compared with Egypt or Syria. Also unusual was the high degree of intra-regional trade with 58 percent of the country's exports going to the Middle East in 1972.[60]

The size and profitability of the services sector was also one of the many reasons why the benefits of economic growth were so badly distributed throughout Lebanese society. Here the IRFED report produces some telling illustrations of sectoral difference. Hence, while commercial, financial, and other services employed 23 percent of the working population, they produced 47 percent of the national product in the late 1950s. By contrast, agriculture then provided work for nearly 50 percent but only contributed 16 percent of GDP.[61] The result was growing rural-to-urban migration, which may well have helped to reduce income differentials without doing much for the overall quality of life. There is also no doubt that the overlap between inequality and ethnicity, and in particular the fact

161

that the poorer districts tended to be inhabited by a majority of Muslim Sunni and Shi'i inhabitants, did much to increase the social tensions, pushing the country towards civil war.

Economic performance during the civil war, 1975–1990

Estimates of the drop in national income from 1975 onward are obviously liable to a considerable margin of error. According to calculations made by Nasser Saidi, GDP had almost halved by the end of 1976 before making a slow recovery until 1980/81, when it stood at some 80 percent of its pre-civil war level.[62] The Israeli invasion then precipitated what Saidi characterizes as another 'downward spiral' in economic activity, followed by a brief recovery and then yet another two years of falling income, in 1989–90. As a result, according to Louis Hobeika of the World Bank, the war ended with GNP down to a third of its 1974 level in constant prices.[63] All sectors of the Lebanese economy were hard hit during the war. Agriculture and industry suffered the most, with the former's contribution to GNP estimated to have fallen from 17 to 14 percent during the war and the latter's from 9 to 7 percent.[64] There was also a huge increase in poverty with rising unemployment and a number of years in the late 1980s when wages tended to lag far behind inflation.[65] To make matters worse, the provision of every type of public and professional service declined precipitously at the same time, whether in the field of education, health, housing, transport, water, and electricity or, above all, personal security.

IRAQ 1946–1990

OIL AND DEVELOPMENT UNDER THE MONARCHY: 1946–1958

After the end of the Second World War, the Iraqi government's economic policy was increasingly dominated by its growing income from oil. This rose steadily from ID 2.3 million ($6.44 million) in 1945 (just over 11 percent of total revenues) to ID 5.3 million ($14.84 million or 15.7 percent) in 1950, and then exploded following the introduction of a 50:50 profit sharing deal with oil companies in 1951, to reach ID 37.4 million ($104.72 million or 47 percent) in 1952 and just under ID 80 million ($224 million or 61.7 percent) in 1958.[66] Control over the expenditure of the entire oil income was given to an eight-man Development Board created in 1950 consisting of six Iraqis and two foreign advisers, one British and one American.

Problems in implementing the board's policies then led to the establishment of a ministry of development in 1953 and a reduction in the proportion of the oil revenues it controlled to 70 percent.[67]

The board soon found itself at the center of a fierce debate about priorities. To begin with it concentrated most of its money and efforts on large works of flood control and water storage on the Tigris and Euphrates. But this led to criticisms that it was neglecting schemes which would lead to an immediate improvement in the lives of Iraq's rural and urban poor. Such arguments found trenchant expression in a report drawn up by the British expert Lord Salter in 1955 in which, after noting the obvious lack of popular support for the board's policies, he called for 'expenditures of a kind that [would] bring quick and clearly visible benefits,' particularly in the fields of housing and the provision of pure drinking water.[68] Some of these suggestions were then incorporated in the revised 1955–59 development plan, re-introduced in 1956, in which the sums allocated to health, welfare, and low-cost dwellings were greatly increased.

Salter also pointed to lack of progress in the government's few pilot schemes designed to provide land for Iraq's 600,000 or so landless families. Six such schemes had only managed to distribute 225,000 dunums (140,000 acres) to 3,434 settlers between 1945 and 1951, while paving the way for people other than peasant cultivators to obtain land.[69] All this suggested to Lord Salter that the government was simply going through the motions in order to divert pressure for a full-scale land reform, a fair comment given the political power of Iraq's landlord class.[70] His observations have since obtained retrospective justification from the fact that, only three years later, in 1958, the monarchy and its supporters were overthrown in a bloody revolution by a regime which, among its first acts, instituted a land reform which swept most of the old landlord class away. Nevertheless, it would only be fair to note that the Development Board was given the almost hopeless task of managing huge sums of money without proper political and administrative support, and in a general environment in which rivalries between international advisory agencies such as the British Development Division based in Beirut, the American Point IV program, and the World Bank, which sent a mission to Iraq in 1951, made consistency of purpose almost impossible.[71]

DEVELOPMENT POLICIES IN A DECADE OF POLITICAL UPHEAVAL, 1958–1968

In the ten years between 1958 and 1968 Iraq experienced four different political regimes: those of Brigadier Qasim (1958–63), the Ba'th Party (1963), 'Abd al-Salam Arif (1963–66), and 'Abd al-Rahman Arif (1966–68). This produced a combination of new policy initiatives and general administrative confusion, as well as forcing successive regimes to cope with a number of problems set in train during the Qasim era, notably confrontations with both the Iraq Petroleum Company (IPC) and the Kurdish population of the north, and an over-ambitious land reform. It was also the case, however, that the frequent change of political regime often left enough space for a few technocratically minded officials to push through a number of quite substantial policy initiatives of their own.[72]

One of the early initiatives of the Qasim regime was the dissolution of the Development Board, a symbolic move designed to signal its intention of adopting radically different policies from its monarchical predecessor. The keystone of these policies was the Land Reform Law of October 1958 which, like the Syrian law of the same year, was much influenced by the Egyptian model, including rigid limits on ownership – 1,000 dunums (618 acres) for irrigated land, 2,000 dunums (1,236 acres) for rain-fed land – and the insistence that its beneficiaries join cooperatives. But as in Syria the land targeted for expropriation was extensive – 8.5 million dunums (5.25 million acres) or 11 times the area appropriated in Egypt in 1952 – and enormously varied in type, while the country had even fewer officials who knew anything about agricultural administration, and almost no one with any experience whatsoever of rural cooperatives. To make matters more difficult, the first stages of the reform were accompanied by fierce resistance in some parts of the country, as well as two years of severe drought. In these circumstances perhaps it was just as well that no effort was made to extend it either to the Kurdish areas, then at the start of a decade and a half of armed rebellion, or to the southern province of Amara where the process of land settlement had long been held up by a series of fierce disputes over title.[73]

Not surprisingly, progress was slow. By September 1963, several months after the violent overthrow of the Qasim regime, only 6 million dunums (3.7 million acres) had been officially sequestered from its former owners, of which less than 6 percent – some 360,000 dunums (222,500 acres) – had been distributed to 29,000 beneficiaries.[74] At the same time the regime had managed to organize just 25 cooperatives, leaving the majority of the new recipients largely unsupported in terms of the provision of

164

seeds, credit, and agricultural machinery. Given problems of this magnitude, the regime soon realized that it had no alternative but to place most of the sequestered land under temporary management, either by the previous owners or their agents, or indeed by almost anyone who could be persuaded to pay a small rent.[75] In these difficult circumstances it seems unlikely that it could have had much success in enforcing the important provisions of the new law regarding rent control, agricultural wages, or the replacement of oral contracts by written sharecropping contracts.

A second major aspect of the Qasim regime's policy was a major reorientation of the development effort towards the investment of much larger sums of money in agriculture, industry, and public housing. These new priorities were set out in a five-year plan, 1961/62–1965/66, directed by a newly created ministry of planning to which 50 percent of oil revenues were assigned.

A final initiative of great future consequence was the passage of Law 80 of 1961 taking back 99.5 percent of the concession areas originally awarded to the IPC group of companies before the Second World War, including what was believed to be the rich North Rumaila field near Basra in the south. This was to initiate over a decade of often acrimonious dispute during which many Iraqis believed that the company was practicing a policy of deliberate under-production in order to reduce revenues and so lower local resistance.[76]

Qasim's successors occupied themselves with the difficult task of trying to complete what he had begun. As far as land reform was concerned, the regime led by 'Abd al-Salam Arif seems to have had considerable success not only in pushing ahead with the program itself but also in continuing another Qasim initiative: the speeded-up distribution of state-owned land in tandem with that seized from the large landowners. By March 1966, the amount of expropriated land had risen to 5.1 million dunums (3.16 million acres) of which 1 million dunums (618,000 acres) had been distributed to 46,292 beneficiaries and a further 2.8 million dunums (1.74 million acres) rented out on, mostly, one-year leases. To this should be added the 1.3 million (800,000 acres) of state land also distributed to 253,835 peasants and the further 4.6 million dunums (2.843 million acres) under temporary management. Progress in the establishment of cooperatives was also accelerated, there being 202 active by March 1966 and another 137 in the process of creation.[77] Two years later, at the fall of the second Arif regime, the figure for sequestrated land had gone up to 3.5 million acres and that for distribution to 1.4 million acres.[78]

Two other initiatives taken during this period are important. The first involved the decision to nationalize 30 large industrial enterprises in 1964, as well as all of the major banks and insurance companies. Once again this was highly imitative of the Egyptian model and, indeed, was designed specifically to meet one of President Nasser's conditions for a union between the two countries, the prior alignment of both countries' systems of economic management and control. Iraqi interest in unity soon cooled, however, leaving the regime with the usual problems of trying to devise an effective mechanism for running a state sector which now produced at least a third of total manufacturing output.[79] Meanwhile, the revised five-year plan called for large sums to be invested in new state factories making a variety of oil derivatives such as petrochemicals, sulfur, plastics, and fertilizer as well as electrical equipment, glass, and pharmaceuticals. However, implementation was slow, often leaving over half of each year's planned allocation unspent.[80]

The second initiative represented an attempt to break the boycott which the IPC had placed on any international cooperation in the development of the North Rumaila field. This involved, first, the creation of the Iraqi National Oil Company (INOC) in 1964, then a deal with the French company ERAP in 1967 to assist INOC in the exploration of the field. However, the second Arif regime was overthrown in July 1968, before further progress could be made.

DEVELOPMENT WITH 'UNLIMITED' CAPITAL, 1968–1980

For some years, the second Ba'thi regime, which seized power in July 1968, was only able to maintain itself by violence and fear, a method of rule which continued even after it had succeeded in creating institutions strong enough to control society and to crush all opposition. Nevertheless, it was soon able to make progress on the all-important oil front, moving quickly to obtain Soviet assistance to develop the North Rumaila field which came into production in 1972. This was closely followed by the nationalization of the IPC's Iraqi assets and then, in 1973, by a final settlement with the company which, among other things, allowed Iraq to market its own oil on international markets.[81] One enormously important result was that the regime was now in a position to profit directly from the first oil price rise of 1973–74, with oil revenues rising dramatically from $6 billion in 1974 to a peak of $26.5 billion in 1980.[82]

Access to funds of such magnitude allowed the Ba'thi regime to spend money on almost anything it wanted: industry and agriculture, education and health, and housing and infrastructure, as well as defense. Targets and priorities were supposed to be established in two successive development plans, 1970–75 and 1976–80, but the available funds were so large that a huge number of different schemes could be pursued all at the same time. This makes it difficult to work out just where the money was going, the more so as, from the mid-1970s onward, the regime's insistence on greater and greater secrecy meant that both the quality and the quantity of official statistics was much reduced.

The major beneficiary of the spending wave was, inevitably, the state sector itself, with the numbers in government employment increasing from 400,000 in 1972 to 600,000 in 1978, of whom 16 percent were to be found in large public industrial establishments and 23 percent in the ministry of the interior, with another 200,000 in the armed forces.[83] Another major beneficiary was the construction sector, where contracts were divided between foreign and local firms, both public and private. To begin with it was the former that received the largest share, winning contracts worth at least $14 billion by 1978 according to a US government estimate.[84] But over time, a substantial Iraqi construction industry came into existence, with many well-connected entrepreneurs able to start up a business with the help of cheap government credit, subsidized raw materials, and access to the import of duty-free machinery.[85] There was also a large knock-on effect in the form of a huge increase in the demand for local inputs of construction materials and interior fitments.

Oil money was also used to push on with the work of completing the agrarian reform. First, the new Law 117 of 1970 put further limits on private ownership while the temporary settlement of the Kurdish insurrection in 1975 allowed the reform to be extended to the north as well. As a result another 4 million dunums (2.47 million acres) was expropriated, bringing the area taken over by the state since 1958 to about half of all Iraq's cultivated land.[86] Second, the process of distribution was once again speeded up. Hence by 1981 a final total of almost 10 million dunums (6.18 million acres) had been handed over to some 264,000 beneficiaries.[87] However, as Habib Ishow notes, many of these same beneficiaries soon abandoned their new plots in the hope of finding better living conditions in the city.[88] Land which remained undistributed was either rented out on short-term contracts or subject to the new experiment of creating eight state and 78 collective farms, most of them in the north.[89] Lastly, there was a parallel emphasis on the creation of new agricultural cooperatives, bringing the total to just under 2,000 by 1979. These contained 355,000 members and controlled 13.2 million dunums (8.16 million acres) of both expropriated and state land.[90]

According to official figures, investment in industry increased from ID 225 million in 1974 to over 1.35 billion in 1978, and agriculture from ID

190 million to ID 495 million.[91] In industry, it is difficult to discern any particular rationale behind this expenditure except to deepen the industrial base by the construction of factories making iron and steel, electronics, and a great variety of petrochemicals. But agricultural policy had the stated aim of reducing the need for imports and of achieving self-sufficiency in food by the early 1980s.[92] An evaluation of such policies follows in the next section.

THE PERFORMANCE OF THE IRAQI ECONOMY 1945–1980

The first detailed estimate of Iraqi national income was made by the government statistician K.G. Fenelon for the years 1950–56.[93] This was followed by a more sophisticated calculation by the economist Khair al-Din Haseeb, for 1953–61.[94] Both series reflect a rapid rate of growth triggered by the increased expenditures out of oil income: 11 percent a year for Fenelon, 7.4 percent for Haseeb. This contrasts with a period of what must have been a low or negative growth in the immediate postwar period characterized by shortages, high inflation, and a serious financial crisis in 1948–49 following a particularly bad harvest and the abnormal government expenditures occasioned by Iraq's participation in the Palestine war of 1948. Rates of growth fell slightly in the 1960s and early 1970s – one estimate gives a 4.8 percent annual increase in GDP 1964–72 – but then took off again in 1974 with national income tripling (at current prices) between 1974 and 1979.[95]

The impact on per capita income was dramatic. In 1950 Iraq had one of the lowest incomes per head in the world, some ID 30 ($84) a year according to the World Bank mission. By 1970 this had risen to ID 103.9 ($290.9) before soaring to ID 825.9 ($2,312.5) in 1979.[96]

Figures for growth in GDP also illustrate the continued dominance of the oil sector over the rest of the economy. Haseeb puts the contribution of oil at 45.7 percent in 1953 and 49.7 percent in 1961.[97] There was then a slight fall in the 1960s – to 35.1 percent in 1964 and 30.3 percent in 1969 – before another period of domination when the contribution of oil reached a high of 61.4 percent in 1979.[98] As far as the other sectors were concerned, the main trend was a continuous decline in the contribution of agriculture, from 32.3 percent in 1953 to 20.8 percent in 1965 and 6.8 percent in 1978. The share of manufacturing remained almost constant, however, starting at 7.1 percent in 1953 (including refining) and ending at 5.3 percent in 1979 (see Table 7.4). The picture in terms of employment is somewhat different, of course, given the fact that the oil sector required so few workers. Here agriculture remained much the largest employer with 42 percent of the labor force in 1981.[99]

Turning to the performance of the different sectors, an evaluation of the agricultural sector is, if anything, even more difficult than in the case of Syria. Similar problems concerning the definition of the cultivated area, the proportion of fallow land, and the enormous annual variations in output due to the weather are exacerbated by the even more unsatisfactory statistical data. A good guess is that the cultivated area had reached some 22 million dunums (13.6 million acres) by the 1980s of which nearly half was under irrigation.[100] But given the government's failure to do anything to reduce the amount of fallow land, it is likely that only some 60 percent was cropped in any one year.[101] In these circumstances probably the best guide to the situation is provided by the figures for the amount of land placed under wheat and barley, crops which were grown on 80 to 90 percent of the available land. Here the picture is very mixed, with only a small increase in the area devoted to wheat between 1948–52 and 1979–81 and the area placed under barley staying more or less the same (Table 7.5). Data concerning production suggest an increase in wheat yields during this same period but not as much as in neighboring Syria and Iran.[102] For the rest, the most noteworthy trends were a small increase in the area allocated to rice during the 1970s and a larger increase in that allocated to fruit and vegetables. Overall the one bright spot is the fact that Iraq kept its lead as by far the largest supplier of dates to the international market, providing 80 percent in the 1970s.[103]

The reasons for this relatively dismal performance are apparent. On the one hand, the productivity of the soil continued to decline due to over-watering, bad management and, sometimes, over-use. On the other, the land reform and other government interventions created enormous disruptions in existing practices without finding a formula which would ensure that the soil was farmed significantly better than before. This was something to which the inadequacy of the cooperative systems, the short-term rental contracts for state land, and, particularly in the 1970s, the heavy-handed party and bureaucratic control over the agricultural administration all made their own harmful contributions.[104]

The performance of the industrial sector was somewhat better, at least in the 1950s, when the early stages of import substitution allowed rapid rates of growth and a structure in which the usual concentration on food processing, textiles, and construction materials was accompanied by the introduction of some more advanced, oil-related technologies. Thereafter the nationalization of the larger factories produced another familiar pattern in which a relatively inefficient public sector coexisted with two quite

169

different types of private sector activity, one producing more or less the same range of goods as the public but more efficiently and in smaller units, the other largely parasitic on the public and encouraged by larger and larger government contracts.[105] In these circumstances it is not difficult to disagree with the Penroses' conclusion, written in 1977, that Iraq's rate of industrial growth was commensurate neither with the size of investments made nor the increase in domestic demand.[106]

How much of this pattern can be explained by reference to some notion of 'rentierism,' in which state access to large revenues from oil distorts developments in the rest of the economy?[107] While recognizing that there is unlikely to be a single set of causes, increased reliance on oil had a significant influence on economic activity on at least two levels. One involved government policy and the ways in which large revenues from oil either allowed successive regimes to avoid serious problems in the non-oil sectors, or to try to solve them simply by throwing money in their direction. The second related to structure and the ways in which, in an oil economy, rising incomes and wages, inflation, and an over-valued currency combine to favor imports over domestically produced goods, services over production, town over country, and consumption over savings. But other, more specifically Iraqi factors, are also important, notably the huge obstacles in the way of creating an efficient system of irrigation and drainage and the particular character of the post-1968 Ba'thi regime with its would-be totalitarian project of bringing all aspects of economic and social life under political control.

It follows that whatever benefits the Iraqis received from the oil-powered development have to be understood in strictly economic terms. From the 1960s onward, increased spending on health, education, and public housing had a progressive impact on levels of literacy, on disease, on life expectancy, and on raising the standards of living of both rural and urban poor. Official statistics show a three-fold increase in the numbers of physicians per 1,000 population between 1960 and 1980, and a move toward a situation in which all children attended primary school and nearly 60 percent went through secondary education as well.[108] But all such progress was then thrown into doubt by the eight-year war with Iran begun with the Iraqi invasion of October 1980.

THE ECONOMY DURING AND AFTER THE IRAN-IRAQ WAR, 1980–1990

Analysis of the performance of the economy during the war with Iran, 1980–88, presents a great number of problems, including the absence of almost any official statistics until the publication of the government's official *Statistical Yearbook* for 1988.[109] Foreign observers have thus had to make do with more than the usual guesses, extrapolations, and estimates. The general consensus seems to be that national income and per capita national income peaked somewhere in the early 1980s and then began a rapid decline. For example, Abbas al-Nasrawi quotes figures which show that per capita GNP dropped from $1,674 in 1980 to $1,148 in 1988 (at constant 1975 prices).[110] The reasons for this were twofold. One was the vast cost of the war itself, which necessitated the mobilization of 44 divisions and up to one million men, over 20 percent of the labor force.[111] The other was the unfortunate combination of falling oil prices and the reduction of Iraq's exports from some 3.5 million barrels a day to no more than 700,00–900,000 as the result of the destruction of its tanker terminal in the Shatt al-Arab, and then the blockage of two of its three major outlets: the Gulf and the trans-Syrian pipeline, which was closed by the Asad regime in 1981.[112] This left only the trans-Turkish pipeline for regular use.

During the first two or three years of the war, Saddam Hussein's regime used its vast financial reserves to practice a policy of 'guns and butter' – or business as usual – as a way of ensuring civilian support. However, once oil revenues began to fall and the war moved back to Iraq's own soil in 1982, it was necessary to cut non-military expenditures as well as to find new sources of funds. Far and away the most important source was loans from the Gulf states anxious to use Iraq as a shield against Iranian expansionism towards the Arab world. Other loans were forthcoming from Western governments and companies anxious to secure the goodwill of the Iraqi regime in the hope of winning lucrative contracts at the war's end. One estimate puts the combined total of all such advances at $80 billion.[113]

Another, small, source of funds was Iraqi private capital, which was gradually encouraged to play a more and more significant role as the war progressed. This began in the agricultural sector in 1983 with the sale of state-owned enterprises and an accelerated program of distributing both state and land reform land to private individuals. The result was that, by 1989, almost all Iraqi land was either privately owned (53 percent) or rented from the state (46 percent) with a concomitant relaxation of most bureaucratic controls.[114] This policy was then greatly expanded, from 1987 onward, in a process of selective liberalization which went much further and much faster than the policy initiated in Syria at just about the same time. Faced with a whole host of problems at the war's end, including the need to maintain payments on its wartime debts as well as to finance a policy of reconstruction, demobilization, and the general transfer to a peacetime economy, the regime initiated a wholesale sell-off of 70 state-owned enterprises accompanied by other measures to encourage private

171

investment, including a ten-year tax holiday and the dissolution of labor unions.[115]

Just how far this policy might have gone if it had been allowed to continue for a few more years was a matter for intense speculation at the time.[116] As in the case of Syria, there was no intention of relaxing state control over the key sectors of the economy, or of allowing any greater degree of political participation. Nevertheless, the speed and wide-ranging nature of the new measures would certainly have produced significant economic consequences had they not been interrupted by the Iraqi invasion of Kuwait in August 1990. As it is, they are now viewed as part of an unsuccessful process of trying to obtain new foreign exchange to meet Iraq's huge international debt as well as to pay for the costs of postwar reconstruction and partial demobilization. And it was Saddam Hussein's impatience with these same policies which is believed to have led him to try to persuade the Gulf states, and Kuwait in particular, to forgive some of their wartime loans, a species of international bullying which rapidly gave way to the invasion of Kuwait and so the second Gulf War.

Notes on Chapter 7
Full details of all sources are in the Bibliography

1   The reserves of gold and foreign currencies held in Paris included those used as backing for the Syrian/Lebanese lira as well as those representing payment for services obtained by the French during the Second World War. See Asfour, *Syria*, pp 45–50.
2   The initial free market exchange rate of the Lebanese lira was LL1 = $0.29. This had moved to $0.31 by 1967; Badre, 'Economic Development of Lebanon,' p 167.
3   Asfour, *Syria*, pp 50–2.
4   Saba, 'The Syro-Lebanese Customs Union,' pp 91–108.
5   *Ibid.*, pp 95–6; Durand, 'La rupture de l'union syro-libanaise,' pp 306–9.
6   Lebanon received 135,000 Palestinian refugees and some LL60 million ($17.4 million) in Palestinian capital (equal to 7 percent of GDP): Basile, 'La Vocation régionale de la place financière de Beyrouth,' p 146. Syria received 85,000 refugees; World Bank, *The Economic Development of Syria*, p 191.
7   According to the World Bank report, 25 percent of Syria's exports went to Lebanon in the early 1950s while Syria was a market for 60 percent of Lebanon's; World Bank, *The Economic Development of Syria*, p 13.
8   *Ibid.*, pp 46–8, 70–1, 129–30.
9   Makdisi, 'Some Aspects of Syrian Economic Growth, 1945–1957,' Table 1.
10 Diab, 'The First Five-Year Plan of Syria,' Table 1.
11 Dabbagh, 'Agrarian Reform in Syria,' pp 6–9.

12 *Ibid.*, pp 11–12.
13 *Ibid.*, p 7.
14 Hannoyer and Seurat, *Etat et secteur public industriel en Syrie*, pp 23–4; Chatelus, 'La Croissance économique: mutation des structures et dynamisme du déséquilibre,' pp 239–41.
15 Meyer, 'Economic Development in Syria since 1970,' p 40.
16 Manners and Sagafi-Nejad, 'Agricultural Development in Syria,' p 272.
17 *Ibid.*, p 274.
18 There were at least 67,000 Syrians working in the Gulf states by the early 1980s; Birks and Sinclair, 'The Socio-Economic Determinants of Intra-Regional Migration,' Table 1.
19 For example, Sadowski, 'Patronage and the Party in Contemporary Syria,' pp 171–2.
20 Heydemann estimates that Arab aid declined from $1.6 billion in 1979 to some $500 million a year in the early 1980s; 'The Political Logic of Economic Rationality,' p 18.
21 See, for example, Heydemann's argument, *ibid.*, p 19.
22 *Ibid.*, pp 17–18.
23 For a good account of the slow progress in creating joint ventures in the agricultural sector see Executive Communicator, *Business Brief: Syria*, No. 96002 (July–September 1996), pp 4, 14.
24 Perthes, 'The Syrian Private Industrial and Commercial Sectors and the State,' pp 211–13.
25 Asfour, *Syria*, pp 15–17.
26 Diab, 'National Income Accounting Practices in Syria,' pp 121–3.
27 Hansen, 'Economic Development of Syria,' pp 336–7n.
28 World Bank, *World Development Report 1984*, Table 19; *World Development Report 1991*, Table 26.
29 Chatelus, 'La Croissance économique,' p 263.
30 Hansen, *Syria*, pp 339, 341–2.
31 Manners and Sagafi-Nejad, 'Agricultural Development in Syria,' pp 264–8.
32 *Ibid.*, Table 14.3, p 265; Metral, 'Le Monde rural syrien à l'ère des réformes (1958–1978),' p 297.
33 Hansen, 'Economic Development of Syria,' p 346.
34 Metral, 'Le Monde rural syrien à l'ère des réformes (1958–1978),' pp 315–16.
35 Meyer, 'Economic Development in Syria since 1970,' p 52.
36 For example, Longuenesse, 'L'Industrialisation et sa significance sociale,' p 349.
37 This is the author's interpretation of the data to be found in Longuenesse, *ibid.*, and Hannoyer and Seurat, *Etat et secteur public industriel en Syrie*, pp 76–7.
38 World Bank, *Economic Development of Syria*, pp 36–7; Hinnebusch, *Peasant and Bureaucracy in Ba'thist Syria*, pp 96–7.
39 *Ibid.*, p 11.
40 Seurat, 'Les Populations, l'état et la société,' p 137; World Bank, *World Development Report 1991*, Table 29.
41 Shehadi, *The Idea of Lebanon*, pp 7–8.
42 Badre, 'The National Income of Lebanon,' Table 1, p 13. The estimate for agricultural production is particularly shaky, as Badre himself acknowledges: *ibid.*, p 13.
43 Dubar and Nasr, *Les Classes sociales au Liban*, p 71.
44 One estimate puts the amount of flight capital at LL110 million from Egypt, LL150 million from Iraq, and LL300–600 million from Syria: quoted in Basile, 'La Vocation régionale de la place financière de Beyrouth,' p 76.

45 Lebanon, Ministère du plan, *Besoins et possibilités de développement du Liban: étude préliminaire*, 1, p 19 and 2, Table 7.

46 For example, Owen, 'The Political Economy of Grand Liban, 1920–1970,' p 30.

47 From study of Intra's 1965 balance sheet by N. Azhari, *L'Evolution du système économique libanais, ou la fin de laissez-faire*, p 28.

48 Hudson, *The Precarious Republic*, p 95.

49 Labaki, 'L'Emigration externe,' p 46 and Table 3; al-Khalil, 'Economic Developments in Lebanon since 1982,' p 86.

50 Abou-Rjaili, 'L'Emigration forcée des populations à l'intérieur du Liban, 1975–1986,' Table 2.

51 Mourad, 'L'Emploi et ses problèmes,' p 37.

52 Saidi, *Economic Consequences of the War in Lebanon*, Table 4.

53 al-Khalil, 'Economic Developments in Lebanon since 1982,' p 87.

54 Badre, 'The Economic Development of Lebanon,' p 180; Khalaf, *Economic Implications of the Size of Nations with Special Reference to Lebanon*, p 163.

55 IMF, *International Financial Statistics*, p 198.

56 Chaib, 'The Export Performance of a Small, Open, Developing Country,' p 11.

57 Badre, 'The Economic Development of Lebanon,' pp 164–5.

58 Bertrand, Boudjikanian, and Picaudou, *L'Industrie libanaise et les marchés arabes du Golfe*, pp 5–8.

59 Ducruet, *Les Capitaux européens*, pp 415–16; Paix, 'La Portée speciale des activités tertiaires de commandement économique au Liban,' p 153.

60 Nasr, 'Backdrop to Civil War,' p 4.

61 Lebanon, Ministère du plan, *Besoins et possibilités de développement du Liban: étude préliminaire*, 1, Table 30.

62 Saidi, *Economic Consequences of the War in Lebanon*, Table 2.

63 Hobeika, 'Key Issues in the Reconstruction of Lebanon,' p 3.

64 *Ibid.*, Charts 1 and 2.

65 al-Khalil, 'Economic Developments in Lebanon since 1982,' pp 87–9; Labaki, 'L'Emigration externe,' p 41.

66 Batatu, *The Old Social Classes and the Revolutionary Movements of Iraq*, Table 6/2.

67 Kingston, 'Pioneers of Development, 1945–1961,' pp 221–93: Penrose and Penrose, *Iraq*, pp 168–81.

68 Quoted in Penrose and Penrose, *Iraq*, p 172.

69 Warriner, *Land Reform and Development in the Middle East*, pp 158–61.

70 Quoted by Ionides, *Divide and Lose*, p 206. Ionides was a former member of the Development Board and one of its strongest critics.

71 Kingston, 'Pioneers of Development,' pp 238–9 and 248; contains a good account of the politics of development in Iraq at this time.

72 This point is noted by Penrose and Penrose, for example, in *Iraq*, pp 460–70. They are particularly valuable witnesses as they were personally acquainted with many of the technocrats in question.

73 *Ibid.*, p 455; Warriner, *Land Reform in Principle and Practice*, pp 92–3, 99–101.

74 Penrose and Penrose, *Iraq*, p 246.

75 Langley, 'Iraq,' pp 186–7.

76 For example, Haseeb, 'Towards a National Oil Policy in Iraq,' pp 1–3.

77 Warriner, *Land Reform in Principle*, pp 89–91; Penrose and Penrose, *Iraq*, p 455.

78 Farouk-Sluglett and Sluglett, *Iraq*, p 101.

79   *Ibid.*, Table 7.3.
80   Owen, 'The Economic Aspects of Revolution in the Middle East,' Table 2; Badre, 'The Economic Development of Iraq,' pp 298–9.
81   The Basra Petroleum Company was not fully nationalized until 1975.
82   Richards and Waterbury, *Political Economy of the Middle East*, Table 3.5.
83   Farouk-Sluglett and Sluglett, *Iraq*, p 249.
84   Springborg, 'Bathism in Practice,' p 195.
85   Farouk-Sluglett and Sluglett, *Iraq*, p 242; Farouk-Sluglett, 'The Meaning of Infitah in Iraq,' p 43; al-Khafaji, 'The Parasitic Basis of the Ba'thist Regime,' pp 75–7.
86   Farouk-Sluglett and Sluglett, *Iraq*, pp 244–5; Penrose and Penrose, *Iraq*, p 454; Ockerman and Samano, 'The Agricultural Development of Iraq,' p 192.
87   Official figures cited in Ishow, 'The Development of Agrarian Policies since 1958,' p 186.
88   *Ibid.*
89   Farouk-Sluglett and Sluglett, *Iraq*, pp 244–5.
90   Ockerman and Samano, 'The Agricultural Development of Iraq,' p 191.
91   Farouk-Sluglett and Sluglett, *Iraq*, Table 7/15.
92   Springborg, 'Bathism in Practice,' p 194.
93   Fenelon, *Iraq*.
94   Haseeb, *The National Income of Iraq, 1953–61*.
95   Penrose and Penrose, *Iraq*, Table V, p 496; Farouk-Sluglett and Sluglett, *Iraq*, p 232.
96   *Ibid.*
97   Haseeb, *The National Income of Iraq, 1953–61*, Table 5, p 20.
98   Badre, 'The Economic Development of Lebanon,' Table 6/2; Farouk-Sluglett and Sluglett, *Iraq*, Table 7/14.
99   Ockerman and Samano, 'The Agricultural Development of Iraq,' p 190.
100 Beaumont, 'Environmental Issues,' p 125.
101 Springborg, 'Bathism in Practice,' p 196.
102 Ockerman and Samano, 'The Agricultural Development of Iraq,' p 200; Beaumont, 'Environmental Issues,' p 127.
103 Ockerman and Samano, 'The Agricultural Development of Iraq,' p 201.
104 Springborg, 'Bathism in Practice,' pp 202–6.
105 Penrose and Penrose, *Iraq*, pp 466–7; Farouk-Sluglett and Sluglett, *Iraq*, p 221; al-Khafaji, 'The Parasitic Basis of the Ba'thist Regime,' pp 75–82.
106 Penrose and Penrose, *Iraq*, pp 423–4.
107 There is a large literature on the subject beginning with Mahdavy, 'Patterns and Problems of Economic Development in Rentier States,' pp 428–67. See also the particular contributions to Beblawi and Luciani (eds), *The Rentier State*.
108 World Bank, *World Development Report* 1984, Tables 24 and 25.
109 The 1988 Statistical Yearbook is used extensively by Chaudhry in her influential 'On the Way to the Market,' pp 14–23.
110 al-Nasrawi, 'Economic Devastation, Underdevelopment and Outlook,' p 82.
111 Iraqi sources quoted by al-Khafaji, 'War as a Vehicle for the Rise and Demise of a State-Controlled Society,' p 11.
112 Farouk-Sluglett and Sluglett, *Iraq*, Table 7/9.
113 Issawi, 'Iraq, 1800–1991,' p 82.
114 Chaudhry, 'On the Way to the Market,' pp 15, 18.
115 *Ibid.*, p 15.
116 For example, *ibid.*, pp 18–23.

8

The Economies of Israel, Jordan, and the West Bank/Gaza 1946–1990

INTRODUCTION

The government of mandatory Palestine began the post-1945 period with a program of reconstruction similar to those introduced in other parts of Britain's colonial empire. This focused on the transition from a wartime to a peacetime economy with special emphasis on the demobilization of the thousands of Jews and Palestinian Arabs who had served in the British armed forces and the management of the pent-up demand for consumer goods in such a way as to allow a continuous reduction in inflation. Meanwhile, the economy benefited considerably from the renewal of citrus exports to Europe as well as from considerable new investment in manufacturing and construction by both Jewish and Arab entrepreneurs.

Such activities had to take place in an increasingly difficult political and military climate, however, as the concerted drive towards Jewish statehood met with growing Arab resistance, manifest, for example, in the imposition of a boycott of Palestinian goods initiated by the Arab League in August 1945. Then, as the conflict intensified, economic activity was hampered still further by the imposition of martial law, the destruction of property, and the sabotage of public utilities, as well as a further pulling apart of the two communities to such an extent that by December 1947, according to the British High Commissioner, Jewish and Arab markets had become 'quite separate.'[1] Finally, as a result of months of internal fighting, followed in May 1948 by the formal establishment of the state of Israel and the military intervention of the surrounding Arab states, the territory of mandatory Palestine was split into three quite separate entities: Israel, the hill country between Tulkarm and Hebron (the West Bank) which passed into Jordanian administration, and the Gaza Strip controlled by Egypt.

The political division of Palestine was accompanied by a huge transfer of population and of the ownership of economic assets, with some 700,000 of the Arab inhabitants of the new Israel fleeing their homes to become refugees in the West Bank, Gaza, and the neighboring Arab countries, leaving their land and property to be confiscated by the Israeli government and over 400 of their villages to be destroyed.[2] All that remained was a population of some 160,000, the majority living in 100 or so villages in the Galilee and around Jerusalem but with some 20 percent in the towns and 15,000 Bedouin in the Negev.[3]

THE ECONOMY OF ISRAEL 1948–1990

The economic history of Israel during this period divides easily in half, with two decades of rapid growth followed by a period of transition between the 1967 and 1973 Middle Eastern wars after which progress was very much slower (see Table 8.1). As Metzer notes, there was a relatively smooth rate of growth of GDP and GDP per capita, from 1952 to 1961 (9.2 and 5.2 percent respectively) and then again from 1962 to 1971 (9.0 and 5.4 percent). But after that a sharp downward trend set in, with GDP only growing at an average 4.2 percent 1972–1981, and 3.2 percent 1980–1989.[4]

1948–1967

The economic performance of the Israeli economy during the first 20 years of the country's existence was largely shaped by two sets of related factors. One was the special character of the new state itself, with its heavy emphasis on Jewish immigration, its strong links with the United States and world Jewry, and its hostile relations with its Arab neighbors. The second was the type of economic structure created before independence combined with its continued domination by certain pre-state institutions and organizations, notably the Histadrut (The General Federation of Jewish Labor) and a variety of large public enterprises grouped together in what was known as the Labor Economy. Let us examine each of these in turn.

From its inception, the new state of Israel actively promoted Jewish immigration, with 100,000 new immigrants arriving in the first six months after independence, another 250,000 in 1949, and a total of 687,000 by the end of 1951, doubling the existing Jewish population to 1.4 million.[5] At first, the majority of these new migrants came from Europe but by 1949–50 nearly half were from the Jewish communities of the Middle East and North Africa, rising to almost three-fourths by 1951. Some were housed in the 50,000 or so abandoned Arab houses, others in 20 'development' towns established between 1948 and 1954 along Israel's new borders and in the Galilee and the Negev.[6] Immigration continued at a high level for the next two decades, redoubling the population again by the end of the 1960s. Although this was a large drain on resources in the first few years, there is strong reason to believe that it was this same wave of immigration which was partly responsible for the high rates of economic growth of these years, through the market it created for housing, public buildings, and consumer durables.[7]

Another important feature of the Israeli economy was the high level of capital inflows from three major sources: world Jewry, the US government, and, from 1953 onward, the reparations paid by West Germany with respect to the loss of Jewish lives and property during the Nazi period. Taken together, these amounted to just over $6 billion during the period 1949–65, of which over two-thirds consisted of unilateral transfers which required no repayment of either interest or principal.[8] The significance of this assistance can be seen easily from the fact that it contributed about a sixth of GNP during the 1950s while allowing Israel to finance a huge import surplus throughout the whole period up to 1967.[9] For most analysts of the Israeli economy, it was this massive capital inflow which was the major factor underlying the first two decades of rapid growth.[10]

The final formative feature was the state of belligerence between Israel and its neighbors. This involved high levels of military spending as well as many other expenses involved in the maintenance of national security, including the willingness to ignore questions of profit and economic advantage when it came to settlement of immigrants or the location of new industrial enterprises. As writers on the Israeli economy repeatedly demonstrate, it is difficult to provide an exact calculation of such expenses, the more so as many of them remain a government secret. This point is made clearly by Nadav Halevi and Ruth Klinov-Malul in support of their estimate that defense (widely understood) took up some 6–7 percent of national resources between 1950/51 and 1965, with a brief jump to 11 percent in the year of the Suez War, 1956/57.[11] Another, more impressionistic, estimate suggests that military-related expenditures accounted for half of the ordinary Israeli budget in the early 1950s.[12] It should also noted that for reasons of national security members of the Palestinian Arab population were placed under military government from 1948 to 1965, losing perhaps two-thirds of their agricultural land in the process, and only being allowed to enter the bottom of the Israeli labor market as wage workers from the late 1950s onward.[13]

Turning to the structure of the Israeli economy, this too had a number of unusual features. To begin with the manufacturing sector provided so large a proportion of the national product – over 24 percent in 1951 – as to place Israel in the category of industrializing nations according to contemporary world standards.[14] Furthermore, Israeli agriculture combined an unusually small share of the labor force – 14 percent in 1948 – with particularly high factor productivity, a reflection of the emphasis placed on intensive methods of production in the mandatory period, particularly dairy farming, vegetables, and poultry.[15] These features continued to dominate after independence in spite of the initial emphasis on the settlement of new immigrants on land taken over from its previous Arab owners. Hence, although there was a huge expansion of the cultivated area from 1.65 million dunums (412,500 acres) in 1949 to 4.13 million (just over 1 million acres) in 1965, and although increased investment in irrigation and mechanization encouraged agricultural output to increase at an extraordinary 12 percent a year during the same period, the sector never employed more than 17 percent of the labor force, while its contribution to NDP fell from 11.4 percent in 1952 to only 8.5 percent in 1965.[16] As for industry, its share increased only slightly – to some 24–25 percent in the early 1960s – leaving government and services as by far the largest sector at around 50 percent.[17]

At the heart of the economy was the labor sector, managed and controlled through the period by a series of Mapai party-dominated governments under the leadership of David Ben Gurion. During the 1950s the Histadrut and its associated enterprises employed some 25 percent of the economically active population and played a key role in the settlement of migrants and the development of Israel's economic resources through such

179

organizations as Sol Boneh, which built over half of the 268,000 housing units put up between 1948 and 1957.[18] Such was its size and impact that Histadrut enterprises alone provided some 18 percent of NDP in 1953 and just over 20 percent between 1957 and 1960.[19] If we add the public sector, with its heavy concentration of capital-intensive industries such as mining, chemicals, and refining, these two major components of the Labor Economy provided just over two-fifths of the national product during the same decade.[20]

Control of this great concentration of economic power also provided the basis for a centralized system of economic management characterized by extensive state intervention and a huge battery of rules and regulations. Hence, although it was necessary to preserve the notion of a 'mixed economy' in order to attract foreign investment, particularly from the United States, the private sector was kept severely in check through the award of import licenses and special subsidies, largely to firms which agreed to undertake investments within the guidelines for economic development established by the government itself.[21] Banks also became part of the same system through their role as intermediaries for the allocation of public funds.[22]

It followed too that Israeli economic goals were defined largely in nation-building terms with a preference for rapid expansion, employment creation, and the dispersal of population, and no particular concern for profit maximization or the question of where the money for future developments was to be found. Such policies, however successful they might have been in the medium term, led inevitably to high rates of inflation and periodic balance of payments crises, triggering off fierce debates between those dubbed the 'idealists,' who were willing to pay any price to achieve their political aims, and those known as the 'economists,' who argued for more orthodox methods of economic management.[23]

By and large, it was the idealists who held the whip hand. But there were two occasions which saw the introduction of what was known as a 'New Economic Policy' in order to deal with a particularly pressing crisis. The first was in 1951–52, when the government engineered a short period of deflation by stopping its borrowing from the banking system and restricting private credit, thus producing a temporary fall in imports.[24] The second began tentatively in 1962 with a devaluation of the Israeli shekel and then continued more forcefully from 1965 onwards as the government made a concerted effort to squeeze the domestic market, including the bloated construction industry, with little regard for rising unemployment or an absolute decline in investment.[25] In retrospect, this can be seen as an attempt to deal with what then seemed like basic features of the Israeli economic scene, notably a great slowing down in the levels of both immigration and outside aid. But, in the event, such concerns were rendered nugatory by the entirely new situation created by unexpected political and military crisis with Egypt in May 1967 and the outbreak of the June war.

1967–1983

The economic impact of the 1967 war was enormous. To begin with, Israel's occupation of the West Bank and the Gaza Strip brought all of the territory of mandatory Palestine once again under a single political authority. In doing so it also opened up these same districts as markets for Israeli goods and as a source of mainly unskilled labor. By 1973 there were 65,000 Palestinians employed in Israel proper, a figure which had grown to some 90,000 by the late 1970s, or just over 7 percent of the total work force.[26] A second consequence of the war was the huge impetus given to defense spending supported, for the most part, by an increase in American aid, much of it tied directly to the purchase of military equipment. Hence, in the three years from 1967 to 1970, Israel received $4.3 billion in official transfers from abroad, a sum equivalent to two-thirds of all the assistance it had been given over the previous two decades.[27] Aid payments continued at the same high level for the rest of the 1970s, averaging just over $3 billion a year between 1971 and 1982, the greater part of it coming from US government grants and loans.[28] This, in turn, helped to push up defense expenditure to some 22 percent of GNP between 1968 and 1972 and then as high as 28–29 percent between 1974 and 1978 in the immediate aftermath of the 1973 war.[29]

The initial impact of these new factors was to pull the economy out of recession as Israel's idle factors of production and underutilized capacities were galvanized by the huge surge in war-induced demand.[30] But then, after only a few years, GDP growth slowed down again and remained at what was, historically, the very low level of 4.2 percent a year between 1972 and 1981 or 1.6 percent per capita.[31] Just why this should have happened became one of the central issues of Israeli economic analysis, leading to a number of interesting hypotheses.

One point on which all are agreed concerns the importance of the external shocks which buffeted the economy between 1967 and 1973, notably the two wars and the continuous increase in the international price of oil which pushed the country's energy bill from something like 1 percent of GNP in the 1960s to over 7 percent between 1973 and 1979.[32] There is general agreement too about the significance of two other new factors: evidence of a considerable underutilization of capital in the manu-facturing sector and of a dramatic fall in the annual rate of increase of productivity from 4.2 percent between 1961 and 1972 to 0.6 percent between 1973 and 1981.[33] In addition, many analysts note the role of gov-ernment policy in encouraging the rapid expansion of an Israeli version of a military-industrial complex dominated by 100 or so large firms, the majority of which were involved, directly or indirectly, in making weapons systems and other defense related equipment.[34] Some, like the Israeli Aircraft Industry (IAI) and the Israeli Military Industry (IMI), were state-owned, others belonged to the Histadrut, while perhaps half were in private hands although with strong links with the government establishment.

How does all this fit together? For some, like Yoram Ben-Porath, the explanation lies quite simply in the difficulty the economy experienced in adjusting to the shocks, particularly at a time of strong inflation (55 per-cent in 1972–80) when the price system was incapable of giving the signals which would allow a rapid adjustment to a new pattern of resource utili-zation.[35] As he notes, the real cost of certain key inputs such as wages, the rate of interest, and the exchange rate of the Israeli shekel, were maintained at levels which led to a serious misallocation of existing resources.[36] For others, the answer lies more directly in the industrial structure itself, with the largest firms being able to maintain their profits and to purchase new equipment regardless of their stagnating output through privileged access to government contracts and ever more generous subsidies.[37] However, cer-tainly the most satisfactory approach is the more multi-dimensional one adopted by Jacob Metzer. He combines an emphasis on the external shocks and the impact of increased defense spending in the 1970s with an exami-nation of some of the more deep-rooted structural changes taking place in the Israeli economy. Chief among these is the end of a long process by which the training and education received by the post-1948 immigrants was translated, over time, into high productivity in the 1960s before more or less working itself out in the early 1970s as immigration slowed almost to a halt.[38]

An emphasis on structure can also be used to illuminate certain other unusual features of the Israeli economy. One influential notion has been that of its growing 'maturity,' an idea which depends in part on certain developments peculiar to Israel itself, in part on the use of various cross-country comparisons.[39] As far as the former aspect is concerned, econo-mists point out that, at its inception, the new state already possessed the basic structure of an industrializing economy and that this permitted rapid growth for over two decades, but at the expense of the creation of many types of vested interests which, just as in the market democracies of

Western Europe, severely constrained the government's ability to negotiate the shocks and changes of the 1970s.[40] As for the use of international comparison, here the first question to be decided is which set of countries to use. As far as the World Bank is concerned, Israel is conventionally located in a band of 'Upper Middle Income' (UMI) economies ranging from Syria to Iraq. But an equally good case could be made for comparing it with the 'Industrial Market Economies' (IME) with which, by 1982, it shared a number of important features. Its per capita income was then only a little less than that of Ireland and Spain while its economic structure, for example the contribution of agriculture, industry, and services to GDP, was much closer to that of the IMEs than to the UMI countries in its own band.[41]

Moshe Syrquin's approach involves the use of both sets of countries in his comparison. He then plots the relationship between their factor inputs and growth of productivity, and then the further relationship of both to increases in their national income. Looked at from this perspective, Israel's performance between 1950 and 1970 is closest to that of a group consisting of Japan and four other industrializing states. But, after 1973, it is more typical of a group of six advanced industrial states (including Britain, the United States, and West Germany) whose growth of productivity also slowed down in the same way in the 1970s. His conclusion, although not clearly stated, would seem to be that the combination of stagnation and inflation which all experienced during this period can be explained in terms of their 'maturity' as manifest in a slowdown in investment and an inability to rein in the growth of public spending where this was supported by powerful vested interests of all kinds. However, this is then qualified by his observation that, in the Israeli case, the jump in public consumption to some 40 percent of GDP following the October war of 1973 was quite exceptional by any standard.[42]

Michael Shalev uses another type of international comparison to make a different, though related, point. Comparing the rates of unemployment in Israel and in seven OECD countries, he finds the Israeli rate to have been high by the latter's standards in the years just before 1973. However, after that, the trends go in the opposite direction, with the Israeli economy in a state of virtual full employment through the rest of the 1970s, something which of the OECD seven only Sweden was able to achieve.[43]

What is common to both comparisons is the attention they pay to public policy. However, whereas Syrquin tends to blame vested interests for the runaway expenditure, Shalev places responsibility fairly and squarely on Israel's Labor-led government, which was in power all the time until its defeat in the 1977 elections. It was Labor which was willing to use the huge increase in foreign aid to subsidize investment in industrial expansion for

183

largely military purposes, and Labor which was responsible for allowing its decision-making process to come under the powerful influence of just those new companies which its own largesse had helped to expand or create.[44]

Matters then deteriorated, according to both authors, under the Likud government which came to power in 1977. It presided over a new burst of inflation which took the annual average rate from 34 percent in 1977 to 54 percent in 1978 and a staggering 140 percent in 1979–83.[45] This is generally ascribed to the 'liberal' policies of the new administration which sought to deal with inflation and the growing balance of payments crisis, not by the previous Labor method of devaluation and freezing wages, but by a new policy of deregulation including the elimination of Israel's multiple exchange rates and the removal of many of the barriers to the holding of foreign currency and the import of capital from abroad. The result was a radical transformation of the entire banking and credit system, with 'hot' money pouring into the country to profit from high interest rates, Israeli citizens exchanging their pounds for dollars, and the government, in response, only able to attract the necessary buyers for its own bonds by increasing these rates as well.

Still more dangerous developments followed as the government lost most of its powers of control over both the money supply and the activities of the three major banks which, together, controlled some 90 percent of bank assets.[46] Inflation then speeded up as a brief period of deflation in 1979 gave way to a policy of increased government spending, and hence growing deficits, first in the run-up to the 1981 election, which again Likud won, and then as a result of the invasion of Lebanon in June 1982. Even worse was to follow. In the autumn of 1983 came a combination of the onset of hyperinflation and a collapse in the price of bank stocks which necessitated a huge government bail-out to prevent further damage.[47] Soon after, there was the 'crisis' election of July 1984 following which neither of the two major coalitions, Labor and Likud, was able to form a government. It was only with the decision to form a 'cabinet of national unity' that it was possible to implement the policies needed to bring the situation under control.

1984–1990: FROM CRISIS TO LIMITED ECONOMIC REFORM

There was general agreement among the chief members of the new cabinet that what was required was a so-called 'package' deal (or social pact) in which measures to constrain spending were agreed in advance between government, capital, and labor. The first of these, involving just a freeze on prices, was put into effect for three months beginning in November 1984, and the second for eight months, with severe limits on increases in wages as well.[48] Such stern measures, though enough to bring inflation down to some 20 percent a month, were still regarded as insufficient, and a proposed third package was quickly replaced by a comprehensive economic plan introduced in July 1985. This involved deep cuts in subsidies and other forms of government expenditure, as well as a further three-month wage and price freeze, the whole supported by a US grant of $1.5 billion. It brought annual inflation down to 20 percent in 1986, and to 16.5 percent in 1987, and had the added advantage of reducing the budget deficit from its all-time high of 13.2 percent of GNP in 1984/85 to only 2.8 percent in 1986/87.[49]

Looked at in terms of similar attempts to halt hyperinflation elsewhere, for example in Latin America, this was an unusual success. Israeli commentators are probably correct to ascribe it to a combination of sensible policies and the type of national unity which encouraged all sections of the Jewish community to work together at a time of national crisis.[50] Its medium-term legacy was more mixed. First, there was a continuation of the economic stagnation of the previous decade. Even though the government permitted a brief boom in the early part of 1987, this was quickly succeeded by another period of depression in which unemployment began to rise again and GNP growth slowed down to 2.7 percent in 1988 and only 1.6 percent in 1989.[51] (see Table 8.2). It should be noted, however, that this stagnation had little do with the widespread disruption caused by the outbreak of Palestinian resistance (the Intifada) in October 1987: the Israeli economy was much too large to be influenced even by the more strenuous Palestinian efforts to conduct a form of economic warfare by means of a boycott of Israeli goods and pressure to prevent laborers from going to work for Israeli firms[52] (see Table 8.3).

A second consequence was a renewed commitment to economic liberalization, including privatization of parts of the public sector. In the event, however, efforts to alter the relationship between public and private proved extremely difficult, given the long history of statist policies and the large number of vested interests involved. Hence, by 1990, only a small number of government enterprises had been sold off, while the public sector's share of employment remained around 30 percent and the old policies of subsidizing failing public enterprises continued.[53] It was only with the entirely changed economic conditions consequent on the Gulf War, in 1990–91, the revival of the peace process, and the massive immigration of Jews from the former Soviet Union that growth revived and some of the obstacles to reform and deregulation were finally put to one side.

185

A final point concerns the distribution of the gains from the economic advances of the whole period 1948–90. In spite of the slowdown in growth during the 1970s, the Israeli economy performed well enough between 1950 and 1980 to increase per capita income from one-fourth of that of the United States to half, or to three-fourths of that enjoyed in Western Europe.[54] Similar progress can be seen in a number of the statistics for national welfare. To give just one set of examples, by 1990, Israel had the highest rate of doctors per head of population, and among the highest rates of life expectancy at birth in the entire world.[55] Such benefits were not distributed evenly, however. Divisions within the labor market, as well as highly unequal access to welfare benefits, meant that wage differentials remained high by West European standards and income levels were becoming more uneven over time.[56]

The reasons for this had much to do with two factors: the existence of divisions within the Jewish community, and between it and the Palestinian. As far as the former were concerned, the bulk of the post-1948 migrants, and particularly those of 'Oriental' origin from Asia and North Africa, could only find jobs at the bottom end of the labor market where incomes were lower and access to senior positions quite limited. Moreover, as Shalev notes, there was nothing like a West European welfare state based on principles of universalism or national uniformity, but instead a system permeated by 'particularisms and selectivity.'[57] In this situation, access to welfare was highly dependent on type of employment, with those in the top jobs well provided for as far as social insurance was concerned and those lower down the scale dealt with by what might be called a simple 'residual' or 'safety-net' system, involving a means test. Only in the 1970s did the situation begin to change with, first, the Labor government introducing a progressive family allowance targeted specifically at the poorer, and larger, families, and then the Likud government bringing in a universal minimum income as well as embarking on a large-scale program of urban renewal.[58]

The situation for the Palestinian Arabs was even worse. Not only did they lose most of their land, and tend to be employed in the least good jobs, but, also as a community, they were discriminated against in terms of government spending and by being excluded from institutions such as the cooperative systems which marketed a significant proportion of Jewish agricultural production.[59] The result, as a 1979–80 income and expenditure survey showed, was that the Arab family income was only just over 70 percent of the Israeli national average.[60]

186

THE ECONOMY OF JORDAN 1946–1990

1945–1967

As a neighbor of Israel, Jordan shared a number of features affecting its economic performance: it suffered from the same lack of natural resources; it was forced to spend an usually large proportion of its budget on defense; and it profited from a similar access to foreign aid owing to international concern about its role in the Arab/Israeli conflict and the presence within its borders of a large and volatile population of Palestinian origin. Indeed, by the mid-1960s Jordan and Israel were estimated to have the highest level of grant aid per head of population in the world: $36.50 and $28.60 a year respectively.[61] This in turn allowed Jordan, like its neighbor, to fund a huge import surplus and to develop at a very much faster rate than would otherwise have been the case. Lastly, both states were intimately involved in the affairs of the West Bank, which Israel took in the June 1967 war.

However, the parallel between the two economies ends there. With only a tiny manufacturing sector, and an average per capita income of some $100 in 1953, post-independence Jordan was at a level of development much more like that of its Arab neighbors, or Asian states such as India and Pakistan, than that of Israel.[62] To make matters worse, the 1948 war created huge new problems for the country: it was cut off from direct access to the ports on the Mediterranean coast such as Haifa and Jaffa, and it was also involuntary host to some 350,000 Palestinian refugees at a time when its own population was estimated at only 375,000. The result was a lowering of wages and an increase in unemployment, with more than half the refugee population still without work in 1954 and many of the rest only able to find work on a seasonal basis.[63]

In time, however, the new situation proved to have some advantages as well. The more prosperous refugees brought funds with them which were used to start businesses in and around the capital city of Amman and to set off a construction boom for new houses. Control over the West Bank with its relatively well developed agricultural sector soon proved to be another asset as did the funds provided by the United Nations Relief and Works Agency (UNRWA) in support of the refugees living in camps in both the West Bank and Jordan itself. Furthermore, the very precariousness of the whole situation attracted increasing levels of budgetary support from outside, first from Britain, and then after the abrogation of the Anglo-Jordanian Treaty in 1957, largely from the United States. Such aid accounted for 58.6 percent of expenditures between 1954 and 1961, and 48.3 percent between 1962 and 1966, allowing the government to make a

187

modest beginning in developing the country's infrastructure as well to invest in the construction of an oil refinery and the expansion of phosphate production.[64] Just as important, aid permitted Jordan to continue to maintain the huge import surplus necessary for economic growth when it could produce so little locally either for domestic consumption or for export. Two sets of figures make the same point. First, between 1950 and 1966 Jordanian exports (mostly of potash) covered only some 11–15 percent of the cost of goods and services purchased abroad.[65] Second, in the period 1959–66, imports provided a staggering 28.3 percent of total GNP.[66]

Given this degree of dependency on aid it was not surprising that the government's advisers, both foreign and local, should urge the introduction of measures designed to promote national self-sufficiency. The problems, however, were considerable. The agricultural sector, which provided employment for about a third of the labor force, continued to be subject to huge fluctuations in rainfall, and so in output. The vestigial manufacturing sector was constrained by the high cost of power, the need to import most raw materials and, above all, the small size of the domestic market. Furthermore, the interests both of state-building and of confrontation with Israel necessitated increasing spending on administration and defense: nearly 15 percent of the budget in 1954, and 22.5 percent in 1964.[67]

In these difficult circumstances three major priorities were identified. One was the expansion of irrigated agriculture in the Jordan Valley by means of the East Ghor canal which, once constructed, permitted a significant increase in the cultivation of vegetables and olives. A second was the development of tourism, particularly around Jerusalem and Bethlehem on the West Bank. The third was to build on the early achievements of the UNRWA school construction program to create a national education system which, by the early 1960s, was already putting a substantially larger proportion of the school-age population through the secondary and tertiary levels than most countries with a similar level of income.[68] Such was the success achieved in these three areas that, by the time Jordan came to draw up its first five-year plan, 1963–67 (later amended to a seven-year plan, 1964–70), there was considerable optimism that the role of foreign aid could be much reduced.[69] However, just as in the case of Israel, the impact of the June 1967 war was so wide-ranging as to produce a radical change in economic direction.

1967–1982: From Recovery to Economic Boom

The immediate impact of the June war was disastrous for Jordan. To begin with, it lost control over the economy of the West Bank which, according to one estimate, was then contributing 30 percent of the country's GDP as well as providing significant amounts of valuable foreign exchange from tourism.[70] There followed four more years of military mobilization, conflict, and destruction as a result of further confrontations both with the Israelis and with the growing power of the Palestine Liberation Organization (PLO), culminating in the fierce fighting between the army and the Palestinian guerrillas in Amman and the north in 1970–71. Worse, there was a new flow of refugees into the East Bank both during and after the 1967 war, which some estimates put as high as 300,000 persons.[71] As a result, there was only a small increase in national product between 1967 and 1972, and perhaps a small fall in per capita income.[72] All that prevented even greater disaster was an increase in Arab aid which brought total foreign assistance to just over JD 50 million ($150 million) in 1967/68, compared with an average of JD 25 million ($75 million) between 1959 and 1966.[73]

The situation began to change for the better in 1971–72, helped by a number of exogenous factors which were to continue for the rest of the decade. First in importance was a series of huge increases in the level of foreign assistance, as first the United States and then the Arab oil states upped their combined contributions to an annual average of JD 123 million ($369 million) in the period 1974–78 and then, following the Baghdad Arab Summit, to JD 372 million ($1.12 billion) between 1979 and 1982 (see Table 8.4). The greater part of this was given, once again, in grants for budgetary support. But it was also sufficient to improve Jordan's international credit rating to such an extent that it could be supplemented by high rates of foreign borrowing from the Euro-dollar market and else-where, raising the country's external debt from JD 68 million ($204 million) in 1973, or 28 percent of GNP, to JD 762.9 million ($2.289 billion) in 1983, equivalent to 41 percent of GNP.[74] To this should be added three other significant sources of foreign currency. One was the increased earnings from tourism, and the second was increased profits from the sale of phosphates as prices more than quadrupled between 1973 and 1976.[75] However, the third and by far the most important new source was the remittances sent home by Jordanians working abroad in increasing numbers in the 1970s, the vast majority in the oil-rich Arab states of the Gulf.[76] The sums transmitted officially through the banking system rose from $454.7 million in 1976 to $1.083 billion in 1982, to which should be added the many hundreds of thousands of dollars remitted

189

unofficially or in the form of imports of consumer durables and other merchandise.[77]

Part of the value of such transfers was lost as a result of the world inflation of the 1970s, including the need to pay more for Jordan's imports of oil. Nevertheless, the rest was sufficient to allow a huge rise both in imports and government expenditure and thus to encourage a relatively high rate of growth. Unfortunately, however, this was at the expense of a return to much the same degree of dependency on outside assistance that had been such a feature of pre-1967 economic life. Hence exports continued to cover only some 20 percent of the value of imports in 1969–79, while the ability to meet budgetary expenditures out of local resources oscillated between 46.4 percent in 1967–72, 57.1 percent in 1976–78, and a low of only 38.3 percent in 1979.[78] Furthermore, even with such a high level of external assistance, the government was still unable to prevent an increasing budget deficit, which had reached some 8.2 percent of GDP in 1980.[79]

The government itself also played an important role in the economic recovery of the early 1970s through such measures as 1972 Law for Encouraging Foreign Investment and then its use of the three-year plan, 1973–75, to establish new priorities for the expansion of public services and the creation of new institutions. Once again there was great emphasis on the expansion of educational facilities, including the establishment of new universities and colleges, measures which ensured that, by 1981, nearly three-fourths of all school-age children completed their secondary education.[80] Other institutional innovations included the opening of the Amman stock exchange in 1978 and the creation of the Social Security Corporation as an instrument for providing disability insurance and pensions for those at work outside the agricultural sector.

Where the government encountered greater difficulty was in its efforts to encourage agricultural and industrial progress. Field crops suffered from repeated droughts during the 1970s as a result of which production slumped from a record 334,100 tons in 1974 to an average of only 90,400 tons for the next three years, before reviving again in 1980.[81] This in turn encouraged a considerable population movement off the land, either into the cities or abroad, reducing the agricultural labor force from a third of the national total in 1970 to only 15 percent in 1980.[82] Indeed, so great was this flight from rural life that Jordan became an importer as well as an exporter of labor, employing nearly 100,000 foreign workers by 1981, most of them Arabs and most of them working in agriculture.[83] As for manufacturing, there was also no real breakthrough, with the sector as a whole still only contributing 15.5 percent to GNP in 1978 and employing a mere 6.3 percent of the labor force[84] (see Table 8.5). The main product line remained chemical, minerals, and metals which provided some 50 percent of total value added in 1977, with food, drink, and tobacco contributing 26.6 percent and shoes, clothes, and textiles another 12.9 percent.[85] If there was a trend, it was one of greater diversification of activities within each of these sectors, for example toward the manufacture of a greater variety of intermediate products such as pumps and household electrical goods.[86]

1983–1990: Stagnation to Recession

Jordan's economic fortunes after 1982 are a perfect illustration of the country's dependence on the health of the regional economy. Once oil prices began to fall, there was the inevitable knock-on effect in terms of steep falls in Arab aid, exports, and remittances. These, in turn, were translated into falling public and private investment, growing domestic unemployment, negative growth in GDP between 1985 and 1989, and, most disturbing of all, a huge increase in the deficit on the balance of payments.[87] One immediate result was the growing problem of meeting interest payments on an international debt which had reached $8 billion by 1988.[88] A series of defaults then led to a banking crisis, a collapse in the value of the Jordanian dinar, and finally a series of negotiations with both the IMF and the Club Paris official bilateral creditors representing the country's main Western creditors. It allowed a much needed rescheduling of the debt but only after the government had promised to implement an austerity program. This involved deep cuts in public expenditure, including reductions in the subsidies allocated to petrol and basic foodstuffs large enough to provoke widespread rioting in the spring of 1989, a forced change of government, and then King Hussein's decision to allow the first national election in 22 years.

Nevertheless, in spite of these political difficulties, the new government adhered to the agreed economic program with such vigor that the sharp fall in GDP experienced in 1989 was quickly replaced by a return to growth in 1990. By then, however, the country was caught up in yet another crisis, this time triggered by the international boycott of Iraq, the country's main trading partner, following its occupation of Kuwait, and the enforced return of some 300,000 of its 340,000 migrant workers from the Gulf states. In the event, however, the effects were not quite as bad as was at first feared and, somewhat to everyone's surprise, the recovery continued into the early 1990s.

THE CHARACTER OF THE JORDANIAN ECONOMY: AN OVERVIEW

Attempts to define the character of the Jordanian economy at the beginning of the 1980s generally focused on the predominant role of the services sector which, as early as 1967, contributed no less than 61.5 percent of GDP.[89] This is certainly an important point and distinguished Jordan from some, although not all, of the other countries with a similar per capita income.[90] It was a reflection partly of the general lack of raw materials and other resources, and partly of the huge role played by trade in goods and services which provided almost half of GNP before 1974 and up to three-fourths from then on.[91] It was also a function of the central role played by a government and administration fortunate enough to be in receipt of increasingly large sums of aid, the greater share of which it was free to distribute as it saw fit. Not surprisingly, a large part of this was spent on the army and public services of one kind or another. This can be seen not only from the budget but also from the major role played by government employment which, by the mid-1970s, involved nearly half of the total labor force of 360,000, with 100,000 persons in the armed forces and another 70,000 either in administration or in special public institutions.[92]

The presence of a government sector of this size with this degree of resources under its control affected the character of the economy in another significant respect as well. Although officially a 'mixed' economy, it was one in which the weight and importance of the public sector and of public initiatives greatly outweighed that of the private.[93] Such was particularly the case after 1973 when the state initiated a program of accelerated growth involving projects so large as to be far beyond the capacity of private entrepreneurs either to finance or to manage. This, in turn, was accompanied by the creation of investment funds connected with such new agencies as the Civil Service Pension Fund or the Social Security Corporation which were used to provide money for the new projects. Then, as more problems emerged in connection with the rising price of food imports in the mid-1970s, the government created a ministry of supply to manage the sale of such necessities as sugar, rice, and wheat at subsidized prices. Other interventions involving the official marketing of certain domestically produced agricultural products soon followed.

The use of a second, related, perspective is also helpful. This derives from the notion of Jordan as a state without oil but having many of the characteristics of a rentier economy owing to its great dependence on oil-related income from the Gulf.[94] Clearly, the post-1974 boom owed almost everything to the moneys received both from the Gulf states themselves and from the huge increase in remittances sent back by the Jordanians working in them. By the same token, Jordan began to experience considerable economic difficulty once the international price of oil began to decline from 1982 onwards. However, there was more to it than that: rentier states can also be characterized in terms of their high wage rates, their high propensity to import, their high rates of inflation, and the high value of their currency in relation to those of their major trading partners. It usually follows that such states also have great problems in developing both their manufacturing and agricultural sectors. Their high-wage, high-cost industry can only survive with a very high degree of protection, as was the case in Jordan. The incomes of their cultivators are not only threatened by cheap food imports but also fall completely out of line with the much higher wages that can be earned in the towns, thus contributing to a powerful rural-to-urban migration. All this took place in Jordan as well.

Managing an economy so dependent on the price of oil and on transfers over which it has little control presents great difficulties. In Jordan, there was one brief period when it sought ways to try to limit the problems posed by fluctuations in income through institutionalizing its relationship with the oil states so as to obtain a regular commitment to provide a fixed amount of aid each year. This was by endorsing a plan known as the 'Strategy for Joint Arab Economic Action' presented to the Amman Summit in November 1980 which would have set just such a set of targets over the next five years.[95] However, this plan was watered down to such an extent that the whole point of the exercise was lost, and aid continued to be disbursed on an ad hoc basis and to be highly dependent on short-term changes in the political arrangements between Jordan and its richer Arab neighbors.

As we have already seen, Jordan's particular economic structure meant that it was ill-suited to weather the downturn in regional activity during the 1980s and, in particular, after 1986. Hence while revenues stagnated, military expenses continued at a high level and the very large public sector continued to grow to incorporate perhaps another tenth of the workforce.[96] Meanwhile, the manufacturing sector stagnated and, in spite of the high rates of public and private investment during the latter part of the 1970s, productivity seems hardly to have grown at all during the following decade, which may well have had something to do with the 'brain drain' consequent on the continued export of many of the country's most highly skilled professionals and workers.[97]

THE WEST BANK AND GAZA, 1948–1990

1948–1967

The establishment of the state of Israel and the division of Palestine in 1948–49 not only created two new entities, the West Bank and Gaza, but also ensured that they would start their new lives with a host of crippling economic problems. In the case of the West Bank, its population was increased by almost 60 percent between 1948 and 1952, as a result of the flood of refugees, all of whom had to be housed in towns and camps.[98] To make matters worse, the new demarcation line which was drawn between West Bank and Israel in 1949 not only cut off the area from access to the cities on the Palestine coast but also deprived some 111 villages of at least half of their agricultural land on the far side of the new border.[99] In 1950, it was officially linked to Jordan, a country much poorer and less developed than itself, whose elite was determined to ensure that it was Amman and not the West Bank cities of Ramallah, Nablus, or East Jerusalem which became the major focus of economic activity.

As in the case of East Bank Jordan, the West Bank became heavily dependent on outside financial assistance, first from the UNRWA and other international agencies, then from tourism (particularly to Jerusalem and Bethlehem) and from the remittances of those of its people who managed to find work abroad. This allowed it to maintain an import surplus of roughly the same proportion as that of Jordan.[100] It also helped shape a roughly similar structure of economic activity so that, by 1967, agriculture is estimated to have contributed 27 percent to GDP, industry and mining 9 percent, and services some 56 percent (see Table 8.6). The most vital part of the economy after tourism was the construction sector which, according to one survey, received some two-thirds of all investments before 1967.[101]

The impact of the 1948–49 division was even more catastrophic for the inhabitants of the tiny area of land which became known as the Gaza Strip. They too lost much of their agricultural and grazing land to Israel. Even worse, the existing population of between 70,000 and 90,000 was overwhelmed by the arrival of between 200,000 and 250,000 refugees.[102] All this created a situation of high unemployment, low wages, and minimal public services, made worse by the fact that, for the first decade or so, there was only scarce assistance from the Egyptian administration which now controlled the strip.

Once again it was the UNRWA which played the dominant role in providing housing, education, and other assistance. However, over time, and especially after the brief Israeli military occupation during the Suez crisis, other sources of income and employment began to grow. The most important local one was agriculture, which became the subject of a considerable Egyptian and international development effort and which, by 1966, provided jobs for over a third of the employed population, contributed 26.2 percent of Gaza's income, and occupied about half the land area of the strip[103] (see Table 8.7). Here the main crop was citrus which, in 1966, occupied 37 percent of the cultivated area and contributed nearly 90 percent of the official exports.[104] Other productive activities included a tiny manufacturing sector and fishing. By far the most important sources of money, however, were remittances and the services provided to the Egyptian administration, the units of the Palestine Liberation Army quartered in the strip, and the contingent of UN peace-keepers established there in 1957. To this should be added the large, and unrecorded, profits from a lively smuggling trade which derived from Gaza's status as a free trade zone with links to markets in both Israel and Egypt.[105]

1967–1987: THE WEST BANK AND GAZA UNDER PROLONGED ISRAELI OCCUPATION

The swift Israeli military victory of June 1967 led to the occupation of the West Bank and Gaza, and their partial reincorporation into a single economic unit with Israel. This had some similarities to a customs union, with a single external tariff and a common currency provided by the Israeli shekel (although the Jordanian dinar continued to circulate on the West Bank as well). There were, however, significant barriers to the internal movement of labor, goods, and services. Palestinians were allowed to travel to work in Israel by day, but not to spend the night there. Meanwhile, although Israeli goods were allowed to circulate freely in the West Bank and Gaza, there were restrictions on the movement of Palestinian agricultural and manufactured goods the other way. Even more important, the West Bank and Gaza were subject not only to military rule but also to separate legal regimes, with a confusing mixture of Ottoman, mandatory, Jordanian, and, in the case of Gaza, Egyptian regulations as well.[106]

Israel used its position of power to control both the political and economic life of the Occupied Territories, employing their resources in whatever way best suited its own interests, limiting Palestinian competition, and preventing the Palestinians from developing any institutions which might have served as a focus for national planning or for initiatives designed to find an alternative path of development. Moreover, the military authorities spent very little money on infrastructure, education, or social

195

welfare.[107] The impact of Israeli control was felt in almost every aspect of economic life but with particular force in the areas of land, water, and industrial development. Concerning land, it has been estimated that by 1991 two-thirds of the surface area of the West Bank had been, or was in the process of being, expropriated for use by the military or the 150 or so Israeli settlements which had been established there since 1967, with a population of some 250,000.[108] At the same time, the Israeli authorities were taking over 70 percent of the available water for use either by the settlers or in Israel itself.[109] To make matters worse, the military government prevented the development of banks and other credit institutions which might have financed investments in the productive sectors of the Palestinian economy while allocating only a small number of licenses for the establishment of new factories other than those working as sub-contractors for Israeli entrepreneurs.[110]

In spite of all such constraints, Palestinian national income began to grow at a substantial rate: some 6 percent a year between the mid-1960s and mid-1980s in real terms.[111] The driving force came from a combination of the export of labor to Israel and the Arab world, and of various types of Arab and international aid. According to the figures in Tables 8.8A and 8B, about a third of the labor force was working outside the West Bank in 1974 and 40 percent outside Gaza, almost all of it in Israel. Out-migration to the Arab world, particularly to the Gulf, then pushed up this proportion to 45 percent for the West Bank and 54 percent for Gaza by 1980, and to 52 and 58 percent respectively by 1987. The wages obtained, though low by Israeli standards, were several times higher than those that could have been earned by unskilled or semi-skilled labor in the Occupied Territories or in neighboring Jordan. As such, they made a significant contribution to the Palestinian national income, providing something like 30 percent of the West Bank's GDP from the early 1970s onward.[112]

The money earned from the export of labor, together with a heavy dependency on imports, combined to increase the share of the services sector as against the two productive sectors, industry and agriculture (Tables 8.6 and 8.7). Given the problems it faced in the form of Israeli competition, as well as from lack of credit, the manufacturing sector remained weak, and contributed only some 5–6 percent of GDP between 1967 and 1987.[113] Almost the only sign of vitality was the growth in the number of small firms working as sub-contractors to larger Israeli enterprises, particularly in the Gaza Strip.[114] As for agriculture, a combination of land loss, labor shortages and lack of local markets led to a decline in its share of employment from 42 to 16 percent in the West Bank between 1970 and 1987, and from 27 to 11 percent in Gaza. Meanwhile, the total cultivated area dropped by some 14 percent below its 1967 level.[115] There was some compensation, however, from an overall increase in productivity and output as farmers switched land to more valuable crops such as fruit and vegetables and used more capital-intensive techniques.[116]

THE ECONOMIC IMPACT OF THE INTIFADA, 1987–1990

The outbreak of the concerted Palestinian resistance to Israeli occupation in October 1987 soon produced a marked deterioration in economic conditions. Demonstrations were followed by curfews, checkpoints, and other barriers to internal movement. Some 2,000 persons were killed and perhaps another 80,000 wounded.[117] Schools and universities were regularly closed. To begin with, the population derived some benefit from an increase in funds from outside, as well as an especially good olive crop in the West Bank in 1988. Nevertheless, as the Intifada continued, Palestinians were able to work fewer hours in Israel, and there was a marked decline in activity in the manufacturing and construction sectors. Just how this translated into a drop in income is a matter for some debate, with the newer estimates from within the Occupied Territories showing a much steeper fall than those provided by the Israeli Central Bureau of Statistics.[118] Hence, while the former indicate a drop of some 26 percent in per capita GNP between 1988 and 1990, the latter see a more gradual decline of 1.8 percent a year between 1987 and 1991.[119] Furthermore, while the Israeli figures show a slight recovery in Palestinian economic life in 1990, Palestinian sources indicate that the slowdown continued into the early 1990s as a result of the new problems posed by the Iraqi invasion of Kuwait, a decline in Arab aid, and the deportation of large numbers of Palestinian workers from the Gulf states.[120]

Notes on Chapter 8
Full details of all sources are in the Bibliography

1   Sir Alan Cunningham to BMEO, Cairo, tg 66, December 1947, Cunningham Papers, Box III/file 1, Middle East Centre, St Antony's College, Oxford.

2   On the flight of the Arab refugees and the disputes about their numbers see Morris, *The Birth of the Palestinian Refugee Problem 1947–1949*, Conclusion and pp 297–8; on the value of the property they left behind see Segev, *The First Israelis*, pp 68–73; on the numbers of villages destroyed see Khalidi (ed.), *All That Remains*, pp xvi (note) and

xx.

3　Carmi and Rosenfeld, 'Israel's Political Economy and the Widening Class Gap Between its Two National Groups,' p 16; Rabieh, *The Negev Bedouin and Livestock Rearing*, pp 7–8.

4　Metzer, 'The Slowdown of Economic Growth,' pp 75–6; World Bank, *World Development Report 1991*, Table 2.

5　Segev, *The First Israelis*, pp 95–6 and note; Ben-Porath, 'Entwined Growth of Population and Product,' p 28.

6　Segev, *The First Israelis*, p 71.

7　This argument is well presented in Ben-Porath, 'Entwined Growth of Population and Product,' pp 27–41.

8　Figures from Halevi and Klinov-Malul, *The Economic Development of Israel*, Appendix 11; Beinin, 'Israel at Forty,' p 437.

9　Shalev, 'Israel's Domestic Policy Regime,' p 131.

10　For example, Halevi and Klinov-Malul, *Economic Development*, p 11.

11　*Ibid.*, p 193. See also Berglas, 'Defense and the Economy,' pp 174–5.

12　Naysmith, 'Israel's Distorted Economy,' p 391.

13　Khalidi, 'The Economy of the Palestinian Arabs of Israel,' p 42; Carmi and Rosenfeld, 'Israel's Political Economy and the Widening Class Gap Between its Two National Groups,' p 29; Shalev, 'Jewish Organized Labor and the Palestinians,' p 107.

14　Szereszewski, *Essays on the Structure of the Jewish Economy in Palestine and Israel*, Table 5.

15　Figure from Halevi and Klinov-Malul, *The Economic Development of Israel*, Table 16.

16　Troen, 'Spearheads of the Zionist Frontier,' Table 1; Carmi and Rosenfeld, 'Israel's Political Economy and the Widening Class Gap Between its Two National Groups,' p 20; Halevi and Klinov-Malul, *The Economic Development of Israel*, Tables 23 and 36 and p 106.

17　Halevi and Klinov-Malul, *The Economic Development of Israel*, Table 36 and pp 112–13.

18　For example, Greenberg, 'The Contribution of the Labour Economy to Immigrant Absorption and Population Dispersal During Israel's First Decade,' pp 286–90.

19　Halevi and Klinov-Malul, *Economic Development*, Table 40.

20　*Ibid.*

21　Shalev, 'Jewish Organized Labor,' p 110; Gross, 'The Economic Regime During Israel's First Decade,' pp 231–7.

22　Gross, 'The Economic Regime During Israel's First Decade,' p 238.

23　For example, *Ibid.*, pp 234–5. The terms come from Naysmith, 'Israel's Distorted Economy,' pp 392–3.

24　Naysmith, 'Israel's Distorted Economy,' pp 401–2; Gross, 'The Economic Regime During Israel's First Decade,' p 231.

25　Shalev, 'Israel's Domestic Policy Regime,' p 121.

26　Metzer and Kaplan, 'The Slowdown of Economic Growth,' pp 80–1.

27　Figures from Yago, 'Whatever Happened to the Promised Land?' p 136n.

28　Beinin, 'Israel at Forty,' Table 1.

29　Ben-Porath, 'Introduction,' p 5.

30　Horowitz, *The Enigma of Economic Growth*, p 27, quoted in Yago, 'Whatever Happened to the Promised Land?' p 141.

31　Metzer, 'The Slowdown of Economic Growth,' p 76.

32　Ben-Porath, 'Introduction,' p 5.

33   Metzer and Kaplan, 'The Slowdown of Economic Growth,' Table 3:1.
34   Shalev, 'Israel's Domestic Policy Regime,' pp 128–9; Beinin, 'Israel at Forty,' pp 443–7.
35   Ben-Porath, 'Introduction' in Ben-Porath (ed.), *The Israeli Economy*, p 6.
36   *Ibid.*
37   Shalev, 'Israel's Domestic Policy Regime: Zionism, Dualism and the Rise of Capital,' pp 127–8.
38   Metzer and Kaplan, 'The Slowdown of Economic Growth,' p 84. As Metzer indicates, this notion is based on research in Israel by Simon Kuznets, published in Hebrew in 1973.
39   This notion in both of its aspects can be found in the subtitle of the collective work edited by Ben-Porath, *The Israeli Economy*, and is used by a number of contributors to it, notably Metzer and Kaplan, 'The Slowdown of Economic Growth,' and Syrquin, 'Economic Growth and Structural Change,' pp 42–74.
40   Syrquin, 'Economic Growth and Structural Change,' especially p 74.
41   World Bank, *World Development Report 1984*, Tables 1 and 3.
42   Syrquin, 'Economic Growth and Structural Change,' particularly pp 49–65 and 73–4.
43   Shalev, 'Israel's Domestic Policy Regime,' p 101.
44   *Ibid.*, pp 129–32.
45   1977 and 1978 figures from *ibid.*, pp 133–4; 1979–83 from Sharon, 'Israel and the Success of the Shekel,' p 115.
46   Ben-Porath, 'Introduction,' pp 17–18.
47   The crisis came when the three major banks were no longer able to continue the practice of buying their own shares to maintain their price and values fell by over 50 percent in September/October 1983 before the government stepped in. For example, Plessner, *The Political Economy of Israel*, pp 257, 261–2.
48   Sharon, 'Israel and the Success of the Shekel,' pp 120–1.
49   *Ibid.*, pp 123–5.
50   This, for example, was the view of the influential governor of the Bank of Israel; Bruno, 'Sharp Disinflation Strategy.'
51   Razin and Sadka, *The Economy of Modern Israel*, pp 41–4.
52   *Ibid.*, p 93.
53   For a good analysis of the barriers to liberalization, see Murphy, 'Structural Inhibitions to Economic Liberalization in Israel,' pp 65–88.
54   Syrquin, 'Economic Growth and Structural Change: an International Perspective,' pp 43, 47.
55   World Bank, *World Development Report 1991*, Tables 1 and 28.
56   Shalev, 'Israel's Domestic Policy Regime,' pp 106–7.
57   *Ibid.*
58   *Ibid.*, p 105.
59   Khalidi, 'The Economy of the Palestinian Arabs of Israel,' pp 46–63.
60   *Ibid.*, p 61.
61   Mazur, *Economic Growth and Development in Jordan*, p 61n.
62   *Ibid.*, p 11.
63   IBRD, *The Economic Development of Jordan*, p 5.
64   Calculations based mainly on official figures in Rivier, *Croissance industrielle dans une économie assistée*, p 22.
65   *Ibid.*, p 18.
66   Mazur, *Economic Growth*, Table III/6.

67 *Ibid.*, Table II/1, p 20.

68 *Ibid.*, p 47.

69 See Jordan Development Board, *Seven Year Program for Economic Development 1964–70*, pp 5–6. The same point is made by the influential Jordanian writing as Talal in his 'Growth and Stability in the Jordanian Economy,' p 98.

70 Mazur, *Economic Growth and Development in Jordan*, p 98.

71 For a discussion of the number of new refugees see Rivier, *Croissance industrielle dans une économie assistée*, p 8. The subject is a controversial one as it relates directly to that part of the Final Status talks between Israel and the Palestinians concerning the rights of certain groups of Palestinian refugees to return to their West Bank homes. Israel claims that only 80,000 such persons were dislodged during the actual fighting in June 1967.

72 The Hashemite Kingdom of Jordan, National Planning Council, *Three Year Development Plan* 1973–1975, pp 6–8.

73 Hammad, 'The Role of Foreign Aid in the Jordanian Economy, 1959–1983,' Table 2.3.

74 *Ibid.*, p 27.

75 Phosphate prices rose from JD 3.7/ton in 1973 to a peak of JD 17.6 at the height of the boom before falling away to between JD 9 and JD 10, 1977–79; Rivier, *Croissance industrielle dans une économie assistée*, Table 2, p 130.

76 Share, 'The Use of Jordan Workers' Remittances,' pp 32–4.

77 Central Bank figures quoted by Saket, 'Economic Uses of Remittances,' Table 1.

78 Rivier, *Croissance industrielle dans une économie assistée*, Tables 5 and 6.

79 IMF: Jordan, 'Staff Report for the 1981 Article IV Consultation,' p 5.

80 World Bank, *World Development Report 1984*, Table 25.

81 Smadi and Asfour, *The Economy of Jordan*, Table 2; Saket and Asfour, *Jordan's Economy*, Table 2.

82 Arabiyyat, 'Performance of the Agricultural Sector in Jordan Within the Regional Context,' pp 174–6.

83 Share, 'Migration and Domestic Labour Market Policies,' p 79.

84 Rivier, *Croissance industrielle dans une économie assistée*, p 1.

85 *Ibid.*, Tables 8 and 14.

86 *Ibid.*, pp 51–3.

87 World Bank, *Peace and the Jordanian Economy*, pp 8–10.

88 *Financial Times*, 25 October 1995.

89 For example, Share, 'Jordan's Trade and Balance of Payments Problems,' p 3.

90 World Bank, *World Development Report* 1984, Table 3. Countries in the same 'Upper Middle Income' band in which services contributed over 60 percent of GDP in 1980 included Chile, Israel, and Singapore.

91 Share, 'Jordan's Trade and Balance of Payments Problems,' Table 2.

92 Official figures cited in Rivier, *Croissance industrielle dans une économie assistée*, Annex 4, Table 8.

93 This point is made forcefully by Sha'sha'a, 'The Role of the Private Sector in Jordan;' I have drawn extensively on this paper for the arguments put forward in this paragraph.

94 For an analysis using this perspective see Chatelus, 'Rentier or Producer Economy in the Middle East? The Jordanian response,' pp 204–20.

95 Sayigh, 'A New Framework for Complementarity among the Arab Economies,' pp 159–65.

96 Gelos, 'Investment Efficiency, Human Capital and Migration,' p 16.

97 *Ibid.*, pp 13–21, 30–3.

98 Mansour, 'The West Bank Economy,' pp 71–2.

99   Plascov, 'The Palestinians of Jordan's Border,' p 205; World Bank, *Economic Development of Jordan*, pp 45–6.
100 Mansour, 'The West Bank Economy,' p 74.
101 *Ibid.*, p 73.
102 There is a small difference in figures between Roy, *The Gaza Strip*, pp 73–5 and Abu-Amr, 'The Gaza Economy 1948–1984,' p 101.
103 Roy, *The Gaza Strip*, Table 3.5, p 83.
104 *Ibid.*, pp 77, 86.
105 *Ibid.*, pp 81, 90.
106 Jordan also continued to pay many West Bank public officials and to provide a conduit for aid and charitable donations sent in from outside.
107 Most calculations show that the Israeli government collected about as much money from Palestinian sources as it spent on public projects. See UNCTAD, 'Health Conditions and Services in the West Bank and Gaza Strip,' p 43.
108 UNCTAD, 'UNCTAD'S Assistance to the Palestinian People,' p 26.
109 *Ibid.*, p 27.
110 For a good summary of Israeli policy, see Shadid, 'Israeli Policy Towards Economic Development in the West Bank and Gaza,' pp 121–37.
111 World Bank, *Peace and the Jordanian Economy*, p 9.
112 UNCTAD, 'UNCTAD'S Assistance to the Palestinian People,' p 19.
113 *Ibid.*, p 13. See also Abu Kishk, 'Industrial Development and Policies in the West Bank and Gaza,' pp 165–90.
114 UNCTAD, 'UNCTAD'S Assistance to the Palestinian People,' p 13.
115 *Ibid.*, pp 9–10.
116 UNCTAD, 'The Agricultural Sector of the West Bank and the Gaza Strip,' pp 27–9.
117 Estimate in UNCTAD, 'Health Conditions and Services in the West Bank and Gaza Strip,' p 43.
118 For a discussion of the various estimates see, UNCTAD, 'Prospects for Sustained Development of the Palestinian Economy in the West Bank and the Gaza Strip, 1990–2010,' pp 23–9.
119 UNCTAD, 'Developments in the Economy of the Occupied Palestinian Territory,' p 17.
120 *Ibid.*, Table 1.

9

The States of the Arabian Peninsula 1946–1990

INTRODUCTION

From 1945 onward, and with increasing speed, the majority of the Gulf Arab states were transformed from a collection of small towns reliant on fishing, herding, and trade to some of the world's leading exporters of oil with high per capita incomes, an unusual level of welfare services, and the beginnings of a modern petrochemical industry. This process started in Kuwait, Bahrain, and Saudi Arabia and then spread down the Gulf to Qatar, which began to export oil in 1949, Abu Dhabi (later to become part of the United Arab Emirates) where oil exports began in 1962, and Oman, where they began in 1967. Examination of this process will begin with a general analysis, first of the forces behind the increase in production and revenues, then of the stages by which control was transferred from the international oil companies to the producer states themselves. A second general section will look at some of the consequences of this process in terms of economic policy and in particular the development of specific patterns of income redistribution which were themselves highly dependent upon the employment of ever-increasing numbers of foreign workers. Later sections will examine the particular growth paths taken by Saudi Arabia, Kuwait, Bahrain, and the states of the lower Gulf and finally their two poor relations, the states of north and south Yemen. A last section will analyze the nature of the economic ties which bound the Gulf states to the rest of the Middle East economy.

OIL: INCREASING REVENUES AND GREATER NATIONAL CONTROL

The oil exporting states of the Gulf obtained increasing revenues from two sources, first a rapid growth in production until the early 1970s, then an equally rapid rise in prices, particularly during the two price explosions of 1973–74 and 1979–80. Both movements are illustrated in Tables 9.1A and 9.1B. They show that, *inter alia*, Gulf oil production grew from some 350 million barrels in 1950 to well over one billion in 1960, over 2.5 billion in 1970 and nearly 5.5 billion in 1980. Meanwhile, total revenues from oil – which included not just those realized through the export of crude but, increasingly, refined products including petrochemicals – rose from some $5 billion in 1970 to just under $160 billion in 1980. Prices then began to drop again, bringing revenues down with them, to a low of $37 billion in 1986 before making a small recovery at the end of the decade.[1]

It should be noted, however, that these figures are in current prices and that if they are converted to constant ones – to offset the impact of the high levels of world inflation during the 1970s – the real price that a producer like Saudi Arabia obtained for its oil did not rise at all between 1974 and 1979 and then, after a second period of growth, fell away again to only half its 1974 level after 1986 (Table 9.2). Lastly, to put the whole thing in inter-national perspective, Saudi Arabia, Kuwait, Qatar, and Abu Dhabi were producing just over 15 percent of the world's oil in 1960, and nearly 25 percent in 1978.[2]

Increases in production were the result of the discovery of new fields and the construction of the necessary apparatus of pipelines (including Tapline which carried Saudi oil to Sidon on the Mediterranean, opened in 1951), tanker terminals, and refineries. They were also the result, until the early 1970s, of the commercial calculations of the international oil companies which held the Middle East oil concessions. Thereafter, as powers over decision-making began to pass to the producer states, additional calculations became important, notably the desire to find a balance between production and conservation as well as, in the Saudi case at least, to maintain a price which was adequate for revenue needs without being so high

203

as to encourage the development of alternative sources of energy. Short-term political considerations were also of occasional significance as will be seen below.

The movement of oil prices requires a somewhat more detailed explanation. From 1945 to the early 1970s, something known as the 'posted' price was set by the international concessionary companies as a general reference point for all Middle Eastern oil transactions. To begin with this was used mainly as the basis for calculating the companies' profits for the purposes of their own national tax authorities. But after 1950, and the replacement of the old royalty agreements, based on a fixed price per barrel, by a 50-50 profit-sharing agreement with the host governments, the posted price was used to calculate the amount paid by the companies to Saudi Arabia and then the other Gulf states. In the event it hardly moved for two decades, being fixed at $1.75/barrel in August 1951 and ending up at just $1.80/barrel in February 1971.[3] As all writers point out, this price was greatly in excess of the real costs of production, then calculated at no more than $0.20/barrel for the oilfields directly along the Gulf coast.[4] However, there is much less agreement about whether the difference between cost and price should be seen as a fair return or, alternatively, a form of rent extracted, first by the companies, then, in the 1970s, by the producer governments themselves.[5] What is clear, though, is that at no time was the posted price more than indirectly influenced by the interplay of short-term movements in supply and demand. Market forces can, at best, can be seen as providing a set of generous parameters within which a price was eventually fixed out of a combination of administrative, political, and other motives.

Considerations of this type become even more significant in discussions of the period from 1971 onward when control over price passed from the companies to a combination of individual producer governments and of their collective instrument, the Organization of Petroleum Exporting Countries (OPEC), which was created in 1960 but only began to play an effective role in the world oil market a decade or so later.[6] Both political and market forces can be seen at play in the two great price rises of the 1970s. During the first, in 1973–74, the temporary disruptions caused by the October Arab-Israeli war, and the brief reduction in Arab oil exports (the so-called 'oil-boycott' aimed at influencing Western policy towards the Arab-Israeli conflict) encouraged producer governments to agree to set higher and higher prices, a process which culminated in the OPEC agreement to charge $11.651/barrel in January 1974.[7]

Later, during the second price explosion, triggered by the Iranian revolution and then the two sudden and unexpected Saudi production cuts in January and April 1979, the individual producing states, though unable to negotiate a common price, did manage to agree a floor price of $18/barrel in June 1979 and then a ceiling of $32/barrel in June 1980.[8] Finally, as prices began to fall in the early 1980s, owing to a decline in world demand, the preferred way of trying to prevent them from dropping still further was for OPEC members to limit production, a policy which was initiated in 1982. Each state was allocated its own quota, with the exception of Saudi Arabia which was expected to act as what was known as the 'swing' producer, with final responsibility for keeping overall output within the agreed limits.[9] But by 1985 the effects of this policy, in terms of lost revenue and a smaller and smaller market share, led the Saudi government to reverse its policy, increasing output again, and selling its oil at a considerable discount, so precipitating a price collapse from $24 to $8/barrel during 1986.[10] After a period of tension and great confusion, the OPEC member states, meeting in July–August and then again in December 1986, agreed to a new system of quotas designed to maintain a 'reference price' of $18/barrel. This was just enough to keep prices in the $15–18/barrel range until the next shock administered by the Iraqi invasion of Kuwait in August 1990.

Let us now look at the changes in ownership and control in somewhat greater detail. After the Second World War, the oil industry outside the Soviet bloc was dominated by seven multinational corporations known colloquially as the 'majors' or the 'seven sisters', five of them American (Standard Oil of New Jersey – later Exxon; Gulf; Texas Oil – later Texaco; SOCAL – later Chevron; and Socony-Vacuum – later Mobil), one Anglo-Dutch (Shell) and one British (Anglo-Iranian – later British Petroleum). In the 1950s, the seven together controlled nearly 90 percent of the non-Soviet oil, and this figure had been reduced to only 72 percent by 1972.[11] Furthermore, all were strongly represented in the Middle East through various local affiliates, for example the Kuwait Oil Company (owned jointly by BP and Gulf) and ARAMCO (SOCAL and Texas joined by Standard Oil of New Jersey and Socony-Vacuum in 1947). The only foothold established by the smaller independents at this time was in the so-called 'Neutral Zone' between Kuwait and Saudi Arabia, where a group of American companies obtained concessions in 1948 and 1949, followed by the Japanese Trading Company which obtained the offshore rights in 1957–58.[12]

The position of the majors remained more or less intact until the late 1960s when a number of factors combined to undermine their position.[13] One was the challenge posed by some of the more radical Arab regimes such as those in Iraq in 1961 and Libya after 1969. Another was the growing presence of so-called 'independent' oil companies who began to offer better terms to local governments to work concession areas uncontrolled or surrendered by one of the majors. A third was the fact that, after about two decades of oil exports, many individual Arab states had developed their own technical expertise to such an extent as to allow them to contemplate running the industry on their own via their own national oil companies such as the Kuwait National Petroleum Company (established in 1960) and the Saudi General Petroleum and Mineral Organization (Petromin, established in 1962). Other factors of importance included the increased international demand for oil which had built up during the boom years of the 1960s and the changing relations between the leading Western governments and the Arab oil producers consequent on the Arab-Israeli wars of 1967 and 1973.

Taken together, it was pressures of this type which facilitated the rapid transformation of relations running from the 1968 OPEC declaration, calling for greater local participation in oil company operations, to the general agreement of October 1972 between the majors and the producers, which provided an agreed framework by which the latter could reach full control in stages over a number of years. Events then speeded up still further as a result of the 1973 Arab-Israeli war, encouraging Kuwait to complete its 100 percent takeover of the Kuwait Oil Company in 1975, followed by Qatar in 1976–77, and then an agreement that Saudi Arabia was to obtain complete control over ARAMCO at some future date.[14]

Once full control was obtained, the Gulf states were in a position not only to set price and production levels in their own national interests but also to formulate policies regarding the structure and shape of the whole of their oil industry. This led, inevitably, to attempts to extend their control over so-called upstream operations (exploration and production) and downstream operations (refining, transport, and marketing). But in each case it was some time before they could create their own companies and develop the necessary expertise, forcing them to reach new agreements with the majors to carry out many of these operations under contract. To make matters more difficult, the fall in oil prices in the 1980s, following the decline in world demand, meant that a number of new projects involving the expansion of locally-owned refining capacity had to be postponed. It was considerations of this type which also accounted for the fact that very little new exploration was carried out from the later 1970s, and that the oil states had still only made small inroads into the refining, transport, and marketing of their own oil by 1980.[15]

DISTRIBUTION AND DEVELOPMENT IN THE OIL-BASED ECONOMIES

If there was one thing that united the ruling families of the Gulf states it was their intention to distribute their newly found oil wealth in ways that provided immediate benefit for their own populations. Proof of this proposition, if proof were needed, came from the few examples of those rulers who tried to slow down expenditures in the interests of preventing rapid change, and who were quickly and easily swept aside.[16] Hence, after what was usually a short period of confusion and mismanagement, plans were implemented, first to develop the local infrastructure in terms of water, roads, schools, etc., then to begin to provide a high level of subsidized welfare services. In this, as in many other areas, Kuwait tended to lead the way with a development program designed to make possible the introduction of a local welfare state.[17] Hence, as early as 1955, according to a British report quoted by Jill Crystal, 'the idea [was] already growing that while paying no taxes, they [the Kuwaitis] [were] entitled to free or state-subsidized education, health, water, electricity, telephone and other services.'[18] The result, in effect, was the implementation of a pattern of negative, or reverse, taxation by which the state, instead of collecting revenues, handed out benefits to its citizens as well as, on a more restricted basis, to its population of migrant workers. Other states tended to follow suit although, in the case of Saudi Arabia, only after a period in which existing taxes had to be phased out, a process which was not finally completed until the early 1970s.[19]

A second area of expenditure concerned the oil sector itself which, though employing relatively few workers, provided a stimulus for oil-based industry, beginning with refining and then moving on to other types of petrochemical products such as propane, butane, methanol, and ammonia for which oil – and later its associated gas – provided not only the feedstock but also a source of cheap energy. Problems soon arose, however, owing to the fact that labor costs rose rapidly during the 1970s, a situation which, allied with low productivity and the high cost of transport to overseas markets, largely negated many of these initial advantages.[20]

Lastly, some attention was paid to the notion of economic diversification on the grounds that oil was a finite resource and could not be expected to act as an engine of economic growth forever. Such a policy was most easily carried out in the larger Gulf states such as Saudi Arabia and Oman, where alternative activities such as agriculture, handicrafts, and locally based industry were easiest to promote. But even in the smaller city-states some effort was made to encourage non-oil industry as well as services such as banking and finance. Nevertheless, the sums each government

207

received from oil sales were often just too large to be absorbed anywhere within the local economy, particularly during the boom period of the 1970s, and here again Kuwait led the way with its decision to invest part of these revenues in other more productive economies abroad, through institutions like the Kuwait Investment Office, which managed the increasingly large sums put aside in the Fund for Future Generations (see below).[21]

However, it is also important to note that the process of redistribution usually went far beyond the formal arrangements required to develop the economy and to create a Gulf version of the welfare state. Other methods ran the whole gamut from handouts of money, land, or, sometimes, quantities of oil for private sale, to jobs in government service and the award of grossly inflated contracts or middle-men commissions to local merchants who provided goods and services for the state. We may also note the way in which some of these activities tended to be justified in terms of the need to create a flourishing private sector or, more generally, an ideology of capitalism in which the crude paternalism of the state and of the ruling family could be justified, as well as camouflaged, as a reward for industry and enterprise.[22]

Policies of development and distribution also raised the question of the relationship between local nationals and the increasing numbers of migrant workers which growth of all kinds required. As is well known, oil tended to be found in states possessing only tiny populations with very low levels of education and skill. In Qatar, for example, when oil was first exported in 1949 only 650 of its 30,000 inhabitants could read and write.[23] A few years later, the first Kuwaiti census of 1957 revealed an indigenous workforce containing just two doctors and eight accountants.[24] Foreign labor was thus required for every type of job from manual labor to the most highly skilled. Here, the oil companies led the way, followed quickly by the local governments with a huge and growing demand for foreign officials, teachers, doctors and, often, policemen and soldiers as well. To begin with, the majority of such migrants came from the Arab world itself. However, as time went on, and particularly when development really took off in the 1970s, increasing numbers of recruits were found in Asia, on the grounds that they were cheaper, less likely to bring their families with them, and easier to control.[25]

Unfortunately, accurate figures to illustrate this process are hard to find due to the fact that so many workers entered the Gulf states illegally, as well as to a general official reluctance to reveal just how dependent on foreign labor each state had become. Two other major problems are provided, first by the Saudi government's consistent exaggeration of the size of its own native population (see later section) and, second, by the difficulty in providing a realistic figure for the very large numbers of Yemenis at work in Saudi Arabia, many of whom were continually moving between the two countries across what, before 1990, was a particularly open border.[26] Table 9.3A gives details of the build-up of a foreign population and a foreign workforce from Kuwaiti statistics which are certainly the best and most reliable of all of the Gulf states, while Table 9.3B gives official figures for both population and labor force for all six Gulf states in 1970–80. It should be noted that this certainly represents a huge underestimate as can be seen from the separate country figures for the employment of Arab and Asian migrant workers given in Tables 9.3C and 9.3D which suggest that the actual number may well have been twice as large. The numbers of foreign workers continued to rise during the 1980s although at a slightly slower rate, reaching 5.54 million by 1985, if we are to believe one set of estimates, or 7.2 million, if we are to believe another.[27]

As these figures show, the numbers of foreign workers exceeded those of the local population in Kuwait by 3.5:1 as early as 1965, a situation which was later repeated throughout the rest of the Gulf, with the exception of Bahrain. This, in turn, led to pressure for two types of laws, the first defining the relationship of locals to foreigners, the second establishing the terms on which non-nationals were allowed to work. As far as nationality was concerned, the Gulf states generally defined their own citizens in terms of whether or not they, or an ancestor, had been resident in the state at a certain date, for example 1920 for Kuwait.[28] There followed another series of laws conferring significant privileges on these citizens, for example, the sole right to own land or to a controlling partnership in a local company, and a monopoly of senior positions within the administration. The effect was to turn citizenship into an enormously valuable economic resource, for it was only persons so defined who were able to gain access to the main mechanisms by which oil wealth was distributed. Lastly, to complete this process, formidable obstacles were placed in the way of any foreigner seeking local naturalization in the Naturalization Law of 1959 and its subsequent amendments.[29]

Measures were also introduced to regulate working conditions and then to define the status of the growing army of migrant workers. These began with the Saudi Labor and Work Regulations of 1947, the Kuwaiti Public Sector Labor Law of 1960 and Private Sector Law of 1964, and the Bahraini Labor Law of 1958. Strikes were not allowed and only in Kuwait were a few foreign workers permitted to join a trade union. In addition, each state introduced measures to regulate foreign labor through the issue of work permits and an increasingly tight set of rules which were supposed to ensure that each migrant worker came to do a specific job for which no local national was available, for a specific period of time, and then returned home.

The aim of all such measures was, of course, to prevent the build-up of a large, permanent foreign population which might threaten the position and privileges of the local community. But in this they only had partial success. In particular, tensions were soon revealed between government policy and the interests of important sections of local business which profited from the presence of foreign workers not only as employees but also as tenants, domestic servants, etc. To make matters more complex, responsibility for ensuring that the regulations regarding the import of migrant labor were properly observed was divided between the state and the potential employees themselves through a continuation of the old 'kafil' system by which each foreign worker employed in the private sector had to have a personal patron or sponsor. The result was the creation of an ambiguous situation. Members of the local population appeared, collectively, to resent the presence of so many foreigners as a threat to their culture and way of life, while as individuals they clearly benefited from their ability to import increasing numbers of migrants without control. It was this situation which, no doubt, accounts for the passage of a series of laws and amendments concerning the status of foreign labor. It is this too which contributed greatly to the permanent state of insecurity in which most migrant workers were forced to live, unsure of the regulations, easily exploited by their patrons, and subject, always, to the threat of instant deportation if they stepped out of line.

SAUDI ARABIA 1945–1990

Saudi revenues from crude oil increased dramatically from $10.4 million in 1946 to $333.7 million in 1960, $1.214 million in 1970, and $104.2 billion in 1980.[30] These were soon large enough to dwarf the contribution from other types of economic activity such as agriculture and trade. Indeed, by 1970, some 88 percent of government revenues came from oil, a figure which had risen to 93 percent in 1973.[31] This at once gave the government a position of dominance within the economy which it was quick to recognize and exploit. The ministry of planning noted in its introduction to the *Third Development Plan, 1980–85*, that 'economic development is to a very large extent government activity' and 'the private sector is dependent on government expenditure.'[32]

Any evaluation of the performance must begin with this fact, even though the necessary data is often incomplete and sometimes deliberately misleading. To take only the most basic statistic necessary for calculating progress, national income per head, official figures consistently overestimated the size of the Saudi population. In an early exercise in 1962–63, the Central Statistical Department established the number of Saudi nationals as 3.3 million, only for this information to be officially suppressed. A second estimate by the Central Planning Organization put it at 5.9 million in 1973, a figure later pushed up to 6.2 million, and then 7 million, by sources elsewhere in the government.[33] Meanwhile, two foreign experts, J. Birks and C. Sinclair, used data for school enrollment to obtain the more realistic figure of 4.3 million for 1974.[34]

There was a similar reluctance to acknowledge the size both of the resident foreign population and of the foreign labor force. While official government figures gave the number of non-Saudi workers as 494,000 in 1975, another calculation, by Birks, put this at 775,000 for the same year.[35] Meanwhile, Birks and Sinclair estimated the total foreign population at 1.5 million in 1974, 2.1 million for 1980 and between 2.6 million and 4.5 million in 1985.[36]

Nevertheless, for better or worse, only those figures the government has provided can be used to try to track the changing pattern of its use of oil revenues over time because it was these expenditures, and these expenditures alone, which were responsible for both the growth and the changing structure of the national economy. Let us begin by looking at this in the pre-plan era, 1945–69, before going on to examine the first two five-year plans and their stated aims and objectives.

For the first decade or so after the Second World War, the government and ARAMCO acted in tandem to spend their oil revenues. Not only did ARAMCO develop the oil sector itself but it also spread money into the rest of the economy through its policy of obtaining increasing amounts of goods and services from local merchants and contractors.[37] It also built and initially operated Saudi Arabia's second railroad, from Dhahran to the capital, Riyadh, between 1947 and 1951.[38] Meanwhile, the government began to build the first macadamized roads as well as to relieve some of the pressing needs of the urban population, although the spread of these benefits, as Edmund Asfour notes, was 'neither pervasive nor equally distributed.'[39] This first effort then came to an end as a result of an acute financial and balance of payments crisis in the period 1957–60, as a result of which the country's second king, King Saud, was forced to transfer most of his power to his half-brother, Faisal.

After a short and successful period of retrenchment, the push to develop the economy began again under Faisal in the early 1960s, with the sums allocated to such expenditures being increased from $24 million in 1960 to

$570 million in 1969, even if not much more than half was actually spent.[40] The major recipient was again the infrastructure, notably roads and public buildings. However, there were also the beginnings of an attempt to diversify activity within the oil sector with the establishment of the Saudi Arabia Fertilizer Company, for which contracts were signed in 1964 and production began in 1970.[41] Meanwhile, King Faisal's government made a start with the creation of important new public institutions such as Petromin, the state oil company, in 1962 and the Central Planning Organization in 1965.

Work on the first five-year plan, 1970–75, encouraged the government to begin to collect the data necessary to give it a sense of the country's resources and then to work out its own investment priorities. Major targets included the further development of the material infrastructure (roads, electricity, communications, and urban construction) and the expansion of the educational system to overcome an acute shortage of local manpower. The planned allocation of moneys to each sector (Table 9.4) provides a good guide to government thinking at this time, even if few of the targets were actually met.[42]

As things turned out, the first plan period also provided a striking example of the difficulties of planning in an oil economy. Begun at a time of some financial stringency, its modest aims were then completely upset by the price explosion of 1973–74 which not only altered expectations entirely but also produced another series of acute bottlenecks – particularly in the overloaded ports where ships' waiting times sometimes lasted as long as 120 days – which the second plan, 1976–79, was then forced to address.[43] Another prominent feature of the second plan was its emphasis on the development of a modern petrochemical sector based on the construction of two huge industrial estates, one at Jubayl near Dhahran, the other at Yanbu on the Red Sea – complete with water, electricity, houses, hospitals, and modern ports, and provided with both feedstock and energy by twin oil and gas pipelines completed in 1981. These were then used as a base for a number of enterprises founded and funded by a new state organization, Saudi Basic Industries Corporation (SABIC, founded in 1976) which, by 1980, had signed contracts for seven major enterprises including two for iron bars and rods, and five for the production of a variety of chemicals including ethane, methanol, and urea.[44] These projects represented a giant step forward in another sense, in that, until the early 1970s, the natural gas associated with the pumping of oil had been simply flared off as being of no economic value.

The period of the second plan also saw impo\rtant initiatives which had a more immediate effect on output. One was the use of yet another new organization, the Saudi Industrial Development Fund (SIDF), to encourage the development of a private industrial sector through the provision of expertise and long-term credit. Its 1979 report indicates that 330 new enterprises were then under way while other figures show that, by the 1980s, SIDF initiatives had helped to make the country more or less self-sufficient in building materials.[45] The second initiative was the subsidies given to local agriculturalists to encourage the production of wheat and other cereals in the interests of 'food security.' These were very effective in the sense that they caused the wheat harvest to increase fourfold during the 1970s.[46] However, as observers were quick to point out, the costs of production were some five times that of the world price while the use of modern pumps led to a considerable depletion of the major ground water resources.[47]

Problems with planning increased during the 1980s with the third five-year plan published in the midst of the oil price explosion in 1980 and the fourth (1985-90) just before the price collapse of 1986. Hence some of their stated aims were rapidly overtaken by events, for instance that of preventing the further expansion of the foreign labor force.[48] But others, such as the diversification of the economy and the encouragement of the private sector, proceeded more or less as planned, although at the expense of drawing down reserves and a growing budget deficit toward the end of the decade. One example is the continued emphasis on wheat production, with annual output increasing from 130,000 to 1.3 million tons during the third plan period (1980-85).[49] Another significant strain on the budget was a build-up of military expenditure occasioned by fears generated by the Iranian revolution and the Iran/Iraq war. This eventually led to a type of barter deal such as in the case of the so-called Al-Yamamah contract finalized in February 1986. Some $15 billion worth of British planes and associated support costs were paid for by the sale of 400,000 barrels a day of oil by Shell and British Petroleum, with the proceeds placed in a London bank account.[50]

It is difficult to evaluate the total impact of all these new initiatives as of the year 1990. Clearly, the expenditure of very large sums of money had created the beginnings of a state industrial sector together with an associated private sector heavily dependent upon it for credit and contracts. But as both remained highly subsidized, as well as highly protected from foreign competition, there is no way of telling how efficient they were or how their products would have fared if sold for profit on the world market.

What can be said with greater certainty is that the 1970s, and the second plan period in particular, witnessed a great increase in welfare both in terms of government expenditure on health, education, and housing as well as subsidies for a wide variety of goods and services. To take just one example, the proportion of school-age children attending school rose from 28 percent in 1970 to 48 percent in 1980.[51] Meanwhile, a general subsidy system introduced in about 1976 to help curb inflation included water (sold at 7 percent cost), electricity, basic foodstuffs such as wheat, sugar, and rice, as well as free education, free medical care in government hospitals, interest-free loans for housing, and welfare support for the poor.[52] By the end of the decade this system was taking up an estimated 12–15 percent of total government expenditure.[53] Later, in the 1980s, it was sufficient to provide a cushion against deteriorating economic conditions as advances in per capita income began to drift down from 1985 onward.

KUWAIT: 1945–1990

Kuwait's early experience with large oil revenues after 1945 made it the archetypal Gulf city state through its establishment of many of the patterns of distribution and development which were later copied by its small neighbors to the south. This began in the 1950s when the country's ruling family was faced with the problem of devising strategies which would allow it to establish its own control over expenditures in the face of competing claims from the British government, which maintained its protectorate until 1961, and the powerful local merchant class. To begin with it was the British who made the running with the creation of two institutions which they hoped would allow them to exercise economic control: the Development Board established in 1953 to draw up plans for capital investment in Kuwait itself, and the Investment Board, also established in 1953, to manage surplus oil revenues banked in London. However, within a matter of only a few years, the Kuwaiti ruler, Shaykh Abdullah al-Sabah, was able either to negate these initiatives with others of his own, for example the creation of the Kuwaiti National Bank in 1952, or to secure the replacement of key British officials with members of his own family and of his fledgling civil service.[54] Meanwhile, a brief financial crisis in 1953–54 provided the occasion to define his relations with the merchants by promising to protect the Kuwaiti private sector, to distribute significant revenues through the local market, and to legitimize the position of the merchants by an endorsement of a free enterprise ideology.[55]

This was the context for the introduction of three different initiatives which combined notions of planning with those of distribution and welfare. The first was the build up of the administration in such a way as to provide, *inter alia*, an increasing number of jobs for Kuwaiti nationals as well as for those migrant workers, mostly Arab, who were employed as teachers, doctors, and skilled advisers. Second, Shaykh Abdullah's government was an early advocate of free welfare services, beginning with the creation of the Social Affairs Department and then the expenditure of such large sums on its own nationals that, by 1961–62, it was spending more per person on social services than Britain.[56] Third, the government used the Kuwait Municipal Plan drawn up by British consultants in 1950 as a mechanism for distributing a significant portion of its oil revenues to local people through its Land Acquisition Policy (begun in 1951), by which the owners of houses in the old city were given money to move to newer quarters outside, while others received equally large sums for land which was purchased for the construction of roads and urban services.[57] According to Ghanim al-Najjar, KD 2.2 billion was distributed in this way between 1951 and 1981, or some 8 percent of total oil revenues and 11 percent of total government expenditure (1951–1978/79), at least half of which went into the pockets of what he terms 'the upper echelon of the power structure,' in other words members of the ruling family and their merchant allies.[58]

Formal planning on a national scale did not begin until the establishment of the Development Board in 1962, followed by the introduction of the first development plan for the period from 1967/68 to 1971/72. As usual, part of the rationale for this process was the need to establish economic and social priorities, in this case the attempt to reduce dependence on migrant labor and oil by policies of diversification and the expansion of the local educational system. In the event, however, the country experienced serious difficulties on both these counts. Diversification in a Kuwaiti context meant a combination of industrialization and downstream expansion as far as oil operations were concerned. However, the former policy was seriously handicapped, first, by the small size of the local market and then, when the government turned to export promotion in the first five-year plan, by high costs including wages well above the international average. Meanwhile, apart from some expansion in refining capacity in the 1970s, other initiatives, such as the beginnings of a petrochemical industry making fertilizer and ammonia, were hampered by weak world demand.[59] Expansion downstream also experienced great difficulties, for example the losses suffered by the Kuwait Oil Tanker Company in 1975–76.[60]

The government gave industrialization one last push in the second five-year plan, 1976–81. But when this ran into difficulties as a result of the high inflation and bottlenecks experienced during the oil price explosion of 1979, it gave increasing attention to an alternative strategy which had been growing in importance through the 1970s: the investment of oil revenues overseas where higher returns were much more easily obtained.[61]

Figures for the relative size of the income earned from foreign investment as opposed to oil provide a graphic illustration of the significance of this shift in policy. In 1978, earnings on the government's foreign investment account were KD 1,265 billion as opposed to oil revenues of KD 2,584 billion; by 1980 these had risen to KD 3.1 billion and KD 5.277 billion respectively.[62] The result was to put an end to the long debate about how to remove those obstacles which were thought to stand in the way of allowing Kuwait to absorb its own oil revenues. For what the new strategy so obviously implied was that the government now believed that it was much more profitable to invest in other countries' industries rather than in building up Kuwait's own. Popular pressure pointed in the same direction. As Crystal notes, the government's decision to create the Reserve Fund for Future Generations in 1976 as a vehicle for investing a proportion of the oil revenues abroad was an obvious response to vocal criticism that the policy of diversification was proving a costly failure.[63]

Kuwait managed to survive the period of falling oil revenues which began in the early 1980s much better than most of its Gulf neighbors. This was largely due to a combination of sound financial management and the fact that income from its foreign investments was sufficient to allow it to absorb most of the shock.[64] It meant that Kuwait enjoyed a period of steady economic growth of some 3 percent a year while maintaining surpluses in both the government account and the balance of payments. The one fly in the ointment was the fallout from the crash of the unofficial stock exchange, the Souk El-Manakh, in August 1982, leaving debts of some $23 billion, most of them in the form of unsecured loans carried by the banks and major investment companies.[65] Government efforts focused on trying to minimize the economic damage as well as on ensuring the viability of existing institutions by purchasing shares in most local financial institutions, a policy which led to a significant expansion of public ownership. Efforts to deal with the losses incurred by individual investors were less successful with no substantial progress having been made by the time of the Iraqi invasion in August 1990.[66]

Government attempts to roll back the tide of labor migration must also be counted a failure. A series of measures aimed both at making entry more difficult and at training Kuwaiti replacement made such little impact that, although the proportion of foreigners in the labor force fell from 70 percent in 1957 to 65 percent in 1970, it then rose again to 72 percent in 1980 and 85 percent in 1990.[67] In these circumstances, a more successful feature of official policy was the maintenance of the barriers it had created between foreigners and local nationals, often underpinned by an emphasis on spatial segregation introduced as early as 1951 when houses in the eight

216

new suburbs designated by the Municipal Plan were to be made available 'exclusively or preferentially' to Kuwaiti nationals.[68]

BAHRAIN AND THE STATES OF THE LOWER GULF

For Bahrain and the states of the lower Gulf the colonial period lasted until the British withdrawal in 1971. In some cases, notably Bahrain, the British presence does not seem to have acted as a particular constraint on the formation of local policy concerning the expenditure of the oil revenues. But in others, such as Qatar and Oman, development planning only began in earnest after formal independence. The United Arab Emirates, formed in 1971 as a federation including Abu Dhabi, Dubai, and five smaller statelets, presents something of a special case in that increasing oil revenues allowed the ruler of Abu Dhabi first to challenge British influence in the late 1960s and then to dominate the process of development planning in the new state.

Revenues from Bahrain's small domestic oil field increased slowly until 1966 when a second, offshore, field at Abu Safeh came on stream, profits from which were shared between Bahrain and Saudi Arabia. A study of the state's finances shows that, between the late 1940s and 1970, these revenues contributed some three-fourths of total state revenue. It also shows that just over half of total revenues were allocated to current expenditure, nearly 30 percent to the ruling family, and the remaining 20 percent to works of capital improvement.[69] From then on the picture becomes more complicated with a huge increase in spending financed by higher oil revenues and increasingly large subventions from Saudi Arabia. This continued until a series of budget deficits from 1976–77 onward forced a policy of retrenchment in which capital expenditure was slashed and many new projects postponed. The problem, as one critic has put it, was that the government was led to develop patterns of expenditure more appropriate to its richer neighbors than a resource poor state like itself.[70]

Like other Gulf states, but with more urgency, Bahrain tried to combine a policy of building up an oil-related industry with diversification into non-oil activities. As far as the former was concerned, the government negotiated a number of joint ventures with various international and local Gulf partners, notably the Aluminum Company (ALBA) established in 1968. As originally planned, the ALBA plant was supposed to benefit from the presence of both cheap oil and gas, and cheap labor. However, by the time it started production in 1972, not only was the international market for aluminum depressed, but the cost of local and imported labor had begun to rise steeply, leading to such heavy losses that the Bahraini government

217

was forced to buy out most of its original partners before managing to sell on 30 percent of its holdings to Saudi Arabia's SABIC.[71]

Plans for economic diversification were based, initially, on the exploitation of such traditional advantages as Bahrain's position as the commercial center of the Gulf.[72] However this was soon eroded by the development of rival ports, leaving no option but to introduce other types of services, for example, the offshore banking facilities begun in 1975. These provided a safe channel for the investment of the surplus oil revenues accumulating in neighboring states. The number of such banks rose from 26 in 1976 to 65 in 1981 when their activities amounted to 8.5 percent of Bahrain's GDP.[73] A somewhat less successful initiative was the establishment of the Arab Ship Building and Repair Yard (opened in 1977) as a result of an OAPEC initiative supported by Bahrain, as well as Kuwait, Qatar, Saudi Arabia, and the UAE. High wage rates in what is a very labor intensive industry made it increasingly uncompetitive and it was only able to stay in business by offering rates at well below cost.[74]

Qatar has much larger oil fields than Bahrain but its revenues only began to increase in a significant way in the early 1970s, growing from $1.8 billion in 1974 to $5.4 billion in 1980 (Table 9.1B). Prior to the adoption of the first development plan in 1973, perhaps a third of the oil money was spent on welfare while much of the rest was allowed to build up as reserves.[75] Thereafter, expenditures were rapidly increased in those areas indicated by the plan, for example health, education, housing, infrastructure (including the international airport), and oil-related industry until inflationary pressures forced the government to cut spending drastically in 1978. As elsewhere, most of the gas associated with oil production was flared until 1975 when the first liquid natural gas plant was completed; a second opened in 1979. Meanwhile, the discovery of a huge field of non-associated natural gas (the 'North Field') became a major focus for efforts at further economic diversification. In 1984 an agreement was signed with two international oil companies for its development and in 1987 work began on offshore production facilities linked to the shore by submerged pipeline. The overall aim was to provide Qatar with a mixture of cheap energy and valuable exports until the end of the twenty-first century.

Further to the southeast, in what was to become the UAE, the first small development plans were implemented by the British in the 1950s before oil production began. These were then succeeded by larger plans drawn up in the 1960s and financed, initially, by money from richer neighbors such as Bahrain and Qatar and then, increasingly, by Abu Dhabi once its own oil revenues began to rise rapidly in the latter part of the same decade (see Table 9.1B). Meanwhile, Abu Dhabi began its own five-year plan, 1968–72, in which nearly one-fourth of expenditure went on infra-structural development.[76] Abu Dhabi continued to provide the bulk of the finance for the UAE after 1971 by virtue of the fact that its revenue from oil was at least four times that of Dubai, the only other significant producer within the new federation. Most of this money was put into the hands of the newly created federal ministries.[77] The separate states were also left free to promote their own particular strategies, with Abu Dhabi tending to concentrate on such oil-related industries as refining and gas liquefaction, and Dubai on its previous expertise in trade and in providing services for Gulf shipping, most notably the construction of a huge dry dock completed in 1979.

The UAE was particularly hard hit by the fall in oil prices after 1980. This produced a series of budget deficits beginning in 1982, the cancel-lation or scaling down of a number of major projects and, most important of all, a decline in GDP of some 4.5 percent a year between 1980 and 1989, the sharpest fall in any of the Gulf states.[78]

Turning lastly to Oman, while the export of oil began in 1967, technical problems meant that increase in output was slow in both the early and the late 1970s (Tables 9.1A and 9.1B). It was only after the British-inspired coup in which Sultan Said Bin Taymur was deposed by his son, Qabus, in 1970, that the Omani government was able to develop the structures necessary to spend its new wealth. To give just one example of its lack of infrastructure at this time, there were only 19 miles of paved roads in the whole country.[79] There were also the problems presented by the fierce guerrilla war conducted against anti-government insurgents in the western province of Dhufar between 1970 and 1975.

The first five-year development plan, introduced in 1976, gave priority to spending on infrastructure (mainly roads, electricity, and water), edu-cation, and health.[80] There was also a nod towards economic diversification in the shape of agriculture, fishing, and industry. However, progress in this area was slow and shortages of both money and skilled labor forced the abandonment of early hopes of establishing both a fertilizer and a gas liquefaction plant.[81] There were further problems in the 1980s when falling oil prices led to decreased revenues and reduced government expenditure. Hence plans to diversify the economy had to wait until the end of the decade when there was new emphasis on tourism, on industry, and on efforts to attract foreign investment, including the opening of the Muscat stock exchange in 1990.

THE POOR RELATIONS: THE YEMEN ARAB REPUBLIC AND THE PEOPLE'S DEMOCRATIC REPUBLIC OF YEMEN

The two states of the Arabian peninsula where no oil was found until the 1980s were those in north Yemen, which became the Yemen Arab Republic (YAR) after the overthrow of the imamate regime in 1962, and in south Yemen where the British colony of Aden together with its associated protectorates gained their independence in 1967 and were thereafter renamed the People's Democratic Republic of Yemen (PDRY).[82] Nevertheless, given their close proximity to Saudi Arabia and the Gulf, their economies were increasingly dominated by the oil revenues they received at second hand via official aid from their richer neighbors and from the remittances sent back by their migrant workers. By 1980 it is estimated that the YAR had some 550,000 short-term migrants at work in the rest of the peninsula sending back remittances worth approximately $1 billion while the PDRY had over 200,000 such workers sending back $180 million (see Table 9.5). In each case these migrants are supposed to have consisted of roughly a third of the total adult labor force.[83]

In the north, there was little economic progress before the overthrow of the imamate government in 1962. This was then followed by some eight years of fighting before the new, Egyptian-backed regime could establish control over the greater part of the country. In these circumstances it was difficult to do more than make a start in confronting the major problems facing a country with a tiny central administration, few literate people, and extremely bad communications between its component parts. But with the establishment of peace in 1970 came a huge expansion in government and government services encouraged by the return of many of the merchant families who had left the country during the imamate period and, even more importantly, the arrival of financial and other assistance from a wide variety of external sources, most notably Saudi Arabia which agreed, first, to lift its ban on the entry of Yemeni migrant labor and then, in 1973, to cover the annual budget deficit. The result was a huge influx of development aid and labor remittances, sufficient to meet the country's entire budgetary expenditure for much of the 1970s and amounting to some 120 percent of GNP in the early 1980s.[84]

From a statistical point of view, the YAR economy grew at an unusually rapid rate during the 1970s with GNP doubling in real terms between 1969/70 and 1976/77.[85] This in turn was the result of a huge increase in government and other services as well as a rapid growth in imports fueled by the increase in remittances from abroad. The impact on the agricultural sector was particularly striking. A combination of labor shortages, rising wages, and competition from imported foods caused a significant shift away from cotton and cereals and toward higher value crops such as fruits, vegetables, and the ubiquitous mild narcotic qat, the chewing of which, according to Shelagh Weir, became near universal in Yemen during the 1970s.[86] Given these powerful trends, government efforts to promote its own economic goals such as industrialization and self-sufficiency in cereals could make little progress. It also found itself in an increasing financial crisis as a result of a growing budget deficit – some 30 percent of GDP by 1982 – which it was forced to cover by the inflationary process of simply borrowing from the Central Bank.[87]

The arrival of the first revenues from oil exports in 1987 provided some temporary relief, permitting increased expenditures on schools, hospitals, and roads. However, this was not sufficient to offset the decline in aid from Arab donors as well as the concomitant reduction of the level of remittances. Hence per capita income began to fall from 1982 onwards. There was also an increasing trade deficit which the government sought to reduce by a severe restriction on imports by means of a strict system of licensing.

South Yemen's entry into the oil era was somewhat longer delayed. During the British period it experienced a very unbalanced form of economic growth due to the disparity between the wealth of the Aden colony and the harsh conditions facing agriculturalists in the rest of the protectorate. Then came a double shock to Aden in 1967 with the closure of the Suez Canal, and the consequent huge reduction in ships using its bunkering facilities, followed immediately by the withdrawal both of British aid and of the British garrison at independence. Something of the losses involved can be gauged from the fact that, until then, British budgetary support had financed approximately two-thirds of government expenditure while the British base had generated some $10 million in wages and services for the local population.[88] To make matters worse, the increasingly radical policies of the new south Yemeni government led to a huge exodus of businessmen and professionals to the north.[89] The result, according to one estimate, was a drop in GNP of some 20 percent between 1966 and 1968.[90]

The new government soon proclaimed itself a Marxist-Socialist one and proceeded to nationalize most areas of business activity in 1969. It also launched a complicated process of land reform in the rural areas of the old protectorates which so disrupted affairs that, according to the World Bank, agricultural production continued to decline 1967–1977.[91] This was a socialism of poverty in which the regime's efforts to create a single-party state and to provide better services for the population were severely constrained by its lack of economic resources. Some initial assistance was provided by the Soviet Union, China, and the states within the Eastern

Bloc. However, over time, a combination of financial and popular pressure forced the regime to look for help from Saudi Arabia and the Gulf, a switch in policy which produced a huge expansion in the sums received from aid and remittances. Indeed, by 1977, it has been estimated that the latter contributed at least 40 percent of GDP.[92] Another bright spot in this otherwise grim picture is the fact that government spending on education was increased to such an extent as to allow a growth in school enrollment rates by over 400 percent between 1966/67 and 1979/80 including a significant proportion of girls.[93]

Growing tensions inside the political leadership intensified the economic difficulties of the 1980s, culminating in a short-lived civil war in January 1986 in which over 10,000 people were killed. This was followed by a marked falling away in Soviet aid as the Soviet Union began its terminal decline. The result was a renewed interest in unity with the somewhat more prosperous north, a process begun in 1988 and completed in May 1990. This was accompanied by new plans to revive the port of Aden as well as to intensify the development of the south's oil fields which had begun production in 1987 and export in 1989.

OIL AND MIDDLE EAST ECONOMIC INTEGRATION

From the moment that Kuwait became a substantial oil exporter in the early 1950s there were people, both British and Arab, who saw its revenues as a potential source of development funding for the poorer but more populous states of the Middle East. However, it was not until the creation of the Kuwait Fund for Arab Economic and Social Development in 1961 that this idea found concrete expression in an institution specifically designed to lend money for Arab projects. In so doing it provided a nice example of enlightened self-interest: by channeling part of its surplus revenues to its more powerful neighbors it was also able to demonstrate its practical commitment to Arabism in a way which helped to reinforce its own legitimacy in the face of the many threats to its independence emanating from Iraq and elsewhere. In its first five years of operation, 1961–66, the fund disbursed some $145 million in development loans to seven Arab countries including Jordan, Lebanon, and Egypt.[94]

More institutions of the same type were soon created. As far as specifically Kuwait initiatives were concerned, these included the African/Arab Bank and the Gulf Permanent Assistance Committee (GUPAC) which was established in 1962 to provide direct grants to the still oil-poor states of the lower Gulf. By such means Kuwait came to spend some 10 percent of its

GDP in development assistance during the late 1960s and early 1970s.[95] Then came the boom years of the early 1970s which saw an explosion of state-owned as well as multi-state organizations. An example of the first type was the Abu Dhabi Fund for Arab Economic Development which administered funds worth $1.25 billion between 1971 and 1980.[96] Examples of the second type include the Arab Fund for Economic and Social Development, which began operations in 1972, and the OPEC Fund, which started up in 1976. In addition, an even larger conduit of direct financial assistance was opened up at the Khartoum Arab summit following the Arab-Israeli war of 1967, during which the oil rich states pledged to provide large sums of money to the so-called front-line states in the struggle against Israel, namely Egypt, Syria, and Jordan.

Attempts to calculate the total amount of Gulf funds transferred to the rest of the Arab world can only yield approximate figures owing to the huge number of agencies involved as well as the difficulty of distinguishing between loans – some part of which were repaid – and grants. One of the more useful attempts is by the British economist, R.S. Porter, who suggests that by 1980 net disbursements from Kuwait, Qatar, Saudi Arabia, and the UAE had reached some $8.3 billion before falling sharply to $4.4 billion in 1984 as oil prices and revenues began to decline (see Table 9.6). Porter's estimates also help to pinpoint the actual distribution of this aid indicating that, during the period 1974–78, by far the largest share – just over two-thirds – was directed towards the three front-line states, with another 17 percent to the rest of the Arab Middle East and another 3.6 percent to North Africa.[97] Later, in the 1980s, much larger sums were either given or loaned to Iraq, in support of its war against revolutionary Iran.

A second, and probably larger, flow of funds resulted from the remittances sent home by the millions of Arab workers in the Gulf. These are if anything even more difficult to estimate owing to the fact that only some of them were transmitted through official banking channels and so recorded in each country's national statistics. Sinclair's study of recorded remittances in 1980 gives figures of $3 billion going to Egypt, over $1 billion to the YAR, and about $0.5 billion to Jordan.[98] It should be noted, however, that some estimates of the unofficial transfers of Arab migrant workers, including the value of the goods they sent home, come to anything up to four or five times the official figures.[99]

Given the economic importance of financial flows of this size it was inevitable that there should be calls for them to be regularized in such a way as to allow planning and predictability in the aid-receiving, migrant-exporting, states. One such was Crown Prince Hassan of Jordan's advocacy of something he called a 'labor-compensation' facility in which the Gulf states would pay a regular subsidy to meet some of the costs of educating those workers who were employed outside their own country of origin. A second, more ambitious, scheme was presented to the Arab economic summit which was convened in Amman in 1980. This would have had the rich oil producers commit themselves to financing a joint Arab economic action program to last for ten years.[100] But all such initiatives immediately ran counter to certain basic political and economic facts. On the one hand, the labor exporters had an interest in sending as many of their nationals abroad as they possibly could, without any let or hindrance. On the other, as Giacomo Luciani notes, the capital rich states were anxious to maintain their freedom of action to spend their revenues where and how they liked.[101] In these circumstances, integration between the Gulf and the rest of the world was achieved not so much by institutionalized exchange as by the creation of a web of pan-Arab institutions which by 1980 had come to constitute what Yusif Sayigh has called a 'Joint Arab Economic Sector' consisting of hundreds of banks, funds, and joint ventures.[102]

Meanwhile, in the Gulf itself, forces were at work creating an interest in economic as well as political and military coordination soon to find expression in the establishment of the Gulf Cooperation Council (GCC) comprising Saudi Arabia, Kuwait, Bahrain, Qatar, the UAE, and Oman in 1981. Given the fact that all six were oil-based economies, it was decided that efforts toward greater economic integration should take the form not of promoting trade between the members but of building joint institutions, harmonizing laws and regulations, and creating joint ventures in the industrial field.[103] There was also an understanding that the states should move towards the creation of a customs union with a common external tariff in order to satisfy the conditions laid down by the European Economic Community as a necessary first step in negotiating privileged access for Gulf petrochemical products to the European market. In the event, however, progress towards integration was slow. It could well be argued that many of the joint projects initiated for infrastructural as well as industrial development would have taken place anyway, whether the GCC existed or not. It was also discovered that the member states often had quite different interests when it came to such matters as tariff policy which some, like Oman, used much more for revenue purposes than others. As a result, most of the targets concerning harmonization of rules and policy were either not met by the agreed time or were met only in part, a problem which continued in even greater form after the Gulf War of 1990–91.

224

Notes on Chapter 9
Full details of all sources are in the Bibliography

1 Organization of Arab Petroleum Exporting Countries (OAPEC), *Secretary General's Fifteenth Annual Report*, Table A7.
2 Congressional Quarterly, *The Middle East*, p 75.
3 Sayigh, *Arab Oil Policies in the 1970s*, p 112. This figure represents the posted price for Arabian Light, a standard oil with a specific gravity of 34°–34.9°.
4 For example, Penrose, 'International Oil Companies and Governments in the Middle East,' p 130n.
5 See, for example, the long discussion in Sayigh, *Arab Oil Policies*, pp 105–10, 131–8. Strictly speaking, economic rent is the difference between the marginal cost of production and the marginal cost of producing the next best alternative.
6 OPEC's founder members consisted of seven Arab states (Algeria, Iraq, Libya, Kuwait, Saudi Arabia, and Abu Dhabi, later joined by Qatar) and six non-Arab ones including Iran. A second organization, OAPEC (Organization of Arab Petroleum Exporting Counties), was established in 1968 with a membership which by 1973 included all the Gulf states except Oman.
7 Golub, *When Oil and Politics Mix*, p 12; Sayigh, *Arab Oil Policies*, p 119. The price was set for something called 'marker' crude, actually Arabian Light 34°.
8 *Ibid.*, pp 25–30; Sayigh, *Arab Oil Policies*, p 120.
9 The first official use of the notion of Saudi Arabia as a 'swing' producer was in 1983. See Yergen, *The Prize*, p 747.
10 OAPEC, *Secretary General's Fourteenth Annual Report*, p 5.
11 Penrose, 'International Oil Companies and Governments in the Middle East.'
12 Longrigg, *Oil in the Middle East*, pp 214–16, 305–12. The leading American independent was the Pacific Western Oil Company which changed its name to Getty Oil in 1956.
13 Penrose, 'International Oil Companies and Governments in the Middle East,' pp 3–35 and Sayigh, *Arab Oil Policies*, pp 19–61, give nicely contrasting accounts of this process.
14 There is some doubt as to exactly when Saudi Arabia's 100 percent participation in ARAMCO was reached but one source suggests that Petromin took over the final 40 percent in 1980. However, it also maintains that ARAMCO changed from acting as a partner to a service company in 1976. See Anthony McDermott in the *Financial Times*, 28 April 1980. But, whatever the case, the successor company, Saudi ARAMCO, was not formally established until 1988.
15 Sayigh, *Arab Oil Policies*, pp 74–5.
16 For example, see Townsend, 'Philosophy of State Development Planning,' p 35.
17 'An Account of Kuwait's Sudden Access to Wealth,' enclosure in A.D.M. Ross, Foreign Office 8 June 1953, PRO POWE 33/1927.
18 Quoted in Crystal, *Oil and Politics*, p 79.
19 Chaudhry, *The Price of Wealth*, pp 76–84, 144–6 and 164.
20 This point is forcefully made in the United Nations Industrial Development Organization (UNIDO) report, *Long Term Prospects for Industrial Development in Bahrain*.
21 For example, Crystal, *Kuwait*, p 52.
22 See, for example, the introduction to the second Saudi five-year plan which states: 'The economic system of Saudi Arabia is based on the principle of free economy where a substantial part of the production and distribution of goods and services is to be left to individuals enjoying freedom in their dealings and transactions.' Quoted in Olsen, 'Saudi Arabia in the 1970s: State, Oil and Development Policy,' p 15.

23 Finnie, *Desert Enterprise*, p 119.
24 Shihab, 'Kuwait,' p 465.
25 For greater detail, see Owen, *Migrant Workers in the Gulf*, pp 4–13.
26 The *Middle East Economic Digest (MEED)* suggested a conservative figure of 400,000 Yemeni workers in Saudi Arabia, 9 May 1980, p 38. Another authoritative work puts it at 600,000. See Shaw and Long, *Saudi Arabian Modernization*, pp 46–7.
27 Both sets of figures come from estimates made by Birks and Sinclair, two of the best-known experts in this field. The main difference between them is that they contain two quite different figures for the immigrant population of Saudi Arabia: 2.6 million versus 4.5 million. Compare Birks, 'The Demographic Challenge in the Arab Gulf,' Table 7.2, with the higher estimates (also by Birks and Sinclair) cited by Findlay, *The Arab World*, Table 5.2.
28 The first Kuwaiti nationality decrees of 1948 spoke of continuous residence since 1899. This was changed to 1920 in a second law of 1959. Crystal, *Oil and Politics*, pp 79, 186n.
29 For a good discussion of the 1959 law, its supporters and its critics, see Russell, 'Uneasy Welcome,' pp 117–20, 159, and 202–5.
30 OPEC, *Annual Statistical Bulletin* 1994, Tables 136 and 140.
31 Olsen, 'Saudi Arabia in the 1970s,' p 120.
32 Kingdom of Saudi Arabia, Ministry of Planning, *Third Development Plan 1400–1405 AH, 1980–1985 AD*, pp 30, 32.
33 Holden and Johns, *The House of Saud*, p 393.
34 *Ibid.*
35 Kingdom of Saudi Arabia, Ministry of Planning, *Third Development Plan 1400–1405 AH, 1980–1985 AD*, Table 2.5; Holden and Johns, *The House of Saud*, p 394.
36 For 1974 see Holden and Johns, *The House of Saud*, p 393; for 1980 and 1985 see reference to Birks and Sinclair in note 27 above.
37 For example, Chaudhry, *The Price of Wealth*, p 91.
38 Finnie, *Desert Enterprise*, p 77.
39 Asfour, 'Prospects and Problems of Economic Development of Saudi Arabia, Kuwait and the Desert Principalities,' p 370. Finnie notes that in 1954 ARAMCO spent as much ($12 million) on paying its local contractors as the government allocated to its school construction budget; Finnie, *Desert Enterprise*, pp 164–5.
40 Asfour, 'Prospects and Problems of Economic Development of Saudi Arabia, Kuwait and the Desert Principalities,' p 371.
41 According to Townsend, construction faults only allowed the fertilizer plant to operate at 30–40 percent capacity, 'L'Industrie en Arabie saoudite,' p 42.
42 Holden and Johns, *The House of Saud*, p 391.
43 Kingdom of Saudi Arabia, Ministry of Planning, *Third Development Plan 1400–1405 AH, 1980–1985 AD*, pp 25–6.
44 See At-Twaijri, *The SABIC Challenge*, Table 1.1, pp 19–20.
45 Townsend, 'L'Industrie en Arabie saoudite,' p 49; sources quoted in Olsen, 'Saudi Arabia in the 1970s,' p 17.
46 Joffe, 'Agricultural Development in Saudi Arabia,' p 209.
47 *Ibid.*, pp 212–17.
48 Kingdom of Saudi Arabia, Ministry of Planning, *Third Development Plan 1400–1405 AH, 1980–1985 AD*, p 16.
49 Kingdom of Saudi Arabia, Ministry of Planning, *Fourth Development Plan Strategy, 1405–1410 AH, 1986–1990 AD*, p 6.

50 'Saudi Arabia notifies Shell and BP that it will take over direct marketing of arms deal oil sales at year end,' *Middle East Economic Survey*, 34/45 (5 August 1996), pp A1-2.

51 Gause, *Oil Monarchies*, p 64.

52 See 'Social Welfare and the System of Consumer Subsidies, Payments and Services,' unclassified report produced by the US Embassy, Riyadh (1 May 1984), pp 4–23.

53 *Ibid.*, Table 7, p 23.

54 This process is still not well understood. For descriptions of some parts of it, see al-Najjar, 'Decision-Making Process in Kuwait,' pp 28–33 and Crystal, *Oil Politics in the Gulf*, pp 75–9.

55 Crystal, *Oil Politics in the Gulf*, p 75.

56 Mallakh, *Kuwait*, p 78.

57 Al-Najjar, 'Decision-Making Process in Kuwait,' pp 91–2.

58 *Ibid.*, pp 92, 99–103.

59 Mallakh and Atta, *The Absorptive Capacity of Kuwait*, p 27.

60 *Ibid.*, pp 28–9.

61 Crystal, *Oil Politics in the Gulf*, pp 51–2.

62 Kuwait, Ministry of Planning, Central Statistical Office, Annual Statistical Abstract 1983, p 205.

63 Crystal, *Kuwait*, p 52.

64 El-Erian, 'Accumulation for Future Generations,' p 3.

65 The gross figure for total losses was $92 billion which netted out to $23 billion, *Financial Times*, 23 May 1995. For a good general account of the whole crisis see Kireyev, 'An Analysis of Kuwait's Debt Collection Program,' p 42.

66 *Ibid.*, pp 42–3.

67 Kuwait, *Annual Statistical Abstract 1983*, p 105; El-Erian, 'Accumulation for Future Generations,' p 3n.

68 Crystal, *Oil and Politics in the Gulf*, p 79.

69 Abdel-Latif, 'Public Finance in Bahrain from 1935 to 1981 with Special Emphasis on the Allocation of Oil Revenues in the Past, Present and Future,' p 97.

70 *Ibid.*, pp 98–102.

71 Yousef, 'An Evaluation of Bahrain's Major Industries and their Future Prospects,' pp 124–5.

72 For example, minute by W.J.S., 26 November 1959, 'Economic Future of Bahrain,' PRO FO 371/132567.

73 Ghantus, 'The Financial Centre and its Future,' pp 133–7.

74 Yousef, 'An Evaluation of Bahrain's Major Industries and their Future Prospects,' pp 126–77.

75 El Mallakh, *Qatar: Development of an Oil Economy*, pp 56–8.

76 El Mallakh, *The Economic Development of the United Arab Emirates*, pp 21–3.

77 *Ibid.*, p 17.

78 World Bank, *World Development Report 1991*, Table 2.

79 *Middle East Review* 1981, p 280.

80 Skeet, *Oman*, p 104.

81 Nyrop et al. (eds), *Area Handbook for the Persian Gulf States*, 2nd revised ed., p 376.

82 Aden and the protectorates were briefly united by the British as the Federation of South Arabia, 1963–67. The YAR and the PDRY were united in 1990 as a single political entity.

83 Steffan and Blanc, 'La Démographie de la République arabe du Yéman,' p 60.

84 Chaudhry, *The Price of Wealth*, p 193 and Table 5.1.
85 World Bank, *Yemen Arab Republic*, 3rd ed., 'Summary and Conclusions,' p i.
86 Mundy, 'Agricultural Development in the Yemeni Tihama'; Kopp, 'Land Usage and its Implications for Yemeni Agriculture'; Weir, 'Economic Aspects of the Qat Industry in North-Western Yemen,' pp 22–3, 32, 46–7, and 64.
87 Claus and Hofmann, *The Importance of the Oil-producing Countries of the Gulf Cooperation Council for the Development of the Yemen Arab Republic and the Hashemite Kingdom of Jordan*, p ii.
88 Nyrop et al. (eds), *Area Handbook for the Yemen*, pp 118–19.
89 *Ibid.*, p 119.
90 *Ibid.*
91 Quoted in Stookey, *South Yemen*, p 83.
92 *Ibid.*, pp 90–1.
93 Lackner, *PDR Yemen*, pp 133–4.
94 El Mallakh, *Kuwait*, Table 3, p 204.
95 *Ibid.*, p 183.
96 El Mallakh, *The Economic Development of the United Arab Emirates*, p 146.
97 Porter, 'Gulf Aid and Investment in the Arab World,' Table 9.2, p 193.
98 Sinclair, 'Migrant Workers,' pp 216–17.
99 For example, see Richards and Waterbury, *Political Economy*, pp 389–90.
100 Sayigh, 'A New Framework for Complementarity,' pp 158–66.
101 Luciani, 'Allocation vs Production States,' pp 80–3.
102 Sayigh, *Arab Oil Policies*, pp 204–5.
103 El-Kuwaiz, 'Economic Integration of the Cooperation Council of the Arab States of the Gulf,' p 77.

Epilogue and Conclusion: The 1990s and Beyond

THE MIDDLE EAST UNTIL 1996: AN OVERVIEW

This book has focused on the national economies as the units of analysis to examine structural change, economic growth, income distribution, and welfare in the Middle East during the twentieth century. As the chapters on individual countries have made clear, the pace of demographic and economic change in the region was quite different in the two periods we have defined for the purposes of this volume; it was relatively limited until 1945 and markedly more rapid afterwards in all countries.

The population of the Middle East excluding Iran increased from some 42 million in 1918 to about 63 million in 1950 at an average annual rate of 1.3 percent per year. The pace of urbanization and the shift from agriculture to the urban economy occurred relatively slowly until mid-century. Oil exploration and production was initiated during the inter-war period in Iraq, Saudia Arabia, and the Gulf but the revenues remained insignificant until after the Second World War except in Iraq. As for economic growth, even though reliable evidence on long term trends in GDP per capita is available only for Turkey and Egypt, it is possible to reach some generalizations for the region as a whole since these two countries accounted for more than 60 percent of the population. In Turkey, per capita production levels in 1950 were approximately 25 percent higher than the levels attained in 1913. In Egypt there was little change from 1913 until 1950. For the region as a whole, then, one can project only a limited upward trend for per capita GDP until mid-century.

A comparison of the Middle East with other regions of the world from 1913 to 1950 indicates that Western Europe, North America, Australia, and Latin America all fared better until mid-century, achieving annual rates of increase in per capita GDP of 1 percent or better. The growth performance of the Middle East is roughly in the same category with Eastern and Southern Europe where long term rates of annual change in per capita GDP varied between 0 and 1 percent per annum. In contrast, Asia excluding Japan actually showed a downward trend in GDP per capita until 1950.[1]

One important reason for the less than stellar performance of the Middle East during the first half of the century was the political change it experienced. The end of the Ottoman Empire, the incorporation of large parts of the region into the British and French colonial empires, and the subsequent creation of new nation states led to the erection of tariff barriers and a variety of other obstacles to the largely free movement of goods and labor which had been a prominent feature of the region during the nineteenth century and before.

The political regimes probably contributed to the relatively weak economic performance as well. Angus Maddison and Alejandro Diaz, amongst others, have argued that developing economies which adopted protectionism and inward-looking policies generally fared better during the Great Depression of the 1930s than those that adhered to the earlier strategy based on primary exports.[2] But the combination of colonial or mandate regimes with the continued power of large agrarian interests in many parts of the Middle East made it very difficult to abandon the earlier formula. The significant exception is Turkey where a political configuration consisting of bureaucratic middle class government elites and mostly small and medium sized agricultural producers facilitated the shift to protectionism in 1929 and the adoption of etatism a few years later. Turkey's industrialization and growth performance during the 1930s was the strongest in the region.

We have even less evidence about income distribution and welfare. Estimates of life expectancy, infant mortality, and literacy are virtually non-existent for the period before 1950. In all likelihood, some progress was made in education and health care, but these gains were limited in view of the trends in GDP per capita and the absence of a major shift in government expenditures towards health and education.

As was the case in many other parts of the developing world, all demographic, economic, and social trends in the Middle East accelerated considerably after 1950. The long term annual growth rate of the population jumped from 1.3 percent in the earlier period to 2.7 percent. Rural-to-urban migration also accelerated, reducing the share of the rural population from about 70 percent in 1950 to less than 45 percent by 1990. This shift was accompanied by the decline in the share of agriculture in overall employment and the rise in the share of the urban economy including the informal sector (see the Statistical Appendix at the end of the volume).

During the second half of the century, industrialization combined with the growing importance of oil to bring about a significant long-term trend of economic growth. Even though the quality of national income accounts in many countries of the region is not very good until the 1960s and GDP estimates for some countries have not been available in recent decades, an annual rate of growth of 3 percent per annum for the entire region can be offered as a rough estimate for the period 1950 to 1990.[3] As a result, per capita production and income levels of the region in 1990 were approximately three times as high as they had been in 1950. This growth rate places the region under study in this volume above other developing regions except East and Southeast Asia. Without the oil revenues, however, the long-term performance of the region would have been close to the averages for the developing countries as a whole.[4]

One important problem for the region was the poor performance of agriculture, often due to the increasing scarcity of land in the face of population growth and the continued tendency of governments to view the agricultural sector primarily as the source of resources for urban development. As a result, self sufficiency in food became increasingly difficult to attain for most countries.

At the same time, there is no doubt that indicators for human development such as life expectancy, infant mortality, and literacy showed significant improvements since the 1950s and the 1960s when they began to be measured on a regular basis.[5] A good part of this improvement was due to the strong correlation between these indices and per capita incomes as well as the fact that, by international standards, income distribution was less unequal in the Middle East than in other regions of the developing world.[6] There is no doubt that that progress in this area would have been much greater if the governments had been willing to allocate a larger share of their budgets to health and education.

231

One important trend that began in the inter-war period, gained momentum in the 1950s and lasted through the take-over of the oil companies in the 1970s was that of nationalization and the transfer of the productive assets from foreigners to states and residents of the region. This shift was accompanied by the rising importance of the public sector. Even though public sector-led ISI performed reasonably well in the early stages, the problems became increasingly apparent in the 1970s. The infant industries had difficulties growing up. They experienced significant problems of stagnation, inefficiency, inability to compete in the export markets, and inability to expand employment. International comparative advantage was often ignored. Heavy industry was favored while agriculture and light industry was neglected.

Since the middle of the 1970s the international agencies have also been pressing for the implementation of a long-term package designed to promote greater reliance on market forces, increased emphasis on the private sector, and greater orientation towards international markets. As a result, most countries of the region have been forced to come to terms with the problems of the inward-looking strategy and to re-orient their economies outward in response to the international forces.[7]

The pace and content of efforts for economic reform showed large variations from one country to another. The uneven progress of structural adjustment programs can best be understood in terms of the interaction of domestic and external forces. While the benefits of reform are always uncertain, various groups easily identify themselves as the losers, at least in the short term. For this reason, those that stand to lose have often been in a better position to act collectively than those that may gain in the longer term. Overcoming the political opposition of the former has depended in most cases on the the availability of external resources to support the transition, the strength of the domestic coalition in favor of the reforms as well as the ability and skill of the governments in charge of the design and implementation of the programs.[8]

Since 1990 many parts of the region have been recovering from the impact of the Gulf War. Economic performance varied greatly from country to country. Some economies were particularly hard hit by the war and its aftermath. Iraqi income declined precipitously as a result of the sanctions imposed by the United Nations while Kuwait had to spend huge sums of money, perhaps as much as $65 billion, on reconstruction before economic activity could return to its pre-war levels.[9] The economies of the Gulf also continued to suffer from the fact that oil prices remained flat while a number of them felt obliged to spend between 5 and 10 percent of their GDP on imports of military equipment.[10] The new Yemeni economy formed from the union of North and South in 1990 was also hurt severely by the expulsion of some one million Yemeni workers from Saudi Arabia at the start of the Gulf War. The Palestinian economy in the West Bank and Gaza remained a victim of the ups and downs of the peace process and the frequent border closures which prevent workers from crossing into Israel. The three largest non-oil economies of the region, Turkey, Israel, and Egypt, were also affected by the war but not as severely. According to World Bank figures, GDP for the region as a whole increased only a little faster than population since the Gulf War, making it the slowest growing region of the developing world between 1990 and 1995.[11]

With the exception of Turkey which had begun its process of structural adjustment in the early 1980s, the Gulf War also provided the fillip to the first serious efforts made by the governments of the region to privatize, to deregulate, and to open up their economies to foreign trade and investment. Progress was most obvious in Egypt and Israel although, in each case, there were difficult technical problems involved in preparing state companies for sale, as well as much opposition from vested interests and a general fear of going too fast and so exacerbating existing social problems such as high levels of unemployment. Elsewhere, in Jordan, Yemen, and a number of Gulf states, the economic reform process was characterized by reduced tariffs and the introduction of new investment laws. Successive governments in Turkey, however, found it politically difficult to sell off state assets to foreigners. They also had little success in controlling public expenditures and inflation rates hovered around 100 percent per year as a result. Syria too made hardly any progress toward reducing the power and importance of the public sector except in the case of new investment where the private sector's share expanded considerably.

In the eyes of many international observers, it was the failure of most governments of the region to grasp the nettle of economic reform which was also responsible for the region's poor economic performance in attracting foreign investment after the Gulf War. According to IMF figures, the economies of the Middle East and North Africa (Turkey, Israel, and the Arab countries along the Mediterranean littoral) received only 1 percent of the total foreign direct investment in the world during the first half of the 1990s, amounting to a little less than 1 percent of the GDP of the region.[12] However, other factors were obviously important, notably the continued political tensions throughout the region and the fact that so many of the economies depended very largely on an uncertain income from oil. There were, however, some encouraging signs: even though many aspects of the structural adjustment process moved slowly, macroeconomic conditions in terms of the maintenance of tight fiscal and monetary policies were beginning to compare favorably with those in other regions of the world, giving hope that the Middle East would not be subject to those sudden reversals of capital flows experienced by the economies of East and Southeast Asia in 1997.[13]

DIVERGING TRAJECTORIES SINCE 1950

The second half of the twentieth century witnessed a significant widening of the differentials in per capita incomes between the countries of the region. For this reason, it has become increasingly difficult to talk about trends for the region as a whole. Below, we provide an admittedly simple, two by two scheme to take into account the diverging trajectories of the countries of the region since 1950, based on population size (small and large) and availability of oil revenues (oil and non-oil).

Small, oil-exporting countries of the Gulf: Kuwait, Oman, United Arab Emirates, Bahrain, and Qatar

From 1945 onward, these states were transformed from a collection of small towns reliant on fishing, herding, and trade to some of the world's leading exporters of oil with high per capita incomes, an unusual level of welfare services and the beginnings of a modern petrochemical industry. With the rise of oil revenues in the early 1970s, these countries rapidly raised the level of domestic activity by accepting a growing volume of immigrant workers and the political risks associated with that strategy. By 1990 more than 40 percent of the population of these countries was made up of foreigners more than half of whom came from other Arab countries. In 1990 the small Gulf countries made up 3.4 percent of the total population of the region as defined for the purposes of this volume but accounted for more than 17 percent of its GNP.[14]

Large oil exporters: Iraq and Saudi Arabia

From mostly agrarian or nomadic economies, these two countries have been transformed in the postwar period into large exporters of oil. In contrast to the small states of the Gulf, their population size has given them greater capacity to absorb oil revenues in various domestic development projects ranging from irrigation and agricultural development to heavy industrialization. At the same time, however, the 'Dutch disease' effect has

234

hurt the competitiveness of the tradables sectors, all but eliminating the possibility of exports outside oil and oil products. Saudi Arabia has relied heavily on labor imported primarily from neighboring Yemen in its development projects since the 1960s. However, political problems have prevented a more efficient use of the oil revenues based on its massive reserves. Similarly, in the case of Iraq, the large oil revenues were squandered in a prolonged war against Iran.

Small non-oil countries: Syria, Yemen, Lebanon, Jordan, and the Occupied Territories

This has been a diverse group. The small population size and limited availability of natural resources have placed serious limitations on industrialization strategies based on the domestic market. As a result, the more successful countries in this group have chosen to keep their economies relatively open and have pursued diverse specialties based on skill in trade, finance, and industry. Jordan and Lebanon have tried to take advantage of their specialties in trade and finance subject to the political and geopolitical constraints they have faced in the postwar period. Syria lagged behind in these respects, remaining more inward-looking. Despite its considerable agricultural resources, Yemen has remained the poorest country of the region and is increasingly dependent on remittances from emigrant workers.

More generally, the emergence of an oil-based growth center in the Gulf and Saudi Arabia since the 1970s attracted large numbers of workers from the Arab speaking countries of the region, especially Egypt, Jordan, and the Occupied Territories as well as Yemen. With the remittances constituting an important source of income in all these countries, the non-oil exporting Arab countries of the region, both small and large, were increasingly linked to the vicissitudes of the oil exporting economies.

Large non-oil countries: Turkey and Egypt

These two countries have had roughly equal populations since 1918, and throughout the century each has accounted for approximately 30 percent of the total population of the region under study in this volume. In both, the basic long-term trend of the century has been the shift of resources, especially labor, from agriculture to the urban economy. While domestic market oriented industry provided jobs to many of these migrants, an even greater share were employed by the informal sector in its variety of forms.

235

The two countries probably had comparable levels of per capita income before the First World War.[15] Per capita incomes remained basically unchanged in Egypt until 1950. Even though Turkey was hit harder by the two world wars, its recovery during the 1920s and the 1930s was considerably stronger due to government interventionism and the emphasis on the non-agricultural sector. As a result, its per capita GDP levels exceeded those of Egypt by mid-century.

Both countries favored inward-looking industrialization strategies during the postwar era in which the public sector played an important role. In Turkey, where the private sector became increasingly important after 1950, the shift towards an external oriented strategy began in 1980. The severity of the crisis of import substituting industrialization (ISI) played an important role in bringing about this shift. Changes in the same direction have been more limited in Egypt where the shortcomings of the industrial sector were compensated, to some extent, by the temporary growth of the petroleum sector and the remittances from workers abroad.

Another important contrast between the two countries concerns the performance of agriculture. Thanks to the availability of land together with supportive government policies after the Second World War, Turkish agriculture performed strongly until the 1970s and increases in output have remained above population growth since then. In Egypt, food production lagged behind population growth due to the inability to expand land under cultivation combined with government policies that favored the urban sector. Available evidence indicates that income distribution has been more unequal in Turkey and the existing disparities increased after the late 1970s. The relatively more equal distribution in Egypt might be linked to the existence of a large public sector and greater government involvement in support of the urban poor.[16]

Israel

Israel is probably the country most difficult to fit into our simple scheme. It has followed a state sector-led ISI strategy that emphasized its highly educated labor force to develop into the technologically most sophisticated economy of the region. Per capita incomes in Israel are now comparable to those of high income industrialized countries. For these reasons, it does not quite fit with the other small non-oil countries. Israel has also been relatively successful in the implementation of the structural adjustment programs in recent decades.

THE MIDDLE EAST AS AN ECONOMIC REGION

One important trend of the world economy during the second half of the twentieth century has been the emergence of regional trading blocs. There have been two waves of regional trading arrangements since the early 1960s. The first wave developed under the impetus of the European common market and spread throughout Africa, Latin America, the Middle East, and other parts of the developing world. Regionalism then came to a halt during much of the 1970s. The second wave began in the middle of the 1980s. In North America, NAFTA has since been expanding towards the southern hemisphere. Another bloc may soon emerge in East Asia with or without the eastern rim of the Pacific. Similarly, throughout the developing world old arrangements are being revived and new ones created.[17]

Because under regionalism preferences are extended only to partners, it can lead to the exclusion of the outsiders. For this reason, it remains to be seen whether the recent wave of regionalism is an intermediate stage towards greater multilateralism, as represented by the GATT until recently, or whether it will replace multilateralism. If each of these blocs begins to favor greater economic, political, and even military linkages within, at the expense of ties with the rest of the world, regionalism will certainly come into conflict with multilateralism or globalization. Before we examine the implications of the recent wave for the Middle East, however, it might be useful to assess the extent to which the Middle East has been an economic region during the twentieth century.

The incorporation of much of the Middle East into the Ottoman Empire in the sixteenth century created a zone of relatively free trade with regular flows between its component parts. This trade was further encouraged during the nineteenth century by better security, the progressive abolition of internal customs duties, and improvements in the transportation system. At the same time, however, it came to be surpassed by the growing trade with Europe in which the region's agricultural goods were exchanged for imported manufactures.

One immediate consequence of the break-up of the Ottoman Empire and the emergence of national economies after the First World War was the rise of tariff barriers to intra-regional trade which were raised further in the early 1930s as governments began to protect their economies against the impact of the Depression. The trend toward reduced intra-regional trade was briefly reversed during the Second World War. For the duration of the war, the Anglo-American Middle East Supply Centre promoted a new division of labor in which countries like Egypt and Palestine were encouraged

237

to become manufacturing centers for the rest of the region and others, like Syria and Transjordan, to develop as its main source of cereals.[18]

The efforts at promoting regional economic cooperation during the 1950s and 1960s emphasized the need to reduce tariffs and facilitate the free movement of goods and labor. Various forms of trading arrangements, blocs, or common markets were envisaged during this period, not only between the Arab countries but also within other sub-regional groupings involving Turkey and Iran. This new phase did not help intra-regional economic flows, however. Countries in the region maintained high levels of tariffs and continued to develop separate commercial and financial linkages with the industrialized countries including the East European bloc.

Many observers are inclined to explain the failure of these efforts in terms of political rivalries, and more generally, by the failure of the political leaders to embrace the goal of unity. One also needs to pay attention, however, to the role of economic factors in this outcome. During the 1960s there were many attempts to create regional trading arrangements between the developing countries. Within the general framework of ISI, however, such strategies of integration amongst the developing countries did not enjoy much success. Governments preferred to continue protecting their own industry rather than open it up to competition from neighbors with similar industrial structures.

There is no doubt that the period from 1973 to 1990 was exceptional in this respect. While oil revenues increased economic diversity and disparity within the region, they also facilitated greater economic integration. Migration, remittances, and cultural exchange also unleashed powerful forces toward economic and social integration not only within the Arab East but beyond, from Iran and Turkey to the Mahgreb. This period also saw the attempt to organize various sub-regional economic groupings of which the longest lasting has been the Gulf Cooperation Council created in 1981. However, progress towards the harmonization of its members' tariff structures has been slow. As mentioned in Chapter 9, only when this has been achieved will the European Union agree to begin discussions concerning access to its market for cheap Gulf petrochemical products.

It is also worth noting that, for a variety of reasons, economic, social, and political, this recent process was based on migration and the related flows of remittances. In contrast, trade flows and direct investment played a much more limited role except for trade associated with the remittances. It is also the case that none of these flows were underpinned by the institutional mechanisms required to encourage their orderly circulation and to protect them from sudden policy changes in one country or another. The Arab oil states, in particular, remained resolutely opposed to treaties or other obligations which might bind their hand as far as policies toward foreign labor and the direction of their investments were concerned.

At the moment, it is not easy to be optimistic about the prospects of increased economic integration within the region. Progress towards creating institutionalized relationships between Israel and its Arab neighbors came to a complete halt in 1996 following the election of the Netanyahu government. The impasse created an opening for a purely Arab economic arrangement as sponsored by Egypt and Syria but various initiatives around this proposal failed to produce concrete proposals for enhanced cooperation.

FUTURE DEVELOPMENTS/FUTURE CHALLENGES

It was the conventional wisdom of the mid-1990s just as it was in the 1890s that economic progress depends on integration with the world economy via the reduction of any and all barriers to international trade and investment. This was certainly the advice given to Middle Eastern regimes which were constantly reminded by the World Bank and other organizations that world trade was estimated to rise at twice the rate of world production for the ten years, 1996–2006, just as it has done for the previous ten. As a significant corollary, World Bank officials pointed out that trade within the Middle East itself was set to grow by only a fraction of this amount, further underlining the necessity for the states of the region to look outward to exports and to the encouragement of further foreign direct investment as the primary mechanism for ensuring their economic well-being. Something of the challenge involved can be seen in the fact that, during the mid-1990s, overall investment in the Middle East and North Africa (MENA) countries was running at just over 20 percent, well below the developing country average of 24 percent.[19]

Beyond this there was also the question of whether states should attempt this integration on their own or by means of membership of an international forum like the World Trade Organization (WTO) or a regional grouping like the European Union (EU). By the end of 1997, Bahrain, Egypt, Israel, and the UAE had joined the WTO with many more negotiating to join. Meanwhile, Turkey had become part of a Customs Union with the EU in 1996 and Israel and Palestine had completed negotiations to enter the proposed Euro-Mediterranean Free Trade Area in which they were promised access to the European market for industrial goods in exchange for a progressive reduction in their external tariffs. Other Middle Eastern states planned to follow. Looking ahead it is possible to see policies subject to two different types of tensions. One is the choice between bilateral arrangements with outside regional markets like that of the EU and the revival, yet again, of the plan to create a Middle Eastern Common Market, with or without Israel. The other is the problem of whether to go for a fully institutionalized type of Middle East economic cooperation or whether just to try to exploit local geographical economies of scale, for example linked electricity grids or water carriers, on a simple state to state basis.

The inevitable impact on the national systems of economic management which such obligations require cannot be overestimated. Whereas previous agreements between Middle Eastern countries and Europe had involved simply the offer of limited entry for certain goods into the European market, the new treaties committed their signatories to a progressive reduction of barriers accompanied by the creation of new legal regimes and the adoption of new standards in accountability and transparency. All this was in addition to the many commitments already made to the World Bank and the IMF with regard to privatization, deregulation, and the creation of open markets. The result will certainly be a revolution in the relations between the private sector and the state as well as a profound change in the economic position of most of the actors involved, whether workers, entrepreneurs, investors, or officials.

Furthermore, at least as far as the non-oil states are concerned, there is the significant challenge of finding those niches in the world market where their own comparative advantages are such that they can hope to export either goods or services in what is an increasingly competitive international context. By and large, the older option of making a start with low skill, low cost exports is no longer open and it is necessary to find alternative routes, perhaps by the development of high-tech industries, as in Israel, perhaps by the development of tourism, perhaps by finding particular luxury markets for quality goods such as Egyptian high grade textiles.

As for the oil producers, they too face serious problems in raising their incomes at a time when the international price of oil looks like remaining stagnant and when their market share is constrained by competitors in the North Sea, Central Asia, and elsewhere. For those who possess large reserves of natural gas, like Qatar, Oman, and the UAE, one answer seems to have been to be to rely on these either to replace oil for local consumption or for export to the fast-growing energy markets of Asia.

However, such developments involve very high capital costs and long gestation periods before the necessary infrastructure can be put in place. And, in most cases, this requires the assistance of foreign companies to provide the relevant technology and investment.[20] Only Saudi Arabia has indicated that it proposes to develop its gas reserves on its own, perhaps, as Fareed Mohamedi suggests, because of a wish to make sure that the profits go to local companies, many of which have been suffering from the lack of opportunities following the end of the oil boom.[21]

One inevitable consequence of the processes of economic transformation already in train will be social dislocation and, on occasions, the eruption of popular opposition to government policy. Liberalization and the creation of markets often lead to greater inequality, insecurity, and the exclusion of the weaker and less skilled members of a society, at least in the short run. One possible flash point for Middle Eastern states may be the growing problem of long-term unemployment made worse by the need to slim government bureaucracies and to lay off many more workers in loss-making state enterprises. Another might be a backlash against such new measures of liberalization as the Egyptian decision to cancel all existing agricultural rent contracts as of October 1997, an initiative which will permit owners to evict tenants for the first time since the Land Reform of 1952.

In the somewhat longer term there is also the need to embark on difficult strategies to ensure that Middle Eastern economies can be made competitive enough to flourish in the global conditions. These include, among many other things, the need to redefine the relations between the public and private sectors, to reform the legal systems and, in the Arab countries at least, to address such problems as the unusually high levels of adult illiteracy and the very low levels of female participation in the non-agricultural labor force. As for the Gulf countries, they face the very special issue of the future of their large foreign workforces and the need to try to ensure that foreigners are replaced by properly trained local citizens. The renewed efforts made by some states after the Gulf War, notably Kuwait and Saudi Arabia, have not proved very successful so far, leaving Saudi Arabia, for example, with a combination of nearly 6 million migrant workers and a growing number of university graduates unable to find work.[22] There are particular problems concerning the private sector which so resolutely prefers foreigners to locals that, in the early 1990s, only 2 percent of its employees were local nationals in the UAE, perhaps 10 percent in Qatar and Oman, and just under 20 percent in Saudi Arabia.[23]

Lastly, there are the more basic issues arising from the further integration of any state with the world economy, such as a perceived loss of sovereignty and state power and a popular fear of foreign economic or cultural invasion. In the Arab/Muslim countries, the notion that the revival of globalization also threatens a new wave of foreign control is already widespread and has found some expression in the political programs of parties and opposition groups.[24] In Israel and Turkey there is the growing realization that further integration with the world economy will leave them open to the possibility of externally generated shocks to the value of both their currency and the share prices on their stock exchange. Should the fears generated by economic and cultural globalization become even stronger, pressures to arrest whatever progress has been made towards greater openness to external forces in the name of protectionism and new regulation could become too powerful to ignore.

Just as important for the region's economic future are the ongoing questions of war and peace and of the balance between population and resources which have dogged many Middle Eastern states for years. What with the uncertainty attending the Arab-Israeli peace process and the economic future of Iraq, political tensions will continue to deter not only foreign investors but also the introduction of schemes to develop trans-regional systems involving water, transportation, or shared gas and electricity grids. The question of augmenting domestic water supplies will also have to be urgently addressed. For the last three decades or so many Middle Eastern states have postponed much of the problem by importing large quantities of meat and cereals as a kind of 'substitute' or 'embedded' water to use J.A. Allan's phrases, but this too will soon reach its limits.[25] It is now necessary to recognize that there are few schemes left that will substantially increase supply, except in eastern Turkey, and that what is now required is a form of demand management aimed at reallocating use away from economically inefficient practices, such as many forms of irrigated agriculture, most probably by imposing a system of tariffs and other charges.

These are daunting challenges indeed. It is more than likely that a number of Arab regimes will find them so demanding as to give up their attempts at reform, while preferring to remain within a largely protectionist cocoon, shored up where possible by access to oil revenues, either their own or from the remittances sent back by their migrant workers. Others, notably the Turkish, the Israeli, and the Egyptian, will see no choice but to continue along their present liberalizing course, backed by elites the majority of which have become convinced that there is no other way forward.

Notes on Epilogue and Conclusion
Full details of all sources are in the Bibliography

1   Maddison, *Monitoring the World Economy, 1820–1992*, pp 62–3.
2   Maddison, *Two Crises*, ch. 2; Diaz Alejandro, 'Latin America in the 1930s.'
3   Because many of the countries whose national income accounts are incomplete are small oil producers whose incomes showed the most rapid increases, the actual long-term trend might be higher than 3 percent. See the Statistical Appendix.
4   Based on the long-term growth rates provided in World Bank, *World Development Report 1992*.
5   See the Statistical Appendix.
6   For the theoretical arguments put forward to support both of these propositions, see Coatsworth, 'Welfare,' pp 1–13.
7   Stallings, 'International Influence on Economic Policy,' pp 41–88.
8   Haggard and Kaufman, 'Institutions and Economic Adjustment,' pp 18–37.
9   Sadowski, 'The End of Counterrevolution?' p 7.
10 Gause, 'Arms Supplies and Military Spending in the Gulf,' p 13, Table 2.
11 Based on GDP figures provided by the World Bank, *World Development Report*, recent volumes.
12 Khalaf, 'World's Slowest Growing Developing Region,' *Financial Times*, 19 September 1997; Shafik, 'Public Policy and Private Initiative,' p 6.
13 This is the argument made by El-Erian and Fennell in *The Economy of the Middle East and North Africa in 1997*, p 5.
14 Based on the GDP figures provided by the World Bank. See also the Statistical Appendix at the end of the volume.
15 Issawi, *An Economic History of the Middle East and North Africa*, pp 104–6.
16 For a more extensive comparison of the two economies during the second half of the twentieth century, see Hansen, *Egypt and Turkey*, pt III, pp 435–547. Also Öncü Keyder and Ibrahim, *Developmentalism and Beyond*.
17 De Melo and Panagriya, 'Introduction,' pp 3–21.
18 Middle East Supply Centre, *Some Facts About the MESC*, Cairo, 1945.
19 David Gardiner, 'Big Rise in Mideast Investment Urged.'
20 Mohamedi, 'Oil, Gas and the Future of the Arab Gulf Countries,' pp 3–4.
21 *Ibid.* See also Corzine, 'Testing Times for Saudi Oil Policy.'
22 Figure for 1994/95 from *Al-Wasat*, 301 (3 November 1997), p 10. According to the same source, the largest contingents of foreign workers in Saudi Arabia are the Indians (1.2 million), the Egyptians (1.1 million), and the Pakistanis (nearly 800,000).
23 Figures quoted in Al-Qudsi, 'The Interaction Between Government Budget, Demography and Labor in the GCC,' p 9.
24 See, for example, some of the views reported in Barnett, 'Regional Security after the Gulf War,' pp 597–618.
25 See his 'Overall Perspectives on Countries and Regions,' p 68.

Tables

Table 1.1　Turkey: basic economic indicators, 1923–46

	1923	1929	1939	1946
Population in millions	13	14	17.5	19
Life expectancy at birth	35	35	35	38
Share of urban population (%)	16	17	18	18
Share of agriculture in the labor force (%)		80	77	77
GNP in current US$m	570	1,000	1,600	2,450
GNP per capita in current US$	43	70	90	130
Share of agriculture in GNP (%)	40	52	39	46
Share of manufacturing in GNP (%)	12	9	17	13
Share of total industry including construction in GNP (%)	16	14	22	18

Sources: Turkey, State Institute of Statistics, *Statistical Indicators*, 1923–1992; Tuncer Bulutay, Yahya S. Tezel, and Nuri Yildirim, *Türkiye Milli Geliri* (1923–1948), 2 vols. (Ankara, 1974).

Table 1.2.　Turkey: a periodization of economic growth, 1923–46, average annual rates for change (in percent)

	1923–46	1923–29	1929–39	1939–46
Population	1.9	1.7	2.2	1.2
GNP	4.6	10.3	5.2	-2.0
GNP per capita	2.6	8.4	3.0	-3.2
Agricultural output	4.9	13.6	4.4	-1.4
Manufacturing output	3.3	7.2	5.2	-3
Total industrial output including construction	4.5	10.2	5.7	2.6

Sources: Calculations are based on Turkey, State Institute of Statistics, *Statistical Indicators*, 1923–1992 and the tables in Bulutay, Tezel, and Yildirim, *Türkiye Milli Geliri*. The latter's estimates for manufacturing output and other related aggregates such as total industrial output and the GNP for 1929–39 were revised downward following the calculations by Zendisayek, 'Large and Small Enterprises in the Early Stages of Turkey's Industrialisation, 1929–1939', ch. 4.

Table 1.3 Turkey: foreign trade, 1924–46

	1924/25	1928/29	1938/39	1945/46
Exports (US$m)	92.6	81.6	107.7	192.1
Imports (US$m)	114.8	118.7	105.7	108.4
Exports/GNP (%)	12.8	11.4	6.9	5.2
Imports/GNP (%)	15.8	14.4	6.8	2.8
Trade balance/GNP (%)	-3.0	-3.0	0.1	2.4
External terms of trade (export prices/import prices; 1928–29=100)	129	100	79	68

Sources: Turkey, State Institute of Statistics, *Statistical Indicators, 1923–1992* and calculations based on Bulutay, Tezel, and Yildirim, *Türkiye Milli Geliri*.

Table 1.4A Turkey: agricultural production, 1928–46 (all indices unless indicated otherwise)

	1929/30	1938/39	1945/46
Labor force	100	119	125
Cultivated land	100	142	135
Total crop output	100	146	120
Total yields	100	103	89
Wheat output (millions of tons)	2.4	3.8	2.6
Wheat output	100	160	110
Wheat yields	100	113	81
Cereal output	100	148	99
Non-cereal output	100	148	146

Table 1.4B Turkey: relative agricultural prices, 1928–46

	1928/29	1932/33	1938/39	1945/46
Agricultural/non-agricultural prices	100	69	81	95
Cereal prices/non-agricultural prices	100	55	57	80
Prices of non-cereal crops/ non-agricultural prices	100	90	104	109

Note: 1928 is excluded from the production indices since it was an exceptionally poor harvest year.

Source: calculations based on Bulutay, Tezel, and Yildirim, *Türkiye Milli Geliri*.

Table 2.1   Egypt: estimates of income and income/capita in selected years, 1912–37

Year	NI (£E millions)[a]	Population (millions)[b]	Income per capita[c] (1886/87=100)
1912			128
1913			
1917		12.75	
1920			124
1927		14.22	
1929			140
1937	165		128

Sources:
a Mahmoud A. Anis, 'A Study of the National Income of Egypt,' *L'Egypte contemporaine*, 261–2 (Nov.–Dec. 1950), p 675.
b Decennial censuses.
c Hansen, 'Income and Consumption in Egypt, 1886/1887 to 1937,' p 29.

Table 2.2   Egypt: the agricultural sector, major indices, 1917–47

Year	Cultivated Area (million feddans)[a]	Crop Area (million feddans)[a]	Chemical fertilizer/cropped feddan (kg)[b]	Cotton Area (million feddans)[a]	Cotton yield (kantar/ feddan)[a]
1917	5.269	6.62		1.7	3.75
1927	5.544	6.61	31.0	1.52	4.01
1937	5.281	8.358	68.0	1.98	5.37
1947	5.761	9.167	47.0	1.3	5.08

Sources:
a Egypt, Ministère de finance, Département de la statistique générale, *Annuaire statistique*, various years.
b Hansen and Marzouk, *Development and Economic Policy in the UAR (Egypt)*, Table 3.10.

Table 2.3   Egypt: agricultural output, 1915–44 (five-year averages: 1895–99=100)

	12 Major Field Crops*	Total Agricultural Production
1915–19	104	107
1920–24	112	112
1925–29	130	131
1930–34	129	133
1935–39	144	152
1940–44	124	135

* Cotton, cotton seeds, rice, wheat, maize, barley, beans, millet, sugar cane, onions, lentils, and helba.

Source: Bent Hansen and Michael Wattleworth, 'Agricultural output and consumption of basic foods in Egypt, 1886/87–1967/68,' *International Journal of Middle Eastern Studies*, 9 (1978), p 457.

Table 2.4   Egypt: domestic production and imports of selected products, 1925 and 1929*

	Domestic production	Imports
1925		
Flour (metric tons)	2,482,419	202,980
Tanned hides (quantity)	250,000	260,000
Leather footwear (pairs)	6,500,000	624,397
1929		
Soap (metric tons)	37,380	9,500
Textiles (square meters)		
workshops	30,000,000	
factory (Filature Nationale)	5,500,000	
Sugar (metric tons)		
refined	108,952	53,072
molasses	56,922	10
Cement (tons)	245,000	60,000
Cottonseed oil (tons)	64,202	

* 1929 was an exceptional year with an unusually large volume of imports in anticipation of the new, and often higher, tariffs which were to go into effect in 1930.

Source: Tignor, *State, Private Enterprise and Economic Change*, Table 3.4.

Table 3.1   Colonial governments in the inter-war period: domestic expenditure by purpose (percent)

	India 1921–30	Cyprus 1923–38[a]	Iraq 1921–30	Trans-Jordan 1924–31	Syria 1923–30	Average[b]
General Administration	19.7	32.0	34.6	20.8	35.4	28.5
Defense and public safety	33.8	17.5	34.4	45.8	28.1	31.9
Economic and environmental services	20.1	16.5	14.5	7.7	7.2	13.2
Public works (development)		13.9	7.0	8.6	15.1	11.2
Social welfare services	7.2	20.1	9.5	10.3	8.9	11.2
Domestic debt service and unspecified expenditure	19.2			6.8	5.4	10.5
Total domestic expenditure	100.0	100.0	100.0	100.0	100.1	
Administration and safety	53.5	49.5	69.0	66.6	63.5	60.4
Economic, environmental, and development	20.1	30.4	21.5	16.3	22.3	24.4

a Average of the years 1923, 1924, 1934, 1935, 1937, 1938.
b Arithmetic mean of each line; last two lines are summations.

Source: Gross, *Economic Policy*, Table 18.

Table 3.2   Iraq: oil production and revenues, 1932–50 (financial years)

	Oil production (1,000 metric tons)	Revenues (ID 1,000)	as % of total government revenues
1932	122	524	12.4
1933	115	540	13.0
1934	1,030	995	19.8
1935	3,664	598	11.2
1936	4,011	600	10.0
1937	4,255	731	10.6
1938	4,298	1,977	25.2
1939	3,693	2,014	21.9
1940	2,514	1,576	16.2
1941	1,566	1,463	14.4
1942	2,595	1,463	10.6
1943	3,572	2,794	15.4
1944	4,146	2,225	11.8
1945	4,607	2,316	11.4
1946	4,680	2,327	9.3
1947	4,702	2,346	9.0
1948	3,427	2,012	7.5
1949	4,067	3,238	11.3
1950	6,479	5,286	15.8

Source: Sassoon, *Economic Policy*, Table 6.3.

Table 3.3   Palestine: government domestic expenditures by purpose, 1920/21–1939/40[a]

	1920/21–1929	1930–1939/40	1920/2–1939/40
Administration and safety	59.2	56.7	58.0
General Administration	32.1	26.9	29.4
Public Safety	20.1	20.9	20.6
Defense	7.0	8.8	8.0
Economic and environmental	20.0	17.5	18.7
Current services	9.3	11.7	10.5
Land survey[b]	2.1	2.3	2.2
Communications and railroads (investment)	8.6	3.5	6.0
Social welfare services	12.6	10.0	11.3
Health	6.0	4.2	5.1
Education and antiquities	6.6	5.8	6.2
Public works (investment)	8.1	15.8	12.1
Total domestic expenditure	100.0	100.0	100.0

a   Budget periods.
b   Considered infrastructure investment (i.e. part of development expenditure).

Source: Gross, *Economic Policy*, Table 17.

Table 3.4 Palestine: population by religions

	Settled population					Total population (including nomads)	
	All religions	Muslims	Jews	Christians	Others	All religions	Muslims
1922 (census)	649,048	486,177	83,790	71,464	7,617	752,048	589,177
1923 (mid-year)	670,381	500,723	89,660	72,090	7,908	778,989	609,331
1924 (mid-year)	709,938	532,636	94,945	74,094	8,263	804,962	627,660
1925 (mid-year)	756,594	550,850	121,725	75,512	8,507	847,238	641,494
1926 (mid-year)	810,885	576,136	149,500	76,467	8,782	898,902	663,613
1927 (mid-year)	834,206	597,616	149,789	77,880	8,921	917,315	680,725
1928 (mid-year)	857,073	616,402	151,656	79,812	9,203	935,951	695,280
1929 (mid-year)	882,511	634,811	156,481	81,776	9,443	960,043	712,343
1930 (mid-year)	921,699	662,289	164,796	84,986	9,628	992,559	733,149
1931 (census)	966,761	693,147	174,606	88,907	10,101	1,033,314	759,700
1932 (31 Dec)	1,007,274	712,250	192,137	92,520	10,367	1,073,827	778,803
1933 (31 Dec)	1,074,388	731,953	234,967	96,791	10,677	1,140,941	798,506
1934 (31 Dec)	1,144,001	747,826	282,975	102,407	10,793	1,210,554	814,379
1935 (31 Dec)	1,241,559	770,135	355,157	105,236	11,031	1,308,112	836,688
1936 (31 Dec)	1,300,139	796,177	384,078	108,506	11,378	1,366,692	862,730
1937 (31 Dec)	1,335,241	816,893	395,836	110,869	11,643	1,401,794	883,446
1938 (31 Dec)	1,368,732	833,697	411,222	111,974	11,839	1,435,285	900,250
1939 (31 Dec)	1,435,145	860,580	445,457	116,958	12,150	1,501,698	927,133
1940 (31 Dec)	1,177,977	881,293	463,535	120,587	12,562	1,544,530	947,846
1941 (31 Dec)	1,518,947	906,551	474,102	125,413	12,881	1,585,500	973,104
1942 (31 Dec)	1,553,452	928,739	484,408	127,181	13,121	1,620,005	995,292
1943 (31 Dec)	1,610,018	962,162	502,912	131,281	13,663	1,676,571	1,028,715
1944 (31 Dec)	1,673,071	994,724	528,702*	135,547	14,098	1,739,624	1,061277

* Revised *de facto* estimate 553,600.

Source: Government of Palestine, *Survey*, vol. 1, p 141.

Table 4.1 Persian Gulf: oil production, 1934–45 (long tons, millions)

	Iraq	Bahrain	Saudi Arabia	Middle East*	World
1934	1.06	0.04		8.85	207
1935	3.66	0.17		11.49	225
1936	4.02	0.62		13.03	244
1937	4.29	1.52		14.76	278
1938	4.32	1.11		14.85	270
1939	4.04	1.01	0.53	15.81	278
1940	2.65	0.94	0.68	13.90	289
1941	1.61	0.91	0.57	10.88	300
1942	3.25	0.84	0.59	15.54	282
1943	3.78	0.90	0.64	16.29	313
1944	4.25	0.91	1.05	20.80	348
1945	4.62	0.95	2.84	26.55	356

* Also includes Egypt and Iran.

Source: Longrigg, *Oil in the Middle East*, Appendix II.

Table 5.1   Turkey: basic economic indicators, 1950–90

	1950	1960	1970	1980	1990
Population in millions	21	28	36	45	56
Life expectancy at birth	44	50	58	62	65
Adult literacy rate (%)		38	52	69	81
Share of urban population (over 5,000; %)	25	32	39	44	59
Share of agriculture in the labor force (%)	80	75	66	58	52
GNP in billions of current US$	3.4	10	19	70	150
GNP per capita in current US$	166	359	539	1,539	2,687
Share of agriculture in GNP (%)	42	38	36	25	17
Share of manufacturing in GNP (%)	10	12	12	13	19
Share of total industry in GNP (%)	14	17	17	18	25

Sources: Turkey, State Institute of Statistics, *Statistical Indicators*, 1923–1992 (Ankara, 1994) and World Bank, *World Development Report*, various years.

Table 5.2   Turkey: long-term trends in agriculture, 1950–90

	1950	1960	1970	1980	1990
Agricultural labor force (millions)	9.0	9.7	9.3	10.0	11.5
Labor force index (1950=100)	100	108	104	111	128
Cultivated area (millions of hectares)	8.2	12.9	13.2	13.3	13.7
Cultivated area index (1950=100)	100	156	160	162	167
Draft animals (millions of pairs)	2.5	2.6	2.2		
Tractors (thousands)	17	42	106	430	620
Wheat yield index (kg/hectare, 1950=100)	100	116	128	195	242
Domestic terms of trade (agricultural prices/non-agricultural prices)	100	102	102	90	92

Source: based on Turkey, State Institute of Statistics, *Statistical Indicators*, 1923–1992.

Table 5.3   Turkey: a periodization of growth in the postwar era, 1947–90, average annual rates of growth percent)

		Population	GNP	GNP per capita	Agriculture	Manufacturing Industry
	1947–90	2.5	5.7	3.2	3.6	7.9
I	1947–62	2.7	6.0	3.3	5.2	7.1
Ia	1947–53		8.7	6.0	11.5	6.5
Ib	1954–62		4.0	1.3	2.1	7.6
II	1963–79	2.4	6.0	3.5	3.4	9.1
IIa	1963–77		6.8	4.3	3.5	10.2
IIb	1978–79		1.3	-1.1	2.8	-0.9
III	1980–90	2.3	4.6	2.3	1.4	7.1

Source: based on Turkey, State Institute of Statistics, *Statistical Indicators*, 1923–1992.

Table 5.4   Turkey: external orientation of the economy, 1947–90 (percent)

	Imports/GNP	Exports/GNP	Manufacturing Exports/GNP
1947/48	8.6	7.0	
1952/53	10.6	7.3	
1962/63	9.5	5.5	1.1
1970/71	5.5	3.3	0.7
1978/79	6.5	2.9	1.3
1984/85	17.6	11.7	7.7
1989/90	14.7	9.7	7.5

Source: based on Turkey, State Institute of Statistics, *Statistical Indicators*, 1923–1992.

Table 5.5   Turkey: urban real wages, 1950–90 (1950=100)

Year	Index
1950	100
1963	119
1970	168
1977	216
1979	175
1987	140
1990	284

Source: Pamuk, 'Long Term Trends.'

Table 6.1   Egypt: growth of population, production, and expenditure, selected
periods, 1939–82 (percent)

Category	1939–55	1959/60–1964/65	1964/65–1973	1973–1981/82	1959/60–1981/82
Population	2.1	2.6	2.4	2.6	2.5
Production Sector					
Agriculture	5.6	6.6	3.3	9.3	6.4
Industry and mining				7.6[a]	
Petroleum				43.6	
Electricity		14.0	15.0	11.3	13.3
Public Utilities		4.8	6.4	[b]	
Construction		16.6	1.2	5.5	6.3
Transport and Communications		11.3	-2.4	22.2	10.0
Trade and finance		2.2	4.1	11.7	6.6
Housing		1.5	1.8	7.5	3.9
Other services		7.6	6.1	6.1	6.4
Gross Domestic Product					
At factor cost	2.5	6.1	3.1	8.1	5.8
At factor cost per capita	0.4	3.5	0.7	5.5	3.3
Gross National Income					
At market prices	3.5[c]	6.7	3.5	7.3	5.7
At market prices per capita	1.4[c]	4.1	1.1	4.7	3.2

Source: Hansen, *Egypt and Turkey*, Table 1.1.

Growth rates are based on various constant price estimates.
a For 1974–1981/82.
b Included in electricity.
c Conjecture.

Table 6.2   Egypt: distribution of agrarian reform land, 1953–1971 ('000 feddans)

Year	Total area requisitioned from 1952 to end of year	Distribution of land (annual)	Distribution of land (cumulative)
1953	211	16	16
1954	294	65	81
1955	374	67	148
1956	434	36	184
1957		42	226
1958	544	43	269
1959		6	275
1960		23	298
1961		28	326
1962		106	432
1963		90	522
1964		122	644
1965		26	670
1966	875	26	696
1967		58	754
1968		20	774
1969		23	797
1970		20	817
1971		5	822

Source: Mabro, *Egyptian Economy*, Table 4.2.

Table 6.3   Egypt: distribution of capital investments by companies operating under Law 43 (as of 30 June 1981) (percent)

Sector	Egyptian public capital	Egyptian private capital	Total Egyptian capital	Arab capital	Foreign capital
Commodities					
Agriculture	35.2	43.2	78.4	9.6	12.0
Petroleum	11.9	2.8	14.7	0.0	85.3
Metals	96.2	1.7	97.9	1.3	0.8
Manufacturing	31.6	35.5	67.1	9.5	23.4
Contracting	47.4	24.1	71.5	5.7	22.8
Total	34.3	34.7	69.0	9.0	22.0
Production Services					
Banking	44.1	37.6	81.7	5.8	12.5
Investment Comps.	34.5	33.1	67.6	24.0	8.4
Transport	4.7	56.9	61.6	14.0	24.4
Tourism and Hotels	7.3	36.7	44.0	13.2	43.8
Consultancy	20.7	43.7	64.4	2.3	33.3
Total	29.9	36.2	66.1	14.5	19.4
Services					
Housing	9.1	52.5	61.6	32.9	5.5
Health	22.5	56.1	78.6	12.3	9.1
Other	3.0	23.4	26.4	1.2	72.4
Total	8.0	39.3	47.3	15.3	37.4
Grand Total	29.1	36.0	65.1	12.4	22.5

Source: Wahba, *Role of the State*, Table 7.11.

Table 6.4   Egypt: exogenous revenue accruing to Egypt, 1974–1981/82 (US$ million, current prices)

Source	1973	1974	1975	1976	1977	1978	1979	1980/81	1981/82
Petroleum Exports[a]		187	289	644	720	802	1,878	3,179	3,329
Tourism[b]	158	265	332	464	728	702	601	712	611
Suez Canal tolls[b]			85	311	428	514	589	780	909
Workers' remittances[b]	86	189	366	755	897	1,761	2,445	2,855	1,935
Total		641	1,072	2,174	2,773	3,779	5,513	7,526	6,784
Total exogenous resources as a % of current a/c receipts		24.95	35.20	51.35	55.89	62.38	66.89	67.64	65.13
Total exogenous resources as a % of current a/c payments		15.39	19.59	38.84	43.21	50.93	54.28	55.85	48.74

a Excluding exports by foreign petroleum companies operating in Egypt, and including a small number of refined products.
b Net receipts.

Source: Wahba, *Role of the State*, Table 7.5 and sources cited there.

Table 6.5   Egypt: trading operations of general authority for supply commodities, 1970/71–1983/84 (£E million)

	1970/1	1972	1973	1974	1975	1976	1977	1978	1979	1980/1	1981/2	1982/3	1983/4
Subsidies	41.8	41.9	136.2	393.2	423.7	281.4	343.2	452.4	996.8	1665.4	1828	1684.5	
Wheat and flour	20.9	15.1	79	216.4	260.9	171.6	149.1	222.8	588.3	776	736	760.9	743.8
Maize	0.8	0.4	4.4	16.5	31.1	23.1	40.6	53.8	38.5	104	141	154.7	235.8
Edible fats and oils (rationed)	10.4	15.8	16.8	55.3	72.2	43.2	54.6	137.4	200.2	133.4	125	243	156.9
Sugar (rationed)	8	6	19	68.9	20.8	6.1				224	132	112.5	23.2
Tea							18.3	12.8	54.6	26.5	29	31.2	47.3
Coffee					5.6								
Other	1.7	4.6	17	36.1	38.7	37.4	75	25.6	115.2	401.5	665	382.3	
Profits	38.6	30.5	47.2	63.1	15	31.2	12.6	29.3	44.5	0.7	2.8	2.4	
Total Net Losses	3.2	11.3	89	330.1	408.7	250.2	330.6	423.1	952.3	1664.7	1825.2	1682.1	
Subsidies as % of total current expenditure	0.4	1.1	7.6	23.3	23.9	14.0	17.6	20.38	27.0	26.8	24.0	19.5	
% of total public expenditure	0.2	0.7	5.5	16.5	16.9	9.8	10.9	11.9	16.2	16.7	14.9	12.7	
Share of GDP	0.1	0.3	2.3	7.6	9.4	4.8	5.3	6.6	8.1	10.0	9.4	8.1	

Source: Commander, *State and Agricultural Development*, Table 2.8.

Table 6.6   Egypt: GDP (current factor costs) by economic sectors, selected years, 1955–87 (percent)

Sector	1955/56	1965/66	1974	1974	1978	1983/84	1986/87
Agriculture	32.3	28.5	31.1	30.5	25.3	20.0	20.1
Industry, petroleum, and mining	17.6	21.6	20.5	20.4	21.6	26.8	
Petroleum only	c	c	c	2.7	6.9	12.0	
Electricity	d	1.1	1.1	1.6	1.3	1.0	28.7
Construction	2.9	4.4	3.3	3.1	5.7	5.3	
Transport and communication	6.4	9.2	4.1	4.2	7.6	7.5	
Suez Canal only				-0.0	3.3	2.8	
Trade and finance	9.5	8.5	11.4	15.1	17.1	20.1	51.2
Housing	9.7	5.1	3.1	4.8	2.9	1.8	
Public utilities	d	0.4	0.4	e	e	e	
Other services	21.6	21.2	25.0	20.4	17.4	17.5	
Total GDP	100	100	100	100	100	100	100
GDP (£E millions)	965	2,138	4,111	4,197	9,021	25,961	43,685

a Comparable with 1955/56 and 1965/66.
b Comparable with 1978 and 1983/84.
c About 1.0 percent.
d Included in industry, petroleum and mining.
e Included in electricity.

Source: Hansen, *Egypt and Turkey*, Table 1.4.

Table 6.7   Egypt: distribution of landholdings by size, 1950–1977/78.

Farm Size (feddans)	Number of Holdings	%	Area ('000 feddans)	%
1950				
0–1	214.3	21.4	111.8	1.8
1–3	410.0	40.9	709.6	11.6
3–5	162.4	16.2	601.4	9.8
5–10	122.4	12.2	818.4	13.3
>10	93.9	9.3	3902.8	63.5
Total	1003.0	100.0	6144.0	100.0
1961				
0–1	434.2	26.4	211.2	3.4
1–3	672.7	41.0	1153.2	18.5
3–5	274.3	16.7	990.0	15.9
5–10	170.0	10.4	1100.7	17.7
>10	90.9	5.5	2767.7	44.5
Total	1642.1	100.0	6222.8	100.0
1974/75				
0–1	1124.3	42.6	739.0	12.4
1–3	949.2	35.9	2023.5	33.6
3–5	354.8	13.4	1185.6	19.8
5–10	148.5	5.6	944.4	15.8
>10	65.2	2.5	1091.2	18.2
Total	2642.0	100.0	5983.7	100.0
1977/78				
0–1	1458.8	48.8	919.9	15.0
1–3	984.3	32.9	2017.4	33.0
3–5	348.7	11.7	1165.6	19.1
5–10	127.6	4.2	785.9	12.9
>10	69.9	2.3	1226.7	20.0
Total	2989.3	100.0	6118.7	100.0

Source: Commander, *State and Agricultural Development*, Table 2.1.

Table 7.1A   Syria: estimates of annual rates of growth of Syrian national and domestic income (percent)

GNP
1936/8–1946/8: 2.5 (Source: Makdisi, 'Some Aspects of Syrian Economic Growth,' pp 46–7)

NDP
1956–68: 4.2 (Source: Hansen, 'Economic Development in Syria,' pp 336–7n)

GDP
1965–80: 9.1 (Source: World Bank, *World Development Report 1991*, Table 2)
1980–89: 1.6 (Source: *Ibid.*)

GDP per capita
1951–68: 3.9 (Source: Chatelus, 'La Croissance économique,' p 263)
1960–76: 2.2 (*Ibid.*)

Table 7.1B   Syria: sectoral contributions to Syrian NDP, selected years, 1956–84* (percent)

Sector	1956	1968	1970	1984
Agriculture	38.3	25.9	20.3	19.7
Industry including extraction/electricity	11.8	13.8	22.0	16.0
Construction	3.3	3.4	3.0	6.6
Transport	9.3	11.2	10.8	8.3
Public Administration	3.1	14.1		

* Categories not necessarily compatible from year to year.

Sources: Hansen, 'Economic development of Syria,' Table 7.2; Meyer, 'Economic development in Syria,' Table 1.

Table 7.2A   Syria: land use, 1963–66 and 1975–80 (annual averages in hectares, '000)*

Category	1963–66	1975–77	1978–80
Cultivable	8,780	5,900	6,053
(of which)			
uncultivated	2,261	391	401
cultivated	6,519	5,551	5,653
fallow	3,143	1,571	1,745
rain-fed	2,826	3,407	3,375
irrigated	550	531	532

* New land use classifications adopted in 1975.

Source: Manners and Sagafi-Nejad, 'Agricultural development,' Tables 14.3, 14.5, and 14.6.

Table 7.2B Syria: cropped area, 1946–80 (annual averages in hectares, '000)

Period/ Average	Wheat	Barley	Cotton	Fruit	Total	Cereals as a % of total
1946–50	884	368	33	184	1,821	76
1951–60	1,392	602	220	217	2,784	75
1961–70	1,249	707	275	259	2,862	70
1971–80	1,490	919	194	380	3,515	70

Source: Manners and Sagafi-Nejad, 'Agricultural development,' Tables 14.3, 14.5, and 14.6.

Table 7.2C Syria: cereal production, 1943–80 (annual averages in metric tons, '000)

	High	Low	Average	Standard deviation	Coefficient of variation
Wheat					
1943–50	909	404	595	±179	30%
1951–60	1,354	438	784	±277	35%
1961–70	1,374	559	930	±264	28%
1971–80	2,226	593	1,445	±485	34%
Barley					
1943–50	357	169	281	±57	20%
1951–60	721	137	365	±203	56%
1961–70	798	203	541	±204	38%
1971–80	1,587	102	629	±423	67%

Source: Manners and Sagafi-Nejad, 'Agricultural development,' Tables 14.3, 14.5, and 14.6.

Table 7.3 Lebanon: structural change, selected years, 1950–73

Percentage shares

	1950	1955	1960	1965	1970	1973
Agriculture	19.7	16.2	14.1	11.6	9.2	9.0
Industry	13.5	12.7	12.1	13.1	15.9	21.0
Construction	4.1	4.3	3.5	5.7	4.5	4.5
Transportation	4.1	5.4	3.9	8.2	8.2	8.5
Trade	28.8	28.8	32.0	30.6	31.4	33.0
Finance and Insurance	3.8	5.1	6.3	3.4	3.4	4.0
Real Estate	9.2	8.4	11.0	7.6	8.8	10.0
Government	6.9	6.0	7.8	8.0	8.7	10.0
Other services	9.6	12.0	9.2	11.3	9.9	

Source: André Emile Chaib, 'The Export performance of a small, open, developing economy: the Lebanese experience, 1951–74' (PhD dissertation, University of Michigan, 1979), p 11.

Table 7.4A Iraq: national income, sectoral contribution, 1953 and 1961
(1956 prices, percent)

	1953	1961
Agriculture, forestry, and fishing	32.3	20.6
Mining and quarrying (including crude oil extraction)	49.6	50.2
Manufacturing (including oil refining)	7.1	10.6
Construction	5.1	5.6
Public administration and defense	8.6	9.1

Source: Haseeb, *National Income*, Table 5.

Table 7.4B Iraq: national income, GDP, 1977 and 1979 (current prices, percent)

	1977	1979
Agriculture, forestry, and fishing	7.3	
Mining and quarrying	49.7	61.4
Manufacturing industries	6.9	5.3
Construction	4.9	3.6

Source: Farouk-Sluglett and Sluglett, *Iraq*, Table 7.14.

Table 7.5 Iraq: area and production of wheat, barley, and rice, 1948–52, 1955–56, 1974–76, and 1979–81 (annual averages)

Years	Wheat area (dunums)	Production (tons)	Barley area (dunums)	Production (tons)	Rice area (dunums)	Production (tons)
1948–52	3,744,000	448000	3,736,000	722,000		203
1955–56	5,700,000	624500	4,752,000	911,500		97
1974–76	6,100,000	1,165600	2,272,100	516,400	160,000	96.6
1979–81	4,860,000		3,432,000		224,000	

Sources: *Oxford Regional Economic Atlas: The Middle East and North Africa*, pp 74–5; Ockerman and Samano, 'Agricultural development' in Beaumont and McLachlan (eds) *Agricultural Development*, p 198; Beaumont, 'Iraq: environmental, resources and development issues' in Hopwood et al. (eds), *Iraq: Power and Society*, Table 2.

Table 7.6   Iraq: oil revenues, 1945–81 and 1984–88

Year	£ Sterling million	Year	US$ million
1945	2.6	1971	840
1946	2.7	1972	575
1947	2.7	1973	1,843
1948	2.1	1974	5,700
1949	3.1	1975	7,500
1950	6.7	1976	8,500
1951	15.1	1977	9,631
1952	33.1	1978	10,200
1953	51.3	1979	21,291
1954	57.7	1980	25,281
1955	73.7	1981	9,800
1956	68.9	1984	11,200
1957	48.9	1985	12,500
1958	79.9	1986	6,600
1959	86.6	1987	11,600
1960	95.1	1988	11,700
1961	94.8		
1962	95.1		
1963	110.0		
1964	126.1		
1965	131.4		
1966	140.8		
1967	131.7		
1968	203.3		
1969	199.6		
1970	213.6		

Sources: OAPEC, *Annual Statistical Bulletin*, 1994, Table 135; OAPEC, *Secretary General's Fifteenth Annual Report*, AH1408/AD 1988 (Kuwait: OAPEC, May 1989), Table A7.

Table 8.1   Israel: leading economic indicators, 1950–83

	1950	1960	1970	1975	1980	1983
Population (000s)	1,370	2,150	3,022	3,473	3,922	4,149
Male unemployment (%)		4.5	3.4	2.5	4.1	4.0
Government consumption/						
GNP (%)	18.6	18.7	36.3	44.2	36.1	33.3
Import surplus/GNP (%)	23.9	16.7	26.6	36.7	21.3	24.7
Net foreign debt (US$m)		676	2,621	6,315	12,010	17,740
Annual inflation rate (%)		12.7	3.66	39.2	131.0	145.7

Source: Ben-Porath, 'Entwined growth' in Ben-Porath (ed.), *Israeli Economy*, Table 1.1.

Table 8.2 Israel: growth of GNP and GDP, 1984–90

	GNP US$ million (1990)	Annual change (%)	GDP US$ million (1990)	Annual change (%)
1984	41,298	-0.3	41,039	2.3
1985	42,659	3.3	42,582	3.8
1986	43,632	2.3	44,151	3.7
1987	47,339	8.5	46,746	5.9
1988	48,486	2.7	47,989	2.7
1989	48,955	1.0	48,757	1.6
1990	50,889	4.0	51,225	5.1

Source: Razin and Sadka, *Economy of Modern Israel*, Table 1.

Table 8.3 Comparative size of Israeli, Jordanian, and West Bank/Gaza economies, 1986

	Israel	Jordan	West Bank	Gaza
Population (000s)	4,298	2,744	826	536
GNP per capita (US$ 1986)	6,615	2,151	1,397	772
GDP per employed person	19,747	7,560	10,100	7,140

Source: World Bank, *Peace and the Jordanian Economy*, Table 1.3.

Table 8.4   Jordan: foreign aid, 1959–83 (JD million)

Year	Official aid (total)	Arab aid	US aid	Other sources	Total foreign aid % of GNP	Total foreign aid % of TRA	Total foreign aid per capita (JD)
1959	25.14		17.32	7.82	31.20	23.43	18.97
1960	25.49		18.20	7.29	25.44	19.14	16.10
1961	25.33		17.05	8.28	20.62	17.18	15.42
1962	23.47		15.48	7.99	19.27	16.37	14.42
1963	22.52		15.51	7.01	17.53	13.88	13.26
1964	26.57	4.54	15.03	7.00	17.76	15.41	15.25
1965	26.78	7.34	11.98	7.46	16.32	14.21	15.42
1966	31.44	9.49	13.37	8.58	18.36	15.41	17.30
1967	51.58	37.57	7.62	6.39	26.19	23.08	26.44
1968	53.07	46.25	1.19	5.63	27.62	22.54	25.94
1969	45.79	41.15	1.25	3.41	20.26	15.92	21.62
1970	39.08	33.07	1.38	4.63	18.27	15.11	17.67
1971	35.94	19.11	12.82	3.56	15.47	12.43	15.38
1972	65.96	23.19	35.95	6.82	25.96	20.69	27.76
1973	61.09	23.66	30.83	6.60	22.17	18.34	25.43
1974	84.43	46.60	25.31	12.52	23.19	18.95	33.11
1975	138.01	105.65	22.44	9.92	37.18	28.28	51.78
1976	122.75	77.59	26.13	19.03	22.50	18.84	45.52
1977	166.94	132.31	15.62	19.01	25.12	20.02	57.38
1978	102.63	66.26	18.56	17.81	13.63	10.94	35.74
1979	318.05	299.66	4.59	13.80	34.13	25.40	101.76
1980	390.85	370.43	6.15	14.27	33.64	27.08	123.10
1981	415.33	394.92		20.41	28.70	22.14	128.21
1982	363.72	335.83		27.89	22.02	17.07	107.57
1983	289.56	258.31		31.75	15.95	12.91	82.38

Source: Hammad, 'Role of Foreign Aid' in Khader and Badran (eds), *Economic Development of Jordan*, Tables 2.2 and 2.4.

Table 8.5   Jordan: sectoral contributions to GDP, 1975, 1977, and 1979 (percent)

	1975	1977	1979
Agriculture, forestry, and fishing	9.7	10.3	7.0
Mining and quarrying	6.2	4.4	4.4
Manufacturing	11.3	16.1	11.9
Electricity and water	1.2	1.0	1.0
Construction	6.0	6.7	9.7
Transport and communication	9.2	8.9	11.4
Trade, finance, and other services	56.4	52.6	54.6

Source: calculations based on data from Jordan, Central Bank, *Seventeenth Annual Report* (np: nd), p 8.

Table 8.6A West Bank: structure of economic activity, 1966

	GDP (%)
Agriculture	27.1
Manufacturing and mining	8.8
Electricity, gas, and water	1.5
Construction	6.4
Services	56.6

Table 8.6B West Bank: structure of economic activity, 1968, 1975, and 1983

	GDP (current price; %)		
	1968	1975	1983
Agriculture	36.3	30.3	26.9
Manufacturing and mining	8.3	8.4	6.9
Construction	3.5	15.5	15.7
Services	51.9	45.8	50.5

Source: Mansour, 'West Bank Economy' in Abed (ed.), *Palestinian Economy*, Tables 4.3, 4.10, and sources cited there.

Table 8.7A Gaza Strip: structure of economy, 1966 (percent)

Agriculture	26.2
Industry	3.3
Construction	4.8
Trade and personal services	20.5
Transport	2.4
Administration and public services	19.0
GDP	76.2
UNWRA and other public transfers	19.0
Remittances	4.8
National Income	100.0

Table 8.7B Gaza Strip: GDP, 1984 (US$ million)

Agriculture	32.9
Industry	29.0
Construction	55.5
Public and community services	75.5
Transport, trade, and other services	56.5
Total	294.4

Sources: Abu-Amr, 'Gaza Economy' in Abed (ed.), *Palestinian Economy*, Table 5.2, 5.3, and sources cited there.

Table 8.8A West Bank and Gaza Strip: Palestinian population, stayers and migrants, 1967–90

Year	West Bank Population ('000)			Gaza Strip Population ('000)			West Bank and Gaza Total Population ('000)	
	Stayers	Migrants	Net emigration rate (%)	Stayers	Migrants	Net emigration rate (%)	Stayers	Migrants
1966				455				
May 1967	846							
Sep. 1967	596			390			966	
1968	586		2.2	381		8.5	967	
1969	583		-0.2	357		0.8	940	
1970	598	-1	0.8		3	0.9	962	2
1971	608	4	0.4	370	6	0.6	978	10
1972	623	6	1.2	379	9	1.1	1001	15
1973	634	14	-0.0	387	13	-0.4	1021	27
1974	652	14	0.4	402	12	0.4	1054	26
1975	670	17	2.3	414	14	0.8	1084	31
1976	675	33	2.1	426	18	1.0	1101	51
1977	683	48	1.5	437	23	0.7	1121	71
1978	696	60	1.4	451	27	1.0	1147	87
1979	708	71	1.8	463	32	1.0	1171	104
1980	719	86	2.4	445	38	1.1	1163	125
1981	724	106	2.2	457	45	1.2	1181	151
1982	733	125	1.1	470	52	0.7	1202	177
1983	749	137	0.4	477	57	0.2	1227	195
1984	772	145	0.8	495	60	1.0	1266	205
1985	793	156	0.6	510	68	0.6	1303	223
1986	816	166	0.6	527	73	0.7	1343	239
1987	838	177	-0.1	545	80	0.6	1383	256
1988	868	182	0.4	566	86	0.5	1434	269
1989	895	192	1.5	589	93	1.2	1484	285
1990	916	213	-0.3	610	104	-0.2	1526	317

Source: Radwan A. Shaban, 'Palestinian Labour Mobility,' *International Labour Review*, 134/5–6 (1993), Tables 1 and 2 and sources cited there.

Table 8.8B   West Bank and Gaza Strip: distribution of Palestinian labor among the
domestic, Israeli, and foreign labor markets ('000)

Year	West Bank				Gaza Strip			
	Domestic	Israel	Other	Total	Domestic	Israel	Other	Total
1968	93	0	0	93	54	0	0	54
1969	115	0	0	115	58	0	0	58
1970	105	14	0	119	56	6	2	64
1971	95	25	2	122	54	8	3	65
1972	94	33	3	130	48	17	5	69
1973	91	37	7	134	46	23	7	76
1974	98	41	6	145	47	26	6	79
1975	96	38	8	142	47	26	7	80
1976	95	36	15	147	48	28	9	85
1977	94	35	22	151	50	27	11	89
1978	97	36	27	160	50	31	13	94
1979	95	39	32	166	46	34	15	95
1980	96	41	38	175	46	35	18	99
1981	95	40	47	182	47	36	21	104
1982	100	43	54	197	46	36	24	106
1983	102	48	58	208	46	40	25	111
1984	110	50	59	219	48	40	26	114
1985	111	48	62	221	50	42	29	121
1986	121	51	65	237	52	43	30	125
1987	119	63	67	249	56	46	32	134
1988	424	64	67	255	56	45	34	135
1989	124	65	69	258	61	40	36	137
1990	135	65	75	275	65	43	39	147

Source: Radwan A. Shaban, 'Palestinian Labour Mobility,' *International Labour Review*, 134/5–6
(1993), Tables 1 and 2 and sources cited there.

Table 9.1A   Arab Gulf states: annual oil production, 1946–90 (barrels '000)

	Saudi Arabia*	Kuwait*	Bahrain	Qatar	UAE	Oman
1946	59,944	5,931	8,010			
1947	89,852	16,225	9,411			
1948	142,853	46,500	10,915			
1949	174,008	90,000	10,985	750		
1950	199,547	125,722	11,016	12,268		
1951	277,963	204,910	10,994	18,009		
1952	301,861	273,433	11,004	25,255		
1953	308,294	314,592	10,978	31,025		
1954	350,843	350,317	10,992	36,450		
1955	356,664	402,917	10,982	41,983		
1956	366,765	405,716	11,014	45,345		
1957	373,751	427,675	11,691	50,798		
1958	385,221	524,389	14,873	63,412		
1959	421,040	526,074	16,473	61,431		
1960	481,368	619,193	16,500	63,088		
1961	540,846	632,803	16,444	64,386		
1962	599,668	713,896	16,446	67,911	5,976	
1963	651,860	762,739	16,503	70,123	17,571	
1964	693,803	840,523	18,000	77,885	67,465	
1965	805,169	857,994	20,788	84,215	102,804	
1966	950,065	907,253	22,521	105,945	131,279	
1967	1,023,841	912,450	25,370	118,428	140,117	23,030
1968	1,114,134	964,486	27,598	124,266	181,756	87,850
1969	1,173,897	1,021,616	27,774	129,746	222,598	119,710
1970	1,387,265	1,090,040	27,973	132,456	283,500	121,210
1971	1,741,149	1,167,329	27,346	156,882	386,655	107,430
1972	2,202,049	1,201,346	25,508	176,545	440,132	103,131
1973	2,772,590	1,102,446	24,948	208,152	559,399	106,926
1974	3,095,641	929,678	24,597	189,348	616,485	106,046
1975	2,582,375	760,660	20,895	159,870	607,360	125,195
1976	3,139,182	785,070	21,288	181,902	708,576	133,956
1977	3,374,425	718,685	21,236	162,425	729,635	124,465
1978	3,029,865	777,815	20,191	177,755	668,315	114,975
1979	3,479,180	912,500	18,741	185,420	668,315	107,675
1980	3,623,400	606,096	17,568	172,752	625,494	103,212
1981	3,582,475	410,625	16,862	147,825	538,010	116,435
1982	2,366,295	300,395	16,068	120,450	456,250	118,260
1983	1,856,390	388,360	15,272	107,675	419,385	136,875
1984	1,706,658	423,462	15,289	144,204	419,436	151,524
1985	1,236,620	373,395	15,330	109,865	435,445	181,770
1986	1,777,550	517,935	16,060	112,420	485,450	204,400
1987	1,556,725	578,525	15,330	106,945	562,465	212,430
1988	1,861,476	546,072	15,738	126,636	572,790	225,822
1989	1,848,360	650,797	15,695	138,700	678,900	233,965
1990	2,339,650	428,875	15,330	148,190	772,705	250,025

*   Including Neutral Zone production.

Source: US Energy Information Administration in DeGolyer and MacNaughton, *Twentieth Century Petroleum Statistics*, 52nd ed., p 9.

Table 9.1B   Arab Gulf states: value of oil exports (crude and refined), 1970, 1975–84, and 1986–90 (US$ million)

	Saudi Arabia	Kuwait	Bahrain	Qatar	UAE*	Oman
1970	2,418	1,582	209	231	523	
1975	29,493	8,593	1,042	1,754	6,806	1,442
1976	38,157	9,090	1,232	2,137	8,383	1,565
1977	43,308	8,981	1,523	2,055	9.258	1,571
1978	40,332	9,557	1,558	2,305	8,661	1,505
1979	62,855	17,294	2,054	2,693	12,862	2,156
1980	198,175	18,935	3,207	5,372	19,390	3,286
1981	118,998	14,229	3,883	5,496	18,761	4,441
1982	78,119	9,066	3,114	4,214	15,956	4,106
1983	44,830	10,069	2,586	2,993	13,016	4,210
1984	36,285	10,996	2,825	4,386	12,037	3,817
1986	18,061	6,378	1,828	6,965	6,965	2,469
1987	20,427	7,523	2,012	7,900	7,900	3,399
1988	20,205	6,840	1,831	7,627	7,627	2,865
1989	20,095	10,432	2,129	10,215	10,215	
1990	40,130	6,385		14,846	14,846	

* Includes natural gas liquids before 1980.

Sources: Saudia Arabia, Kuwait, Qatar, and UAE: Arthur Anderson/Cambridge Energy Research Associates, *World Oil Trends 1997*, Table 24; Bahrain and Oman: F. Gregory Cause III, *Oil Monarchies: Domestic Security and Challenges in the Arab Gulf States*, Table 2a (figures in Bahraini Dinars converted at BDI = US$2.66) and Table 2c (figures in Omani Riyals converted at US$1 = OR 0.345, 1975–85, and OR 0.384 thereafter).

Table 9.2   Current and real price of crude oil, 1970–88 (US$/barrel)

	Current price	Real price (1974 US$)
1970	1.3	2.1
1971	1.7	2.6
1972	1.9	3.1
1973	2.7	3.3
1974	11.2	11.2
1975	10.9	9.8
1976	11.7	10.4
1977	12.8	10.3
1978	12.9	9.1
1979	18.6	11.5
1980	30.5	17.2
1981	34.3	19.3
1982	31.0	17.7
1983	28.1	16.4
1984	27.5	16.4
1985	26.5	15.6
1986	13.5	6.7
1987	17.4	7.3
1988	14.0	5.5

Source: OAPEC, *Secretary General's Fifteenth Annual Report*, Table 1.1.

Table 9.3A Kuwait: population and labor force according to nationality, 1957, 1965, 1975, and 1980

	Population Kuwaiti	Non-Kuwaiti	Labour force Kuwaiti	Non-Kuwaiti
1957	113,622	92,851		
1965	220,059	247,280	43,108	141,279
1975	472,088	522,749	91,844	212,738
1980	565,613	792,339	107,760	383,749

Source: Kuwait, Ministry of Planning, Central Statistical Office, *Annual Statistical Abstract 1983*, pp 25, 105.

Table 9.3B Arab Gulf states: estimates of Arab migrant workers 1970, 1975, and 1980 ('000)

	1970	1975	1980
Bahrain	5.6	6.2	9.0
Kuwait	121.5	143.0	241.0
Oman	2.0	8.5	9.0
Qatar	12.7	14.9	23.0
Saudi Arabia	345.0	699.9	820.0
UAE	35.5	62.0	89.0
Total Arab	522.3	934.5	1192.1
Total non-national	677.2	1387.3	2102.0
Arabs as a % of non-national workers	77.1	67.4	56.7

Source: Ian J. Seccombe, 'International Migration, Arabisation and Localisation in the Gulf Labour Market' in Pridham (ed.), *Arab Gulf and the Arab World*, Table 8.1 and sources cited there.

Table 9.3C Arab Gulf states: estimates of population and labor and ratio of citizens to migrants, c.1980

State	Population Citizens	%	Expatriates	%	Total	Labour Citizens	%	Expatriates	%	Total
Kuwait	562,065	41.5	793,762	58.5	1,355,827	109,170	22.4	378,710	77.6	487,875
Qatar	52,200	26	147,800	74	200,000	10,341	20.6	39800	79.4	50,141
UAE	96,630	17.5	460,257	82.5	557,887	55,162	17.5	260,049	82.5	315,211
Bahrain	242,596	67.6	116,261	32.4	358,857	98,764	67.5	47,553	32.5	146,317
Saudi Arabia	510,0675	70.5	2,134,325	29.5	7,235,000	1,262,393	39.3	1,981,810	60.7	3,208,203
Oman	635,000	70.6	265,000	29.4	900,000	1,16,500	45.7	137,200	54.3	253,200
Total	6,055,166	62.4	3,652,405	37.6	9,707,571	1,535,830	36.2	2,707,922	69.8	4,243,752

Source: Owen, *Migrant Workers in the Gulf*, Table 2 and sources cited there.

Table 9.3D Arab Gulf states: estimates of numbers of Asian migrant workers in Saudi Arabia and in all the GCC states in the early 1980s

Country of Origin	At work in Saudi Arabia	Total in 6 GCC states
India		800,000
Pakistan	1,200,000	1,700,000–2,300,000*
Bangladesh	57,834	178,824**
Sri Lanka		50,000
Philippines	253,080	342,310
Korea (South)	102,305	171,040
Thailand		159,000
Indonesia	20,000	20,000
Turkey	40,000	250,000*

*   GCC plus Libya and Iraq.
** All migrants abroad.

Source: Owen, *Migrant Workers in the Gulf*, Table 2 and sources cited there.

Table 9.4   Saudi Arabia: sectoral allocation of expenditures in the first and second Five-Year Plans 1970–9

	First Plan Saudi Riyals (m)	%	Second Plan Saudi Riyals (m)	%
Agriculture	1.468	3.6	4.685	1.1
Manufacturing	1.099	2.7	45.058	10.4
Electricity and urban development	4.572	11.1	107.896	24.8
Transport and communications	7.477	18.1	40.353	9.3
Social and health	1.921	4.7	31.951	7.3
Education and culture	7.378	17.8	79.161	18.2
Administration	7.714	18.6	38.179	8.8
Defense	9.550	23.1	78.157	18.0
Other	0.127	0.3	9.312	2.1

Source: Gorm Rye Olsen, 'Saudi Arabia in the 1970s: State, Oil and Development Policy,' Table 4, p 14 and sources cited there.

Table 9.5   Yemen: estimates of numbers of short-term Yemeni migrant
             workers and their remittances 1970–80

	YAR numbers	Remittances (US$ m)	PDRY numbers	Remittances (US$ m)
1970	144,000	53		
1971				44.9
1973				33.4
1975	385,000	457[a]		
1976		842[b]	125,000	
1977		1,411[c]		180
1978				
1979				
1980	548,000	1,000	210,000	

a 1975/76
b 1976/77
c 1977/78

Sources: Lackner, *P.D.R. Yemen: Outpost of Socialist Development in Arabia*, pp 128–9; Hans Steffan
and Olivier Blanc, 'La Démographie de la République arabe du Yémen' in Paul Bonnenfant (ed.),
La Peninsule arabe d'aujourd'hui, Table 13 and p 102; Stookey, *South Yemen: A Marxist Republic in
Arabia*, p 89; Nyrop et al. (eds), *Area Handbook for the Yemens*, Table 4.

Table 9.6   Arab Gulf states: aid and official investment in the Arab World,
             1970–84 (net disbursements, US$ million)

	Kuwait	Qatar	Saudi Arabia	UAE	Total
1970	148		173		320
1975	965	317	2,665	1,046	4,984
1980	1,140	386	5,775	1,052	8,262
1984	1,018	13	3,315	43	4,389

Source: Porter, 'Gulf Aid and Investment in the Arab world' in Pridham (ed.), *The Arab Gulf and the
Arab World* , Table 9.1.

Statistical Appendix

	1925	1950
Total population of the Middle East (millions, estimated)	55	80

	1925–1950
Annual rate of population growth (%)	1.5

Data for Egypt and Turkey only:

	Egypt		Turkey	
	1925	1950	1925	1950
Population (millions)	14.2 (1927)	19 (1947)	13.2	20.8
Annual rate of population growth 1925–50 (%)	1.5		1.8	
Share of urban population (above 5,000, %)	27	33	24	25
Share of agriculture in the labor force	67	61	80	78
GNP (millions of current US $)		2,470	810	3,450
GNP per capita (current US $)		130	60	165
Share of agriculture in GDP (%)		43	48	42
Share of industry in GDP (%)		6	10	15
Exports (millions of US $)		504	103	263
Imports (millions of US $)		613	129	286
Exports/GDP (%)		20.4	12.6	7.6
Imports/GDP (%)		24.8	15.9	8.3

Sources: Mead, *Growth and Structural Change in the Egyptian Economy*, Homewood; Turkey, State Institute of Statistics, *Statistical Indicators* 1923–1992.

PART II: 1950–90

	1950	1970	1990
Total population of the Middle East (millions)	80	135	240

	1950–70	1970–90
Annual rate of population growth (%)	2.7	2.9

The table below begins with the statistics for Egypt and Turkey. They are followed by the other countries of the region, in alphabetical order. Bahrain and Qatar are added to the end since only a limited number of series are available for these two countries. The data for Yemen is obtained by aggregating the figures from the North and the South.

Sources: World Bank, *World Development Report*; United Nations Development Programme, *Human Development Report*, various years.

	Egypt	
	1960	**1990**
Population (millions)	25.9	52.1

	1965–80	1980–90
Annual rate of population growth (%)	2.1	2.4

	1960	1990
Crude birth rate per 1000 (1965 in parentheses)	45	31
Crude death rate per 1000 (1965 in parentheses)	19	10
Life expectancy at birth (years)	46	60

	1965	1990
Total fertility rate	6.8	4.0

	1960	1990
Infant mortality (per 1,000 live births)	179	66
Adult illiteracy (%) (1965 in parentheses)	74	52
Female adult illiteracy (%)		66
Share of urban population (%)	38	47
GDP (billions of current US$)	4.6	33.2

	1965–90
Average annual growth of GDP per capita (%)	4.1

	Egypt (continued)	
	1960	1990
GDP per capita in 1990 (US$)		600
GDP per capita (purchasing power parity adjusted: 1990 US$)	550	2,000
Agriculture in the labor force (%)	58	34
Share of agriculture in GDP (%)	30	17
Share of industry in GDP (%)	24	29
Share of manufacturing in GDP (%)	20	16
Share of exports (billions of US$)	0.9	3.0
Imports (billions of US$)		10.3
Exports/GDP (%)	20	10

	Turkey		Iraq		Israel	
	1960	1990	1960	1990	1960	1990
Population (millions)	27.5	56.1	6.8	18.9	2.1	4.7
Population growth (%)	2.4	2.4	3.4	3.6	2.8	1.8
Crude birth rate (per 1,000)	44	28	51	42	26	22
Crude death rate (per 1,000)	17	7	19	8	8	6
Life expectancy (years)	51	67	49	65	69	76
	1965	1990	1965	1990	1965	1990
Fertility rate	5.7	3.5	7.2	6.2	3.8	2.8
	1960	1990	1960	1990	1960	1990
Infant mortality (per 1,000 live births)	190	60	139	65	35	10
Adult illiteracy (%)	62	19	82	40	16	5
Female illiteracy (%)		29		51		7
Urban population (%)	30	61	43	71	77	92
GDP (US$ billions)	7.7	96.5	2.4		3.6	53.2
	1965–90		1965–90		1965–90	
Growth of GDP per capita (%)	2.6				2.6	
	1960	1990	1960	1990	1960	1990
GDP per capita (in 1990 US$)		1,630				10,920
GDP per capita in 1990 US$ (PPP adjusted)	1,650	4,650		3,500	3,950	10,850
Share of agriculture in labor Force (%)	78	46	53	13	14	5
Share of agriculture in GDP (%)	41	18	17		11	
Share of industry in GDP (%)	21	33	52		32	
Share of manufacturing in GDP (%)	13	24	10		23	
Exports (US$ billions)	0.2	13	1	16.8	0.5	12
Imports (US$ billions)		22.3		4.3		15.2
Exports/GDP (%)	3	14	42		14	32

273

	Jordan		Kuwait		Lebanon	
	1960	1990	1960	1990	1960	1990
Population (millions)	1.7	3.2	0.3	2.1	1.9	2.8
Population growth (%)	4.3	3.7	7.1	4.4	1.7	
Crude birth rate (per 1,000)	48	43	44	25	43	
Crude death rate (per 1,000)	20	6	10	3	14	
Life expectancy (years)	47	67	60	74	60	66
	1965	**1990**	**1965**	**1990**	**1965**	**1990**
Fertility rate	8.0	6.3	7.4	3.4		
	1960	**1990**	**1960**	**1990**	**1960**	**1990**
Infant mortality (per 1,000 live births)	135	51	89	14	68	38
Adult illiteracy (%)	68	20	53	27	(31)	20
Female illiteracy (%)		30		33		27
Urban population (%)	43	61	72	96	44	
GDP (current US$ billions)		3.3	2.1	23.5	1.2	
	1965–90		**1965–90**		**1965–90**	
Average annual rate of growth of GDP per capita (%)			4.0			
	1960	**1990**	**1960**	**1990**	**1960**	**1990**
GDP per capita (US$)		1,240				
GDP per capita (purchasing power parity adjusted: 1990 US$)	1,300	2,350		15,200		2,300
Agriculture in labor force (%)	44	10	2	1	38	14
Agriculture in GDP (%)		8	0	1	12	
Industry in GDP (%)		26	70	56	20	
Manufacturing in GDP (%)		12	3	9	13	
Exports (US$ billions)		1.1		8.3	0.3	
Imports (US$ billions)		2.7		4.8		
Exports/GDP		33		35	27	

	Oman		Saudi Arabia		Syria	
	1960	1990	1960	1990	1960	1990
Population (millions)	0.5	1.6	4.1	14.9	4.6	12.4
Population growth (%)	3.6	4.7	4.6	4.7	3.4	3.6
Crude birth rate (per 1,000)	(50)	44	51	43	47	44
Crude death rate (per 1,000)	(24)	6	28	7	26	7
Life Expectancy (years)	40	66	44	64	50	66
	1965	1990	1965	1990	1965	1990
Fertility rate	7.2	7.0	7.3	7.0	7.7	6.5
	1960	1990	1960	1990	1960	1990
Infant mortality (per 1,000 live births)	214	32	170	65	135	43
Adult illiteracy (%)			97	38	70	36
Female illiteracy (%)				52		49
Urban population (%)	4	11	30	63	37	50
GDP (current US$ billions)	0.1	7.7	2.3	80.9	1.5	14.7
	1965–90		1965–90		1965–90	
Average annual rate of growth of GDP per capita (%)	6.4		2.6		2.9	
	1960	1990	1960	1990	1960	1990
GDP per capita (US$)		5,650		7,050		1,000
GDP per capita (purchasing power parity adjusted: 1990 US$)		9,950	7,600	11,000	1,800	4,800
Agriculture in labor force (%)	66	49	71	48	54	22
Agriculture in GDP (%)	(61)	3	(8)	8	(29)	28
Industry in GDP (%)	(23)	80	(60)	45	(22)	22
Manufacturing in GDP (%)	(0)	4	(9)	9		
Exports (US$ billions)		0.5		31.1		4.2
Imports (US$ billions)		2.6		24.1		2.4
Exports/GDP		7		38		2

275

	UAE		Yemen	
	1960	1990	1960	1990
Population (millions)	0.1	1.6	5.2	11.3
Population growth (%)	16.5	4.3	2.3	3.1
Crude birth rate (per 1,000)	(41)	22	52	53
Crude death rate (per 1,000)	(14)	4	30	18
Life expectancy	53	71	36	52
	1965	1990	1965	1990
Fertility rate	6.8	4.6	7	7.7
Infant mortality (per 1,000 live births)	145	23	214	124
Adult illiteracy (%)			(92)	62
Female illiteracy (%)				74
Urban population (%)	37	78	10	29
GDP per capita (US$)		19,860		540
GDP per capita (purchasing power parity adjusted: 1990 US$)		16,750		1,550
Agriculture in labor force (%)	24	5	75	63
Agriculture in GDP (%)		2		20
Industry in GDP (%)		55		28
Manufacturing in GDP		9		8
Exports (US$ billions)				
Imports (US$ billions)				
Exports/GDP				

	Bahrain		Qatar	
	1960	1990	1960	1990
Population (millions)	0.2	0.5	0.1	0.4

	1960–90		1960–90	
Population growth (%)	3.9		7.4	

	1960	1990	1960	1990
Life expectancy	56	71	53	69
Infant mortality (per 1,000 live births)	130	15	145	30
GDP per capita (US$)		6,830		15,870
GDP per capita (purchasing power parity adjusted: 1990 US$)		10,700		

Bibliography

UNPUBLISHED MATERIAL

PUBLIC RECORD OFFICE

FO Series 371 and 406, POWE Series 33.

BODLEIAN LIBRARY, OXFORD

Milner Papers: Sir Owen Thomas, 'Agricultural and economic position of Egypt,' 26 April 1920, p 21, Box 164.

PRIVATE PAPERS, MIDDLE EAST CENTRE,
ST ANTONY'S COLLEGE, OXFORD

Cunningham Papers
Dickson Papers
Holden Papers
Murray, Dr K.M., 'Land tenure in the Fertile Crescent,' nd (1945?), MESC HD 2061
Philby Papers

THESES/DISSERTATIONS

Chaib, André Emil, 'The Export Performance of a Small, Open, Developing Country: the Lebanese Experience, 1951–74,' PhD dissertation, University of Michigan, 1979.
Kingston, Paul W.T., 'Pioneers of Development: The British Development Division and the Politics of Technical Assistance, 1945–1961,' DPhil. dissertation, University of Oxford, Michaelmas 1990.
al-Najjar, Ghanim Hamad, 'Decision-Making Process in Kuwait: The Land Acquisition Policy as a Case Study,' PhD dissertation, University of Exeter, January 1984.
Özel, Işik, 'The GNP for Turkey, 1907–1939: A Quantitative Study Based on Ottoman and Turkish Statistics,' MA thesis, Atatürk Institute, Boğaziçi University, Istanbul, 1997.
Russell, Sharon Stanton, 'Uneasy Welcome: The Political Economy of Migration Policy in Saudi Arabia,' PhD dissertation, Massachusetts Institute of Technology, September 1987.
Sadowski, Yahya M., 'Political Power and Economic Organization in Syria: The Course of State Intervention 1946–1958,' PhD dissertation, University of California at Los Angeles, 1984.
Whitaker, James Long, 'The Union of Demeter with Zeus: Agriculture and Politics in Modern Syria,' PhD dissertation, University of Durham, 1996.

Yüçel, Yelda, 'Macroeconomic Policies in Turkey during the Great Depression, 1929–1940,' MA thesis, Department of Economics, Boğaziçi University, Istanbul, 1996.

Zendisayek, Beril, 'Large and Small Enterprises in the Early Stages of Turkey's Industrialisation, 1929–1939,' MA thesis, Department of Economics, Boğaziçi University, Istanbul, 1997.

OTHER

Butter, David, 'Debt and Financial Policies,' paper presented to the conference 'Politics and the Economy under Mubarak,' School of Oriental and African Studies, London University, 18 May 1987.

Hobeika, Louis, 'Key Issues in the Reconstruction of Lebanon,' paper prepared for the meetings of the Allied Social Sciences Associations, Anaheim, California, 5 January 1993.

Metzer, Jacob and Oded Kaplan, 'The Jewish and Arab Economies in Mandatory Palestine: Production, Employment and Growth,' unpublished English summary of original Hebrew *Meshek Yehudi u-meshek Aravi be-Erets Yisrael: totsar, taasukahu-tsemihah bi-tekufat ha-mandat*, Jerusalem, The Maurice Falk Institute for Economic Research in Israel, 1990.

Olsen, Gorm Rye, 'Saudi Arabia in the 1970's: State, Oil and Development Policy,' paper prepared for the workshop on 'The Middle East in the 1980s: Current Structures and Prospects,' ECPR Joint Sessions, Lancaster, March/April 1980.

Share, Dr M., 'Jordan's Trade and Balance of Payments Problems,' paper presented to the Conference on the Politics and the Economy of Jordan, School of Oriental and African Studies, London University, May 1987.

Sha'sha'a, Zeid J., 'The Role of the Private Sector in Jordan,' paper presented to the Conference on Politics and the Economy of Jordan, School of Oriental and African Studies, London University, May 1987.

PUBLISHED MATERIAL

OFFICIAL

Egypt

Commission of Commerce and Industry, *Rapport de la commission du commerce et de l'industrie*, 2nd ed., Cairo, Imprimerie nationale, 1922.

Madabit majlis al-shuyukh wa-al-nuwwab, Cairo, 1933 and 1937.

Ministry of Finance, Statistical Department, *Annuaire statistique*, Cairo, Imprimerie nationale, various years.

Ministry of Finance, Statistical Department, *The Census of Egypt Taken in 1917* II, Cairo, Government Press, 1920.

Ministry of Finance, *Twenty Years of Agricultural Development in Egypt (1919–1939)*, Hussein Kamel Selim, Cairo/Bulaq, Government Press, 1940.

France

Ministère des affaires étrangères, *Rapport à la Société des Nations sur la situation de la Syrie et du Liban*, 1929.

International Monetary Fund

World Economic Outlook, May 1997, *Globalization: Opportunities and Challenges*, Washington DC, IMF, 1997.
International Financial Statistics, Washington, February 1969.

Iraq

Government of El-'Iraq, *An Inquiry into Land Tenure and Related Questions: Proposals for the Initiation of Reform*, by Sir Ernest Dowson, Letchworth, Garden City Press, nd (Introduction 1931).

Jordan

Central Bank, *Seventeenth Annual Report*.
The Hashemite Kingdom of Jordan, National Planning Council, *Three Year Development Plan 1973–1975*.
Jordan Development Board, *Seven Year Program for Economic Development 1964–70*, Amman, nd.

Kuwait

Ministry of Planning, Central Statistical Office, *Annual Statistical Abstract 1983*.

Lebanon

Ministère du plan, *Besoins et possibilités de développement du Liban: étude préliminaire*, Beirut, Mission IRFED, 1960–1961.

Palestine

Government of Palestine, *A Survey of Palestine: Prepared for the Information of the Anglo-American Committee of Inquiry*, Jerusalem, 1946.
— *National Income of Palestine 1944*, by P.J. Loftus, Jerusalem, Government Printing Office, 1946.

Saudi Arabia

Ministry of Planning, *Third Development Plan 1400–1405AH, 1980–1985AD*, np, Ministry of Planning, nd (1980?).

Ministry of Planning, *Fourth Development Plan, 1405–1410AH, 1986–1990AD*, np, Ministry of Planning, nd (1984?).

Syria

Ministry of Agriculture, Cotton Bureau, *A Report on the Cotton Situation in Syria*, Paris, June 1955.

Turkey

State Institute of Statistics, *The Industrial Census of 1927*, Ankara, 1928.
— *Statistical Indicators*, 1923–1992, Ankara, 1991–94.
— *Statistical Yearbooks*, various years.

United Kingdom

Colonial Office, *Annual Report on Aden and Aden Protectorate for the Year 1946*, London, HMSO, 1948.
Naval Intelligence Division, *Western Arabia and the Red Sea*, np, June 1946.
Department of Overseas Trade, *Egypt: Review of Commercial Conditions*, May 1945.
— 'Economic Conditions in Syria,' London, May 1934.
'Administrative Report on the Persian Gulf Political Residency and Muskat Political Agency for 1901–1902,' in *Selections from the Records of the Government of India*, Foreign Department, No. 392, Calcutta, Government Printing Office, 1902.

United Nations

United Nations Conference on Trade and Development (UNCTAD), *Health Conditions and Services in the West Bank and Gaza Strip* by Rita Giacaman, UNCTAD/ECDC/SEU/3, 28 September 1994.
— *Prospects for Sustained Development of the Palestinian Economy in the West Bank and the Gaza Strip, 1990–2010: A Quantitative Framework: Technical Supplement*, UNCTAD/ECDC/SEU/6/Add. 1, 11 November 1994.
— *Developments in the Economy of the Occupied Palestinian Territory*, UNCTAD/TD/B/40 (1)/8, 26 July 1993.
— *Prospects for Sustained Development of the Palestinian Economy in the West Bank and Gaza*, UNCTAD/DSD/SEU/2, 27 September 1993.
— *The Agricultural Sector of the West Bank and the Gaza Strip* by Hisham Awartani, UNCTAD/DSD/SEU/Misc. 5, 12 October 1993.

United Nations Industrial Development Organization (UNIDO), *Long Term Prospects for Industrial Development in Bahrain*, Vienna, 1981.

United States

Department of State, 'Annual Economic and Financial Review (Syria-Lebanon) 1942,' Beirut, 27 February 1943/2. A copy can be found at the Centre for Lebanese Studies, Oxford, US Archives on Lebanon, Box 50.
— 'Study of the Financial Situation of Syria and Lebanon' by William Wilman II, sent from Beirut, 1 March 1944. A copy can be found at the Centre for Lebanese Studies, Oxford, US Archives on Lebanon, Box 49.
Congressional Quarterly, *The Middle East: US Policy, Israel and the Arabs*, 4th ed. Washington DC, July 1979.
US Embassy, Riyadh, 'Social Welfare and the System of Consumer Subsidies, Payments and Services,' unclassified report, 1 May 1984.

World Bank/IBRD

IBRD, *The Economic Development of Syria*, Baltimore, Johns Hopkins University Press, 1956.
— *The Economic Development of Jordan*, Baltimore, Johns Hopkins University Press, 1957.
— *The Economic Development of Iraq*, Baltimore, Johns Hopkins University Press, 1952.
— *Yemen Arab Republic, Development of a Traditional Economy*, 3rd ed., Washington DC, World Bank, 1983.
World Bank, *Claiming the Future: Choosing Prosperity in the Middle East and North Africa*, Washington DC, World Bank, 1995.
— *Peace and the Jordanian Economy*, Washington DC, World Bank, 1994.
— *World Development Report 1984*, New York, Oxford University Press, 1984.
— *World Development Report 1991*, New York, Oxford University Press, 1991.
— *World Development Report 1992*, New York, Oxford University Press, 1992.

BOOKS AND ARTICLES

Abdalla, Ahmed, *The Student Movement and National Politics in Egypt*, London, Al-Saqi Books, 1985.
Abdel-Fadil, Mahmoud, *Development, Income Distribution and Social Change in Rural Egypt 1952–1970*, Cambridge and New York, Cambridge University Press, 1975.
Abdel-Latif, Abla, 'Public Finance in Bahrain from 1935 to 1981 with Special Emphasis on the Allocation of Oil Revenues in the Past, Present and Future' in Jeffrey B. Nugent and Theodore H. Thomas (eds), *Bahrain and the Gulf: Past Perspectives and Alternative Futures*, London and Sydney, Croom Helm, 1985.
Abou-Rjaili, Khalil, 'L'Emigration forcée des populations à l'intérieur du Liban, 1975–1986,' *The Beirut Review* 3 (Spring 1992).
Abramovitz, Moses, 'Catching up, forging ahead, and falling behind,' *Journal of Economic History* 46/2 (1986), pp 385–406.

Abu-Amr, Ziad, 'The Gaza Economy 1948–1984' in George T. Abed (ed.), *The Palestinian Economy: Studies in Development under Prolonged Occupation*, London, Routledge, 1988.

Abu Kishk, Bakir, 'Industrial Development and Policies in the West Bank and Gaza' in George T. Abed (ed.), *The Palestinian Economy: Studies in Development under Prolonged Occupation*, London, Routledge, 1988.

Abu Rabieh, Aref, *The Negev Bedouin and Livestock Rearing: Social, Economic and Political Aspects*, Oxford and London, Berg, 1994.

Ahmad, Feroz, 'War and Society Under the Young Turks,' *Review* 11 (1988), Binghamton NY, Fernand Braudel Center.

— *The Turkish Experiment in Democracy, 1950–1975*, London, Hurst and Company, 1977.

Aktar, Ayhan, 'Varlik Vergisi ve Istanbul,' *Toplum ve Bilim* 71 (1996).

Aldcroft, Derek, 'Eastern Europe in the Age of Turbulence, 1919–1950,' *Economic History Review* 2nd series, 41/4 (1988).

Allan, J.A., 'Overall Perspectives on Countries and Regions' in Peter Rogers and Peter Lydins (eds), *Water in the Arab World: Perspectives and Progress*, Cambridge MA, Harvard University Press, 1994.

Almana, Mohammed, *Arabia Unified: A Portrait of Ibn Saud*, London, Hutchinson, 1980.

Al-Qudsi, Sulayman, *The Interaction Between Government Budget, Demography and Labor in the GCC*, Working Paper 9708, Cairo, Economic Research Forum, November 1996.

Amadouny, Vatan M., 'Infrastructural Development under the British Mandate' in Eugene Rogan and Tariq Tell (eds), *Village, Steppe and State: The Social Origins of Modern Jordan*, London and New York, British Academic Press, 1994.

Amawi, Abla M., 'The Consolidation of the Merchant Class in Transjordan during the Second World War' in Eugene L. Rogan and Tariq Tell (eds), *Village, Steppe and State: The Social Origins of Modern Jordan*, London and New York, British Academic Press, 1994.

Amin, Galal, *Egypt's Economic Predicament*, Leiden and New York, E.J. Brill, 1995.

Anderson, Irvine H., *ARAMCO, the United States and Saudi Arabia: A Study in the Dynamics of Foreign Oil Policy*, Princeton NJ, Princeton University Press, 1982.

Anis, M.A., 'A Study of the National Income of Egypt,' *L'Egypte contemporaine* 261–2 (November–December 1950).

Anon. 'Saudi Arabia Notifies Shell and BP That It Will Take Over Direct Marketing of Arms Deal Oil Sales At Year End,' *Middle East Economic Survey* 34/45 (5 August 1996).

Antonius, George, *The Arab Awakening: The Story of the Arab Nationalist Movement*, London, H. Hamilton, 1938.

Arabiyyat, Dr Suleiman, 'Performance of the Agricultural Sector in Jordan Within the Regional Context' in Monther Share (ed.), *Jordan's Place Within the Arab Oil Economies*, Irbid, Yarmouk University, 1986. Proceedings of the seminar held at Yarmouk University's Liaison Office, Amman, March 12–13 1983, under the auspices of the University of Jordan, Amman, the Middle East Centre of St Antony's College, Oxford, and Yarmouk University, Irbid.

Aricanli, Tosun and Dani Rodrik, 'An Overview of Turkey's Experience with Economic Liberalization and Structural Adjustment,' *World Development* 18 (1990).

Arrighi, Giovanni, *The Long Twentieth Century*, New York and London, Verso, 1994.

Asfour, Edmund Y., 'Prospects and Problems of Economic Development of Saudi Arabia, Kuwait and the Desert Principalities' in Charles A. Cooper and Sidney S. Alexander (eds), *Economic Development and Population Growth in the Middle East*, New York, American Elsevier, 1971.

— *Syria: Development and Monetary Policy*, Cambridge MA, Harvard University Press, 1959.

Atran, Scott. 'Le masha'a et la question foncière en Palestine 1858–1948,' *Annales* 6 (November–December 1987).

Azhari, N.L., *Evolution du système économique libanais, ou la fin de laissez-faire*, Paris, Librairie général du droit et de jurisprudence, 1970.

Badre, Albert Y., 'The Economic Development of Lebanon' in Charles A. Cooper and Sidney S. Alexander (eds), *Economic Development and Population Growth in the Middle East*, New York, American Elsevier, 1972.

— 'The National Income of Lebanon,' *Middle East Economic Papers* (1956).

Bagh, A.S., *L'Industrie à Damas entre 1928–1958: étude de géographie économique*, Damascus, Imprimerie de l'université, 1961.

Barkey, Henry J., *The State and the Industrialization Crisis in Turkey*, Boulder CO, Westview Press, 1990.

Barlow, Robin and Fikret Şenses, 'The Turkish Export Boom: Just Reward or Just Lucky,' *Journal of Development Economics* 48 (1995).

Barnett, Michael, 'Regional Security after the Gulf War,' *Political Science Quarterly* 111, 4 (1996–97).

Basile, A., 'La Vocation régionale de la place financière de Beyrouth,' *Proche-Orient: études économiques* 77–78 (January–December 1973).

Batatu, Hanna, *The Old Social Classes and the Revolutionary Movements of Iraq*, Princeton NJ, Princeton University Press, 1978.

Baxter, J. 'Notes on the Estimate of the National Income of Egypt for 1921–1922,' *L'Egypte contemporaine* 14/73 (May 1923).

Beaumont, Peter, 'Environmental Issues' in D. Hopwood, H. Ishow, and Thomas Koszinowski (eds), *Iraq: Power and Society*, Reading, Ithaca Press, 1993.

Beblawi, Hazem and Giacomo Luciani (eds), *The Rentier State*, London, Croom Helm, 1987.

Behar, Cem, *The Population of the Ottoman Empire and Turkey, 1500–1927*, Ankara, State Institute of Statistics, 1995.

Beinin, Joel, 'Israel at Forty: the Political Economy/Political Culture of Constant Conflict,' *Arab Studies Quarterly* 10/3 (1988).

Beinin, Joel and Zachary Lockman, *Workers on the Nile: Nationalism, Communism, Islam and the Egyptian Working Class*, Princeton NJ, Princeton University Press, 1987.

Belgrave, Charles, *Personal Column*, London, Hutchinson, 1960.

Ben-Ami, O., 'The Palestinian Diamond Industry,' *The Palestine Economist: A Review of Palestine's Economy*, Jerusalem, 1948.

Ben-Porath, Yoram, 'Entwined Growth of Population and Product' in Yoram Ben-Porath (ed.), *The Israeli Economy: Maturing Through Crises*, Cambridge MA and London, Harvard University Press, 1986.

Berger, Morroe, 'The Middle Class in the Arab World' in Walter Laqueur (ed.), *The Middle East in Transition*, London, Routledge and Keegan Paul, 1958.

Bertrand, Jean-Pierre, Aïda Boudjikanian, and Nadine Picaudou, *L'Industrie libanaise et les marchés arabes du Golfe*, Beirut, CERMOC, 1979.

Berglas, Eitan, 'Defense and the Economy' in Yoram Ben-Porath (ed.), *The Israeli Economy: Maturing Through Crises*, Cambridge MA and London, Harvard University Press, 1986.

Betts, Raymond F., *France and Decolonisation*, London, Macmillan, 1991.

Birks, J.S., 'The Demographic Challenge in the Arab Gulf' in B.R. Pridham (ed.), *The Arab Gulf and the Arab World*, New York, Croom Helm, 1988.

Birks, J.S. and C.A. Sinclair, 'The Socio-Economic Determinants of Intra-Regional Migration' in UNECWA, *International Migration in the Arab World*, Beirut, United Nations Economic Commission on Western Asia, 1982. Proceedings of an ECWA Population Conference, Nicosia, Cyprus, 11–16 May 1981.

Birtek, Faruk and Çağlar Keyder, 'Agriculture and the State: An Inquiry into Agricultural Differentiation and Political Alliances: the Case of Turkey,' *Journal of Peasant Studies* 2 (1975).

Block, Fred L., *The Origins of International Economic Disorder*, Berkeley and Los Angeles, University of California Press, 1977.

Bocco, Richard and Tariq Tell, 'Pax Britannica in the Steppe: British Policy and the Trans-jordanian Bedouin' in Eugene L. Rogan and Tariq Tell (eds), *Village, Steppe and State: The Social Origins of Modern Jordan*, London and New York, British Academic Press, 1994.

Boratav, Korkut, *Türkiye Iktisat Tarihi, 1908–1985*, Istanbul, Gerçek Yayinlari, 1988.

— 'Inter-Class and Intra-Class Relations of Distribution Under Structural Adjustment: Turkey During the 1980s' in Tosun Aricanli and Dani Rodrik (eds), *The Political Economy of Turkey: Debt, Adjustment and Sustainability*, London, Macmillan, 1990.

— 'Kemalist Economic Policies and Etatism' in A. Kazancigil and E. Özbudun (eds), *Atatürk: Founder of a Modern State*, London, C. Hurst, 1981.

Boratav, Korkut, Oktar Türel, and Erinç Yeldan, 'Dilemmas of Structural Adjustment and Environmental Policies Under Instability: Post-1980 Turkey,' *World Development* 24 (1996).

Bowen, R., 'The Pearl Fisheries of the Persian Gulf,' *Middle East Journal* 5/2 (Spring 1951).

Bresciani-Turroni, Professor Costantino, 'Relations entre la récolte et le prix du coton égyptien,' *L'Egypte contemporaine* 21 (1930).

Bruno, Michael, 'Sharp Disinflation Strategy: Israel 1985,' *Economic Policy* 2 (April 1986).

Buheiry, Marwan, *Beirut's Role in the Political Economy of the French Mandate*, Papers on Lebanon No. 4, Oxford, Centre for Lebanese Studies, 1986.

Bulutay, Tuncer, Yahya S. Tezel, and Nuri Yildirim, *Türkiye Milli Geliri (1923–1948)*, 2 vols., Ankara, Üniversitesi Siyasal Bilgiler Fakültesi Yayinlari, 1974.

Burns, Norman, *The Tariff of Syria, 1919–1932*, Beirut, American University of Beirut Press, 1933.

Burns, Norman and Allen D. Edwards, 'Foreign Trade' in Said B. Himadeh (ed.), *The Economic Organization of Syria*, Beirut, American University of Beirut Press, 1936.

Bury, G. Wyman, *Arabia Infelix or the Turks in Yamen*, London, Macmillan and Co., 1915.

Carmi, Shulamit and Henry Rosenfeld, 'Israel's Political Economy and the Widening Class Gap Between its Two National Groups,' *African and Asian Studies* 26/1 (March 1992).

Çeçen, A. Aydin, A. Suut Doğruel, and Fatma Doğruel, 'Economic Growth and Structural Change in Turkey, 1960–88,' *International Journal of Middle East Studies* 26 (1994).

Celasun, Merih, 'Income Distribution and Domestic Terms of Trade in Turkey, 1978–1983,' *Middle East Technical University Studies in Development* 13 (1986).

Celasun, Merih and Dani Rodrik, 'Debt, Adjustment and Growth: Turkey' in Jeffrey D. Sachs and Susan Collins (eds), *Developing Country Debt and Economic Performance*, Chicago, University of Chicago Press, 1989.

Charani, M. 'Points de vue successifs sur l'économie syrienne' in *Mélanges Proche-Orientaux d'économie politique*, Annales de la faculté de droit, Beirut, Université Saint-Joseph de Beyrouth, 1956.

Chatelus, Michel, 'Rentier or Producer Economy in the Middle East? The Jordanian response' in Bichara Khader and Adnan Badran (eds), *The Economic Development of Jordan*, London and Wolfeboro NH, Croom Helm, 1987.

— 'La Croissance économique: mutation des structures et dynamisme du déséquilibre' in André Raymond (ed.), *La Syrie d'aujourd'hui*, Paris, CNRS, 1980.

Chaudhry, Kiren Aziz, 'On the Way to the Market: Economic Liberalization and Iraq's Invasion of Kuwait,' *Middle East Report* (MERIP) 170 (May–June 1991).

— *The Price of Wealth: Economics and Institutions in the Middle East*, Ithaca and London, Cornell University Press, 1997.

Chayanov, A.V., *The Theory of Peasant Economy*, D. Thorner, R.E.F. Smith, and B. Kerblay (eds), new ed., Madison, University of Wisconsin Press, 1987.

Chenery, H., S. Robinson, and M. Syrquin, *Industrialization and Growth*, New York, Oxford University Press for the World Bank, 1986.

Claus, Burghard and Michael Hofmann, *The Importance of the Oil-producing Countries of the Gulf Cooperation Council for the Development of the Yemen Arab Republic and the Hashemite Kingdom of Jordan*, Berlin, German Development Institute, September 1984.

Coatsworth, John H., 'Welfare,' *American Historical Review* 101/1 (February 1996).

Commander, Simon, *The State and Agricultural Development in Egypt Since 1973*, London, Ithaca Press, 1987.

— *The Political Economy of Food Production and Distribution in Egypt: A Survey of Developments since 1973*, Overseas Development Institute Working Paper No. 14, London, July 1984.

Corzine, Robert, 'Testing Times for Saudi Oil Policy,' *Financial Times*, 31 October 1997.

Couland, Jacques, *Le Mouvement syndical au Liban 1919–1946*, Paris, Editions sociales, 1970.

Crafts, Nicks, 'The Golden Age of Economic Growth in Europe, 1950–1973,' *Economic History Review*, vol. 48

Crouchley, A.E., *The Investment of Foreign Capital in Egyptian Companies and the Public Debt*, Egypt, Ministry of Finance, Technical Paper No. 12, Cairo, 1936.

Crystal, Jill, *Kuwait: The Transformation of An Oil State*, Boulder CO, Westview, 1992.

— *Oil and Politics in the Gulf: Rulers and Merchants in Kuwait and Qatar*, Cambridge and New York, Cambridge University Press, 1990.

Dabbagh, Salah M., 'Agrarian Reform in Syria,' *Middle East Economic Papers* (1962).

Dasuqi, Asim, *Kibar mullak al-aradi al-zira'iyya wa dawrahum fi-al-mujtama' al-misri, 1914–1952*, Cairo, Dar al-thaqafa al-jadida, 1975.

DeGolyer and MacNaughton, *Twentieth Century Petroleum Statistics*, 52nd ed., Dallas, DeGolyer and MacNaughton, 1996.

De Melo, Jaime and Arvind Panagriya, 'Introduction,' in Jaime De Melo and Arvind Panagriya (eds), *New Dimensions in Regional Integration*, Cambridge and New York, Cambridge University Press, 1993.

Derviş, Kemal and Sherman Robinson, 'The Structure of Income Inequality in Turkey, 1950–1973' in Ergun Özbudun and Aydin Ulusan (eds), *The Political Economy of Income Distribution in Turkey*, New York, Holmes and Meier, 1980.

Diab, Muhammad, 'National Income Accounting Practices in Syria' in Taufiq M. Khan (ed.), *Middle East Studies in Income and Wealth*, London, Bowes and Bowes, New Haven, International Association for Research in Income and Wealth, 1965.

— 'The First Five-Year Plan of Syria: An Appraisal,' *Middle East Economic Papers* (1960).

Diaz Alejandro, Carlos F., 'Latin America in the 1930s' in Rosemary Thorp (ed.), *Latin America in the 1930s: The Role of the Periphery in the World Crisis*, London, Macmillan, 1984.

Dubar, Claude and Salim Nasr, *Les Classes sociales au Liban*, Paris, Presses de la Fondation nationale des sciences politiques, 1976.

Ducruet, Jean, *Les Capitaux européens au Proche-Orient*, Paris, Presses universitaires de France, 1964.

Durand, Huguette, 'La rupture de l'union syro-libanaise' in *Mélanges Proche-Orientaux d'économie politique*, Université Saint-Joseph de Beyrouth, Annales de la faculté de droit, Beirut, 1956.

Economist Intelligence Unit, *Iran and the Arabian Peninsula: Economic Structure and Analysis*, London and New York, Economist Intelligence Unit, 1991.

— Country Report, *Oman / Yemen 1990–91*, London, Economist Intelligence Unit, 1991.

Edens, G., *Oil and Development in the Middle East*, London and New York, Praeger, 1979.

El-Barawy, Rashed, *Economic Development in the United Arab Republic (Egypt)*, Cairo, The Anglo-Egyptian Bookshop, preface dated 1970.

Eldem, Vedat, *Osmanli Imparatorluğu'nun Iktisadi Şartlari Hakkinda Bir Tetkik*, Istanbul, Iş Bankasi Publications, 1970.

El-Din, Gamal Essam, 'Privatization at a Crossroad,' *Al-Ahram Weekly*, 23–29 October 1997.

— 'Cabinet Boosts Privatization,' *Al-Ahram Weekly*, 30 October–5 November 1997.

El-Erian, Mohamed A., 'Accumulation for Future Generations: Kuwait's Economic Challenges' in Nigel Andrew Chalk et al., *Kuwait: From Reconstruction to Accumulation for Future Generations*, Occasional Paper 150, Washington DC, International Monetary Fund, April 1997.

El-Erian, Mohamed A. and Susan Fennell, *The Economy of the Middle East and North Africa in 1997*, Washington DC, Middle East Department, International Monetary Fund, November 1997.

El-Ghonemy, M.R., 'The Egyptian State and Agricultural Land Market 1810–1986,' *Journal of Agricultural Economics* 43/2 (May 1992).

El-Gritly, A.A.I., 'The Structure of Modern Industry in Egypt,' *L'Egypte contemporaine* 241/2 (November/December 1947).

El-Kuwaiz, Abdullah Ibrahim, 'Economic Integration of the Cooperation Council of the Arab States of the Gulf: Challenges, Achievements and Future Outlook' in John A. Sandwick (ed.), *The Gulf Cooperation Council*, Boulder CO, Westview Press, Washington DC, American-Arab Affairs Council, 1987.

El Mallakh, Ragaei, *The Economic Development of the United Arab Emirates*, London, Croom Helm, 1981.

— *Qatar: Development of an Oil Economy*, London, Croom Helm, 1979.

— *Kuwait: Economic Development and Regional Cooperation*, Chicago and London, University of Chicago Press, 1970.

El Mallakh, Ragaei and Jacob M. Atta, *The Absorptive Capacity of Kuwait: Domestic and International Perspectives*, Lexington MA, Lexington Books, Toronto, D.C. Heath, 1981.

El-Shanawany, E., 'The First National Life Tables for Egypt,' *L'Egypte contemporaine* 162 (March 1936).

Epstein, Eliahu, 'The Bedouin of Transjordan: Their Social and Economic Problems,' *Journal of the Royal Central Asian Society* 25, pt 2 (April 1938).

Executive Communicator, *Business Brief: Syria*, No. 96002 (July–September 1996).

Exxon Corporation, *Middle East Oil*, 2nd ed., New York, Exxon Background Series, September 1980.

Farouk-Sluglett, Marion, 'The Meaning of Infitah in Iraq,' *Review of Middle East Studies* 6, London, Scorpion Publishing, 1993.

Farouk-Sluglett, Marion and Peter Sluglett, *Iraq Since 1958: From Revolution to Dictatorship*, London and New York, KPI International, 1987.

Fenelon, K.G., *Iraq, National Income and Expenditure 1950–56*, Baghdad, Al-rabita Press, 1958.

Findlay, Allan M., *The Arab World*, London, Routledge, 1994.

Finnie, David J., *Desert Enterprise: The Middle East Oil Industry in Its Local Environment*, Cambridge MA, Harvard University Press, 1958.

Firestone, Ya'akov, 'The Land Equalising Musha' Village: A Reassessment' in Gad G. Gilbar (ed.), *Ottoman Palestine 1800–1914: Studies in Economic and Social History*, Leiden, E.J. Brill, 1990.

Fischbach, Michael R., 'British Land Policy in Transjordan' in Eugene L. Rogan and Tariq Tell (eds), *Village, Steppe and State: The Social Origins of Modern Jordan*, London and New York, British Academic Press, 1994.

Foreman-Peck, James, *A History of the World Economy Since 1850*, 2nd ed., New York and London, Harvester Wheatsheaf, 1995.

Fouad, Ashraf, 'Gulf Arabs Move Closer to Unity,' Reuters, quoted in *Daily Star* (Beirut), 18 December 1997.

Gallagher, Nancy Elizabeth, *Egypt's Other Wars: Epidemics and the Politics of Public Health*, Syracuse, Syracuse University Press, 1990.

Gardiner, David, 'Big Rise in Mideast Investment Urged,' *Financial Times*, 12 November 1996.

Gause, F. Gregory III, 'Arms Supplies and Military Spending in the Gulf,' *Middle East Report* 27/3, 204 (July–September 1997).

— *Oil Monarchies: Domestic and Security Challenges in the Arab Gulf States*, New York, Council on Foreign Relations Press, 1994.

Gavin, R.J., *Aden under British Rule 1839–1967*, London, C. Hurst, 1975.

Gelos, Gaston, 'Investment Efficiency, Human Capital and Migration: A Productivity Analysis of the Jordanian Economy' in *Middle East and North Africa Series*, World Bank Discussion Paper No. 14, Washington DC, World Bank, May 1995.

Gershenkron, Alexander, *Economic Backwardness in Historical Perspective*, Cambridge MA, Harvard University Press, 1962.

Ghali, Mirrit, 'Un Programme de réforme agraire pour l'Egypte,' *L'Egypte contemporaine* 236/7 (January/February 1947).

— *Al-islah al-zira'i*, Cairo, Jama'a al-nahda al-qawmiyya, 1945.

Ghantus, Elias T., 'The Financial Centre and its Future' in Jeffrey B. Nugent and Theodore H. Thomas (eds), *Bahrain and the Gulf: Past Perspectives and Alternative Futures*, London and Sydney, Croom Helm, 1985.

Golub, David B., *When Oil and Politics Mix: Saudi Oil Policy, 1973–1985*, Cambridge MA, Harvard Center for Middle Eastern Studies, 1985.

Grafftey-Smith, Lawrence, *Bright Levant*, London, John Murray, 1970.

Granott, A., *The Land System of Palestine: History and Structure*, trans. M. Simon, London, Eyre and Spottiswoode, 1952.

Greenberg, Yitzhak. 'The Contribution of the Labour Economy to Immigrant Absorption and Population Dispersal During Israel's First Decade' in S. Ilan Troen and Noah Lucas (eds), *Israel: The First Decade of Independence*, Albany, State University of New York Press, 1995.

Gross, Nachum T., 'The Economic Regime During Israel's First Decade' in Ilan Troen and Noah Lucas (eds), *Israel: The First Decade of Independence*, Albany, State University of New York Press, 1995.

— *The Economic Policy of the Mandatory Government in Palestine*, Jerusalem, The Maurice Falk Institute for Economic Research in Israel, 1984.

— 'Some New Light on the Palestine Census of Industries 1928,' *Asian and African Studies* 13 (1979).

Gross, Nachum T. and Jacob Metzer, 'Palestine in World War II: Some Economic Aspects' in Geoffrey T. Mills and Hugh Rockoff (eds), *The Sinews of War: Essays on the Economic History of World War II*, Ames IO, Iowa State University Press, 1993.

Grunwald, Kurt and Joachim Ronall, *Industrialization in the Middle East*, New York, Council for Middle Eastern Affairs Press, 1960.

Güran, Tevfik, *Agricultural Statistics of Turkey During the Ottoman Period*, Ankara, State Institute of Statistics, 1997.

Haggard, Steven and Robert R. Kaufman (eds), *Politics of Economic Adjustment*, Princeton NJ, Princeton University Press, 1992.

— 'Institutions and Economic Adjustment' in Steven Haggard and Robert R. Kaufman (eds), *Politics of Economic Adjustment*, Princeton NJ, Princeton University Press, 1992

Hakim, George, 'Fiscal System' in Said B. Himadeh (ed.), *The Economic Organization of Syria*, Beirut, American University of Beirut Press, 1936.

Halevi, Nadav and Ruth Klinov-Malul, *The Economic Development of Israel*, New York, Frederick A. Praeger, 1968.

Halliday, Fred, *Revolution and Foreign Policy: The Case of South Yemen 1967–1987*, Cambridge and New York, Cambridge University Press, 1990.

Hammad, Khalil, 'The Role of Foreign Aid in the Jordanian Economy, 1959–1983' in Bichara Khader and Adnan Badran (eds), *The Economic Development of Jordan*, London, Wolfeboro NH, Croom Helm, 1987.

Handoussa, Heba, 'Crisis and Challenge: Prospects for the 1990s' in Heba Handoussa and Gillian Potter (eds), *Employment and Structural Adjustment: Egypt in the 1990s*, Cairo, American University in Cairo Press, 1991.

— Reform Policies for Egypt's Manufacturing Sector,' in Heba Handoussa and Gillian Potter (eds), *Employment and Structural Adjustment: Egypt in the 1990s*, Cairo, American University Press, 1991.

Hanna, Sami A. and George H. Gardiner (eds), *Arab Socialism*, Leiden, E.J. Brill, 1969.

Hannoyer, Jean and Michel Seurat, *Etat et secteur public industriel en Syrie*, Beirut, CERMOC, Lyons, Lyons University Press, 1979.

Hansen, Bent, 'Economic Development of Syria' in Charles A. Cooper and Sidney S. Alexander (eds), *Economic Development and Population Growth in the Middle East*, New York, American Elsevier, 1972.

— *Egypt and Turkey*, Oxford and New York, Oxford University Press for the World Bank, 1991.

— 'Income and Consumption in Egypt, 1886/1887 to 1937,' *International Journal of Middle Eastern Studies* 10 (1979).

— 'Planning and Growth in the UAR (1960–5)' in P.J. Vatikiotis (ed.), *Egypt Since the Revolution*, London, George Allen and Unwin, 1968.

Hansen, Bent and Girgis A. Marzouk, *Development and Economic Policy in the UAR (Egypt)*, Amsterdam, North-Holland Publishing Company, 1965.

Hansen, Bent and Michael Wattleworth, 'Agricultural Output and Consumption of Basic Foods in Egypt, 1886/7–1967/8,' *International Journal of Middle East Studies* 9 (1978).

Hasan, Muhammad Salman, 'The Role of Foreign Trade in the Economic Development of Iraq, 1864–1964: A Study of Growth in a Dependent Economy' in M.A. Cook (ed.), *Studies in the Economic History of the Middle East*, London, Oxford University Press, 1970.

— *Al-tatawwur al-iqtisadi fi al-'Iraq: al-tijara al-kharijiyya wa-al-tatawwur al-iqtisadi, 1864–1958*, Saida/Beirut, al-Maktaba al-'Asriyya, 1965.

Haseeb, Khair al-Din, 'Towards a National Oil Policy in Iraq,' *Middle East Economic Survey* (Beirut) 11/28 (10 May 1968).

— *The National Income of Iraq 1953–1961*, London, Oxford University Press for Royal Institute of International Affairs, 1964.

Heard-Bey, Frauke, *From Trucial States to United Arab Emirates: A Society in Transition*, London and New York, Longman, 1982.

Helbaoui, Youssef, *La Syrie: mise en valeur d'un pays sous-développé*, Paris, Librairie générale de droit et de jurisprudence, 1956.

Hershlag, Z.Y., *Turkey: The Challenge of Growth*, Leiden, E.J. Brill, 1968.

Heydemann, Steven, 'The Political Logic of Economic Rationality' in Henry J. Barkey, *The Politics of Economic Reform in the Middle East*, New York, St Martin's Press, 1992.

Heyworth-Dunne, Gamal Eddine, *Al-Yemen: A General Social, Political and Economic Survey*, Cairo, The Renaissance Bookshop, 1952.

Himadeh, Said B., 'Industry' in Said B. Himadeh (ed.), *The Economic Organization of Palestine*, Beirut, American University of Beirut Press, 1938.

Hinnebusch, Raymond F., *Peasant and Bureaucracy in Bathist Syria: The Political Economy of Rural Development*, Boulder CO, Westview, 1989.

Hirschman, Albert O., 'The Political Economy of Import-Substituting Industrialization in Latin America,' *Quarterly Journal of Economics* 82 (1968).

Hirst, Paul and Grahame Thompson, *Globalisation in Question*, Cambridge, Polity Press, 1996.

Hogarth, David George, *Hejaz Before World War I*, new ed., Naples, Falcon, Cambridge and New York, Oleander, 1978.

Holden, David and Richard Johns, *The House of Saud*, London and Sydney, Pan Books, 1982.

Hopkins, A.G., *An Economic History of West Africa*, London, Longman, 1973.

Hopkins, Lester G., 'Population' in Said B. Himadeh (ed.), *Economic Organization of Palestine*, Beirut, American University of Beirut, 1938.

Horowitz, David, *The Enigma of Economic Growth: A Case Study of Israel*, New York, Praeger, 1972.

Hudson, Michael, *The Precarious Republic: Political Modernization in Lebanon*, New York, Random House, 1968.

Hunter, Guy, 'Economic Problems: The Middle East Supply Centre' in George Kirk (ed.), *The Middle East at War, 1939–1946*, London, Oxford University Press, 1952.

Ikram, Khaled, *Egypt: Economic Management in a Period of Transition*, Baltimore and London, Johns Hopkins University Press, 1980.

Ionides, Michael, *Divide and Lose: The Arab Revolt of 1955–1958*, London, Geoffrey Bles, 1960.

Ishow, Habib, 'The Development of Agrarian Policies since 1958' in D. Hopwood, H. Ishow, and Thomas Koszinowski (eds), *Iraq: Power and Society*, Reading, Ithaca Press, 1993.

Issawi, Charles, *An Economic History of the Middle East and North Africa*, London, Methuen and Co., 1982.

— *Egypt at Mid-Century: An Economic Survey*, London and New York, Oxford University Press, 1954.

— 'Iraq, 1800–1991: A Study in Aborted Development,' *Princeton Papers in Near Eastern Studies* 1 (1992).

— 'The economic development of Egypt, 1800–1960' in Charles Issawi (ed.), *The Economic History of the Middle East 1800–1914: A Book of Readings*, London and Chicago, Chicago University Press, 1966
— (ed.), *The Economic History of the Middle East, 1800–1914: A Book of Readings*, London and Chicago, Chicago University Press, 1966.
Joffe, George, 'Agricultural Development in Saudi Arabia: The Problematic Path to Self-Sufficiency' in Peter Beaumont and Keith McLachlan (eds), *Agricultural Development in the Middle East*, London, John Wiley and Sons, 1985.
Kahler, Miles, 'External Influence, Conditionality and Political Adjustment' in Stephan Haggard and Robert R. Kaufman (eds), *The Politics of Economic Adjustment*, Princeton NJ, Princeton University Press, 1992.
Karshenas, Massoud, *Structural Adjustment and Employment in the Middle East and North Africa*, Department of Economics, School of Oriental and African Studies, University of London, Working Paper Series No. 50, November 1994.
Kazgan, Gülten, 'Türk Ekonomisinde 1927–35 Depresyonu, Kapital Birikimi ve Örgüt-leşmeler' in Iktisadi ve Ticari Ilimler Akademisi Derneği, *Atatürk Döneminin Ekonomik ve Toplumsal Sorunlari*, Istanbul, Iktisadi ve Ticari Ilimler Akademisi Derneği, 1977.
Kemp, Tom, *Industrialization in the Non-Western World*, 2nd ed., London and New York, Longman, 1983.
Kenwood, A.G. and A.L. Lougheed, *The Growth of the International Economy, 1829–1990*, London and New York, Routledge, 1992
Keyder, Çağlar, *State and Class in Turkey*, London and New York, Verso, 1987.
— *The Definition of a Peripheral Economy, 1923–1929*, Cambridge and New York, Cambridge University Press, 1981.
Keyder, Çağlar and Ayhan Aksu-Koç, *External Labour Migration from Turkey and Its Impact*, Report No. 185e, Ottawa, International Development Research Centre, 1988.
Keyder, Çağlar and Şevket Pamuk, '1945 Çiftçiyi Topraklandirma Kanunu Üzerine Tezler,' *Yapit* 8 (1984).
Keynes, John Maynard, *Indian Currency and Finance*, London, MacMillan, 1913.
al-Khafaji, 'Isam, 'War as a Vehicle for the Rise and Demise of a State-Controlled Society: The Case of Ba'thist Iraq,' *Amsterdam Middle East Papers* 4, University of Amsterdam, December 1995.
— 'The Parasitic Basis of the Ba'thist Regime' in CARDRI (Committee Against Repression and For Democratic Rights in Iraq), *Saddam's Iraq: Revolution or Reaction?* London, Zed Press, 1986.
Khalaf, Nadim G., *Economic Implications of the Size of Nations with Special Reference to Lebanon*, Leiden, E.J. Brill, 1971.
Khalaf, Roula, 'Middle East States Urged to Deregulate,' *Financial Times*, 7 March 1997.
— 'World's Slowest Growing Developing Region,' *Financial Times*, 19 September 1997.
Khalidi, Raja, 'The Economy of the Palestinian Arabs of Israel' in George T. Abed, *The Palestinian Economy: Studies in Development under Prolonged Occupation*, London, Routledge, 1988.
Khalidi, Walid (ed.), *All That Remains: The Palestinian Villages Occupied and Depopulated by Israel in 1948*, Beirut, The Institute for Palestine Studies, 1992.
al-Khalil, Yusif, 'Economic Developments in Lebanon since 1982,' *Beirut Review* 3 (Spring 1992).
Khuri, Albert, 'Agriculture' in Said B. Himadeh (ed.), *The Economic Organization of Palestine*, Beirut, American University of Beirut Press, 1938

Khuri, Fuad I., *Tribe and State in Bahrain: The Transformation of Social and Political Authority in an Arab State*, Chicago and London, University of Chicago Press, 1980.

Kidron, Peretz, 'Closure: The Shape of Things to Come,' *Middle East International* 24 (October 1997).

Kindleberger, Charles P., *The World in Depression, 1929–39*, revised and enlarged ed., Berkeley and Los Angeles, University of California Press, 1986.

Kireyev, Alexei P., 'An Analysis of Kuwait's Debt Collection Program' in Nigel Andrew Chalk et al., *Kuwait: From Reconstruction to Accumulation for Future Generations*, Occasional Paper 150, Washington DC, International Monetary Fund, April 1997.

Konikoff, A., *Trans-Jordan: An Economic Survey*, Jerusalem, ACHUA Cooperative Printing Press, 1943.

Kopp, Hans, 'Land Usage and its Implications for Yemeni Agriculture' in B.R. Pridham (ed.), *Economy, Society and Culture in Contemporary Yemen*, London and Dover NH, Croom Helm, Exeter, Devon, Centre for Arab Gulf Studies, University of Exeter, 1985.

Kostiner, Joseph, 'On Instruments and Their Designers: The Ikhwan of Najd and the Emergence of the Saudi State,' *Middle Eastern Studies* 21/3 (July 1985).

— *The Making of Saudi Arabia, 1916 to 1936: From Chieftaincy to Monarchical State*, New York and London, Oxford University Press, 1993.

Kuznets, Simon, *Modern Economic Growth*, New Haven, Yale University Press, 1966.

— *The Income Growth of Nations*, Cambridge MA, Harvard University Press, 1971.

Labaki, Boutros, 'L'Emigration externe,' *Maghreb/Machrek* 125 (July/August/September 1989).

Lackner, Helen, *PDR Yemen: Outpost of Socialist Development in Arabia*, London, Ithaca Press, 1985.

Landen, Robert Geran, *Oman Since 1856: Disruptive Modernization in a Traditional Arab Society*, Princeton NJ, Princeton University Press, 1967.

Langley, Kathleen M., 'Iraq: Some Aspects of the Economic Scene,' *Middle East Journal* 18/2 (Spring 1964).

Latron, A. 'La Production et le commerce de soie au Levant,' *L'Asie française* (March 1935).

Lévi, I.G., 'Evaluation du revenu national de l'Egypte: réponse à Monsieur J. Baxter,' *L'Egypte contemporaine* 14/73 (May 1923).

— 'L'Augmentation de revenues de l'état: possibilités et moyens d'y parvenir,' *L'Egypte contemporaine* 68 (December 1922).

Lloyd, E.H.M., *Food and Inflation in the Middle East 1940–45*, Stanford CA, Stanford University Press, nd, Introduction 1956.

Lockman, Zachary. 'Railway Workers and Relational History: Arabs and Jews in British-Ruled Palestine,' *Comparative Studies in Society and History* 35/3 (July 1993).

Longrigg, Stephen Hemsley, *Oil in the Middle East: Its Discovery and Its Development*, London, Oxford University Press, 1968.

Longuenesse, Elisabeth, 'L'Industrialisation et sa significance sociale' in André Raymond (ed.), *La Syrie d'aujourd'hui*, Paris, CNRS, 1980.

Lorimer, J.G., *Gazetteer of the Persian Gulf, Oman and Central Arabia* 2, *Geographical and Statistical*, reprint Farnborough Hants, Gregg International, 1970.

Luciani, Giacomo, 'Allocation Vs Production States: A Theoretical Framework' in Giacomo Luciani (ed.), *The Arab State*, London, Routledge, 1990.

Mabro, Robert, *The Egyptian Economy: 1952–1972*, London, Oxford University Press, 1976.

Mabro, Robert and Samir Radwan, *The Industrialization of Egypt 1939–1973: Policy and Performance*, Oxford, Clarendon Press, 1976.

McCarthy, Justin, *The Population of Palestine: Population Statistics of the Late Ottoman Period and the Mandate*, New York, Columbia University Press, 1990.

— *Muslims and Minorities: The Population of Ottoman Anatolia and the End of Empire*, New York and London, New York University Press, 1983.

de Macedo, Jorge Braga, Barry Eichengreen, and Jaime Reis (eds.), *Currency Convertibility: The Gold Standard and Beyond*, London and New York, Routledge, 1996.

McGregor, R., 'Saudi Arabia: Population and the Making of the Modern State' in J.I. Clarke and W.B. Fisher (eds), *Populations of the Middle East and North Africa: A Geographical Approach*, New York, American Publishing Corporation, 1972.

Maddison, Angus, *Monitoring the World Economy, 1820–1992*, Paris, Development Centre of the OECD, 1995.

__ *The World Economy in the 20th Century*, Paris, Development Centre of the OECD, 1989.

— *Two Crises: Latin America and Asia, 1929–38 and 1973–93*, Paris, Development Centre of the OECD, Washington DC, OECD Publications and Information Center (distributors), 1985.

Mahdavy, Hossein, 'Patterns and Problems of Economic Development in Rentier States: the Case of Iran' in M.A. Cook (ed.), *Studies in the Economic History of the Middle East*, London and New York, Oxford University Press, 1979.

Makdisi, Samir A., 'Syria: Rate of Economic Growth and Fixed Capital Formation 1936–1968,' *Middle East Journal* 25/2 (Spring 1971).

— 'Some Aspects of Syrian Economic Growth, 1945–1957,' *Middle East Economic Papers* (1961).

Malone, J.J., 'Involvement and Change: The Coming of the Oil Age to Saudi Arabia' in Tim Niblock (ed.), *Social and Economic Development in the Arab Gulf*, London, Croom Helm, New York, St Martin's Press, 1980.

Manners, Ian R. and Tagi Sagafi-Nejad, 'Agricultural Development in Syria' in Peter Beaumont and Keith McLachlan (eds), *Agricultural Development in the Middle East*, London, John Wiley and Sons, 1985.

Mansour, Antoine, 'The West Bank Economy: 1948–1984' in George T. Abed (ed.), *The Palestinian Economy: Studies in Development under Prolonged Occupation*, London, Routledge, 1988.

Mazur, Michael P., *Economic Growth and Development in Jordan*, London, Croom Helm, 1979.

Mead, Donald C., *Growth and Structural Change in the Egyptian Economy*, Homewood IL, Richard D. Irwin, 1967.

Meredith, David, 'The British Government and Colonial Economic Policy, 1919–1939,' *Economic History Review*, 2nd series, 28 (1975).

Metral, Françoise, 'Le Monde rural syrien à l'ère des réformes (1958–1978)' in André Raymond, *La Syrie d'aujourd'hui*, Paris, CNRS 1980.

Metzer, Jacob, *The Divided Economy of Mandatory Palestine*, Cambridge, Cambridge University Press, 1998.

— 'The Slow-down of Economic Growth: A Passing Phase on the End of the Big Spurt' in Yoram Ben-Porath (ed.), *The Israeli Economy: Maturing Through Crises*, Cambridge MA and London, Harvard University Press, 1986.

Metzer, Jacob and Oded Kaplan, 'Jointly but Severally: Arab/Jewish Dualism and Economic Growth in Mandatory Palestine,' *Journal of Economic History* 45/2 (January 1985).

Middle East Supply Centre, *Some Facts About the MESC*, Cairo, MESC, 1945.

Mikesell, Raymond F., 'Monetary Problems in Saudi Arabia,' *Middle East Journal* 1 (July 1947).

Milward, Alan S., *The Reconstruction of Western Europe, 1945–51*, Berkeley and Los Angeles, University of California Press, 1984.

Meyer, Gunther, 'Economic Development in Syria since 1970' in J.A. Allan (ed.), *Politics and Economy in Syria*, London, School of Oriental and African Studies, 1987.

Mohamedi, Fareed, 'Oil, Gas and the Future of the Arab Gulf Countries,' *Middle East Report* 27/3, 204 (July–September 1997).

Morris, Benny, *The Birth of the Palestinian Refugee Problem 1947–1949*, Cambridge, Cambridge University Press, 1988.

Mourad, Jean, 'L'Emploi et ses problèmes,' *Le Commerce du Levant* (Spécial Economie: 1985–1986), Beirut 1986.

Mundy, Martha, 'La Propriété dite mushâ' en Syrie: à propos des travaux de Ya'akov Firestone,' *Revue du Monde Musulman* 79–80, pt 1–2 (1996).

— 'Village Land and Individual Title: Musha' and Ottoman Land Registration in the Ajlun District' in Eugene L. Rogan and Tariq Tell (eds), *Village, Steppe and State: The Social Origins of Modern Jordan*, London and New York, British Academic Press, 1994.

— 'Agricultural Development in the Yemeni Tihama' in B.R. Pridham (ed.), *Economy, Society and Culture in Contemporary Yemen*, London and Dover NH, Croom Helm, Exeter, Devon, Centre for Arab Gulf Studies, University of Exeter, 1985.

Munif, 'Abd al-Rahman, *Mudun al-milh: riwaya*, Beirut, Al-mu'assasa al-'arabiyya li-al-dirasat wa-al-nashr, 1985.

— *Cities of Salt*, trans. Paul Theroux, London, Cape, 1988.

Munir, Metin, 'Exception to the Rule,' *Financial Times*, Turkey Supplement, 26 May 1997.

Murphy, Emma, 'Structural Inhibitions to Economic Liberalization in Israel,' *Middle East Journal* 48/1 (Winter 1994).

Mutlu, Servet, 'The Southeastern Anatolia Project (GAP) in Turkey,' *Orient* 37/1 (1997).

Nasr, Salim, 'Backdrop to Civil War: The Crisis of Lebanese Capitalism,' MERIP Reports 8, 10, 73 (December 1978).

al-Nasrawi, Abbas, 'Economic Devastation, Underdevelopment and Outlook' in Fran Hazelton (ed.), *Iraq since the Gulf War: Prospects for Democracy*, London and Atlantic Highlands NJ, Zed Books, 1994.

Nathan, R.R., O. Gass, and D. Creamer, *Palestine: Problem and Promise*, Washington, Public Affairs Press, 1946.

Naysmith, Jenny, 'Israel's Distorted Economy,' *Middle East Journal* 8/4 (Fall 1954).

Nelson, Joan (ed.), *Economic Crisis and Policy Choice: The Politics of Adjustment in the Third World*, Princeton NJ, Princeton University Press, 1990.

Nyrop, Richard F., *Area Handbook for the Persian Gulf States*, 2nd revised ed., Washington DC, Department of the Army, 1984.

Nyrop, Richard F. et al. (eds), *Area Handbook for the Yemens*, Washington DC, US Government Printing Office, 1977.

O'Brien, Patrick, *The Revolution in Egypt's Economic System: From Private Enterprise to Socialism 1952–1965*, London, Oxford University Press, 1966.

Ockerman, Herbert W. and Shimoon G. Samano, 'The Agricultural Development of Iraq' in Peter Beaumont and Keith McLachlan (eds), *Agricultural Development in the Middle East*, London, John Wiley and Sons, 1985.

Ökçün, Gündüz, *The Ottoman Industrial Census of 1913, 1915*, Ankara, State Institute of Statistics, 1997.

Okruhlik, Gwenn and Patrick Conge, 'National Autonomy, Labor Migration and Political Crisis: Yemen and Saudi Arabia,' *Middle East Journal* 51/4 (Fall 1997).

Öncü, Ayse, Çağlar Keyder, and Saad Eddin Ibrahim, *Developmentalism and Beyond: Society and Politics in Egypt and Turkey*, Cairo, American University in Cairo Press, 1994.

Öniş, Ziya and James Riedel, *Economic Crises and Long Term Growth in Turkey*, Washington DC, World Bank, 1993.

Öniş, Ziya and Steven B. Webb, *Political Economy of Policy Reform*, The World Bank Working Papers, WPS 1059, 1992.

Organization of Arab Petroleum Exporting Countries, *Secretary General's Fourteenth Annual Report* 1407AH/1987AD, Kuwait, OAPEC, 1989.

— *Secretary General's Fifteenth Annual Report*, 1408AH/1988AD, Kuwait, OAPEC, May 1989.

Organization of Petroleum Exporting Countries, *Annual Statistical Bulletin, 1994*, Vienna, Austria, OPEC, 1994

Oweiss, Ibrahim, *The Underground Economy with Special Reference to the Case of Egypt*, National Bank of Egypt, Commemoration Lecture Programme, Cairo, 19 December 1994.

Owen, Roger, 'Aspects of Ottoman Law in Mandatory Palestine, 1918,' *Harvard Middle Eastern and Islamic Review* 1/2 (November 1994).

— *The Middle East in the World Economy 1800–1914*, London and New York, Methuen 1981, reprint by I.B. Tauris and Co., 1993.

— 'Economic Development in Mandatory Palestine, 1918–1948' in George T. Abed (ed.), *The Palestinian Economy, Studies in Development under Prolonged Occupation*, London, Routledge, 1988.

— 'The Silk-Reeling Industry of Mount Lebanon, 1840–1914: A Study of the Possibilities and Limitations of Factory Production in the Periphery' in Huri Islamoglu-Inan (ed.), *The Ottoman Empire and the World Economy*, Cambridge and New York, Cambridge University Press, Paris, Editions de la maison des sciences de l'homme, 1987.

— 'Large Landowners, Agricultural Progress and the State in Egypt, 1800–1970: An Overview with Many Questions' in Alan Richards (ed.), *Food, States and Peasants: Analyses of the Agrarian Question in the Middle East*, Boulder CO and London, Westview Press, 1986.

— *Migrant Workers in the Gulf*, Report No. 68., London, The Minority Rights Group Ltd., September 1985.

— 'The Economic Aspects of Revolution in the Middle East' in P.J. Vatikiotis (ed.), *Revolution in the Middle East: And Other Case Studies*, London, Allen and Unwin, 1972.

— 'The Political Economy of Grand Liban, 1920–1970' in Roger Owen (ed.), *Essays on the Crisis in Lebanon*, London, Ithaca Press, 1976.

Özmucur, Süleyman, *Gelirin Fonksiyonel Dagilimi, 1948–1991*, Bogaziçi University Research Paper ISS/EC 91-06, Istanbul, Bogaziçi University, 1991.

Paine, Suzanne, *Exporting Workers: The Turkish Case*, Cambridge, Cambridge University Press, 1974.

Paix, C., 'La Portée speciale des activités tertiaires de commandement économique au Liban,' *Revue Tiers-Monde* 16/61 (January–March 1975).

Pamuk, Şevket, 'Long Term Trends in Urban Wages in Turkey, 1850–1990' in Vera Zamagni and Peter Scholliers (eds), *Labour's Reward: Real Wages and Economic Growth in 19th and 20th Century Europe*, Aldershot, England, Brookfield VT, E. Elgar, 1995.

— *The Ottoman Empire and European Capitalism 1820–1913: Trade, Investment and Production*, Cambridge, Cambridge University Press, 1987.

— 'War, State Economic Policies and Resistance by Agricultural Producers in Turkey, 1939–1945' in Farhad Kazemi and John Waterbury (eds), *Peasants and Politics in the Modern Middle East*, Miami, Florida International University Press, 1991.

Penrose, Edith, 'Oil and State in Arabia' in Derek Hopwood (ed.), *The Arabian Peninsula: Society and Politics*, London, George Allen and Unwin, 1972.

— 'International Oil Companies and Governments in the Middle East' in John Duke Anthony (ed.), *The Middle East: Oil, Politics and Development*, Washington DC, American Enterprise Institute for Public Policy, 1975.

Penrose, Edith and E.F. Penrose, *Iraq: International Relations and National Development*, London, Benn, Boulder CO, Westview, 1978.

Perthes, Volker, 'The Syrian Private Industrial and Commercial Sectors and the State,' *International Journal of Middle East Studies* 24/2 (May 1992).

Pinder, John, 'Europe in the World Economy, 1920–1970' in Carlo M. Cipolla (ed.), *Fontana Economic History of Europe: Contemporary Economies*, London, Fontana-Collins, 1976.

Plascov, Avi, 'The Palestinians of Jordan's Border' in Roger Owen (ed.), *Studies in the Economic and Social History of Palestine in the Nineteenth and Twentieth Centuries*, London and Basingstoke, Macmillan, 1982.

Plessner, Yakir, *The Political Economy of Israel: From Ideology to Stagnation*, Albany, State University of New York Press, 1994.

Pool, David, 'From Elite to Class: The Transformation of the Iraqi Political Leadership' in Abbas Kelidar (ed.), *The Integration of Modern Iraq*, London, Croom Helm, 1978.

Porath, Yehoshuah, 'The Land Problem as a Factor in Relations among Arabs, Jews and the Mandatory Government' in Gabriel Ben-Dor (ed.), *The Palestinians and the Middle East Conflict*, Ramat Gan, Israel, Turtledove Publications, 1978.

Porter, R.S., 'Gulf Aid and Investment in the Arab World' in B.R. Pridham (ed.), *The Arab Gulf and the Arab World*, London and New York, Croom Helm, 1988.

Radwan, Samir, *Capital Formation in Egyptian Industry and Agriculture, 1882–1967*, London, Ithaca Press, 1974.

Radwan, Samir and Eddy Lee, *Agrarian Change in Egypt: An Anatomy of Rural Poverty*, London and Dover, NH, Croom Helm, 1986.

Rasheed, Guzine A.-K., 'Development of Agricultural and Taxation in Modern Iraq,' *Bulletin of the School of Oriental and African Studies* (London) 25, pt 2 (1962).

Razin, Assaf and Efriam Sadka, *The Economy of Modern Israel: Malaise and Promise*, Chicago and London, University of Chicago Press, 1993.

Richards, Alan, 'Agricultural Employment, Wages and Government Policy During and After the Oil Boom' in Heba Handoussa and Gillian Potter (eds), *Employment and Structural Adjustment: Egypt in the 1990s*, Cairo, American University in Cairo Press, 1991.

— *Egypt's Agricultural Development, 1800–1980: Technical and Social Change*, Boulder CO, Westview Press, 1982.

Richards, Alan and John Waterbury, *A Political Economy of the Middle East: State, Class and Economic Development*, 2nd ed., Boulder CO, San Francisco, and Oxford, Westview, 1996.

Rivier, François, *Croissance industrielle dans une économie assistée: le cas jordanien*, Beirut, CERMOC, Lyons, Lyons University Press, 1980.

Rodrik, Dani, *Premature Liberalization, Incomplete Stabilization: The Özal Decade in Turkey*, Discussion Paper No. 402, London, Centre for Economic Policy Research, 1990.

Rothermund, Dieter, *The Global Impact of the Great Depression, 1929–1939*, London and New York, Routledge, 1996.

Roy, Sarah, *The Gaza Strip: The Political Economy of Development*, Washington DC, Institute for Palestine Studies, 1995.

Royal Institute of International Affairs (RIIA), *The Problem of International Investment*, London and New York, Oxford University Press, 1937.

Saad, Reem, 'Social History of an Agrarian Reform Community in Egypt,' *Cairo Papers in Social Science* (American University at Cairo) 11, 4 (Winter 1988).

Saba, Elias, 'The Syro-Lebanese Customs Union,' *Middle East Economic Papers*, Economic Research Institute, American University of Beirut, 1960.

Sadowski, Yahya M., 'The End of Counterrevolution? The Politics of Economic Adjustment in Kuwait,' *Middle East Report* 27/3, 204 (July–September 1997).

— 'Patronage and the Party in Contemporary Syria' in Peter J. Chelkowski and Robert J. Pranger (eds), *Ideology and Power in the Middle East: Studies in Honor of George Lenczowski*, Durham NC and London, Duke University Press, 1984.

Saidi, Nasser H., *Economic Consequences of the War in Lebanon*, Papers on Lebanon 3, Oxford, Centre for Lebanese Studies, September 1986.

Saket, Bassam K., 'Economic Uses of Remittances – The Case of Jordan' in Monther Share (ed.), *Jordan's Place Within the Arab Oil Economies*, Proceedings of the seminar held at Yarmouk University's Liaison Office, Amman, March 12–13 1983, under the auspices of the University of Jordan, Amman, the Middle East Centre of St Antony's College, Oxford, and Yarmouk University, Irbid, Irbid, Yarmouk University, 1986.

Saket, Bassam K. and Bassam J. Asfour, *Jordan's Economy: 1980 and Beyond*, Amman, Economics Department, Royal Scientific Society, 14 July 1980.

Sassoon, Joseph, *Economic Policy in Iraq 1932–1950*, London, Frank Cass, 1987.

Sayigh, Yusif A., *Arab Oil Policies in the 1970s*, London and Canberra, Croom Helm, 1983.

— 'A New Framework for Complementarity Among the Arab Economies' in Ibrahim Ibrahim (ed.), *Arab Resources: The Transformation of a Society*, London, Croom Helm, Washington DC, Center for Contemporary Arab Studies, 1983.

Schilcher, Linda Schatkowski, 'The Famine of 1915–1918 in Greater Syria' in John P. Spagnolo (ed.), *Problems of the Modern Middle East in Historical Perspective: Essays in Honour of Albert Hourani*, Reading, Ithaca Press, 1992.

Seccombe, Ian J., 'Labour Migration in the Arabian Gulf: Evolution and Characteristics,' *BRISMES Bulletin* 10 (1983).

Seccombe, Ian J. and Richard Lawless, *Work Camps and Company Towns: Settlement Patterns and the Gulf Oil Industry*, Centre for Middle Eastern and Islamic Studies, University of Durham, Occasional Papers No. 36, 1987.

Segev, Tom, *The First Israelis*, New York, The Free Press, London, Macmillan, 1986.

Seurat, Michel, 'Les Populations, l'état et la société' in André Raymond (ed.), *La Syrie d'aujourd'hui*, Paris, CNRS, 1980.

Shaban, Radwan A., 'Palestinian Labour Mobility,' *International Labour Review* 134/5–6 (1993).

Shadid, Mohammed K., 'Israeli Policy Towards Economic Development in the West Bank and Gaza' in George T. Abed (ed.), *The Palestinian Economy: Studies in Development under Prolonged Occupation*, London, Routledge, 1988.

Shafir, Gershon, *Land, Labor and the Origins of the Israeli-Palestinian Conflict 1882–1914*, Cambridge, Cambridge University Press, 1989.

Shafik, Nemat, 'Public Policy and Private Initiative: Towards New Partnerships in the Middle East and North Africa,' *ERF Forum* 4/2 (September 1997).

Shalev, Michael, 'Israel's Domestic Policy Regime: Zionism, Dualism and the Rise of Capital' in Francis G. Castles, (ed.), *The Comparative History of Public Policy*, Cambridge, Polity Press, New York, Oxford University Press, 1989.

— 'Jewish Organized Labor and the Palestinians: A Study in State/Society Relations in Israel' in Baruch Kimmerling (ed.), *The Israeli State and Society: Boundaries and Frontiers*, Albany, State University of New York Press, 1989.

Sharaf, Hussein A., 'The Development and Present Structure of National Income Accounts in the United Arab Republic' in Taufiq M. Khan (ed.), *Middle East Studies in Income and Wealth*, London, Bowes and Bowes, New Haven, International Association for Research in Income and Wealth, 1965.

Share, Monther, 'The Use of Jordan Workers' Remittances' in Bichara Khader and Adnan Badran (eds), *The Economic Development of Jordan*, London and Wolfeboro NH, Croom Helm, 1987.

— 'Migration and Domestic Labour Market Policies – The Case of Jordan' in Monther Share (ed.), *Jordan's Place Within the Arab Oil Economies*, Proceedings of the seminar held at Yarmouk University's Liaison Office, Amman, March 12–13 1983, under the auspices of the University of Jordan, Amman, the Middle East Centre of St Antony's College, Oxford, and Yarmouk University, Irbid, Irbid, Yarmouk University, 1986.

Sharon, Emmanuel, 'Israel and the Success of the Shekel: The Key Years, 1984–1987' in Pamela S. Falk (ed.), *Inflation – Are We Next? Hyperinflation and Solutions in Argentina, Brazil, and Israel*, Boulder CO and London, Lynne Rienner Publishers, 1990.

Shaw, John A. and David E. Long, *Saudi Arabian Modernization: The Impact of Change on Stability*, New York, Praeger, 1982.

Shehadi, Nadim, *The Idea of Lebanon: Economy and State in the Cénacle Libanais 1946–54*, Papers on Lebanon 5, Oxford, Centre for Lebanese Studies, May 1987.

Shihab, Fakhri. 'Kuwait: A Super-Affluent Society,' *Foreign Affairs* 42/3 April 1964.

Shimizu, Hiroshi, *Anglo-Japanese Trade Rivalry in the Middle East in the Inter-war Period*, London, Ithaca Press, 1986.

Shorter, Frederic C., 'The Population of Turkey After the War of Independence,' *International Journal of Middle Eastern Studies* 17 (1985).

Sinclair, C.A., 'Migrant Workers' Remittances in the Arab World' in B.R. Pridham (ed.), *The Arab Gulf and the Arab World*, London and New York, Croom Helm, 1988.

Skeet, Ian, *Oman: Politics and Development*, New York, St Martin's Press, 1992.

Smadi, Mohammad and Bassam Asfour, *The Economy of Jordan: A Sectoral Review, 1977*, Amman, Economics Department, Royal Scientific Society, May 1978.

Smith, Barbara J., *The Roots of Separatism in Palestine: British Economic Policy 1920–1929*, Syracuse, Syracuse University, 1993.

Spagnolo, John P. (ed.), *Problems of the Modern Middle East in Historical Perspective: Essays in Honour of Albert Hourani*, Reading, Ithaca Press, 1992.

Springborg, Robert, 'Bathism in Practice: Agriculture, Politics and Political Culture in Syria and Iraq,' *Middle Eastern Studies* 17/2 (April 1981).

Stallings, Barbara, 'International Influence on Economic Policy: Debt Stabilization and Structural Reform' in Stephan Haggard and Robert R. Kaufman (eds), *The Politics of Economic Adjustment*, Princeton NJ, Princeton University Press, 1992.

Steffan, Hans and Olivier Blanc, 'La Démographie de la République arabe du Yéman' in Paul Bonnenfant (ed.), *La Peninsule arabique d'aujourd'hui*, Paris, CNRS, 1982.

Stein, Kenneth W., *The Land Question in Palestine, 1917–1939*, Chapel Hill, and London, University of North Carolina Press, 1984.

Stocking, George W., *Middle East Oil: A Study in Political and Economic Controversy*, London, Allan Lane, The Penguin Press, 1971.

Stookey, Robert W., *South Yemen, A Marxist Republic in Arabia*, Boulder CO, Westview, London, Croom Helm, 1982.

Syrquin, Moshe, 'Economic Growth and Structural Change: an International Perspective' in Yoram Ben-Porath (ed.), *The Israeli Economy: Maturing Through Crises*, Cambridge, MA and London, Harvard University Press, 1986.

Szereszewski, Robert, *Essays on the Structure of the Jewish Economy in Palestine and Israel*, Jerusalem, The Maurice Falk Institute, 1968.

Talal, H., 'Growth and Stability in the Jordanian Economy,' *Middle East Journal* 21/1 (Winter 1968).

Taylor, Alan M., 'On the Costs of Inward-looking Development: Price Distortions, Growth and Divergence in Latin America,' *Journal of Economic History* 58/1 (March 1998).

Tekeli, Ilhan and Selim Ilkin, *Uygulamaya Geçerken Türkiye'de Devletçiliğin Oluşumu*, Ankara, Orta Dogu Teknik Universitesi, 1982.

— *1929 Dünya Buhraninda Türkiye'nin Iktisadi Politika Arayişlari*, Ankara, Orta Doğu Teknik Universitesi, 1977.

Tezel, Yahya S., *Cumhuriyet Döneminin Iktisadi Tarihi (1923–1950)*, 2nd ed., Ankara, Yurt Yayinevi, 1986.

Thornburg, Max Weston, Graham Spry, and George Soule, *Turkey: An Economic Appraisal*, New York, The Twentieth Century Fund, 1949.

Tignor, Robert L., *Egyptian Textiles and British Capital 1930–56*, Cairo, American University in Cairo Press, 1989.

— *State, Private Enterprise and Economic Change in Egypt, 1914–1952*, Princeton NJ, Princeton University Press, 1984.

Toprak, Zafer, *Türkiye'de Milli Iktisat, 1908–1918*, Ankara, Yurt Yayinlari, 1982.

Townsend, John, 'Philosophy of State Development Planning' in M.S. El-Azhary (ed.), *The Impact of Oil Revenues on Arab Gulf Development*, London and Sydney, Croom Helm, 1984.

— 'L'Industrie en Arabie saoudite,' *Maghreb/Machrek* 89 (July/August/September 1980).

Toye, John, *Dilemmas of Development*, 2nd ed., London and Cambridge MA, Basil Blackwell, 1993.

Troen, S. Ilan, 'Spearheads of the Zionist Frontier: Historical Perspectives on Post-1967 Settlement Planning in Judea and Samaria,' *Planning Perspectives* 7 (1992).

Tute, Hon. Mr Justice, 'The Law of State Lands in Palestine,' *Journal of Comparative Legislation and International Law*, 3rd series, 9 (November 1927).

At-Twaijri, Muhammad Ibrahim, *The SABIC Challenge: A Strategic Perspective*, Dhahran, Saudi Arabia, King Fahd University of Petroleum and Minerals, 1993.

Twitchell, K.S., *Saudi Arabia with an Account of the Development of its Natural Resources*, Princeton NJ, Princeton University Press, 1947.

Vallet, J., *Contribution à l'étude de la condition des ouvriers de la grande industrie du Caire*, Valence, Imprimerie valentinoise, 1913.

Van der Wee, Herman, *Prosperity and Upheaval: The World Economy, 1945–1980*, Berkeley and Los Angeles, University of California Press, 1977.

Vitalis, Robert, *When Capitalists Collide: Business Conflict and the End of Empire in Egypt*, Berkeley, University of California Press, 1995.

— 'On the Theory and Practice of Compradors: The Role of 'Abbud Pasha in the Egyptian Political Economy,' *International Journal of Middle Eastern Studies* 22/3 (August 1990).

— 'The End of Third Worldism in Egyptian Studies,' *Arab Studies Journal* 4/1 (spring 1966).

Waardenburg, Jean-Jacques, *Les universités dans le monde arabe actuel*, The Hague, Mouton and Co, 1966.

Wade, Robert, *Governing the Market: Economic Theory and the Role of Government in East Asian Industrialization*, Princeton NJ, Princeton University Press, 1990.

Wahba, Mourad M., *The Role of the State in the Egyptian Economy 1945–1981*, Reading, Ithaca Press, 1994.

Walpole, G.F., 'Land Problems in Transjordan,' *Journal of the Royal Central Asian Society* 35 (1948).

Warriner, Doreen, *Land Reform and Development in the Middle East: A Study of Egypt, Syria and Iraq*, London and New York, Royal Institute of International Affairs, 1957.

— *Land and Poverty in the Middle East*, London, Royal Institute of International Affairs, 1948.

Waterbury, John, *Exposed to Innumerable Illusions: Public Enterprise and State Power in Egypt, India, Mexico and Turkey*, Cambridge and New York, Cambridge University Press, 1993.

— 'Export-Led Growth and the Center-Right Coalition,' *Comparative Politics* 24 (1991/92).

— *The Egypt of Nasser and Sadat: The Political Economy of Two Regimes*, Princeton NJ, Princeton University Press, 1983.

— *Hydropolitics of the Nile Valley*, Syracuse NY, Syracuse University Press, 1979.

— *Egypt: Burdens of the Past/Options for the Future*, Bloomington IN, Indiana University Press, 1978.

Weir, Shelagh, 'Economic Aspects of the Qat Industry in North-Western Yemen' in B.R. Pridham (ed.), *Economy, Society and Culture in Contemporary Yemen*, London and Dover NH, Croom Helm, Exeter, Devon, Centre for Arab Gulf Studies, University of Exeter, 1985.

Weulersse, Jacques, *Paysans de Syrie et du Proche Orient*, 2nd ed., Paris, Gallimard, 1946.

Widmer, Robert, 'Population' in Economic Organization of Syria' in Said B. Himadeh (ed.), *The Economic Organization of Syria*, Beirut, American University of Beirut Press, 1936.

Wilmington, Martin W., *The Middle East Supply Centre*, Albany NY, State University of New York Press, London, University of London Press, 1971.

Yago, Glenn, 'Whatever Happened to the Promised Land? Capital Flows and the Israeli State,' *Berkeley Journal of Sociology* 21 (1996).

Yapp, M.E, *The Near East Since the First World War*, London and New York, Longman, 1991.

Yergen, Daniel, *The Prize: The Epic Quest for Oil, Money and Power*, New York, Simon and Schuster/Touchstone, 1993.

Yousef, Abdullah Ali, 'An Evaluation of Bahrain's Major Industries and their Future Prospects' in Jeffrey B. Nugent and Theodore H. Thomas (eds), *Bahrain and the Gulf: Past Perspectives and Alternative Futures*, London and Sydney, Croom Helm, 1985.

Zahlan, Rosemarie Said, *The Making of the Modern Gulf States*, London and Boston, Unwin Hyman, 1989.

Zahra, M.A. and M. al-Darwish, *A Statistical Study of Some of the Factors Affecting the Price of Egyptian Cotton*, Technical Bulletin, No. 1, Cairo, Cotton Bureau, 1930.

Zimmerman, L.J., 'The Disribution of World Income 1860–1960' in Egbert De Vries (ed.), *Essays on Unbalanced Growth: A Century of Disparity and Convergence*, S-Gravenhage, Mouton and Co, 1962.

Zürcher, Erik J., Turkey, *A Modern History*, London and New York, I.B. Tauris, 1993.

Index